ATLANTIC COAST CONFERENCE FOOTBALL

ATLANTIC COAST CONFERENCE FOOTBALL

A History Through 1991

by

Tom Perrin

McFarland & Company, Inc., Publishers

Jefferson, North Carolina, and London

.

British Library Cataloguing-in-Publication data are available

Library of Congress Cataloguing-in-Publication Data

Perrin, Tom, 1928–
    Atlantic coast conference football : a history through 1991 / by
Tom Perrin.
        p.   cm.
    Includes index.
    ISBN 0-89950-749-2 (lib. bdg. : 50# alk. paper) ∞
    1. Atlantic Coast Conference – History.   2. Football – United
States – History.   I. Title.
    GV958.5.A75P47   1992
    796.332'63'0975 – dc20   92-50315
                                                                    CIP

Manufactured in the United States of America

McFarland & Company, Inc., Publishers
  Box 611, Jefferson, North Carolina 28640

To my brother, Keith,
who overcame much

Contents

Acknowledgments

Many thanks to the sports people who helped with information: Sam Blackman and Donna Strickland at Clemson; Duke's Warren Miller; Lori Cover at Georgia Tech; Maryland's Chuck Walsh; Lee Snyder and Pamala Jeffries at North Carolina; Caffie Darden and Carter Cheves at North Carolina State; Jane Desjardins at Virginia; Barbara Dery and Heather Ackerman at Wake Forest; and Brian Binette at South Carolina. Equally helpful in the archives were Dennis Taylor and Karen Jones at Clemson; Doris Parrish, Bill King, and Tom Harkins at Duke; Anne Bartlow, Nancy Gauss, Jim Dodd, and Michael Branch at Georgia Tech; Anne Turkos at Maryland; H. G. Jones at North Carolina; Maurice Toler and Virginia Hughes at North Carolina State; Laura Endicott at Virginia; and John Woodard and Myrtle Lytle at Wake Forest. Elizabeth Holsten and Martha Mills in the alumni office at North Carolina, and Nancy Priddy in Wake Forest's alumni office also helped resurrect many players in old records. Cheryl McLean in the state library of North Carolina at Raleigh also provided much research that was above and beyond.

Sports information directors who provided photos were Clemson's Tim Bourret, Duke's Mike Cragg, Georgia Tech's Mike Finn, Maryland's Herb Hartnett, North Carolina's Rick Brewer, North Carolina State's Mark Bockelman, Virginia's Rich Murray, Wake Forest's John Justus, and South Carolina's Kerry Tharp. Fred Banks of Circle Book Service provided extra photos of Maryland, North Carolina, and North Carolina State.

Introduction

In the South, football began in the round-robin games of 1888–89 between North Carolina, Trinity (now Duke), and Wake Forest. The game quickly spread from Maryland to Texas, and one conference after another was formed to facilitate better grouping. The last one born was the Atlantic Coast Conference, and this is the story of its best football teams: Clemson, Duke, Georgia Tech, Maryland, North Carolina, North Carolina State, Virginia, and Wake Forest.

Clemson is nestled in the foothills of the Blue Ridge mountains near the Georgia border, and the tiger paws painted on the roads make the return to I-85 easier. The school is built around Fort Hill, the plantation home of John C. Calhoun, Vice President to Andrew Jackson. His son-in-law, Tom Clemson, left the land to be used as an agricultural school, and in 1893 Clemson opened its doors as a land-grant school, thanks to the efforts of Ben Tillman. Today the tiny town of Clemson becomes one of the largest cities in South Carolina when the stadium is filled on autumn afternoons.

Duke was founded in 1924 by tobacco magnate James B. Duke as a memorial to his father, Washington Duke. Originally the school was called Trinity, a Methodist institution started in 1859. In 1892, Trinity moved to west Durham where the east campus with its Georgian architecture now stands. Nearby are Sarah P. Duke gardens, and further west the Gothic spires of Duke chapel overlook the west campus. Next is Wallace Wade Stadium, the home of Duke football, and on the western edge of the campus is Duke Forest, a natural study resource with 30 miles of trails.

Hard by I-85 in downtown Atlanta stands Georgia Tech, founded in 1885. Its first students came to pursue a degree in mechanical engineering, the only one offered at the time. Tech's strength is not only the red clay of Georgia, but a restored gold and white 1930 model A Ford cabriolet, the official school mascot. The old Ford was first used in 1961, but a Ramblin' Wreck had been around for over three decades. The Ramblin' Wreck fight song appeared almost as soon as the school opened, and it is not only American boys that grow up singing its rollicking tune, for Richard Nixon and Nikita Khrushchev sang it when they met in Moscow in 1959.

Maryland opened in 1856 as an agricultural school nine miles north of Washington, D.C., on land belonging to Charles Calvert, a descendant of Lord Baltimore, the state's founding father. The school colors are the same as the state flag: black and gold for George Calvert (Lord Baltimore) and red and white for his mother, Alice Crossland. Maryland has been called the school that Curley Byrd built, for he was its quarterback, then football coach, athletic director, assistant to the president, vice president, and finally its president. He also designed the football stadium and campus layout, and suggested the nickname Terrapin, a local turtle known for its bite, when students wanted to replace the name Old Liners with a new one for the school.

North Carolina, located in Chapel Hill, has been called "the perfect college town," making its tree-lined streets and balmy atmosphere what a college should look and feel like. Its inception in 1795 makes it one of the oldest schools in the nation, and its nickname of Tar Heels stems from the tar, pitch, and turpentine that were the state's principal industry. The nickname is as old as the school, for it was born during the Revolutionary War when tar was dumped into the streams to impede the advance of British forces. A ram called Rameses, however, is the school mascot. Introduced in 1924, Rameses has traveled from Yankee Stadium to the Gator Bowl, but his main chore is to outwit the Duke students who try to ram-nap him during "Beat Dook" week each year.

North Carolina State, located in Raleigh, is the third school in the triangle area with Durham and Chapel Hill which boasts more Ph.D.s than any other part of the country. It opened in 1889 as a land-grant agricultural and mechanical school and was known as A&M or Aggies or Farmers for over a quarter-century. The school's colors of pink and blue were gone by 1895, brown and white were tried for a year, but the students finally chose red and white to represent the school. An unhappy fan in 1922 said State football players behaved like a pack of wolves, and a term that was coined in derision became a badge of honor. Chancellor J. W. Harrelson reminded the students that Nazi subs ran in wolfpacks during the Second World War, but he was outvoted by the students who replied that a wolf was a scrappy, tough animal like their team.

Virginia was founded in 1819 by Thomas Jefferson and is one of three things on his tombstone for which he wanted to be remembered. James Madison and James Monroe were on the board of governors in the early years. The Rotunda, a half-scale version of the Pantheon which faces the Lawn, is the focal point of the grounds as the campus is called. Jefferson wanted his school to educate leaders in practical affairs and public service, not just to train teachers. Another feature of Mr. Jefferson's school is the student-run honor system that expels anyone found guilty of lying, cheating, or stealing.

Wake Forest was started on Calvin Jones' plantation amid the stately pine forest of Wake County in 1834. The Baptist seminary is still there, but the school was moved to Winston-Salem in 1956 on a site donated by Charles H. and Mary Reynolds Babcock. President Harry S Truman attended the ground-breaking ceremonies that brought a picturesque campus of Georgian architecture and patined roofs. Wake's colors have been black and gold since 1895, thanks to a badge designed by John Heck who died before he graduated.

I. Football Goes South
(Origins to 1952)

Football is as ancient as the first severed head of an enemy which was thrown or kicked back and forth by the victors. The Greeks gave it respectability by adding goal lines, side lines, and calling it harpaston. The Romans adopted it and passed it on to the Italians who called it *calcio*. Despite several royal edicts banning the game in medieval England, football was taken up by many town teams who challenged each other to a match with the mayor or sheriff often making the kickoff.

Since field sports were considered unscholarly by English colleges, football was popularized by the secondary schools of Charterhouse, Eton, Harrow, Rugby, Shrewsbury, and Winchester. These public schools had played the game as an intramural sport as early as the seventeenth century until one November day in 1823 at Rugby when William Webb Ellis changed the game forever. As the five o'clock bell tolled the end of a scoreless contest, Ellis ran with the ball instead of driving a heel into the turf to signal a fair catch and free kick. In a boyish burst of enthusiasm, he stiff-armed would-be tacklers, wrenched free from others, sidestepped a few more, and ran the ball over the goal.

"Walk-ker," the in-saying of the day, fell from the lips of the startled onlookers.

After the initial indignation had died down, running with the ball became the distinctive feature of football as it was played at Rugby. But Ellis became more than the prototype of the open-field runner, for he had also brought into being the stiff-arm, tackling, the touchdown, linemen, and a method for putting the ball into play when the runner was downed called a scrummage or scrum. After the tackle, the ball was thrown between two opposing lines who tried to heel it out, or kick it to a back in the rear who ran with the ball until he was again tackled. Since the ball could be heeled back either way in a scrummage, control of it was haphazard at best.

Other secondary schools in England contributed to the game. At Eton, the fifty men who formed the team on which Ellis played were trimmed to eleven. Eton also gave credit for a touchdown in the event either team kicked a goal from the field or after crossing the goal; otherwise, the only value of a touchdown was that it gave the team which made a touchdown a chance to kick a goal after it. In 1863, Charterhouse and Westminster played the first match between two schools anywhere, and developed a game which included an "outside" rule that later was called "offside."

Two distinct games emerged: soccer football, in which running with the ball was forbidden and kicking predominated; and rugby football, in which running with the ball was permitted. Soccer is derived from the word "association," as the game with no running was called after the London Football Association came into being in 1862. A few years later in 1871 the Rugby Football Union was formed, and in the following year Cambridge and Oxford played the first intercollegiate game in England.

Football came to America in the same way it was played in England. By 1609, the colonists in Jamestown kicked a blown-up bladder between two teams which included anyone who wanted to play, and before the Revolutionary War freshmen at Harvard were required to furnish footballs for the students. Freshmen and sophomores played each other at Harvard in 1827, followed by interclass games at Yale and Princeton in 1840. But the first and best of the early teams was the Oneida Club of Boston which included men who had played high school football in the Boston area. It was captained by Gerrit Miller, and from 1862 to 1865 it was unbeaten and unscored on. When a monument on Boston Common commemorated their feat in 1925, there were seven surviving members, including captain Miller, Edward Arnold, Edward Bowditch, Robert Lawrence, James Lovett, Francis Peabody, and Winthrop Scudder. After the Civil War, Henry Alden patented the first football cover in 1867.

The first football game between two schools at the college level took place on November 6, 1869. Still smarting from a 40–2 shellacking by Princeton in a baseball game three years earlier, Rutgers captain William Leggett challenged the Princeton captain, William Gummere, to a football game. At ten o'clock the train from Princeton pulled into New Brunswick, and the two captains began to clarify the rules. The rules of the London

Football Association were followed, with twenty-five men on each side, and the round ball had to be kicked or batted but not carried.

The site of the game, College Field, today is a parking lot behind the Rutgers gym. Long before game time at three o'clock, spectators were seated atop the fence which surrounded the field. The crowd was treated to a cheer taken from the Seventh New York Regiment when it passed through Princeton during the Civil War: "Hurrah! Hurrah! Hurrah! Siss! Boom! Ah!" The Rutgers section replied by singing "Oh, Susanna" and "Wait for the Wagon." As the players took off their jackets to tussle in street clothes, the Rutgers side wrapped scarlet scarves around their heads, and a coin was tossed to see who got the ball or the wind. Both of the captains shook hands and the game was on.

While both teams placed half their men in defensive positions around the field and the others were to chase the ball, two men known as "captains of the enemy's goal" patrolled the area in front of the opposition goalpost. For Princeton these players were George Billmeyer and Homer Boughner, while George Dixon and Stephen Gano attacked the enemy goal for Rutgers.

Rutgers won the toss and chose the wind as Princeton kicked off. Princeton tried an onside kick, but it dribbled off to the side. The smaller Rutgers players surrounded the ball and deftly kicked it back and forth until Dixon and Gano were able to drive it home in the first five minutes of play.

When the teams changed goals, captain Gummere told one of his biggest men, Jacob Michael, to break up the Rutgers players who were always around the ball. "Big Mike" scattered them so effectively that he tied the score soon after. Dixon put Rutgers ahead after he took a kick from Madison Ball, but Gummere tied it when he got the ball on a "Big Mike" power play.

Rutgers went ahead on a goal by Gano, and then pushed the score to 4–2. But the Rutgers lead was overshadowed when Jacob Michael and George Large of Rutgers charged into the fence and leveled it and its load of students. The taller Princeton men kept the ball in the air and batted the game into another tie, so Rutgers kept the ball on the ground and with their superior kicking ability scored the final two goals for a 6–4 win. The day ended with a supper for both teams at a local hotel before the men of Nassau took a late train back to Princeton.

After Rutgers defeated Princeton in the first soccer-style football game, Columbia and Yale, at the urging of ex–Rugby man David Schley Schaff, joined them in some games that were clearly soccer. By this time the number of players was down to twenty, and when some Etonians came to play Yale in 1873, their captain, G. C. Allen, persuaded captain Bill

Walter Camp of Yale, the father of American football.

Halsted's Elis to use eleven men. A year later, captain David Roger's rugby fifteen of McGill University in Montreal played captain Henry Grant's Harvard squad to a scoreless draw. In 1875, captain William Whiting's Harvard fifteen introduced Yale to the rugby game with a 4–0 whitewash. Three of the Harvard goals were kicked from the field by Augustus Tower, William Seamans, and Benjamin Blanchard's drop-kick on the run, and the other on Herbert Leeds' conversion after a "try" or touchdown. Captain William Arnold's Yalemen were won over to the running and tackling game and so was Princeton, thanks to two of its players in the stands, Jotham Potter and Earle Dodge.

Potter and Dodge sent out invitations for a meeting at the Massasoit House in Springfield, Massachusetts, to standardize the rules. Attending were captain Edward Price and Charles Brower of Columbia, Herbert Leeds and Charles Eaton of Harvard, captain Gene Baker and J. B. Atwater of Yale, and Potter and Dodge of Princeton. After a stormy session, the Intercollegiate Football Association was formed in 1876 with a modified Rugby Union code. An oval-shaped ball was used on a field 140 yards by 70 yards, playing time was equal halves of 45 minutes, fifteen men were on a side, as in rugby, but unlike English rugby, touchdowns counted in the scoring as did goals.

Columbia dropped out of the IFA for a few years, and Yale's 1878 captain, Walter Camp, got Yale voted into the Association one year later. From the year he was captain until his death in 1925, Camp served on every rules committee and became the "Father of American Football." By the time he was captain, the flannel suits he had played in as an underclassman were replaced by canvas uniforms laced up the front. They were worn for the first time by Princeton in the Harvard game of 1877 and were called "smocks" after their inventor, Ledou Smock, while the players were called canvasbacks. It was also at the end of the 1870s that the names for the positions of the players, which were borrowed from rugby, came into general use.

American football was born in 1880 when Camp was able to get Bob Bacon of Harvard and Bland Ballard of Princeton to accept eleven men on a side, a scrimmage line, a center who snapped the ball with his foot, and a quarterback who handled the ball first on every play, including punts and field goal tries. Ball control and planned plays now replaced the game of chance inherent in the rugby scrum. Ballard was an innovator himself, for as last year's Tiger captain, he first conceived the idea of using interference to block for the ball carrier. It was disallowed at first, since anyone ahead of the ball carrier was offside in rugby, but it was quickly accepted as part of the American game.

Although Princeton and Yale played a scoreless tie in 1879, the Intercollegiate Football Association awarded Princeton the championship pennant on the basis that it had won the title in 1878. The new scrimmage line was hampered in the Princeton-Yale title game of 1880 when Tiger captain Francis Loney thought his team could keep the crown with another tie. The scrimmage line was also hurt by the safety rule, for a team which touched the ball down safe behind its goal was allowed to bring it out to the 25-yard line and retain possession. It was possible, therefore, to keep the ball indefinitely if it wasn't fumbled away.

The Princeton-Yale title games of 1880 and 1881 were both scoreless and were called the "block games." In the first game Princeton had eleven safeties and Yale five, but the IFA awarded no title because the public thought the championship should be settled on the field and not at a conference table. In the next rules meeting, Camp got an amendment passed which stated that if there was no scoring, the team with four fewer safeties would be the winner. Camp also got the playing field reduced to 110 yards by 53 yards. The second block game provoked even greater unrest. Princeton kept the ball throughout the first half and moved it only a few yards, and Yale did the same thing in the last half. The newspapers ridiculed a ho-hum game in which the object was not to score but to block the other team's effort to do so.

Camp put offense into American football with a system of downs for the 1882 season. If a team didn't gain five yards in three tries, the ball went to the other team. When Harvard's Ed Cabot asked how one could tell when five yards had been gained, Camp suggested putting chalk lines across the field.

"It'll look like a gridiron," said Princeton's Ned Peace, and American football was almost off the drawing board.

A system of downs brought planned plays and signals which were called at the line of scrimmage by the captain. At first, they were sentences, phrases, or words. Talking to players in sequence indicated the play for a while. Finally, each play was numbered, with a separate number used for the snap of the ball.

One flaw still remained, for the scoring system had a rule which boggles the mind: "A match shall be decided by a majority of touchdowns; a goal shall be equal to four touchdowns, but in case of a tie a goal kicked from a touchdown shall take precedence over four touchdowns."

The Harvard-Princeton game of 1882 underscored this jargon. Frank Mason of Harvard scored a touchdown, missed the goal (or conversion) after it, but kicked a goal from the field. Princeton made a touchdown, and Jim Haxall converted the goal. Both teams claimed the superiority of their goal. When referee Bob Watson, 1880 Yale captain, awarded Harvard the win, the Tigers protested vehemently and claimed victory for years.

With Camp's scoring system of 1883, the basic structure of American football was complete. A field goal, or goal from the field, was five points, and a goal after touchdown was four points. A touchdown was two points, and a safety, or downing the ball behind your goal, was no longer safe territory but gave one point to the opposition. A year later, a touchdown became four points, and a conversion and safety both became two points. In 1885, the first penalty appeared when Camp proposed a five-yard penalty for offside. In order to stem the desire to win at any price, another rule in the following year stated that all college players must be regularly enrolled students in school.

A new rule in 1888 made offensive linemen keep their arms at their sides. It was intended to stop slugging and made them stand closer together instead of spreading out in rugby fashion. Backfield men also lined up in a tight T-formation, and the long lateral passes from one back to another disappeared. The game was changed for decades as blockers were concentrated in front of the ball carrier, and mass-formation plays which attempted to gain a few yards at a time became popular for a few years. At Princeton, the "boxing the tackle" maneuver was devised in which end Dave Bovaird and tackle Bill Cook formed a two-man box around Yale's left tackle, Charley Gill. Simultaneously, Tiger backs Snake Ames and Jerry Black wiped out left end Kid Wallace, and Hector Cowan went through the hole for a large gain before Billy Bull brought him down. This game also saw the Princeton quarterback instead of the captain call signals for the first time.

Football came to the South that same year when Wake Forest met North Carolina at the state fair on October 18 in Raleigh. It was soccer football with 15 men on a side, and a goal counted two points. North Carolina scored first, but Wake took a 6–4 win in three frames. Among those taking part for Wake were captain Carey Dowd, Frank Mitchell, Hubert Royster, B. T. Williamson, Junius Beckwith, Bill Devin, Jim McDaniel, Charles Richardson, D. B. Oliver, and Del Upchurch. Carolina's team included captain Bob Bingham, George Graham, Charlie Mangum, John Holmes, Andy Patterson, George Ransom, Henry Gilliam, and John Morehead, after whom the campus planetarium is named.

Wake Forest's first football team in 1888. Notice the pugnacious stance of the linemen and center Bob Burns ready to kick the ball back to quarterback Fred Merritt.

Rugby football appeared one month later on Thanksgiving Day when Dr. John Crowell, a Yale man and president of Trinity College (now Duke University), challenged North Carolina to a contest in Raleigh. North Carolina made a valiant attempt to learn the new game, but Trinity's expertise prevailed as quarterback Stonewall Durham, halfback Tom Daniels, and right guard Hal Crowell scored touchdowns in a 16–0 win. Trinity's fullback was Albert Sharpe, with Frank Rahders at halfback. Rushers, or linemen, were Blake Nicholson, Will Cranford, Robert Durham, Bob Mitchell, Will Fearrington, and captain Whit Johnston. The North Carolina team had quarterback Reuben Campbell, halfbacks George Graham and Henry Gilliam, and fullback Edgar Love. Rushers were Sam Blount, Lacy Little, Henry Wharton, Palmer Dalrymple, William Shaffner, captain Steve Bragaw, and Logan Howell, who replaced injured William Headen. Not long after Trinity, North Carolina, and Wake Forest formed the North Carolina Inter-Collegiate Football Association.

North Carolina's football team improved greatly when Hector Cowan came to the campus in the spring of 1889. New faces were linemen John Burroughs, Fred Fearrington, Sloan Huggins, Bob Johnston, Bill Snipes, end Linwood Corpening, and back Joe Rhem. The result was a 33–0 victory over Wake Forest, but Trinity beat Carolina 25–17 as captain Bragaw suffered a broken leg. Bill Riddick and John White joined the Wake Forest

The 1892 North Carolina football team. Front row, left to right: Louis Guion, Al Barnard, Bill Devin, Charles Baskerville. Middle row: Jim Biggs, Mike Hoke, Pete Murphy, Bill Merritt. Back row: Ben Stanley, William Wooten, Norfleet Gibbs, David Kirkpatrick, Eugene Snipes, George Little, James Pugh.

team which like Trinity had a win and loss in the round-robin schedule, and the schools divided the state championship. In the fall of the year, the three teams split their games and again divided the state title. Wake Forest traveled to Richmond in December and on successive days lost to Virginia 46–4 but beat Richmond 32–14. Carolina's George Graham suffered a broken collarbone, and the trustees banned the sport in 1890. Wake Forest also outlawed the game that year, and in 1890 Trinity played a single game with Virginia in Richmond and lost 10–4.

Duke's veteran team was the South's best in 1891. The line had Ed Whitaker, Doc Caviness, Tim Plyler, and Will McDowell, with backs Fred Harper, Robert Durham, Tom Daniels, and Stonewall Durham, who took over for Billie Rowland. New men were Plato Durham, Jake Haynes, and Erwin Avery, supported by Ben Black, Carl Bandy, Will Flowers, Luther Hartsell, Tom James, Alva Plyler, and Pink Turner. They beat Furman 96–0, North Carolina 6–4, as a 95-yard run by Sam Ashe set up the Carolina score, and Virginia 20–0.

North Carolina, known as the University until out-of-state games were scheduled the following year, played another game in 1891. Wake Forest was the opponent, and the record shows a 1–0 forfeit in favor of Wake, but the Tar Heel team that ex–Yale back Billy Graves had put together was ahead when the forfeit occurred. A North Carolina player named Herb Ferguson bulldogged left half Claude Wilson to the turf and a few plays later brought Roy Powell down hard with a necktie tackle. Sam Hall at guard had enough and threw a punch at Ferguson, but Ferguson punched Hall in return. As so often happens the second player was penalized, this one by umpire Dave Prince. The penalty did not please captain Mike Hoke of the University who argued that both men should be disqualified according to the rules. When he took his team from the field, referee Howard Shaw awarded the game to Wake Forest.

Backs Hoke, Ferguson, and Ashe aided the North Carolina cause, as did quarterback Al Barnard. Interior linemen were 235-pound center Dan Hudgins, Eugene Snipes, Rufus Austin, William Pinckney Martin Currie, and George Little, with Jim Biggs and Harry Whedbee at end rush. The substitutes who sometimes got in the game were Norfleet Gibbs, Ken Jones, Henry Clay Houston, and Jim Gaither.

Wake's 235-pound center, Rufus Fry, made the middle like a sumo wrestler stand-off. Flanking him were Walter Sikes at guard, tackles Edwin Webb and Bill Garland, with Job Cook and John Payseur at end. George Blanton was at quarterback, and at right half was captain Vernon Howell who would later earn a master's degree at North Carolina. The subs who got in against the Tar Heels were Silas Boyles, Raleigh Daniels, John Mills, and Carl Pridgen.

Football took hold across the land in 1892. Ex–Yalemen Amos Alonzo Stagg coached and played on Chicago's pioneer eleven, and Lee McClung coached California in its first meeting with Walter Camp's Stanford squad. Georgia Tech fielded a team for the first time, and in 1893 player-coach Leonard Wood took it to its first win, a 28–6 defeat of Georgia. North Carolina A&M (later North Carolina State) and the Maryland Aggies (later Maryland) also put a team on the field for the first time. North Carolina had its first real season and best team so far. After losing the initial game in the long rivalry with Virginia at Charlottesville 30–18, Carolina, led by 200-pound linemen Bill Merritt, Pete Murphy, William Wooten, and David "Baby" Kirkpatrick, shut out Trinity 24–0, Auburn 64–0, Vanderbilt 24–0, and Virginia 26–0 in a return match in Atlanta.

It was in Atlanta that the forerunner of the Atlantic Coast Conference was born in 1894. Dr. William L. Dudley of Vanderbilt asked representatives from Alabama, Auburn, Georgia, Georgia Tech, North Carolina, and the University of the South (Sewanee) to meet in order to regulate athletics in the South. The result was the Southern Intercollegiate Athletic Association (SIAA). North Carolina and Virginia declined to join because of the distance between them and the other schools. Within a few years, most of the biggest schools in the South became members of the SIAA, including Clemson, which fielded its first football team in 1896.

But it was too late for Trinity, which lost its only game of 1894 and did not play again for a quarter-century. Wake Forest also gave up the sport after a lone game in 1895 and did not resume play until the 1908 season. In addition to the "ringers" or players who were not students, the brutality of the game became a vital issue at Wake Forest. Offered as proof was Walter Sikes of the 1895 team who had played in Wake Forest's first game in 1888 and was a campus landmark because of his flattened nose.

A famous wrinkle in the development of American football took place in the Georgia–North Carolina game of 1895. A Georgia rush threatened to block a punt by Joel Whitaker, the Carolina quarterback. Whitaker sidestepped the charging line and threw the ball forward to get rid of it. Halfback George Stephens caught the illegal forward pass and sprinted 70 yards for the game's only score. Georgia coach Pop Warner protested loud and long, but the referee let the play stand because he had not seen the ball thrown forward. First year Auburn coach, John Heisman, saw the play and began his campaign to improve the game by making a forward pass legal.

Stephens was no ordinary halfback. In a 1910 article, Joel Whitaker put him in the all-star lineup of early UNC players. His running mates were halfback Hunter Carpenter and quarterback Will Jacocks, both from the 1904 team. At fullback was Arthur Belden (1897). The ends were Ed Gregory and Herman Koehler, and at center was Herbert "Mink" Cunningham, all from the 1898 squad. The guards were Louis Guion (1894) and Harris "Bear" Collier (1895), with Bob Wright (1896) and Romy Story (1906) at tackle.

The 1898 North Carolina team was well represented because it was the school's only unbeaten and untied team. Under coach Will Reynolds, UNC had seven shutouts and allowed only eight points in winning nine games. In addition to Gregory, Koehler, and Cunningham, the team usually lined up with Sam Shull and Frank Bennett at tackle, with Sam Cromartie and Ike Phifer playing guard. Handling the ball were Frank Rogers at quarter,

A youthful John Heisman became Georgia Tech's first paid coach in 1904.

halfbacks Vernon Howell and Jim MacRae, and fullback Ernest Graves. Reserves were Cameron Buxton, Jim Copeland, Fred Coxe, Warren Kluttz, and Evan McIver.

While UNC's 1898 squad was carving a niche in gridiron lore, an incident the previous year almost killed southern football. In the Virginia game, Georgia fullback Richard Von Gammon was injured and died in a hospital the next morning. In special session, the Georgia legislature voted overwhelmingly to banish football from the state. But the dead boy's mother wrote the governor requesting him not to abolish the game her son had loved so much.

Governor Atkinson did not sign the bill.

The new century found John Heisman coaching at Clemson. He won six of six in 1900, beating South Carolina 51–0, Georgia 39–5, and Alabama 35–0. Linemen from left to right were C.A. Bellows, Joe Duckworth, Jack Woodward, John Kinsler, A.P. George, Norman Walker, and Jim Lynah. The halfbacks were Buster Hunter and Will Forsythe, with Claude Douthit at full and Gus Lewis at quarter.

Mass-formation plays and two-on-one blocking in order to gain a few yards had made the game dangerous. The closely bunched line made it difficult for the center to kick the ball back, so in 1890 it became legal to center it with the hands. Flying wedge formations were outlawed after the 1893 season, but the guards-back formations of George Woodruff at Pennsylvania in 1894 and tackle-back of Henry Williams at Minnesota in 1900 often put more men in the backfield than on the line. In 1898 the value of a touchdown was raised to five points and a conversion was reduced to one point. A field goal became four points in 1904, and six men on the offensive scrimmage line with a seventh man a yard out and a yard back curtailed further use of guards-back and tackle-back plays. The first man who handled the ball could not run forward unless he was five yards from the center, so the checkerboard that appeared last year between the 25-yard lines now covered the entire field.

Further change was needed because 18 players were killed in 1905, and President Theodore Roosevelt threatened to abolish the sport. Columbia quit the game from 1906 to 1914 due to the action of its president, Nicholas Murray Butler, California and Stanford played rugby during these nine years, Northwestern had no team for two years, South Carolina fielded no team for one, and Western Conference schedules were cut in half.

A conference called by chancellor Henry M. McCracken of New York University formed the American Intercollegiate Football Rules Committee headed by Captain Palmer E. Pierce of West Point (1906). Four years later the name was changed to the National Collegiate Athletic Association (NCAA). The forward pass was legalized, but the man who threw it had to be five yards behind the center. To keep the foot in football, an incomplete forward pass was given a 15-yard penalty. A neutral zone the length of the ball was introduced, the game was shortened to equal halves of 30 minutes, and ten yards gained in three tries was necessary for a first down.

Like Princeton, Harvard, and Yale, Virginia had its alumni coach in the early years. Merritt T. "Empty" Cooke, who was captain of the 1905 team, coached Virginia to seven wins and no losses, had seven shutouts, including a scoreless tie with Sewanee, and gave up only nine points in 1908. Halfback Forrest Stanton's 30-yard end run beat North Carolina State 6–0, and another last-half run by fullback Kemper Yancey overcame Georgetown in a snowstorm 6–0.

Captain Bill Gloth at center, guard Bill Calfee, and quarterback Sam Honaker were gone from the 1908 squad, but in their place were center Oscar Thraves, guard Malcolm Harris, and quarterback Stapleton Gooch. Returning were ends Hedley Bowen and John Elliott, tackles Horace Geyer and Byron Cecil, guard Matt Murphy, fullback Kemper Yancey, and halfback Forrest Stanton. Ed Holladay went in at left half when Archer Christian was fatally injured in the 21–0 win over Georgetown. He was driven back on a cross buck with no pile-up, but his head bounced hard when he hit the ground. In the aftermath of this tragedy, Virginia's game with North Carolina was cancelled. Curley Byrd, 1907 Maryland captain, who played for George Washington in 1908, was not allowed to play for Georgetown against Virginia because of the one-year residence rule between the two schools. It was also in 1909 that a field goal first became three points.

Johnny Neff, who captained the 1907 Virginia team, coached the 1909 squad to seven victories, had seven shutouts, and permitted only 11 points in the 11–7 loss to Lehigh. The Lehigh contest started poorly as captain Lloyd Treat blocked Hedley Bowen's punt, caught it on the bounce and went 35 yards to a touchdown before the game was a minute old. Stape Gooch tied it on a 10-yard pass to John Elliott, but Don Gordon's 10-yard run in the last half put Lehigh ahead again. Charles Martin added the conversion, and Gordon was later downed behind the goal by Horace Geyer for a safety. The fumbles that had plagued the Lehigh game continued against Navy, as Kemper Yancey lost the ball going over tackle at the goal and Matt Murphy fell on it in the end zone for a 5–0 victory.

The deaths of Army tackle Eugene Byrne, Navy quarterback Earl Wilson, and a dozen others in 1909 brought more changes next year. With halfbacks deeper to defend against a forward pass, the tackle position was vulnerable to mass interference. In order to reduce injuries, seven men had to be on the offensive line at the snap of the ball, and for two years a pass could not exceed 20 yards. The game was divided into quarters, and any player who left the game could return at the start of the next quarter. The ball could be run or thrown across the line at any point by the first back who touched it, so the checkerboard reverted to a gridiron again. The field was shortened to 100 yards in 1912, and a ten-yard end zone was added at both ends. A touchdown was upped to six points, and a fourth down to gain ten yards and maintain possession was added.

North Carolina's 1914 team was its first to win ten games. With assistants Tal Pendleton, Tom Wilson, and Art Bluethenthal from Princeton's 1911 national champions, coach Doggie Trenchard turned the Tar Heels into one of the South's best teams. After drubbing Richmond 41–0, a reverse from quarterback Rey Allen to end Roy Homewood to right half Walter Fuller highlighted a 65–0 whitewash of Virginia Medical College. Sam Hines started at left half in place of captain Dave Tayloe in a Thursday contest that produced a 53–0 victory over Wake Forest. Mel Parker's 35-yard stolen pass keyed a 48–0 defeat of Norman Edgerton's South Carolina squad four days later, but Gamecock captain Luther Hill was lost with a broken leg. A trip to Atlanta saw Alex Cunningham's Georgia team lose 41–6 as Parker scored on the third play. Tayloe went 62 yards on the next series for the first of his three touchdowns, and Ed Reid added two more. Dave Paddock squirmed in for the Georgia score, but Ed Broyles failed to convert. A 40–0 win over Riverside Academy completed the swing to the deep South.

The game in Nashville with Vanderbilt was the roughest one of the season. Chili Carman scored for the Commodores near the sideline, so Sam Chester tried a puntout from behind the goal to get better position for the ball on the conversion. Glen Reams heeled the ball, or caught it, at the 25-yard stripe, but Rabbit Curry missed the free kick. Center Yank Tandy halved the score with a field goal, but tackle Josh Cody's kick made it 9–3. The Vandy line of center Chet Huffman, guards Chuck Brown and Dutch Phillipp, tackle Doc Warren, and ends Russ Cohen and Emmett Putnam had the game under control until tackle Graham Ramsey broke through to block a second-half punt. He recovered it in the end zone, and Tandy drop-kicked the conversion for a 10–9 Carolina win.

Giles Long completed a touchdown to Bob Winston in the 16–3 win over Davidson, and Bill McKinnon kicked the three points for captain Jim Howell's men. Jim Bain ran in a fumble and Laurence Oakes converted for the VMI points, but Winston returned the ensuing kickoff to beat Frank Gorton's eleven 30–7. Wilbur Smith had Wake Forest ready this time, as they led 7–6 at the half on a Gil Billings pass to Bob Holding that set up a score by George Trust. The Deacon line of center John Carrick, guards Laurence Stallings and Hubert Olive, tackles Lonnie Blackman and captain George Moore, and ends Julius Powell and John Abernethy battled Carolina in the mud until Fuller scored for a 12–7 Tar Heel win.

A crowd of 15,000, the largest ever to watch a football game in Richmond, was at Broad Street Park for the joust with Virginia on Thanksgiving Day. On hand were Secretary of the Navy Josephus Daniels, who spoke to both teams at halftime, Virginia governor Henry C. Stuart, and governor Locke Craig of North Carolina. It was another knock-down, drag-out game as neither team attempted a pass, and Virginia emerged victorious 20–3. Trenchard complained about the poor officiating, but the Tar Heels were lucky to get a field goal by Tandy against Virginia's clear-cut superiority.

Others not previously referred to on the North Carolina team were linemen Frank Jones, Archie Gay, Horace Cowell, Henry Foust, and George Tennent, ends Bill Huske and Bob Wright, Jr., and Carl Ervin, Leroy Bridges, and Bob Burnett in the backfield.

Virginia had three great years before its first losing season in 1916. Coached by Rice Warren, the 1913 club won seven and lost to Georgetown, 8–7, when Ed Heiskell and Bill Cusack blocked John Ray's punt back through the end zone. Next year's team won eight under coach Joe Wood. They lost only to Frank Hinkey's Yale team, 21–0, as the lateral passes of Alex Wilson, Harry Legore, Carroll Knowles, and Foggy Ainsworth were too much. This squad lost centers Shelby Jett, John Brown, and Tom Creekmore, guards Jim Redus and captain Aubrey Carter, tackles Bill Maiden and Pichegru Woolfolk, halfback Bob Randolph, and Warwick Landes at full.

Coming back for 1914 were ends Jim Gillette and James White, guard Harris Coleman, quarterback Bobby Gooch, and captain Gene Mayer at left half. New men were centers Peyton Evans and George Anderson, guard Claude Moore, tackles Reuben Barker and Jim Ward, end Bill Flannagan, Norborne Berkeley at quarter, Ed Anderson and Bill Word at right half, and Harold Sparr and Knox Walker at full.

Harry Varner coached the 1915 team to eight wins, including 10–0 over Yale and 35–10 over Dan McGugin's Vanderbilt team that had eight shutouts in ten games. They lost only to Percy Haughton's Harvard eleven, 9–0, on three Eddie Mahan field goals.

The 1915 team had ends Jim Ward, James White, and Rich Stillwell, tackles George Anderson, Bill Stuart, and Claude Moore, Al Thurman, John Calhoun, and captain Harris Coleman at guard, and centers John Brown and Tom Coleman. Backs were quarterback Norborne Berkeley, Harold Sparr at full, and halfbacks Gene Mayer, Ed Anderson, and Ed

Tippett, whose field goal beat Georgia 9–7. After Mayer's 35-yard dash, the 25-yarder sailed over at the gun to erase John Powell's 80-yard run. Mayer ended with 312 career points and 48 touchdowns, six of them in Richmond's 74–0 defeat.

Southern football came into full bloom with John Heisman's national champions at Georgia Tech in 1917. Gone were fullback Tommy Spence, guard Bob Lang, and end Jim Senter who had buried Cumberland the previous year, 222–0. Utilizing Heisman's "jump shift" in which the team lined up behind the center and jumped into place at the snap of the ball, they were unbeaten for the last two years with only a tie each season to mar their record.

This year they won all nine games while averaging over 54 points per game. Leading this whirlwind group were quarterback Al Hill with 22 touchdowns, halfback Ev Strupper with 20 scores, and Carlisle transfer Joe Guyon at halfback who had 344 yards in 12 carries in the 83–0 trouncing of Vanderbilt. At fullback was Judy Harlan. The center was Pup Phillips, Ham Dowling and Dan Welchel at guard, tackles Bill Fincher with 49 conversions and captain Walker Carpenter, with Si Bell and Ray Ulrich at end.

With quarterback Jack McDonough, halfbacks Buck Flowers and Red Barron, and Judy Harlan at full, new coach Bill Alexander at Georgia Tech lost only to Pitt, 10–3, in 1920. Interior linemen were Al Staton, Oscar Davis, Bad Dad Amis, Dummy LeBey, and Bill Fincher, flanked by John Staton and George Ratterman, whose son later quarterbacked at Notre Dame and in the pros.

After World War I, the Southern Intercollegiate Athletic Association suffered from growing pains. By 1920, the SIAA had grown to 29 members, many of them smaller schools. The biggest problem was the same hurdle that haunts college football today: freshman eligibility. The larger schools wanted the "freshman rule" to control questionable recruiting practices, "ringers" or migrant athletes, and unauthorized subsidies. The smaller schools needed freshmen on their teams to help them compete on an equal basis when they played the bigger universities. Out of this discord came the Southern Conference in 1922.

The coaching team of brothers Bill and Bob Fetzer took North Carolina to nine wins in 1922 and a single loss to Yale, 18–0, at New Haven. The loss was a bitter pill to swallow. Halfback Red Johnston led a drive to the Yale goal, but after ramming it over three times they came up empty as a penalty nullified each score.

Carolina had center Bill Blount, Charles Poindexter and captain Grady

Pritchard at guard, Pierce Matthews and Herman McIver at tackle, and ends Suey Cochran, Casey Morris, and Tom Shepard. Backs were Alan McGee, Fred Morris, Moose Tenney, and passer Monk McDonald.

At Maryland Agricultural College, Curley Byrd took over as football coach in 1912 and began to create a school in his own image. He was instrumental in getting the state to take over MAC and turn it into Maryland State in 1916. After lobbying in the legislature for a bill which merged Maryland State with a professional school in Baltimore, the University of Maryland was born in 1920. With Leroy Mackert and Untz Brewer in the backfield that year, the stage was set for future greatness with a 10–7 win over one of Chick Meehan's strong Syracuse teams in the early 1920s.

An even greater win came three years later when quarterback Boots Groves' kick overcame Penn at Franklin Field 3–0. The 1923 team was Byrd's best to date—if not the best. Jack McQuade was at full, with halfbacks Tubby Branner and Ed Pugh. At center was Rosy Pollock, Tony Hough and Bottle Hall at guard, Joe Burger and Walter Bromley at tackle, and ends Bill Supplee and Pat Lanigan.

A month later, Maryland almost had another great win at the Yale Bowl in New Haven. With Mack Brewer and Arthur Bonnett in for injured Hough and Hall at guard, and Downey Osborn and George Heine replacing runners Branner and McQuade, Maryland had 9-0-0 Yale hanging on 16–14 as Groves missed a last-period field goal.

"It was eight feet inside the post," screamed Heine. Byrd agreed, and another team found it tough to beat Yale at home.

Coach Hank Garrity's 1924 Wake Forest squad had seven wins and was also state champion for the first time. They beat North Carolina, 7–6, on halfback Murray Greason's 70-yard scoring run. Howard Jones' Trinity team (which had resumed play in 1920) lost, 32–0, as end Bill Riley blocked two punts that resulted in touchdowns, and North Carolina State went under 12–0. Regular linemen were Fred Emmerson at center, guards Clyde Jones and DeVere Lentz, Bill Ellerbe and captain Bill Moran at tackle, and Pete Pagano at end. The backs were Matt Karleskint at full, Blainey Rackley at quarter, and halfback Frank Armstrong, the World War II general portrayed by Gregory Peck in the movie, "Twelve O'Clock High."

It was also in 1924 that the first girl cheerleader was seen on the sidelines, as Ziegfeld Follies showgirl Marian Draper led the cheers in the Tulane-Vanderbilt game. Two years later future bandleader Kay Kyser was leading cheers at North Carolina.

North Carolina State under Gus Tebell reached nine wins for the first

Left: **In addition to his many hats at Maryland, Curley Byrd was also a sports-writer for the** ***Washington Star*** **for 20 years while coaching.** *Right:* **Bill Alexander coached Georgia Tech to its second national championship in 1928.**

time, lost only to Furman 20–0, and was champion of the sprawling Southern Conference. Halfback Jack McDowall made 1927 the year of the wolf as he ran back a punt 58 yards for a score to down Wake Forest 30–7. His 75-yard interception beat Florida 12–6, as the Gators, with linemen Louis Bono, Bert Grandoff, Joe Bryan, Jus Clemons, ends Dale Van Sickel and Dennis Stanley, and backs Clyde Crabtree, Carl Brumbaugh, Royce Goodbread, and Rainey Cawthon were but a year from greatness. McDowall's two drop-kick extra points defeated Jimmy DeHart's Duke squad 20–18. His running mates were halfbacks Bill Outen and George Hunsucker, Sparky Adams at quarter, and Bob Warren at full. Linemen were center Bill Metz, guards Fred Vaughan and captain Nick Nicholson, tackles Bob Evans and John Lepo, and ends Frank Goodwin and Tom Childress.

Georgia Tech had another national champion in 1928 when Bill Alexander took them all the way to Pasadena and an 8–7 Rose Bowl victory over California. The game featured the run of Cal center, Roy "Wrong-Way" Riegels, who grabbed a fumble and ran 66 yards to his own goal. On the next play, tackle Vance Maree blocked a punt for the safety that proved to be the winning margin.

A late rally on a pass from quarterback Benny Lom to end Irv Phillips and Stan Barr's conversion came up a point short for Cal.

The Tech line-up had all–American Pete Pund at center, guards Raleigh Drennon and Joe Westbrook, tackle Ken Thrash with Maree, and ends Frank Waddey and Tom Jones. Bob Durant and Izzy Shulman were at quarter, Roy Lumpkin at full, with halfbacks Warner Mizell and Stumpy Thomason. Regular tackle Frank Speer did not play.

Two years after William Rand Kenan, a football letterman at Carolina in 1893 and noted engineer, donated money to build Kenan Stadium, UNC had another 9-1-0 season in 1929. Chuck Collins, an end on the Four Horsemen team at Notre Dame, saw his squad score 346 points to 60 while losing only to Georgia, 19–12. They were known as "The Team with a Million Backs" and were famed for their long distance passers: Jim Ward, Jim Magner, Jim Maus, who threw 67 yards to Chuck Erickson for a touchdown in the North Carolina State game, and Phil Jackson, who had scoring passes of 78 yards to Yank Spaulding and 60 yards to Johnny Branch against Maryland. Other backs were Pete Wyrick, Strud Nash, Henry House, Pap Harden, and Rip Slusser. Linemen were center Ned Lipscomb, Ellis Fysal and captain Ray Farris at guard, tackles Fenton Adkins and Bill Koenig, and ends Julian Fenner and Don Holt. Ezra Rowe only did kickoffs and had a good claim as the first college specialist.

After a long drought, Josh Cody coached Clemson to its best season in three decades. The 1930 team won eight and lost to Tennessee and Charley Bachman's Florida Gators by like scores, 27–0. They lined up with ends Foggy Woodruff and Bob Jones, tackles Mule Yarborough and Footsie Davis, guards Reuben Siegel and Vic Fleming, and center Red Fordham. Maxcey Welch and captain Johnnie Justus were halfbacks, Lionell Harvin at full, and blocker Grady Salley.

Two years prior to the Southern Conference division, Curley Byrd had another good team at Maryland in 1931. He used a double wing formation with Shorty Chalmers coming across from his left wing spot to do the passing, but it was blocking back Al Woods who started them off right with an 80-yard run up the middle in the 13–0 win over Washington College. After Charlie May's score tied Virginia, Chalmers kicked the winning conversion 7–6. Rip Miller's Navy squad was scuttled 6–0 on a pass to end Al Pease who got behind Joe Tschirgi. They tied Kentucky 6–6, with its great backs, Shipwreck Kelly, Cecil Urbaniak, and Ralph Kercheval, on a reverse from May to Chalmers who threw to end John Norris. Halfback Bosey Berger on the right wing had two first-half scores as VMI was beaten 41–20, and Ray

Poppelman scored twice in the 20–0 win over Virginia Tech. Vanderbilt led only 13–12 at the half, but knocked them from the conference lead as their heavier team rolled to a 39–12 victory. Maryland rebounded with a 13–7 win over Washington and Lee on a pair of Poppelman touchdowns, and Berger scored three times in the 35–14 defeat of Johns Hopkins. In the 41–6 victory over Dick Harlow's Western Maryland eleven, Poppelman's 201 yards rushing mark stood for 43 years, and his 1,350 yards broke Snitz Snyder's season record of 1,255 yards.

Starters were centers Skip Faber and John Mitchell, guards Jess Krajcovic and Courtney Hayden, tackles Charles Keenan and Ernie Carliss, with reserves Paul Kiernan and Ray Koelle.

In order to reduce travel time and expense because of great distance, the Southeastern Conference separated from the Southern Conference in 1933. The SEC encompassed 13 members: Alabama, Auburn, Florida, Georgia, Georgia Tech, Kentucky, Louisiana State, Mississippi, Mississippi State, Sewanee, Tennessee, Tulane, and Vanderbilt. Sewanee withdrew after 1940, Georgia Tech after 1963, and Tulane two years later. These schools were in the deep South or west of the Appalachian Mountains, while those in the Southern Conference were on the coast in the mid–Atlantic states.

The Southern Conference kept ten schools: Clemson, Duke, Maryland, North Carolina, North Carolina State, South Carolina, Virginia, Virginia Military Institute, Virginia Tech, and Washington and Lee.

Three years later The Citadel, Davidson, Furman, Richmond, Wake Forest, and William and Mary joined the Southern Conference. Virginia withdrew in 1936, but the addition of George Washington in 1941 and West Virginia in 1949 raised the membership to 17.

With the coming of Wallace Wade, the heroic years of Duke football began. He was no stranger to the Rose Bowl. He was in the second Rose Bowl game at guard for Brown when they lost to Washington State, 14–0. He coached Alabama in three Rose Bowl games: His 1925 team beat Washington, 20–19, he tied Stanford the next year, 7–7, and his 1930 team evened the score with Washington State, 24–0. He almost made three trips as Duke coach. Behind all–American tackle Fred Crawford in 1933, Duke won nine games, but lost the finale to Georgia Tech on a Wink Davis score, 6–0, and the Rose Bowl scouts in Atlanta continued their search. On this team were ends Tom Rogers, Earle Wentz, and back-up Ed West, tackle Gus Durner, Jack Dunlap and captain Carl Schock at guard, and Jack's brother, E. B. Dunlap at center. At quarter was Horace Hendrickson, Corky

Carl Snavely coached North Carolina in its golden era of football after World War II.

Cornelius, Nick Laney, and Harry Rossiter at halfback, with Bob Cox and Jack Alexander at full.

Duke was Southern Conference champion again in 1935 after a big win over Carl Snavely's Carolina team. UNC had won all seven games and was lauded for the Rose Bowl in spite of president Frank Graham's de-emphasis that made Snavely leave at year's end. After Jule Ward's 47-yard scoring run, Don Jackson rolled a punt out-of-bounds on the Duke 2. Carolina was set to catch the 6–0 lead as John Hennemier, Duke's 160-pound center, snapped the ball. With Andy Bershak, Dick Buck, Jim Hutchins, and Herman Snyder closing in on him, Ace Parker punted out of danger to Carolina's 41-yard line where Dick Talliaferro downed it. Parker later scored on a 30-yard run to maintain Duke's reputation as the "home run" team.

Another good team in 1935 was Maryland. Gone were Norwood Sothoron and John Simpson, but 19 talented lettermen returned to take the Terps to a 7-2-2 record. Leading them was halfback Bill Guckevson, a triple-threat player worthy of all–American honors. He carried four times for 100 yards and a touchdown and averaged 57 yards on seven punts in a 39–6 triumph over St. John's. His touchdown beat Virginia Tech 7–0. After losing to North Carolina 33–0, his 29-yard run set up the score by Jack Stonebraker that beat VMI 6–0. His punt return led to a score by Charlie Ellinger against Dutch Stanley's Florida Gators, he hit Vic Willis for another, and Stonebraker made the final tally in a 20–6 victory.

Guckeyson and Ellinger scored to overcome Virginia 14–7, and Guckeyson's pass set up a John Gormley score to lead Indiana 7–6. Bo McMillan's Hoosiers scored in the last minutes for a 13–7 win, then named Guckeyson the best back they'd seen all year, despite the fact they had faced Chicago and Jay Berwanger, the first Heisman winner. LeRoy Day had Washington and Jefferson ready in a 0–0 knot, but Guckeyson scored twice to down Jack Hagerty's Georgetown Hoyas 12–6. After another scoreless tie with Syracuse in a pouring rain, Guckeyson scored one touchdown, passed for another, and ran in a 60-yard pass theft in the 22–7 win over Western Maryland.

Guckeyson's supporting cast included center Frank DeArmey, guards Ed Minion and Mike Surgent, tackles John Birkland and Carl Stalfort, end Lou Ennis, and halfback George Sachs. In addition to those already mentioned reserve linemen were Charley Callahan, Ed Fletcher, Bill Garrott, Tom McLaughlin, and Bill Wolfe, Bernie Buscher at end, and Ed Daly and Coleman Headley in the backfield.

Duke was conference champ again in 1936 with an even better team. They won eight and lost only to Tennessee, 15–13, as Red Harp scored on a 70-yard punt return late in the game. They did another job on North Carolina, 27–7, this time with Ray Wolf as coach. After tying it at seven, Tom Burnette kicked off five yards deep into the end zone. Ace Parker went all the way, as his escort of end Dick Talliaferro, tackle Tom Power, and guard Woody Lipscomb screened off safety Crowell Little.

Suiting up were center Dan Hill, guards Fred Yorke, Clarence Badgett, and Bob Alabaster, tackles Joe Brunansky and Joe Cardwell, and end Frank Liana. Backs were Eric Tipton, Sam Gardner, and Elmore Hackney. Linemen Bill Bailey, Willard Earngey, Fred Edwards, Charlie Fischer, Bob Haas, and backs Herb Hudgins, Johnny Johnston, Bob O'Mara, Bob Spangler, and Harwood Smith also played.

All–American Ace Parker was captain, leading scorer, and most valuable player for Duke in 1936.

Maryland was back in 1937 with eight wins, but "Jarrin' Jim" Meade, a bruising runner and powerful punter, was now the star. Frank Dobson's men beat St. John's 28–0 in the last meeting between the two schools, but Penn—minus its Four Furies, Fran Murray, Lew Elverson, Bill Kurlish, and Ed Warwick, outlasted the Terps 28–21. Charlie Weidinger completed to end Blair Smith for the lead, but Bob Dougherty tied it only to have Meade put Maryland ahead at the half. Bill Kirkleski's pass to Ed Fielden evened it again, but two more third-quarter catches by Bob Schuenemann, one from fullback Jim Connell, put Harvey Harman's Quakers in the win column.

Maryland shut out the next three opponents. Frank DeArmey at guard led the 6–0 win over Charlie Havens' Western Maryland squad, and Pershing Mondorff's last-period field goal overcame Virginia 3–0. Marty Glickman gained only 25 yards for Syracuse, while John McCarthy's catch and Frank Skotnicki's interception scored for the Terps, and Ossie Solem's Orangemen left town with a 13–0 deficit.

Florida finally scored against the Terp line of tackles Bob Brown and

The man with the magic punting shoe was Eric Tipton of Duke.

Ralph Albarano and guards Mike Surgent and Bill Wolfe. Bill Bryant's catch set up a blast by Meade, and Weidinger went in for a 13–7 win after end Nick Budkoff carried to the two on a lateral. VMI's slim halftime lead held up until the final minute when Mondorff's toe won it 9–7 over Pooley Hubert's Keydets.

Penn State jumped in front on touchdowns by Alex Barantovich and John Skemp, but the Terps came back to tie it. Wendy Wear and Harry Harrison won it late for coach Bob Higgins 21–14, but Maryland kept the last two foes out of the end zone with victories over Georgetown 12–2 and Tex Tilson's Washington and Lee Generals 8–0.

Besides those named, Jim Forrester and Bob Walton were at center, and backs were Fred Hewitt, John Boyda, and Bob Brand.

Not many people would disagree that Wallace Wade's 1938 Duke team was his finest. They had a national following on defense as Michigan's Tom

Wallace Wade's quiet demeanor belied the tough defense he built as coach at Duke.

Harmon had on offense two years later, for they were unbeaten, untied, and unscored on. It was the 19th and last major team to do so except for Bob Neyland's Tennessee Vols a year later.

They were called the "Iron Dukes" and lined up from the left with Bolo

Perdue, Frank Ribar, Fred Yorke, Dan Hill, Allen Johnson, Bob Haas, and Bill Bailey. At quarterback was Bob Spangler, Willard Eaves and Eric Tipton at halfback, and Bob O'Mara at full. Guards Bob Alabaster and Bob Baskervill, tackle Alex Winterson, end Jim Marion, and halfbacks Wes and George McAfee also lettered.

In the third game, Colgate advanced to the 1-yard line but stalled because of a penalty and lost, 7–0. Next week they beat Georgia Tech, 6–0, and were rated ninth by the Associated Press poll. Then they dedicated Bowman Gray Stadium at Wake Forest with a 7–0 win. George McAfee, out because of an operation for a wart on his foot, finally got in to help beat North Carolina, 14–0. After a 21–0 win over Syracuse, the AP ranked them third.

Jock Sutherland brought his defending national champion Pitt team to Durham and was met by an unseasonal snowfall. After an exchange of punts, Pitt's Dream Backfield marched down the field to five first downs. Behind blocking back John Chickerneo, Marshall Goldberg at full went through the line on a spinner, around end on a spin-fake, and over guard before the Iron Dukes dug in.

At the 10-yard line, halfback Dick Cassiano tried Leonard Darnell at end but was dragged down for no gain. Another attempt at end was stopped by Spangler. A pass to Bill Daddio in the end zone sailed over his head. On fourth down, halfback Hal Stebbins tried end again and was dumped by Tipton. Then Tipton hammered the Panthers back with a stupendous 65-yard punt.

Pitt never came as close again. Another second-quarter drive of four first downs took them to the Duke 20 where it conked out. Tipton's 56-yard punt to the 1-foot line stung them once more.

Tipton kept the pressure on in the last half with his surgical punting. On fourth-and-one at the start of the final quarter, he put one out at the 5-yard line. Bolo Perdue blocked the return punt and fell on it in the end zone for the game's only touchdown. Tony Ruffa replaced halfback Jap Davis and added the extra point.

Pitt never made a first down after the intermission. In the stands, Bob Neyland and Herman Hickman nodded in admiration at the Duke defense and Tipton's once-in-a-lifetime performance. Here is the log of his amazing performance against Pitt that day:

First quarter:
52-yard punt downed on 10-yard line

Dead-eye passer, long-range punter, 9.7 speed, shifty hips, sure-handed receiver, and bear-trap tackler made the *NY Sun* call George McAfee of Duke "the nation's most versatile back" in 1939.

50-yard punt downed on 8-yard line
65-yard punt downed on 18-yard line
Second quarter:
  24-yard punt out-of-bounds on 12-yard line
  47-yard punt downed on 14-yard line
  48-yard punt downed on 35-yard line
  56-yard punt downed on 1-foot line
Third quarter:
  45-yard punt downed on 16-yard line
  53-yard punt downed on 11-yard line
  30-yard punt out-of-bounds on 9-yard line
  42-yard punt downed on 13-yard line
  41-yard punt downed on 31-yard line
Fourth quarter:
  26-yard punt out-of-bounds on 5-yard line
  34-yard punt out-of-bounds on 11-yard line
  31-yard punt out-of-bounds on 7-yard line
  36-yard punt out-of-bounds on 9-yard line.

Duke's first bowl game was in the Rose Bowl against Southern California. Duke tackle Tom Maloney blocked two kicks early on, but for three quarters the game was a punting duel between Tipton and Grenny Lansdell and Mickey Anderson of the Trojans.

The game seesawed back and forth until Duke fullback Robbie Robinson gained five yards as the third period ended. With last down and one on the 17-yard line, Tony Ruffa put some points on the scoreboard with a field goal. Moments later, Spangler fumbled an Ollie Day punt. Two running plays failed as did a halfback-to-halfback pass from Bob Peoples to Bob Hoffman. A field goal attempt by Phil Gaspar also failed but Troy kept coming.

Howard Jones sent in Doyle Nave, a fourth-string quarterback. His third completion to end Al Krueger won it 7–3 with 41 seconds to go, but the Iron Dukes were as famous in defeat as in victory.

Clemson and Duke both lost a game in 1939 by one point. Charlie Bowser's Pitt squad beat Duke 14–13, and Clemson lost 7–6 to Tulane on tackle Bill Kirchem's blocked PAT. Last-year coach Jess Neely took the Tigers to the Cotton Bowl where they downed Frank Leahy's Boston College Eagles, 6–3. After a smash by fullback Charlie Timmons had overtaken an Alex Lukachik field goal, all–American tailback Banks McFadden held off BC with his last-half punts, and Clemson had its first all–American and a win in its first bowl game.

Clemson lined up left to right with Joe Blalock, Tom Moorer, center Bob

Defensive backfield coach Banks McFadden was Clemson's first all–American in 1939.

Sharpe, Walter Cox, Bill Hall, George Fritts, and Carl Black. Backs were Shad Bryant and captain and blocker Joe Payne.

Bill Alexander at Georgia Tech also had a good team in 1939, as they won eight and lost two close ones. Notre Dame beat them, 17–14, on Harry Stevenson's field goal, and Duke scored a 7–6 win after tailback Johnny Bosch quick-kicked into his own guard and the ball bounded back to Tech's goal. Assistant coach Bobby Dodd devised the razzle-dazzle that beat Missouri in the Orange Bowl. After a Paul Christman score put Missouri ahead, Tech scored on a 59-yard end-around by Bob Ison and a triple reverse from Bosch to Howard Ector to Earl Wheby. Roy Goree's conversions made it 21–7.

Other backs were Cowboy Shaw, Billy Gibson, Bobby Beers, Bob Pair, and captain Buck Murphy. Linemen who held a block to make the magic work were tackles Charlie Wood and Eston Lackey, guards Bob Aderhold and Hawk Cavette, and centers Jim Wright and Roane Beard. Ends were Paul Sprayberry, Joe Bartlett, and George Webb.

Wallace Wade was back in 1941 with his best offensive team at Duke.

They won nine games with an average of 32.7 points per game, were first in total offense with 372.2 yards per game, and finished second in the AP poll, highest ever for a Duke team.

After Pearl Harbor was bombed on December 7, no large crowds on the West Coast were permitted. Wade invited officials to play the Rose Bowl in Durham, and a plaque on Wallace Wade Stadium commemorates it as the only Rose Bowl game not played in Pasadena.

Oregon State represented the Pacific Coast. They lost to Southern Cal 13–7 on a 25-yard touchdown pass from Ray Woods to Doug Essick with 13 seconds left. They also lost to Washington State 7–0, which had two punishing backs in Bob Kennedy and Dick Renfro and the finest pair of ends in Cougar history, Dale Gentry and Nick Susoeff, as Billy Sewell got the lone score.

Coach Lon Stiner had put together a big, mobile line that held its own with Duke. Shortly after the kickoff, left-handed wingback Don Durdan took a spinner from right-handed tailback Bob Dethman, faded to pass, found no one open and ran it over. Warren Simas place-kicked it to 7–0. In the second period, the Duke halfbacks got their reverse rolling. Tom Davis gained 29 yards, Steve Lach got 22, and then Lach scored – all on reverses. Bob Gantt's kick tied it. Before they headed for the lockers, Bobby Rute's long pass to Moffat Storer just missed for Duke.

The second half opened with Gene Gray breaking free for 23 yards behind a big block by George Peters. Another Durdan toss to George Zellick for a score put the orange-jersied visitors ahead. After another reverse by Lach, fullback Winston Siegfried scored for Duke. Tommy Prothro converted for 14–14. The Beavers pulled in front for good on Dethman's 70-yard pass play to Gray, and a safety closed it 20–16. It was only the second time that anyone had scored 20 points on a Duke team coached by Wallace Wade.

Duke's line from the left had Jim Smith, Mike Karmazin, Tom Burns, captain Bob Barnett, Pete Goddard, Bob McDonough, and Al Piasecky. Reserves seeing action were linemen Bob Beatty, Blake Fawcett, Ralph Felty, Aubrey Gill, Jim Lipscomb, Art Miller, Bob Nanni, Jake Poole, Clyde Redding, Wade Talton, Paul Thompson, and Harry Troxell. At end were Ernest Beamer, Luther Dempsey, Ralph Morgan, with backs George Bokinsky, Leo Long, and Bill Wartman.

For the first time in a quarter-century, Virginia won eight games in 1941 but lost to Yale 21–19. Bill Dudley and Yale's Ed Taylor exchanged punts all day, as Frank Murray's men got all the first-half points and Yale got the

rest. Captain Dudley won the extra-point job when Eric Schlesinger missed the first two conversions against Yale. He was also first in all-purpose running with 1,674 yards and in scoring with 134 points. He led the first win over VMI in seven years 27–7. His pass to end Bill Preston began the rout of North Carolina for the first win in nine years 28–7. Dudley added three touchdowns, two on runs of 67 and 79 yards.

The team lined up in a T-formation with the quarterback as a man-in-motion and Dudley passing from tailback. UVa linemen were tackles Ed Steckmesser, Dan Oehmig, Milt Parlow, guards Jim Baer, Jack Saurbeck, Tony Lakin, Charles Cooper, Bob Fuller, and center Bill Suhling. Ends were Larry Abbott, Howard Goodwin, Billy Hill, and Jim White. Backs were Ed Bryant, Herb Munhall, Don Niklason, John Neff, and Ed Kreich. Assistants were line coach Ralph Heikkinen, end coach Bunny Corcoran, and backfield coach Art Guepe.

At South Carolina, center Lou Sossamon and backs Dutch Elston and Stan Stasica won league honors on a team with only four wins.

With many players serving in the military during the first year of wartime football, Georgia Tech was good but thin in 1942. A scintillating 160-pound freshman, Clint Castleberry, who lost his life in World War II, made his one year at tailback a memorable one. After Ralph Plaster dived in, Castleberry left-handed the toss to Pat McHugh that beat Notre Dame 13–6. Against Navy, he intercepted Gordon Studer and returned it 92 yards in a 21–0 win. In the Alabama game, Plaster went in from fullback for the only score after Castleberry got it close on a pass to McHugh.

Georgia Tech won nine games but lost the final two. They didn't have the horses to run with number-two Georgia, which had Heisman winner Frank Sinkwich, and got beat up 34–0. They also lost to Texas in the Cotton Bowl. Texas scored on a Roy McKay pass to Max Minor and on a 60-yard punt return by Jackie Field. A Davey Eldredge score and Bob Jordan conversion ended it 14–7.

Their backfield also had halfback Bobby Sheldon, Jim Kuhn on the wing, and blockers Jack Faulkner and Bill Stein. In the line were Mutt Manning at center, Ed Ryckeley and all–American Harvey Hardy at guard, Preston West and Tom Anderson at tackle, and Jack Helms and captain Jack Marshall on the flanks.

Opposite: **North Carolina's Fred Stallings (89) and Harry Dunkle (20) fail to flag the fast express as Bill Dudley of Virginia sets his sights on the goal 79 yards away.**

The number 19 of Clint Castleberry is the only retired jersey at Georgia Tech.

Georgia Tech continued to win in 1943. Their losses were to national champion Notre Dame 55–13, fourth-place Navy 28–14, and number-seven Duke 14–7. Their eighth win was over Henry Frnka's Tulsa team in the Sugar Bowl, 20–18, and made Tech the first team to appear in all four major bowls. Tulsa built an 18–7 halftime lead on a fake place-kick and screen pass to Ed Shedlosky, Jimmy Ford's 76-yard run after a fake pass, and a short dash by Clyde LeForce. A pass from tailback Eddie Prokop to Walt Kilzer at end set up Georgia Tech's first score by quarterback Frank Broyles.

Another pass from Prokop to all–American end Phil Tinsley in the third quarter, a last-period plunge by Ed Scharfschwerdt, and two extra points by Prokop gave Tech the come-from-behind win.

Squad members were center Mutt Manning, Frank Beall, Charlie Hoover and captain John Steber at guard, tackles W. N. Smith and Bill Chambers, end Jim Wilson, and Mickey Logan at fullback.

With Wallace Wade serving in the Army in France, basketball coach Eddie Cameron led Duke footballers to eight wins. They had a 14–13 loss to Navy on a missed extra point in the last minute, while Vic Finos converted twice after scores by Hillis Hume and Joe Sullivan. Their 37.2-point average led the nation in scoring and passed the highballing 1941 team in total points. Duke also led in scoring defense with 3.8 points, rushing defense with 39.4 yards, and total defense with 121.7 yards allowed each game.

Most players were in the Navy V-12 program, the Marines, or in the Army ROTC. Bob Gantt, Benny Cittadino, and Ernest Beamer were ends, Frank Irwin and Pat Preston at tackle, Bill Milner and ex–Vol Jim Myers at guard, and Fletcher Wall at center. The backs were Tom Davis, Leo Long, Bobby Rute, Buddy Luper, and Jim Wolfe.

The 1944 Dukes lost four in a row and were called "the best losing team in the nation." But they won the next four and ended the regular season with a 5-4-0 mark. In the 27–7 loss to Army and its touchdown twins, Glenn Davis and Doc Blanchard, they led at the half, 7–6, and were the only team to lead Army all year.

With over 200 colleges suspending football during the war, Duke met Alabama in the Sugar Bowl. Grantland Rice later called the game "one of the greatest thrillers of all time." Agreeing with him were 20,000 military personnel in the New Orleans area who had been given tickets that were purchased by businessmen and citizens in Alabama, Louisiana, and North Carolina.

After halfback George Clark turned left end for 52 yards on the first play, he faked a pass a few plays later and scrambled 14 yards to a score. Harold Raether converted to make it 7–0. Freshman Harry Gilmer led Alabama down the field, and on third-and-goal he hit Hal Self in the flat on one of his spectacular leaping throws. Fullback Norwood Hodges took it in from there, but Hugh Morrow missed the extra point and Duke still led, 7–6. Hodges scored again after Gilmer's 55-yard completion to Ralph Jones. Morrow's PAT was blocked, but Alabama had a 12–7 lead.

In the second period, Jones scored on a pass from Gilmer, and Morrow's conversion stretched it to 19–7. Cliff Lewis went in at tailback and led a drive to the Alabama goal where fullback Tom Davis ran in. Raether's missed PAT left it 19–13.

After the half, Davis carried the ball ten straight times on power plays. He scored on the last one, and Raether booted Duke into the lead, 20–19. Lee Spears took over for Davis and sparked a drive, but Alabama held and punted out of danger.

Charlie Justice follows Haywood Fowle through the Tennessee line.

In the last period Duke was on the move, but Morrow intercepted a pass to captain Gordon Carver at halfback and raced 78 yards down the sideline to score. His conversion made it 26–20. Duke kept coming, but Alabama held at the goal and coach Frank Thomas took a safety making it 26–22. After the free kick, Jim LaRue went 19 yards on a wingback reverse and George Clark ran 20 yards to the winning score. Raether's conversion ended it 29–26.

Duke had center John Crowder, guards Ernie Knotts and Fred Sink, tackles Frank Irwin and Lloyd Eisenberg, ends Reece Harry and Ed Austin, and blocking backs Bob Smith and John Krisza.

Wake Forest lost its first three games in 1945, but most of coach Peahead Walker's veterans were back, including wingback Bo Sacrinty who had played on Duke's V-12 powerhouse two years ago, and tailback Nick Sacrinty who took them to 8-1-0 the previous year until sidelined by mid-season surgery. This year they got on target with five wins and a 13–13 tie with South Carolina.

In the play-off, Wake Forest and South Carolina met in the first Gator Bowl in Jacksonville. Captain Nick Sacrinty made the first touchdown, but a score by halfback Bobby Giles gave South Carolina a 7–6 halftime lead. Behind Wake Forest's heavier line, fullback Rock Brinkley racked up two touchdowns and halfback Bob Smathers made the other. Dutch Brembs ended it 26–14 for Johnnie McMillan's Gamecock club on a late 90-yard interception. Of Wake Forest's 396 yards total offense, 378 were gained on the ground.

Wake Forest linemen were center Dick Foreman, Jim Harris and Buck Garrison at guard, Dewey Hobbs and Pride Ratteree at tackle, and Dave Harris and John Bruno at end. Blocking back Nick Ognovich won the best-blocker award in the Southern Conference.

On the sideline as a guest of returning Gamecock coach Rex Enright was Charlie Justice, whom he hoped to enroll at Columbia.

North Carolina football was enriched by the coming of Charlie "Choo-Choo" Justice, so named because his gait had the chug of a choo-choo train. He had career totals of 234 points, 42.5 yards on punts, and 4,883 yards total offense, a school record. He took Carolina to its first bowl game and followed it with two more. He avenged the pair of beatings the Blue Devils had given UNC in 1943 with four straight wins, and great Duke players like tackles Louis Allen and all–American Al DeRogatis, guard Bill Davis, and punter-halfback Fred Folger would never know the joy of beating Carolina.

Coach Peahead Walker went out of his way to recruit Bill George for Wake Forest.

Justice began his fabulous career with a 68-yard run to knot VPI 14–14, and outdid Miami punter Harry Ghaul with a fake punt for 66 yards to beat Jack Harding's Hurricanes 21–0. He had a 70-yard punt return and a 90-yard kickoff return to stop Florida 40–19, and a 74-yard scoring run in a 20–14 Tennessee win, a team that lost to Wake Forest and made Peahead Walker coach of the week. He finished the season with runs of 54 and 45 yards to overcome Virginia 49–14.

In the Sugar Bowl, North Carolina met number-three Georgia which was coached by Wally Butts and led by all–American tailback Charley Trippi. After Georgia's Joe Geri stopped one drive and UNC's Bob Mitten stole a screen pass, Carolina moved behind guard Sid Varney and took a 7–0 lead on a plunge by fullback Walt Pupa. Carolina was marching again as wingback Jim Camp took a handoff from Justice on a fake kick and ran to mid-field. Justice faked a pass and got to the 42. Joe Romano's end-around gained seven.

The game turned around abruptly as Pupa faked to Justice and threw a long pass that end Joe Tereshinski intercepted on his 24. He bumped into his own man, Gene Chandler, and tossed the ball to fullback Dick McPhee. Most people thought the ball went forward.

Field judge Gabe Hill threw down his handkerchief but quickly picked it up. McPhee ran to the Carolina 14 before Tar Heel center Dan Stiegman caught him from behind. Johnny Rauch wedged in three plays later and George Jernigan converted to tie it.

Bob Cox kicked Carolina ahead 10-7. Georgia came back on a pass to Dan Edwards who outran John Clements to the goal, but the play was disputed again on an alleged offside. After Georgia's final score gave them a 20–10 margin, Carolina suffered another apparent injustice. Pupa tossed to Ken Powell for a score, but the official ruled that defender Rabbit Smith had been bumped. The newspapers said Carolina won a moral victory, and officials George Gardner, Wiley Sholar, Alvin Bell, and Hill got as much coverage as the game. "I don't like those moral victories," said trainer Morris Mason. "I like those scoreboard victories."

Returning veterans also gave Beattie Feathers a strong team at North Carolina State in 1946. They lost only twice during the regular season. Virginia Tech downed them 14–6 as Maynard Bruce lateraled to Ralph Beard who left-handed a toss to Jim Ransone at end, and Beard ran in after a blocked punt by tackle Jack Ittner. Ross Orr added both conversions. Vanderbilt stopped them 7–0 on Jimmy Allen's score, but eight wins put them in their first bowl.

Tailback Charlie Richkus started them off against Duke with a pass to wingback Oscar Bozeman that tied the game, and then won it 13–6 on a short run with ten seconds to go. Duke was held to only two yards rushing by the fine line play of co-captains Curt Ramsey at tackle and end Al Phillips, tackles Taylor Moser, Fred Wagoner, guards Bernie Watts, Ralph Barksdale, and John Wagoner, Fred's twin brother, center Hal Saunders and end George Blomquist.

Tailback Howard Turner kept it going with a 98-yard kickoff return that tied Clemson and then scored the tie-breaker to win 14–7. Wake Forest was beaten 14–6 after Gwynn Fletcher's interception set up the winning pass from Richkus to end Bobby Courts. Fullback George Allen scored three times in the 49–7 win over VMI.

In the Gator Bowl, fullback Eddy Davis had three touchdowns, Charlie Sarratt threw to end Jim Owens, and Dave Wallace added a score in Oklahoma's 34–13 win. Phillips and punter-fullback Les Palmer scored for the Pack, and Jim Byler kicked the extra point.

Others in for State were end Paul Gibson, tackles Tom Gould and Billy Smith, guard Bill Manning, Dick Peacock at center, and backs Ogden Smith, Bill Stanton, Harloe Sheets, and Bob Bowlby.

North Carolina opened 1947 without linemen Ernie Williamson, Ralph Strayhorn, Baxter Jarrell, Max Spurlin, and halfback Billy Britt. Some pride was saved in a 14–7 win over Georgia, but they were flat in a 34–0 loss to Texas, which had Bobby Layne and Tom Landry in the backfield. A week later Peahead Walker had another of his surprises ready as Wake Forest dumped them 19–7. Carolina regrouped to win its last seven games but turned down the Orange Bowl because it was refused 3,000 tickets for alumni and backers.

Although Justice was a marked man, he was aided by blocking backs Joe Wright, Eddie Knox, Don Hartig, Bobby Weant, center Al Bernot, guard Emmett Cheek, tackles Stan Marczyk and Bill Smith, and ends Dan Logue and George Sparger. Hosea Rodgers at full ran 76 yards to a score in the 35–7 win over Florida. Next week Justice scored once and tossed touchdowns to ends John Tandy and Bob Cox to take Tennessee 20–6. Jack Fitch and Bob Kennedy got more work as ball carriers, but Justice picked up 123 yards to subdue North Carolina State 41–6. He had 106 yards against Maryland to win 19–0, and ended the year with 141 yards to down Virginia 40–7.

In his second year as head coach at Georgia Tech, 1946, Bobby Dodd guided them to the Oil Bowl and a 41–19 win over Herman Wedemeyer and Jimmy Phelan–coached St. Mary's. This year Tech won ten and lost to Alabama 14–7, as Harry Gilmer scored one and completed to Rebel Steiner for the other. Ray Smith, Ev Frizzell, and Buck Doyal got in when center Lewis Hook was hurt in Duke's 7–0 defeat.

Opening day Dodd beat Tennessee and his old coach Bob Neyland 27–0. Tulane lost 20–0 on Frank Ziegler's dive and catches by Bob Jordan and George Brodnax at end, and George Mathews threw to ends Jack Griffin and Jim Castleberry in VMI's 20–0 loss. Jimmy Jordan caught one in Auburn's 27–7 defeat, with Travis Tidwell going over for Auburn, and The Citadel under Quinn Decker yielded 38–0. Navy went down 16–14 on Bob McCoy's 62-yard run, Red Patton's diagonal pass to quarterback Jim Southard, and a Dinky Bowen field goal. A Jack Peek toss, and runs by Joe

Brown, Jack Bills, Morris Harrison, and Buster Humphreys beat Furman 51–0. Georgia lost 7–0 as Breezy Reid reached Tech's 25 only in the last five minutes.

Dodd continued his bowl mystique with a 20–14 Orange Bowl win over George Sauer's Kansas squad. Quarterback Jim Still bowed out with two scoring tosses to Patton and one to halfback Billy Queen. With Kansas fullback Forrest Griffith banging ahead, all–American halfback Ray Evans scored twice and guard Don Fambrough converted. Red Hogan hit Otto Schnellbacher after Dick Monroe nabbed a fumble near game's end, but Lynn McNutt dropped the ball on a quarterback sneak and Tech guard Rollo Phillips covered it on the 2-yard line.

Georgia Tech's trenches had guards Ewell Pope and captain Bill Healy, and tackles Ralph Slaten and all–American Bob Davis. Backups were Bob Bossons, Dan Bradach, Bill Busbin, Tom Coleman, Clay Matthews, Ralph McKinney, and backs Jim Petit and Rumsey Taylor.

Maryland was in a bowl game for the first time in 1947 under its new coach, Jim Tatum. Lu Gambino scored 16 touchdowns, three of them in the 19–13 win over South Carolina. Bishop Strickland and Jack Couch scored late for the Gamecocks. Gambino had three more in Delaware's 43–19 loss to snap their win streak at 26 games. Delaware led 7–6 on Billy Cole's score and Joe Coady's conversion, but Gambino returned the kickoff 92 yards to go in front for good. The score went to 30–7 before Cole's 90-yard kickoff runback and Mariano Stalloni's fourth-quarter touchdown for coach Bill Murray.

Hubie Werner had a 44-yard punt return against Richmond, and Walt Bolen returned a punt 85 yards for the Richmond score, but Gambino scored twice and completed to George Simler to stop Johnny Fenlon's squad 18–6. Duke gave Maryland its first setback, 19–7, as Tom Hughes came in for John Montgomery and scored to nail down the win. Dick DeShazo and Ray Beasley ran in to give VPI an early lead, but Vic Turyn threw to Elmer Wingate to make it 12–7 at the half. A Floyd Bowles pass to Orin Hopkins and Jack Cooke conversion opened it up to 19–7, but two last-quarter scores on Turyn's toss to Simler and Johnny Idzik's 32-yard run pulled it out 21–19.

Gambino's three scores beat Bill Kern and West Virginia 27–0, and he had three more to quell Kass Kovalcheck and Duquesne 32–0. North Carolina won 19–0, but Gambino scored twice, once after Lee Nalley stopped Jim Larue's 52-yard run at the goal, to outdo Vanderbilt 20–6. Dean Davidson tossed to Jimmy Allen for Vandy, but tackle Ray Krouse, center Gene Kinney, end Fred Davis, and three interceptions by Idzik helped turn back Red Sanders' Commodores.

After a 0–0 tie with the Wolfpack, Gambino scored three times behind the blocking of Harry Bonk and Tom McHugh converted twice to lead Georgia 20–7 in the Gator Bowl. But with three minutes left John Donaldson scored, and Earl Roth fumbled the center snap on a punt and Johnny Rauch threw to Joe Geri to even it at twenty.

Terp linemen were Al Phillips, Ed Schwarz, Joe Drach, and Jim Goodman, backed by Jim Brasher, Paul Broglio, Bill Everson, Rudy Gayzur, Chet Gierula, and Jake Rowden. Other reserves were ends Pete Augsburger and Frank Evans, and John Baroni, Sam Behr, Stan Lavine, Vernon Seibert, and Joe Tucker in the backfield.

North Carolina won the 1948 rematch with Texas 34–7, as end Mike Rubish, tackles Len Szafaryn and Ted Hazlewood, guard Larry Klosterman, and center Chan Highsmith never gave quarterback Paul Campbell time to pass. Justice scored two and threw for two more. Georgia was beaten again, 21–14, as Justice had 106 yards rushing. After their third win, UNC was in the top spot for one brief week. Bill Maceyko's interceptions of 66 and 59 yards silenced Maryland 49–20. Justice piled up 120 yards to beat Duke 20–0. His 80-yard touchdown run and 159 yards rushing set down Virginia 34–12.

With only a 7–7 tie by Rube McCray's William and Mary eleven, UNC met Oklahoma in the Sugar Bowl. Linebacker Myrle Greathouse intercepted to set up a score by quarterback Jack Mitchell, but the Tar Heels came back quickly. They had the go-ahead points in hand when defender Darrell Royal fell down and the ball bounced off Art Weiner. Lindell Pearson's third-period score for OU took it 14–6.

Justice had punts of 65, 65, 57, and 53 yards to show why he was the nation's top punter this season with a 44-yard average.

With 22 lettermen missing, North Carolina's 1949 edition was the weakest of the Justice teams. Justice was all–American again and was second in the Heisman vote to Notre Dame's Leon Hart as he had been last year to SMU's Doak Walker. Ends Ken Powell and Art Weiner also won all–American honors, with Weiner the country's top receiver on 52 catches for 762 yards. Center was now handled by Irv Holdash, supported by Joe Neikirk. They lost to Gus Tinsley's Louisiana State squad 13–7 and were blasted by Tennessee 35–6.

UNC was also blown out by Notre Dame at Yankee Stadium 42–6. Frank Leahy's team was in its fourth unbeaten year and on the way to its

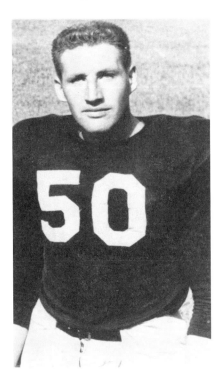

Art Weiner became the country's leading receiver when North Carolina went to its passing game in 1949.

record of 39 games without defeat, but Carolina held them to a 6–6 halftime tie before the Irish legions wore them down.

One week later Duke came close to beating them. On the first play quarterback Billy Cox put Duke ahead with a 75-yard dash, but Powell and Ed Bilpuch blocked the kick. Justice, who saw little action against Notre Dame, came in with a heavily taped ankle and tossed to Weiner for a 7–6 halftime lead. Then he caught a pass from halfback Billy Hayes and found Weiner again for a 21–6 bulge. Tom Powers quickly cut it to 21–13 on a 93-yard kickoff return.

The last minutes were hectic. Duke fullback Louis Viau fell on George Verchik's fumble on the Carolina 4-yard line, and it was 21–20 four plays later. George Skipworth returned a punt by Justice, but Duke lost the ball on halfback Dick Bunting's interception. Justice punted poorly, and Cox threw an incomplete pass as time apparently ran out. Hundreds of fans in the record crowd of 57,500 poured onto the field, but Duke still had one

Frank Howard seconded his own nomination as Clemson coach and held the job for 30 years, a tenure at the same school not matched by many coaches.

play left. Mike Souchak attempted a field goal, but Weiner stormed in and plopped on the ball and was kicked instead.

Seven wins put Carolina in the Cotton Bowl against the Rice Owls. Quarterback Tobin Rote threw touchdowns to Billy Burkhalter and Froggie Williams, and Burkhalter and Bobby Lantrip swept over before Carolina scored. Then Justice threw to blocking back Paul Rizzo and lateraled to him for another to make the final 27–13.

Frank Howard, line coach for Jess Neely, took over at Clemson when Neely left for Rice and in 1948 brought them their first perfect season in

Fred Cone led Clemson to two unbeaten seasons and two bowl-game wins in 1948 and 1950.

almost half a century. They won eleven games, including a 24–23 win over Missouri in the Gator Bowl. The only close shave was in the Big Thursday game with South Carolina. Behind 7–6 late in the contest, tackle Phil Prince blocked a punt by South Carolina quarterback Bo Hagan on the 28-yard line. End Oscar Thompson scooped up the ball and carried it over to win the game 13–7.

Clemson kicked off in the Gator Bowl, but on the third play blocking back Bob Martin recovered a fumble on the Missouri 19. Five plays later, fullback Fred Cone crashed over and Jack Miller kicked it to 7–0. Wingback Ray Mathews captured another Missouri fumble, and before long it was 14–0. After the kickoff, Missouri capped a drive with Bus Entsminger's quarterback sneak and Frank Dawson's conversion. On the next series, Wilbur Volz intercepted a pass at mid-field and it was soon a new ball game at 14–14.

Clemson took the second-half kickoff and drove to a score on a flea-flicker from Cone to Bobby Gage at tailback to John Poulos at end. After a Mizzou punt rolled dead on the 1-yard line, they got two points as Gage's pass hit the ground in the end zone for a safety. Miller's 32-yard field goal extended it to 24–16. Dave Ashley returned the kickoff to his 40, and seven plays later Don Faurot's club scored on a pass from halfback Rich Braznell to end Ken Bounds, but Clemson ran out the clock for a one-point victory.

Clemson lined up with center Gene Moore, guards Ray Clanton and Frank Gillespie, and tackle Tom Salisbury, sustained by guard Jack Cox and tackles Luke Deanhardt and Chick Gainer. Others were ends Gene Carson and John Childress, and backs Bunny Brodie, Rocky Carothers, Carol Cox, Dick Hendley, Jim Reynolds, and Jim Whitmire.

In two years Howard had Clemson in the Orange Bowl against Miami. Both were 8-0-1 and had 14–14 ties: Clemson with South Carolina and Miami with Louisville. There was no score until the second period when tailback Billy Hair's 45-yard toss to end Bob Hudson led to a Fred Cone score and Charlie Radcliff conversion. After a completion to Ray Mathews, Hair upped the lead to 13 for Clemson with a pass to end Glenn Smith. Two minutes later, Miami defender Jack Delbello intercepted a pass in the end zone and ran it out to mid-field. Frank Smith's reverse was good for 45 yards. Harry Mallios took a pitch from quarterback Bob Schneidenbach and ran five yards for the score. Miami zipped 95 yards in five plays for its second score. Ed Lutes caught a pass at mid-field but was not stopped until he reached the Clemson 17. On fourth down, Jack Hackett threw to Frank Smith for the score. Gordon Watson again converted to give Miami the lead for the first time, 14–13. With six minutes left, Frank Smith took a pitch-out but was downed by guard Sterling Smith in the end zone for a 15–14 Clemson margin. Linebacker Don Wade's interception preserved the one-point win.

Clemson's offense had tackles Dick Gillespie and two-way Jack Mooneyham, guards Pete Manos and Dan DiMucci, center Jack Brunson, blocking back–linebacker Windie Wyndham, and tailback Jackie Calvert. On the defensive unit were ends George Withers and Dreher Gaskins, tackle Billy Grigsby, guard Barclay Crawford, cornerback Jimmy Ward, safety Pete Cook, and right half Gil Rushton.

At Wake Forest, the nation's leading receiver in 1948, Jack "Red" O'Quinn, was gone, and last year's all–American tackle, Bill George, was out of school for a year, but Peahead Walker's final team in 1950 was one of his best. They won six, lost to Clemson on a missed conversion 13–12, tied Boston College 7–7, and tied North Carolina State 6–6 on another missed conversion, as tackle Jim Staton blocked Ed Mooney's quick kick and halfback Guido Scarton later scored. State almost won on a 70-yard pass play in the last two minutes, but Ray Barkouskie's extra point was wide.

Three quarterbacks led the team: Carroll Blackerby, Ed Kissell, and Dickie Davis, who connected with halfback Nub Smith on a 60-yard score in the 43–0 win over Richmond and threw to end Jack Lewis for the score that beat Duke 13–7. Larry Spencer's 83-yard scoring interception beat George Washington 13–7. They stopped South Carolina in the finale 14–7, as Gamecock halfback Steve Wadiak set a Southern Conference record with 998 yards rushing, including 256 yards in the mud on Big Thursday against Clemson.

Wake had centers Jim Zrakas and Bob Gaona, guards Bill Link, Bill Finnance, and captain Bob Auffarth, with Bud Pickard in reserve, tackles Ed Listopad, Wood Beasley, and Ed McClure, and Ken Bridges at end, Bill Miller at full and Bozo Roberson at half.

Art Guepe also had good teams at Virginia in his last years. In 1949 they won seven and lost two. The ends were Carlton Eliot, Bob Weir, and Ed Bessell, tackles Boris Goldberg and Bill Johnson, guards Joe Palumbo and John Thomas, and center Bill Walsh. Fullback John Papit led in all-purpose running with 179 yards per game and went on to be UVa's career rushing leader with 3,237 yards.

The 1950 outfit went 8-2-0 but the next year was even better as they won eight but were beaten by Gator Bowl–bound Washington and Lee 42–14. The movers in the backfield were Rufus Barkley at quarter,

A triple-threat back at North Carolina State in the early 1950s, Alex Webster starred for 10 years with the New York Giants.

halfbacks Bobby Pate and Bob Tata, Gerald Furst at full, punt returner Jim Lesane, and punter Hal Hoak. At tackle was Bob Miller with captain Joe Palumbo at guard. His last team in 1952 also finished 8-2-0 and had Charlie Harding at quarter. The ends were Tom Scott and captain Bill Chisholm, tackles Joe Mehalick, Pete Gay, and Preston Harrison, guards Don Alexander and Tom Ford, center Stuart Harris, and linebackers Bob Gut and Herman Gatling.

In five years Jim Tatum had Maryland at the top. The 1951 team won all ten games, stomped number-one Tennessee in the Sugar Bowl, 28–13,

Jim Tatum said Maryland's Bob Ward was "ounce for ounce" the greatest player he had seen.

and had their first perfect season. They were tops in scoring with 39.2 points per game, second with 382 yards total offense, and third with 76 yards rushing defense per game.

In the 54–14 thrashing of Washington and Lee, all–American guard Bob Ward jarred the ball from punt returner Randy Broyles and guard Pete Ladygo fell on it for a score to start the season. Seven different Terrapins scored, including Ed Barritt and Hank Fox, while Gil Bocetti and Bob Thomas tallied for W&L. George Washington lost 33–6, with Andy Davis running in an interception after Maryland had scored all its points. Left half Chet Hanulak scored twice and right half Ed Fullerton had an 86-yard touchdown run in the 43–7 defeat of Georgia. After the game, Georgia coach Wally Butts had his team on the field scrimmaging. Tatum pointed it out to his men with the words, "That's what happens to losers."

North Carolina gave Maryland its toughest game of the year. Ralph Felton put the Terps ahead with a 28-yard run, but Carolina scored and Abie Williams converted to tie it. Quarterback Jack Scarbath threw 11 yards to end Lou Weidensaul to regain the lead in the second quarter. The Terrapin secondary of Joe Petruzzo, Bernie Faloney, and Fullerton was put to the test after the half. Petruzzo stole two passes and shook the ball loose from Bob Gantt in the end zone with 1:05 left to save the 14–7 lead, and Maryland had its first win over the Tar Heels in a quarter-century.

North Carolina State was bombed 53–0 as they gained only 40 yards rushing, less than half the amount fullback Ed Modzelewski had in 11 carries. Maryland beat West Virginia and Art Lewis 54–7 in the finale. They ran for 523 yards and threw only seven times, two for touchdowns to ends Lloyd Colteryahn and Paul Lindsay.

Although Maryland was the underdog, Tennessee was outplayed in the Sugar Bowl. Triple-threat tailback Hank Lauricella, who was second in the Heisman vote to Dick Kazmaier, was ineffective, and the great Tennessee line of Pug Pearman, John Michels, Doug Atkins, Ted Daffer, and linebackers Bill Jasper and Gordon Polofsky became porous. Maryland swept through, around, and over it as Fullerton went off guard for one score, threw to halfback Bob Shemonski for another, and Scarbath ran over on a split-T keeper for 21–0. Wingback Bert Rechichar's catch trimmed it to 21–7.

After the intermission, John Alderton and Paul Nestor spread wide on the Terp flanks and Tennessee tried to run inside where tackles Bill Maletzky, middle man Dick Modzelewski, Bob Morgan, and linebackers Dave Cianelli, Ed Kensler, and Roy Martine shut down the single wing. The Vols had to pass, and Maryland's last score came on Fullerton's 43-yard return of a Lauricella toss.

Meanwhile, center Tom Cosgrove, guards Bob Ward and Pete Ladygo, and tackles Stan Jones and Bob Moss forced Neyland to a 5-4 defense. Scarbath saw the change and called an audible on almost every play. A last-quarter score by tailback Herky Payne made it 28–13, as Don Decker was true on all four conversions.

Like Maryland, Bobby Dodd's separate offensive and defensive units at Georgia Tech outgunned the opposition. In 1951 they won 11 of 12, and in 1952 they won all 12. Dodd credited line coach Ray Graves, end coach Tonto Coleman, and backfield coach Frank Broyles for building a team that didn't beat itself with errors.

After its first two wins in 1951, Tech edged Bear Bryant's Kentucky Wildcats and their brilliant passer, Babe Parilli, 13–7. Then quarterback Darrell Crawford tied a school record with four touchdown tosses to beat Auburn, 27–7. One week later, another great passer, Bill Wade of Vanderbilt, came close, but fullback Glenn Turner's score and a safety by all–American guard Ray Beck and Ed Carithers on Richard Foster in the end zone won it 8–7.

Maryland tackle Dick Modzelewski won the Outland Trophy as the year's best lineman in 1952.

The only non-victory in two years was a 14–14 tie with Duke. Blaine Earon scored to put Duke ahead at the half, but Tech caught them in the third period as Crawford scored and Beck ran 60 yards with a blocked punt. After Dudley Hager intercepted late, Worth "A Million" Lutz went in and Ray Green converted for the tie.

Crawford threw two touchdowns and scored one to beat Harold "Red" Drew's Alabama team 27–7. Harry Babcock's catch scored for Georgia in their 48–6 loss, as the Jackets picked off eight Zeke Bratkowski passes. George Maloof scored four times close in, Leon Hardeman ran 35 yards

Bobby Dodd became a coaching legend in his own time at Georgia Tech.

for another, Buck Martin pulled one in, and Larry Morris returned an interception 55 yards to end the scoring.

Once again it was Bobby Dodd and George Sauer in the Orange Bowl, only Sauer was now coaching Baylor. Tech short-circuited the passes of Larry Isbell to Stan Williams and Hal Riley with three interceptions and came back twice to tie it. After the third theft, Pepper Rodgers untied it with a field goal 17–14.

The loss of Crawford, Maloof, Beck, tackles Lamar Wheat and Lum Snyder, end Pete Ferris, and defensive end Sid Williams didn't show. The 1952 squad had six all–Americans: defensive back Bobby Moorhead, linebacker George Morris, center Pete Brown, tackle Hal Miller, end Buck Martin, and Leon Hardeman. The all–SEC team had end Sam Hensley, tackle Bob Sherman, guards Jake Shoemaker, Orville Vereen, Ed Gossage, and backs Bill Teas and Charlie Brannon.

The Ramblin' Wreck mowed down a dozen opponents with only three hitches. In the second game Bob Woodruff's Florida squad, which had tackle Charlie LaPradd and Doug Dickey at safety but lost Haywood Sullivan to the Boston Red Sox, went ahead on Buford Long's short run and Dave Hurse conversion. Bill Brigman's pass to Martin tied it, but Papa Hall took a handoff from Rick Casares and sprinted 64 yards for the lead. Brigman's pass to Jeff Knox evened it, but a late field goal by Rodgers won it 17–14, and no one scored two touchdowns on the Wreck again.

The second tussle was with an improved Alabama team that had backs Bobby Marlow, Corky Tharp, Tommy Lewis, and linemen Jerry Watford, Travis Hunt, and Ralph Carrigan. In this rugged defensive game, Jakie Rudolph's fourth-down tackle stopped one threat, and a Dick Pretz score outranked a Bobby Luna field goal 7–3.

In the last toughie, Bob Clemens put Georgia ahead 7–3 until Chappell Rhino took a lateral and tossed a third-period pass to Martin for 10–7. An intentional safety narrowed it to one, but two scores made the final 23–9 and Tech was in a bowl game again.

Behind tackle Kline Gilbert, Mississippi scored early in the Sugar Bowl on Jimmy Lear's passing and Wilson Dillard's running to give Johnny Vaught's Rebs a 7–0 lead. But Tech soon took control, as their company of two-platoon men made the final 24–7.

Henry Hair sat out the year, but also serving in the Tech platoons were linemen Bill Thaden, Roger Frey, Frank Givens, Dick Inman, Matt Lyons, Milford Bennett, ends Cecil Trainer and Dave Davis, and backs George Humphreys, Larry Ruffin, and Joe Hall.

The increase of college athletics after World War II brought gambling and "fixing" of games. Americans were shocked to learn that 86 basketball games had been fixed in 22 cities from 1947 to 1950. The investigation that followed resulted in the jailing of five players and 13 gamblers. In 1951, 90 cadets were dismissed from the U.S. Military Academy at West Point for violating the honor code by "cribbing" or passing information on coming exams.

The NCAA recommended that the number of games should be curtailed because of the pressures they were creating. Among these were postseason games. The presidents of the Southern Conference met and passed a recommendation to cancel bowl games. Maryland's top team of 1951 was invited to play in the Sugar Bowl, but the conference voted against it 14–3. They also adopted a resolution by a 12–5 vote that any member playing in a bowl game be put on a one-year probation that prohibited games with member schools.

Clemson also went to the Gator Bowl and lost 14–0 to Miami. The only conference games for Clemson in 1952 were with Maryland and South Carolina, while Maryland played only Clemson.

Scheduling was also an issue. The larger schools with 40,000-seat stadiums found it impractical to schedule games with smaller schools that had 10,000-seat stadiums. In addition, a conference champion was seldom clear-cut when it was impossible for all teams to play each other. Another issue was freshmen on varsity teams which had been waived in 1951 and 1952 because of the Korean War.

It was in this atmosphere that the Atlantic Coast Conference was born.

II. The ACC Starts at the Top (1953–1962)

1953

On May 7, 1953, the representatives of the Southern Conference met at the Sedgfield Inn in Greensboro, North Carolina, for their annual spring meeting. At 9:30 that night the members from Clemson, Duke, Maryland, North Carolina, North Carolina State, South Carolina, and Wake Forest passed the following resolution:

> In view of the increasing problems in intercollegiate athletics it is the opinion of the group present that the formation of a smaller conference is desirable.
> We, therefore, propose to recommend that a new conference be formed consisting of the seven colleges and universities present.
> That the colleges and universities present clear through proper channels the approval of this action.
> That a meeting of the seven schools shall be called as soon as possible after proper clearance is obtained.

When president Max Farrington called the conference to order next morning, Dr. James T. Penney of South Carolina presented the previous night's resolution. After discussing it all day, the new conference was viewed as the best solution for all and went into effect that night. By the end of the month schedules were drawn up, and by the end of the year Virginia became the eighth member.

The other big news this year was the return of one-platoon football. The NCAA Rules Committee abolished two-platoon football on behalf of many

Stan Jones (left) and Bob Morgan anchored the Maryland line at tackle in 1953.

smaller schools which had abandoned big-time football because they could no longer compete financially. They were not able to afford large coaching staffs with offensive and defensive specialists, and the cost of larger squads with more scholarships that did not fill their small stadiums.

Maryland was number one and co-champs of the ACC in its first year. They won ten games, and their rushing defense of 83.9 yards and scoring defense of 3.1 points per game led the country. They never trailed or tied until the bowl game. Starters were centers John Irvine and Charlie Lattimer, guards Jack Bowersox and George Palahunik, and tackles Stan Jones, Bob Morgan, and Tom Breunich.

Others on the national champion Terrapins were linemen Ralph Baierl, Ray Blackburn, Don Brougher, Herb Hoffman, Tom McLuckie, Bob Pellegrini, and Dick Shipley. Ends were George Albrecht, Russ Dennis, Tim Flynn, Fred Heffner, Jim Kilgallen, Paul Kramer, and Jim Parsons. Backs were Lynn Beightol, Dick Burgee, and Ed Vereb.

Maryland coach Jim Tatum and one of his prize pupils, lineman Bob Pellegrini.

After defeating Missouri 20–6, Ron Waller scored three times in the 52–0 wasting of Washington and Lee. Dick Nolan had touchdowns on a 65-yard pass play from quarterback Bernie Faloney and a 90-yard punt return in the 20–0 win over Clemson. Eight Zeke Bratkowski passes to John Carson, one for a score, and another to Jimmy Campagna could not keep Georgia from a 40–13 loss. A 26–0 win over North Carolina followed. Maryland had 27 points in 20 minutes and went on to beat Miami (Florida) 30–0, with end Marty Crytzer scoring on a rollout pass made up in the huddle.

South Carolina had the second-best offense in the conference, but Carl Brazell and Gene Wilson made only 37 yards rushing. The great air arm of Johnny Gramling to ends Clyde Bennett and Warren Clark gained 122 yards, but it was 17–0 when Bill Wohrman scored for the Gamecocks in the first half before going down 24–6.

Bo Sherman's George Washington Colonials played inspired ball as end George Dancu, linebacker Steve Korcheck, and a Lou Donofrio interception held Maryland to 7–6 at halftime. Ralph Felton scored first, and Bob Sturm pitched to Bill Weaver who threw to Dick Gaspari for GW. End Bill Walker blocked a punt and caused a fumble to tear it open, and Joe Horning made a last-period score for 27–6.

Mississippi had stopped Maryland's 19-game win streak last year and feeling was high to avenge the 21–14 loss. With center Ed Beatty and guard Crawford Mims out front, the Rebels averged 188 yards rushing from Hal Lofton, Allen Muirhead, Jimmy Patton, Earl Blair, and Lea Paslay, and had 345 yards total offense per outing on the passing of sophomores Eagle Day and Houston Patton. But six interceptions and eight Ole Miss fumbles did them in, as fullback Dick Bielski had a score and field goal in the 38–0 win.

Alabama quarterbacks Al Elmore and Bart Starr got nowhere in the 21–0 Maryland win. Chet Hanulak scored early on an 81-yard run and finished the year with 753 yards on 77 carries for a 9.8 average. Good news followed the game, for Iowa tied front-runner Notre Dame 14–14 that same day, and the Terps moved into the top spot. The bad news was that Faloney went out with torn ligaments in his knee on a hit by tackle Sid Youngleman.

Charlie Boxold took over against Oklahoma in the Orange Bowl. Oklahoma had lost its opener to Notre Dame, 28–21, and tied Pitt one week later 7–7. With end Max Boydston, guard J. D. Roberts, Merrill Green at half, and quarterback Gene Calame, they won the rest of their games, led with a rushing average of 306.9 yards per game, and began the longest win streak in college football.

After stopping Maryland at the goal and again on the six, Oklahoma won on a second quarter, 25-yard run by halfback Larry Grigg. It was not a good omen for Curley Byrd. He resigned as president the next day, ran for governor and lost the election.

Duke shared the ACC title and was 7-2-1 overall. They came close to winning all ten. Army edged them 14–13 on a conversion by guard Ralph Chesnauskas, Georgia Tech slipped by 13–10 on a late punt return by Bill Teas, and Navy tied them zip-to-zip.

South Carolina lost 20–7 in the first game of the new ACC and Wake Forest 19–0 the next week. All the points in Tennessee's 21–7 loss came in the second period, as Red Smith and Bob Pascal scored for Duke. Lloyd Caudle went in after Byrd Looper recovered a Ted Schwanger fumble, and Jimmy Wade ran over after his pass to Jerry Hyde. The Vols threatened late when Bill Barbish fell on a fumble but were held at the 1-yard line.

Purdue's Roy Evans threw to Rex Brock behind center Walt Cudzik and guards Fred Preziosio and Tom Bettis, but Pascal ran in for a halftime tie. Smith's last-quarter catch put Duke in front, but Karl Herkommer knotted it again. Jim Reichert failed on three field goal attempts for Stu Holcomb's Boilermakers, but Jerry Barger won it 20–14 on a keeper with 39 seconds showing.

The Polo Grounds was the scene of Duke's first setback. Tom Bell went in behind blocks by center Norman Stephen, tackle Bob Farris, and end Lowell Sisson to cap a 76-yard drive. Pete Vann tossed to Pat Uebel for a 14–7 Army lead, but quarterback Worth "A Million" Lutz, who was hurt in the second game, scored again for Duke after guard Bob Burrows recovered Jerry Hagan's fumble. Fred Attaya's quick kicks, the running of Gerry Lodge, and Army's five-man line, led by tackle Ron Melnik and guard Dick Ziegler, stopped the Duke backs repeatedly. In the last minute, Smith, who failed to convert the second time, broke free for a 73-yard run but was overtaken by end Bob Mischak on the seven. Lutz burrowed straight ahead and disappeared into a pile-up. The stands were silent as the players were peeled off one-by-one, but when the ball was spotted at the one-inch line the Cadet cheer filled the New York skyline from east side to west.

North Carolina State fell 31–0, as senior Dave Lerps got in for the first time and dashed 75 yards for a score. Virginia was buried 48–6 in the Oyster Bowl at Norfolk on three touchdowns by Caudle and one by W. D. McRoy. Bernie Jack and W. D. Fesperman both converted three times. Defensive stars in the cold, wind, and mud were Navy's Don Fullam and John Hopkins and ends Sonny Sorrell and Howard Pitt for Duke. Lutz threw three times after a second-half call for offside, but linesman J. Walter Coffee said Duke had used up its four plays and Navy took over inside its 20.

Georgia Tech won after Duke's Jack Kistler bucked in for the lead, but North Carolina was beaten 35–20 on a frigid day in Durham. Caudle scored twice, but Norman Lane's catch made it 15–7 at halftime. Caudle scored again on a lateral from Lutz, but Ken Keller stepped in front of the next one and scored for Carolina, and Bill Conner went in with 50 seconds left to end the scoring.

In addition to those named, starters were center John Palmer, guard Ralph Torrance, and tackles Ed Meadows and Jesse Birchfield. Others who donned pads were linemen Fred Campbell, Ronnie Falls, Doug Knotts, Jim Logan, Jim Nelson, Marty Rose, and Walter Smith. Ends were Joe Hands,

Jerry Kocourek, and Tracy Moon. Backs were Bryant Aldridge, Dale Boyd, Sam Eberdt, and Nick McKeithan.

South Carolina was one of three teams to tie for third with two wins and three losses. High winds postponed a Saturday night game with The Citadel until Monday night, but Carl Brazell scored twice and Johnny Gramling threw to Warren Clark and Hal Lewis hit Larry Gosnell to end it 25–0. Virginia lost 19–0 on second-period scores by Mike Caskey, Gene Wilson, and Brazell, with Roland Barefoot and Jim Boyle scoring for Bill Young's Furman squad in their 27–13 defeat. Jim Jarrett converted twice against Clemson after Gramling threw to Clyde Bennett and Lewis threw to Joe Silas for 14–0. The Tigers' Tommy Williams tossed late to Scott Jackson, and Pooley Hubert, Jr., converted to cut the final score in half.

After Maryland won, Dick Lackey's runs and punts kept the Tar Heels in the game before losing 18–0. West Virginia, anchored by center Bob Orders, had wins over Lowell Dawson's Pitt Panthers and Penn State, but Gramling went over twice and Fred Wyant tossed to Jack Stone and then to Joe Papetti to cut it to 14–6 at halftime. Gramling's toss to Wilson and Joe Marconi's dive ended it 20–14.

Behind center Leon Cunningham, guards Frank Mincevich and Bob King, and tackles Hugh Merck and Harry Lovell, the Gamecocks beat Wofford easily 49–0. South Carolina had a chance to beat the 1903 team with eight wins, but they lost to Wake Forest 19–13 in the finale and were 7-3-0. Wilson went the final yards on the opening kickoff, but Joe White tied it on a pass to Bob Ondilla. White's toss to Jim Bland and Bob Frederick's run pushed it to 19–7, and Gramling's completion to Blackie Kincaid concluded the scoring.

Gramling and Bennett closed their careers with record-making marks for the Gamecocks. Gramling's 1,045 yards passing were the first to exceed 1,000 yards in a season, and his 2,007 yards were first to pass 2,000 yards in a career. Bennett established marks for most catches in a season (34), most yards from receptions in a season (502), and most passes caught in a career (64).

Reserves were linemen Hugh Bell, Ned Brown, Charlie Camp, Dick Covington, Gene Kopec, Bob Schwartz, Ed Wilson, end Spec Granger, and backs Bobby Drawdy and Bob Korn. Others in a suit were Joe DeFore, Buddy Griffin, Crosby Lewis, and George Martin.

North Carolina also tied for third. Flo Worrell scored on a 32-yard run to lead North Carolina State, and Ken Keller ran over after Dan Mainer fell on a fumble. A safety made it 16–0 at the half as John Zubaty was downed in the end zone. Don Langston ran in for the Pack, but two fourth-quarter scores by Billy Williams made the final 29–7. Five fumbles by Carl Wise's Washington and Lee Generals led to five touchdowns in a 39–0 win, and last-half scores by Charlie Motta and Keller beat Wake Forest 18–13.

Maryland's 26–0 goose-egg launched a five-game losing streak. After John Carson and Charlie Madison scored for Georgia, a catch by Gene White set up a Bob Clemens dive for 20–0 at intermission. Larry Parker ran over for Carolina, but Zeke Bratkowski threw to Jimmy Campagna to open it up again. After Will Frye recovered an Al Bishop fumble, Len Bullock's sneak closed it 27–14. The Vols marred homecoming with 20 third-quarter points as Darris McCord's recovery led to a Jimmy Wade toss to Mack Franklin, and Tom Tracy scored on runs of 20 and 62 yards. Connie Gravitte's score ended it 20–6. South Carolina aided the downhill slide 18–0, and Notre Dame added a 34–14 loss. Neil Worden and Tom McHugh both scored twice and Don Schaefer once for the Irish, and Marshall Newman hit Jeff Newton for Carolina. Dick Keller's 78-yard sprint for Notre Dame was called back, and Gravitte got the last Tar Heel touchdown.

A 24-yard run by Nick Marcopulos jump-started the first of two scores by Bullock in a 33–7 win over Virginia. End Dick Kocornik blocked and recovered a punt in the end zone, Keller and Worrell added the others, and Tom Adler converted. Herb Hartwell set up a UVa score by Harry Strempek and Pete Potter ran in the extra point, and Duke ran down the curtain on a season that started so brightly.

North Carolina had center Bill Kirkman, guards George Foti and Jimmy Neville, tackles Ken Yarborough and Frank Fredere, and Dick Starner at end. Reserves were linemen Will Alexander, Thad Eure, Bill Koman, John Lambert, Jack Maultsby, Roland Perdue, and back Ed Patterson. Others were Miles Gregory, Billy Hawks, Steve Marcinko, Sonny Ridenhour, Howard Seawell, and Van Weatherspoon.

Wake Forest was also in a three-way tie for third. Bill Bowman put William and Mary ahead on a 71-yard run up the middle, but John Parham's run tied it at the half. Hadacol Hines kicked it to 10–7, and two plays later Charlie Sumner ran in an interception. Bill Churm's 55-yard run led to Parham's second touchdown as Jack Freeman's club won 16–14, and Duke won 19–0 the following week.

Bruce Hillenbrand threw to Bob Ondilla, but Ralph Cecere made it 6–6 at halftime for Art Raimo's Villanova eleven. Joe White's score was tied by Gene Filipski's 64-yard punt return, but White scored again after Jack Behrmann's catch for an 18–12 win. After Carolina won, Hillenbrand scored one and threw for one to beat the Wolfpack 20–7. Ed Merrick's Richmond Spiders gained a 13–13 tie on second-half scores by Ralph Scarpo and Bill Bauder's passes to Ed Elliott on the touchdown and extra point in the final minute.

The Deacs also experienced a late decline. Clemson won 18–0, and Mike Holovak's Boston College Eagles took a 20–7 win. Sonny George ran in a 55-yard interception of Bill Stuka, but Frank Marr blocked a punt and Lou Florio recovered in the end zone to start a fourth-quarter rally. Two miscues put the game away: Dan Brosnaham dived over after a Dick Myles recovery, and Tom Magnarelli leaped in after Dick Charlton's theft. Frank Morze and Dick Zotti converted. Gus Pringles and John Popson kicked Furman to a 21–19 win, and Wake climbed into a tie with the win over South Carolina.

Starters were center Joe Dupree, guards Gerald Huth and Tony Trentini, tackles Bob Bartholomew and Rocky Littleton, and ends Ed Stowers and Tom Whims. Reserves were linemen Don Garrison, J. C. Turner, and Mark Viola, ends Dave Lee and Earl Ware, and backs Jim Bland, Bob Brincefield, and John Herrlein. Others were Cliff Brookshire, John Coles, Tommy Frank, Wes Ledford, and Mike Soltis.

1954

Returning for their second year of coaching in the ACC were Clemson's Frank Howard, Duke's Bill Murray, Maryland's Jim Tatum, George Barclay at North Carolina, Rex Enright at South Carolina, Ned McDonald at Virginia, and Tom Rogers at Wake Forest. Earle Edwards, an end coach under Michigan State's Biggie Munn for six years, replaced Horace Hendrickson at North Carolina State.

Duke won the ACC title outright this year. They ruined Steve Sebo's debut, who succeeded George Munger at Penn, with a 52–0 win at Philadelphia. It was all downhill for the Quakers after a Jim Manley pass for the first touchdown was nullified, although Walt Hynoski gained 75 yards for Penn. Back home, Harvey Robinson's Vols were edged 7–6, and Pat Oleksiak's late interception turned away another Duke threat. The win over Tennessee marked the first time either team had won three in a row. The nation's top passing team, Purdue, trailed by two touchdowns, but Froncie Gutman and Bill Murakowski scored and Len Dawson converted for a 13–13 knot.

The devastation of Hurricane Hazel was continued in Durham by Earl Blaik's Army team a day later as Billy Chance, Flay Goodwin, and Godwin Ordway opened holes for Tom Bell and Pat Uebel. After Pete Lash in Army's number-two backfield of Russ Mericle, Joe Cygler, and Fred Knieriem scored first, Pete Vann's prodigious toss of 58 yards to Don Holleder set up another score by Mike Zeigler. Bernie Blaney and Bob Pascal scored on pitches for Duke, but Vann sneaked in twice for a 28–14 Cadet win. George Marinkov returned the opening kickoff to set up a score by John Zubaty for the Wolfpack, but Pascal scored twice, once on a 51-yard run, and Jerry Barger and Ed Post connected on a 62-yarder for a 21–7 victory.

A mid-year highlight was the 21–20 comeback win over Georgia Tech. Jimmy Thompson sprinted 51 yards to bring a score by Dick Mattison, Bill Brigman tossed a 53-yarder to Paul Rotenberry, and Wade Mitchell threw 18 yards to Bill Sennett for the Tech margin. Duke was out of it late in the third period when Barger passed to end Jerry Kocourek for one score, fullback Bryant Aldridge drove over 2:42 into the final quarter, and Post took a pitch and ran four yards for the tie. Only 42 seconds remained when Jim Nelson sent his 11th straight conversion of the year over the bar as bedlam broke loose. "The stadium crowd was a roaring, howling mob," wrote sports editor Wilton Garrison of the *Charlotte Observer*.

The Oyster Bowl in Norfolk saw 850 Navy first-class Midshipmen parade on the field preceding the game. Navy continued the show as Vince Monto slammed over, Dick Echard connected with Jim Owen for a 45-yard touchdown, Bob Craig added two more, and George Welsh and Bob Hepworth also scored. Jack Garrow averaged eight yards per carry but didn't score, and George Textor kicked two extra points for coach Eddie Erdelatz. Guard Len Benzi kept a Navy drive going by recovering a Joe Gattuso fumble, and seven interceptions fell into Middie hands: two by John Weaver, and one each by Bob Davis, Wilson Whitmire, Craig, Echard, and Hepworth in a 40–7 Navy win.

Duke finished with three conference wins to take the title. The first was a victory over Wake Forest. The Barger-to-Pascal pitch worked again, and Barger's toss to Tracy Moon and a 42-yard keeper made it 21–0 early in the third quarter. Dick Daniels ran six yards for the Deacs, but Sonny Jurgensen's 65-yarder to Post made it 28–7. Nick Maravic dived in twice, and Joe White kicked two extra points and Dick Travagaline one in the 28–21 finish.

The rain and mud didn't stop Duke's air game as Pascal threw 37 yards to Moon on the fourth play, and Barger tossed 39 yards to Buddy Bass to lead South Carolina. Bass and Pascal hooked up for a score and Bass ran left end for another tally. Carolina's Frank Mincevich fell on a bobbled end zone punt for a 26–7 final.

The Tar Heels trailed 14–6 to make their traditional game close, but Aldridge scooted 20 yards to start a 19-point third-quarter rally. Bill Conner ran over after Len Black intercepted, Worth "A Million" Lutz added another, and Rich Sebastian toed an extra point. Bill Kirkman grabbed a Bob Murray pass, and Larry Parker ran in from the three as the clock ran out in a 47–12 win.

The ACC and Big Seven Conference had signed to play in the Orange Bowl last year, but a no-repeat clause kept Oklahoma from a return visit. Bill Glassford's runner-up Nebraska squad came to Miami instead, and Duke went ahead on Pascal's end run. Then Aldridge intercepted a Don Erway missile, and Barger completed to Kocourek just before the halftime festivities. After a freak punt bounded back from mid-field to the Duke 35, two yards behind the original line of scrimmage, Nebraska made it 14–7 as Don Comstock struggled in and Bob Smith converted. The Blue Devils matched the third-quarter score on Sonny Sorrell's 17-yard reception. A pair of short runs by Nick McKeithan and Sam Eberdt closed it 34–7.

John Palmer was again Duke's center, Ralph Torrance was back at guard with Jesse Birchfield, and Fred Campbell and Doug Knotts were tackles. Other linemen were yell guy Dan Cox, Sid Deloatch, Ronnie Falls, W. D. Fesperman, Roy Hord, Charlie Klinger, Milt Konicek, Marty Rose, and Don Snowberger. The ends were Bob Benson and Riley Stallings, with Fred Beasley at halfback.

Maryland beat Blanton Collier's Kentucky Cats 20–0 and North Carolina 33–0 but choked badly in between. Wake Forest tied them 13–13 as tackle Bob Bartholomew and ends Ed Stowers and Tom Whims upset the Terp blocking. John Parham and Dick Daniels scored for the Deacs, and Joe White added the conversion. They lost to UCLA 12–7 and Miami 9–7. UCLA led in rushing defense with 73.2 yards and scoring defense with 4.4 points per game, and Red Sanders' defense of four linemen and four linebackers shut off Maryland's quick openers through the line. Bob Davenport scored after a bad center snap and again after a poor punt. Miami won when halfback Ron Waller was nailed in the end zone by Jack Losch and Bob Nolan.

Jim Tatum had learned a valuable lesson in the Orange Bowl loss. Oklahoma's Bud Wilkinson had kept the pressure on with two lines of similar ability, and just as important, his offense did not suffer when Buddy Leake replaced Gene Calame at quarterback. This had been Maryland's downfall, so Tatum's first step was to take a good look at sophomore Frank Tamburello, and by mid-season he was getting as much playing time as veteran Charlie Boxold.

It was Tamburello at quarterback who ignited the Terrapins against South Carolina with two touchdowns on keeper plays for a 20–0 victory. South Carolina quarterback Mackie Prickett marched his team to the 1-yard line in the waning moments, but fullback Crosby Lewis fumbled the ball and George Albrecht recovered it to end the 41-game scoring streak of the Gamecocks.

Maryland made it 21–0 at halftime over North Carolina State on three big plays. Waller scored on a 61-yard scurry, Dave Nusz took a lateral from Howie Dare and went 37 yards, and Boxold completed a 34-yarder to end Russ Dennis. Albrecht's 20-yard interception capped another 21-second-half points for a 42–14 triumph.

On the following weekend Waller scored on first-half runs of 61 and 51 yards, and late in the last quarter Dick Bielski tacked on a 36-yard field goal to seal Clemson's fate 16–0.

Maryland continued to score on big plays. In the 48–6 win over George Washington, Tamburello tossed 76 yards to end Paul Kramer and 37 yards to end Jim Parsons. Halfbacks Joe Horning and Ed Vereb had 40-yard runs, and Lynn Beightol hit Tim Flynn on a 27-yarder. Maryland raised its third-quarter total to 29 points when fullback Len Ciemniecki fell and lost the ball out of the end zone. After the kickoff, GW scored on Arnie Tranen's pass to Mike Sommer as they crossed mid-field for the first time.

The Terps were torrid, and less than a week later on Thanksgiving Day they blistered Missouri before a national TV audience 74–13. Maryland had three touchdowns in 12½ minutes, including a 70-yard interception of Vic Eaton's pass by Tamburello, and scored eight of the first nine times they had the ball. After Boxold's 35-yard scoring pass to Kramer, Missouri quarterback Tony Scardino threw to Hank Burnine and added another one after the half to Bill Curley. But it was all Maryland again as Bielski bolted 31 yards, Waller had an 80-yard run, and Dare, Albrecht, and fullback Tom Selep scored on short yardage. The last scores came on a 27-yard interception by Jim Skarda and a 90-yard theft by Dick Burgee.

No one had scored 70 points on Missouri before. The number-eight Terps made 601 yards total offense and 492 overland, but the Wake Forest tie put them one-half game behind and Duke in Miami.

John Irvine was back at center in his final year at Maryland. At guard were Jack Bowersox, George Palahunik, and Bob Pellegrini; tackles were Ralph Baierl, Ray Blackburn, and Don Brougher, with Bill Walker at end. Others were linemen Jack Davis, Ed Heuring, Herb Hoffman, George Kolarac, Joe Lazzarino, Mike Sandusky, Dick Shipley, and Al Wharton, and Jean Waters at end.

North Carolina was 4-2-0 in conference play, but big losses to Maryland and five in a row to Duke made them a distant third. The first win was over North Carolina State 20–6. Ted Kilyk fell on a fumble but Eddie West lost the ball and Marshall Newman ran in. After Newman intercepted Bill Franklin, he threw 50 yards to Connie Gravitte, and Don Klochak scored with 1:13 remaining. The Wolfpack huffed and puffed inside the 20 six times but scored only when guard Mike Nardone ran 32 yards with a deflected pass. A 7–7 stand-off took place as Gravitte scored on the third play and Klochak converted after Roland Perdue's recovery. Tulane hung on until the last period when Fred Wilcox returned Larry Parker's punt, then hit Harry Duvigneaud and Emmett Zelenka kicked it to a tie.

Charlie Madison's score for Georgia was matched by Len Bullock for a halftime knot. Jim Harper threw only two second-half passes as Bob Clemens and Howard Kelly ran in for a 21–7 Georgia win. The defending national champs continued to pound on them in College Park with a shutout for the second straight year.

Ed Sutton scored on runs of 21 and 77 yards and had a 65-yard run called back because of clipping in a 14–7 win over Wake Forest. Nick Maravic scored and Chuck Topping converted for Wake. Sutton fell on Leo Ward's fumble to stop a late Deacon threat, and Will Frye was ejected. On the next play a fight started and Burt Harrison was ejected as both benches emptied. The fight didn't end at the gun but resumed outside the dressing rooms after the game.

Tennessee continued to dominate the Tar Heels with a 26–20 win at Knoxville. Tom Tracy ran 43 yards for the first score and Bobby Brengle's 80-yard punt return let the crowd sit back. Tom Cloar's toss to Terry Sweeney swelled the Vol lead, but Al Long's pass to Ken Keller cut it to 19–7 at the half. The fans became uneasy on scores by Keller and Larry Muschamp, but Tracy put on the clincher with a 71-yard sprint in the final quarter.

The Tar Heels avenged last year's whitewash with a 21–19 win over South Carolina. Mackie Prickett ran over on the sixth play, but Keller put UNC ahead 7–6. Mike Caskey scored for 13–7 at the half, but Bullock's pass to Parker teetered North Carolina ahead 14–13. Buddy Frick zipped 70 yards late in the last period, but Bullock threw to Norman Lane with 90 seconds left for the win.

The heavyweights hung another beating on Carolina as Terry Brennan, who replaced Frank Leahy, and his Irish climbed to fourth place with a 42–13 win. Ralph Guglielmi tossed to Jim Morse and set up a pair of touchdowns by Joe Heap. Then Tom Carey came in and threw to Jim Munro for 28–0 at the half. Paul Hornung made his debut as the Notre Dame signal caller and directed the final scores by Jack Witucki and Frank Pinn. Long's pass to Parker and Doug Farmer's pass to Larry McMullen scored for the Tar Heels.

North Carolina's fourth victim was Virginia 26–14. Long and Parker connected again, and Klochak ran in twice and Keller once as UNC scored 26 second-period points. Charlie Modlin and Fred Moyer scored for UVa and Bill Clarke and Chuck Knowles converted, and Duke drove in the last nail on another suicide schedule.

South Carolina finished fourth with 3-3-0. They surprised New Yorkers with a 34–20 win over Army in Michie Stadium at West Point. Tom Bell ran the end and Mike Zeigler intercepted for a 14–14 halftime tie to make Lieutenant General Blackshear Bryan's first game as Academy superintendent enjoyable. Then blocking fullback Bill Wohrman said "Follow me," and Carl Brazell and Mike Caskey both scored twice and Tom Woodlee once as the Gamecocks pulled away. One week later, West Virginia, led by tackles Sam Huff and Bruce Bosley, shot them down with a 26–6 beating as Fred Wyant threw to Bill Hillen and pushed over twice. Jack Rabbits made the other score and Chick Donaldson converted for the win.

After disposing of Furman 27–7, Clemson made the annual trek to the Big Thursday game at the state fair and lost 13–8. Wingo Avery recovered an early fumble, but South Carolina held. Bill Tarrer fumbled his punt in the end zone for two points, but Bill Floyd and Mackie Prickett ran in for a 13–2 halftime lead. Joel Wells took a lateral from Don King and threw to Joe Pagliei who ran 60 yards for the Clemson score, but a Bob Paredes conversion was wide. Buck George lost a fumble and Willie Smith recovered a fumble for Clemson before the hard-hitting game was over.

Carolina's three league losses came in the next four games, but they shut out Virginia 27–0. Wohrman ran over to lead Wake Forest, and Prickett nosed in after a Harry Lovell interception, but Nick Consoles threw to Bill Barnes for 13–7 at intermission. An Ed Stowers catch brought the tying touchdown by Burt Harrison in the third quarter, but Wohrman bucked in again and Jim Jarrett converted. Nick Maravic ran in behind Bob Bartholomew and Gerald Huth, but John Parham's extra point sailed wide for a 20–19 final. Dick Miles swept end to put The Citadel ahead, but touchdowns by Wohrman, Prickett, and Tarrer beat Johnnie McMillan's squad 19–6.

1955

Maryland fullback Tom Selep was lost for the season with a bad knee, but the rest of last year's reserve backs that Tatum had brought along with Frank Tamburello were ready. Bob Pellegrini went from guard to center and continued to back up the line that led everyone in rushing defense with 75.9 yards per game.

Maryland's opener with Missouri was closer this time. Ed Vereb's 14-yard sprint put Maryland ahead on the first series. Tamburello's 22-yard toss to end Bill Walker, and Bob Laughery's conversion made it 13–0. Mizzou missed by one in the last half, as Jim Hunter hit Sonny Stringer and Hank Burnine for touchdowns.

The Terps' big line kept the UCLA single wing in check all day. The left was held by 230-pound end Ed Cooke and 245-pound tackle Al Wharton, and the right had 210-pound end Russ Dennis and 240-pound tackle Mike Sandusky. Left guard Gene Dyson and right guard Jack Davis both scaled 200 pounds. UCLA threatened once early in the game. Four passes from left half Ronnie Knox to ends Rommie Loudd and Tom Adams took them to the 3-yard line, but fullback Doug Peters lost the ball on Pellegrini's hit and Dyson recovered it. On fourth-and-one Vereb turned end 17 yards for the only score, and Maryland was number one for a few weeks.

Maryland downed Baylor 20–6 on Tamburello tosses to Dennis and right half Jack Healy, and a halfback-to-halfback pass from Dave Nusz to Howie Dare. After Baylor's Jim Davenport replaced a hurt Bobby Jones, he hit Tony DeGrazier for 20 yards. Charley Dupre rammed to the 2, where Del Shofner ran end for the score.

Maryland held Wake Forest to nine yards rushing and coasted to a 28–7 win. An interception of a Nick Consoles pass by fullback Fred Hamilton led to a third score just before intermission. North Carolina was held to 18 yards rushing and lost 25–7. Vereb scored three times and passed for one after intercepting Carolina quarterback Dave Reed. The Tar

Heels scored when center Jim Jones stole the ball from Tamburello and ran 35 yards to a touchdown.

Two scores by Ben Schwartzwalder's Orangemen were not enough as Syracuse lost 34–13. Fullback Jim Brown scored once and the other came on a fancy buck lateral. Fullback Gus Zaso tore into the line and handed the ball to quarterback Ed Albright. A pitch to right half Mark Hoffman followed, and Hoffman left-handed one to end Don Althouse who had circled to the left in the secondary.

Louisiana State was a little tougher but finally lost 13–0. Four interceptions by Maryland, one by fullback Phil Perlo in the end zone, kept Paul Dietzel's squad from scoring. Clemson took the opening kickoff and drove to a score on a pass by quarterback Don King to end Dalton Rivers. A 50-yard run by halfback Joel Wells put the Tigers up by twelve. Two passes from Lynn Beightol to Vereb and Laughery's third-quarter conversion put Maryland in front for good. The Terrapin line stiffened and held Clemson to 22 total yards in the last half for a 25–12 win. Two scores by Vereb in the 19–0 George Washington defeat ran his total to 16 to tie Lu Gambino's 1947 school mark.

In the Orange Bowl, it was Maryland's top-rated rushing defense against Oklahoma's number-one offense that led in rushing, total yards, and scoring. The Sooners had not lost a conference game since Bud Wilkinson took over in 1947 and were riding a wave of 29 straight victories. In addition, they had a flock of all-conference players in center Jerry Tubbs, guards Bo Bolinger and Cecil Morris, tackles Ed Gray and Cal Woodworth, quarterback Jim Harris, and halfbacks Tommy McDonald and Bob Burris.

Maryland had pointed all year for a rematch with Oklahoma and now the number-three Terps were in with the national champs. But they were no match for Oklahoma's team speed that ran 20 more plays a game than Maryland, and like North Carolina in the Sugar Bowl against Georgia, the Terps were burned out by game time with too much practice. Vereb broke loose for 66 yards, but quarterback Jay O'Neal caught him from behind at the ten. Don Stiller at end grabbed a fumble to halt the threat. The Terps took a 6–0 lead into the locker room when Vereb later scored from the 15.

Early in the third quarter, McDonald's 33-yard punt return and 19-yard halfback option pass set off the Sooners. Two plays later he scored, and Billy Pricer's conversion put OU ahead for keeps. McDonald led the team in running back to the huddle and up to the line of scrimmage. On one series, center Bob Harrison blocked Pellegrini in the back while he was still

Sonny Jurgensen quarterbacked Duke in 1955–1956 and then spent 17 years with the Philadelphia Eagles and Washington Redskins.

calling defensive signals. O'Neal later scored at the end of a 51-yard march, and halfback Carl Dodd's 82-yard interception ended it 20–6.

In for Maryland at left end were Jim Parsons and Jean Waters, left tackle Ed Heuring and Dick Bittner, left guard Paul Tonetti, George

Kolaric, and Bob Suchy, center Fred Tullai and Gene Alderton, right guard Nick DeCicco and Ron Athey, right tackle Joe Lazzarino, Don Healy, and Tom Stelf, and right end Tim Flynn and Bill Turner. Backs were John Fritsch at quarter, John McVicker at left half, Dick Burgee at right half, and Jim Skarda at full.

Like Maryland, Duke was 4-0-0 in league play and shared the title. North Carolina State, Tennessee, and William and Mary were dispatched with relative ease. Eddie West lost the opening kickoff to center Ronnie Falls, and eight plays later Duke scored on Sonny Jurgensen's quarterback sneak to start the 33–7 touchdown parade. The Vols were stopped on the Duke 6 in the first period, and from then on it was all Duke. Jurgensen tossed to halfbacks Bob Pascal and Ed Post in a 55-yard march that ended with Sonny Sorrell's catch at the close of the half. Bernie Blaney sliced off tackle early in the third quarter and outraced Johnny Majors 80 yards to the goal. Pascal scored later in a 21–0 win. William and Mary was beaten 47–7 for the first time in seven tries.

Ohio State took a 14–0 lead on Jim Roseboro's 44-yard touchdown run and Hopalong Cassady's 38-yard punt return, but Blaney scored before the half and Pascal tied it in the third quarter. With 82,254 Columbus fans screaming wildly, Jurgensen directed an 82-yard drive in the final frame and scored to win it 20–14.

Duke was toppled from its fifth-place perch by a 26–7 loss to Pitt. Duke led 7–6 at the half on Blaney's 75-yard pass play from Jurgensen, and quarterback Corny Salvaterra threw 37 yards to end Joe Walton. A 15-yard pass from Darrell Lewis to Walton gave Pitt a lead it never surrendered. Duke fumbled seven times as end John Paluck led a rush that thwarted the Blue Devil backs.

Georgia Tech made 14 first-quarter points as George Volkert set up one touchdown and scored on a 22-yard run. Johnny Mengert ran back a Bob Murray pass from mid-field in the last period, and a touchdown by Jimmy Thompson destroyed the Dukes 27–0.

Navy and Duke traded third-quarter touchdowns. Quarterback George Welsh tossed to end Ron Beagle, and Ned Oldham converted. Duke's Bryant Aldridge dived over, and Jim Nelson added the PAT.

It was 41–7 over South Carolina, as Bill Tarrer scored late for the Gamecocks. Wake Forest was taken 14–0, and Skitch Rudy's 35-yard second-quarter sprint held up to beat North Carolina 6–0.

Regulars were guards W. D. Fesperman and captain Jesse Birchfield, tackles Doug Knotts, Dan Cox, Sid Deloatch, and Buddy Bass at end.

Linemen were Charlie Klinger, Milt Konicek, Johnny Long, Bill Recinella, Marty Rose, Buddy Stanley, and Tom Topping. Ends were Bob Benson, Dave Hurm, Jerry Kocourek, John Thompson, with backs Fred Beasley, Dale Boyd, Nick Kredich, and Eddie Rushton.

Clemson was third with 3-1-0. They beat Georgia 26–7 for the first time since 1914 on two Billy O'Dell scores and a Walt Laraway interception. Georgia scored on Dick Young's pass to Laneair Roberts. After Clemson's Frank Griffith was knocked down hard, 1,000 fans swarmed on the field and fought until the band played the national anthem. Clemson had an easy time in conference play except for Maryland, but Rice won 21–7 on two first-half scores by James Peters and Virgil Mutschink. Auburn took a 21–0 win as Howell Tubbs threw to Jim Phillips and Fob James punched in, and Furman's Jim Boyle scored once and threw for two in a 40–20 loss.

1956

With Jim Tatum taking over at North Carolina, Maryland's new coach was Tommy Mont. Other new coaches were Wake Forest's Paul Amen, Virginia's Ben Martin, and Warren Giese at South Carolina.

With eight starting seniors in the line-up, Clemson claimed its first title with four conference wins, no losses, and a tie. After Frank Howard's annual warmup with Presbyterian 27–7, Clemson and Florida slugged out a 20–20 tie. Clemson's 14–0 lead flitted away as Joe Brodsky and John Symank ran in and Harry Spears and Joe Hergert converted. Howell Boney fell on a fumble, and Symank scored to put Florida ahead. Then Willie Smith covered a fumble, and Clemson marched 68 yards to tie it with 28 seconds remaining.

All the scoring in the North Carolina State game came in the last period. A Joel Wells plunge and Charlie Horne's 10-yard end run outdistanced Dick Hunter's lateral to Wally Prince 13–7. Wake Forest never got inside the 30-yard line and was blanked 17–0, as Horace Turbeville contributed a 20-yard field goal. In the 54th state fair game with South Carolina on Big Thursday in Columbia, Charlie Bussey went in on a quarterback sneak after Jim Coleman's 39-yard punt return. South Carolina's 75-yard drive in the final period ended when Don Johnson fumbled into the end zone for a touchback. Don Divers scored for Virginia Tech in their 21–6 loss, and Bob Spooner and Tom Selep swapped scores in the 6–6 Maryland tie.

Quarterback Sam Scarnecchia scored twice in a 21–0 win, as Clemson could not penetrate the Miami defense. Andy Gustafson's nine-man line brought up halfbacks John Varone and Porky Oliver to stand with ends Don Johnson and Phil Bennett, tackles Charley Diamond and Gary Greaves, guards Bob Cunio, Don Wallace, and Tom Pratt, backed by Don Bosseller and Mike Hudock. This no-give line led in total and rushing defense and took Miami to sixth place.

Clemson closed with wins over Virginia 7–0 and Furman 28–7. Bussey's quarterback sneak and extra point beat Virginia. Furman drew even on Jackie Powers' run and John Edge's conversion. Another Wells score, a Dalton Rivers catch, and Spooner slam won it.

Clemson earned the right to play Big Seven runner-up Colorado in the Orange Bowl even though Miami had trounced them earlier in the same stadium. Dallas Ward's Buffaloes exploded in the second period as John "the Beast" Bayuk scored close in. Then Bob Stransky's interception led to a Boyd Dowler score. Howard Cook went over on the first play after Frank Clarke blocked a punt for 20–0.

The Tigers replied with 14 third-period points as they drove to a score after the kickoff, and Wells scored again on a 58-yard run. They took the lead when Tommy Sease fell on a fumble at the ten and Spooner carried it in. Colorado came back 27–21 as Bayuk scored at the end of a 53-yard march and Ellwin Indorf converted.

In Clemson's line were tackles Dick Marazza and Bill Hudson, guards Earle Greene and John Grdijan, and center Donnie Bunton. Others who lettered were Billy Breedlove, Henry Bruorton, Jack Bush, Dick DeSimone, Bill Few, Leon Kaltenbach, and Shot Rogers.

Duke lost its first ACC game in four years to South Carolina 7–0, but four wins put them second. They also lost to number-two Tennessee, number-four Georgia Tech, Pitt, and tied Navy.

Duke rebounded in game two to beat Virginia 40–7. End Bert Lattimore scored on a 35-yard interception and 9-yard pass from Pryor Millner. Captain and end Buddy Bass had a 23-yarder from Sonny Jurgensen, and halfback Eddie Rushton scored on a 24-yard pass from Bob Brodhead. Center Johnny Long returned an interception 25 yards, and Jurgensen closed it with a quarterback sneak. Virginia made it into Duke territory once in the third period and scored on Nelson Yarbrough's 14-yard pass to end Bob Gunderman.

Bowden Wyatt had recast Tennessee in the mold of Bob Neyland and crushed everyone, including Duke. Tailback Johnny Majors put the Vols in front on first-quarter runs of 18 and 28 yards. Duke kept pace with short-yardage scores by Brodhead and halfback Bob Honeycutt, but Tennessee took a 20–13 halftime lead on Tommy Bronson's run. Al Carter's plunge and toss to wingback Bill Anderson scored for the Vols, and Millner squeezed over for a 33–20 count.

Southern Methodist went ahead 6–0 on a Charlie Arnold score after Charlie Jackson's 34-yard run to the 2. Duke bounced back for a 7–6 lead when Jurgensen and fullback Hal McElhaney worked a 22-yard screen pass and Rushton dived in at the half. McElhaney went 31 yards on a last-quarter draw play for the clincher 14–6.

Bernie Blaney raced 98 yards up the middle on the opening kickoff, but Corny Salvaterra's 7-yard run and 27-yarder to end Joe Walton put Pitt ahead for good. Two minutes later a 59-yard Darrell Lewis to Walton pass made it 20–7 at the half. Rushton trimmed off seven when he stole a Salvaterra lateral and ran 77 yards, but Ray DiPasquale's last-period plunge secured it 27–14.

After North Carolina State lost 42–0, Dick Mattison's fourth-quarter score gave Georgia Tech a 7–0 win, and Paul Gober's short run gained Navy a 7–7 tie. George Dutrow opened the scoring with a 52-yard run in the 26–0 win over Wake Forest, and two touchdowns by Wray Carlton after Jurgensen's toss to end Bob Benson put North Carolina in a hole. Curt Hathaway's quarterback sneak cut it to 14–6 at intermission, but Jurgensen wedged in late for a 21–6 win.

Tackles Dan Cox and Sid Deloatch flanked guards Roy Hord and Charlie Klinger. Wade Byrd, Mel Guy, Jim Harrison, John Kersey, Milt Konicek, Bob McGaughey, Bill Recinella, Phil Scudieri, Buddy Stanley, and Tom Topping were linemen. George Atherholt, Jim Bartal, Doug Padgett, and John Thompson were at end, with backs Phil Dupler, Bill Hagie, Jim Harris, Nick Kredich, and Skitch Rudy.

South Carolina was third with 5-2-0. Conley Snidow's Wofford squad lost 26–13, but Miami's rugged front stopped them 14–6. The Tar Heels lost 14–0, Virginia fell 27–13, and Bob Barrett ran in Billy Baker's wayward pass to defeat Furman and Homer Hobbs 13–6. The Wolfpack knocked them from the ACC race as John Lowe's conversion tied it and a last-period score won it 14–7, but the defense came on at the end to blank both Maryland and Wake Forest 13–0.

The Gamecocks had center Lawton Rogers, guards Nelson Weston and Tommy Addison, tackles Sam DeLuca and John Kompara, ends Buddy Frick and Julius Derrick, with Alex Hawkins and King Dixon at halfback, Don Johnson at full, and Mackie Prickett at quarter.

Reserves were linemen Don Rogers, Dwight Keith, Corky Gaines, and Jimmy Merck, Weems Baskin, Eddie Beall, and Buddy Nidiffer at end, and backs Jack Hall and John Dorsett. Others who suited up were Bill Bullard, Tony Byers, Frank Destino, Rich Ericsson, Bill Floyd, Charlie Johnson, Billy Rivers, and Sam Vickers.

Most of Maryland's line were back, but with Frank Tamburello drafted into the military they ended fourth and had a dismal year. They dropped the first game to Syracuse 26–12 as Jim Brown scored twice and Charley Zimmerman threw to Jim Ridlon for another. Dick Lasse snatched a hand-off, got a block from Tom Stephens, and rambled 68 yards to a score. After stopping Wake Forest six times in close, they squeezed out a 6–0 win on Ted Kershner's pass to Jack Healy but lost the next five games. Sam Boyd's Baylor Bears beat them as Del Shofner turned end to lead at intermission. After a touchdown from Doyle Traylor to Earl Miller was nullified, tackle Bill Parsley covered a fumble and Art Beall took it in for a 14–0 win. The Terps averted another shutout with a last-minute score, while Miami won 13–6 on tosses from Sam Scarnecchia to John Bookman and Bonnie Yar-brough's left-hander to Jack Johnson.

The season worsened as North Carolina and Tennessee beat the Terps badly. Ed Sutton gave to Larry McMullen on a punt return to set up a Tar Heel score, Charles Robinson added one in a 34–6 win, while Maryland scored on Fred Patella's late pass to Al Beardsley. The Vols won as Johnny Majors threw to Buddy Cruze, Bobby Sandlin, and Bill Anderson to put the game out of reach. The second score came after Charles Rader and John Gordy blocked a punt, Roger Urbano ran in an 84-yard interception, Carl Smith dived in, and Bob Smithers and Sammy Burklow both converted twice in a 34–7 victory.

Ben Scotti recovered two first-period fumbles by Bob Cravens and Ken Robertson against Kentucky, but the Terps couldn't score. Two Delmar Hughes conversions after Billy Mitchell's 78-yard punt return and Ivan Cur-nutte's run gave Kentucky a 14–0 win. After the Clemson tie and South Carolina's win, the Terps salvaged the season with a 25–14 defeat of the Wolfpack on a 103-yard Dickie Lewis interception late in the game.

1957

North Carolina State was undefeated in conference play and won its first ACC grid crown with a 5-0-1 mark. Due to NCAA basketball violations, the Wolfpack was kept from post-season play.

It will be quite a few more years before someone breaks Dick Christy's average of 45.4 yards on kickoff returns at North Carolina State in 1957.

With only starting tackle John Szuchan gone from last year's team, State opened with a second straight win over North Carolina. Behind the blocking of tackle Darrell Dess and guard Frank Tokar, quarterback Frank Cackovic ran 52 yards after a lateral from Wally Prince. Two plays later, Dick Hunter scored in the 7–0 victory.

Dick Christy scored three times in the 48–13 win over Maryland, one on a 96-yard kickoff return. End John Collar started the scoring on Hunter's 14-yard pass. Captain Hunter kicked five conversions and John Lawrence had one. Fourth-quarter touchdowns were added by Ken Trowbridge's 49-yard run and Ernie Driscoll's pass to Finley Read. Howie Dare's

90-yard kickoff return and Ted Kershner's short pass to halfback Bob Layman scored for Maryland.

Christy had another long return against Clemson as he went 97 yards on the opening kickoff, and fullback Don Hafer scored in the 13–7 win. Clemson drove to the goal at the end of the first half, and threatened again on quarterback Bill Barbery's 50-yard pass to George Usry. Florida State was beaten 7–0 on a halfback-to-halfback 46-yard pass play from Hunter to Christy.

Next came ties with Miami and Duke. In Miami's 0–0 game, Don Miketa's tackle forced Miami to punt but it was blocked, and Miami blocked Jim Sciaretta's field goal. A last-minute interception by Joe Plevel got Miami to the 8-yard line, but they lost the ball on downs. In Duke's 14–14 tie, Bob Brodhead squirmed over and also threw 53 yards to end John Thompson, but Christy scored on a Tom Katich pass at the half and again on Hunter's third-quarter toss.

In the 19–0 win over Wake Forest, Hunter scored on a short run after holding for a fake field goal. Last-half scores came on Christy's burst up the middle and Ron Podwika's 16-yard dash.

Don Hafer's 70-yard sprint started off the William and Mary game, but he fumbled the ball on the hit. Christy recovered in the end zone, and State led 6–0 in the first two minutes. The Wolfpack drove deep into William and Mary territory three times in the second half but couldn't score. After a halfback pass to Jack Yohe from halfback Dave Edmunds, Edmunds scored in the last quarter. Bob Hardage converted, and State had its only loss of the year. Virginia Tech lost 12–0 on Driscoll's pass to end Bob Pepe and Hunter's 58-yard fourth-quarter dash. Hunter gave the fans a treat with three quick kicks of 80, 64, and 53 yards.

It was Christy who treated the crowd in the South Carolina game. The score was 19–19 at the end of three as Christy nosed in three times to match a Sam Vickers quarterback sneak and runs by Stan Spears and Don Johnson. Christy scored straight ahead once more, but with 1:09 left Alex Hawkins hit Julius Derrick on a 16-yarder for a 26–26 knot. After a pass was intercepted far downfield by Hawkins, he was belted out of bounds by center Paul Balonick. The fans ran on the field, but Carolina was penalized for pass interference. With one play left, Christy booted a 36-yard field goal and set a new ACC one-game mark of 29 points.

In the Wolfpack line were end Jim Crain, tackles Larry Dixon and Dick DeAngelis, guards Bill Rearick and Joe Rodri, centers Jim Oddo and Bob Paroli, with Tony Guerrieri at full. Others were Jay Beacon, Julius

Compton, Dick Goudie, Tom Guerrieri, Ed Hordubay, Bob Kennel, Kelly Minyard, Jim Sherron, and Steve Vitek.

Duke's 5-1-1 mark was second. Dan Lee starred in the first game, while King Dixon and Heyward King's pass to Carroll McClain scored for South Carolina in a 26–14 Duke win. Wray Carlton's 26 points in the 40–0 victory over Virginia broke the one-game mark of 20 points set last year by Wake Forest's Bill Barnes, only to have it surpassed by Christy's 29 points later in the year.

Duke scored in the first and last quarters to beat Maryland 14–0. Carlton's 68-yard touchdown scamper on the first play and extra point held off eighth-place Rice 7–6, as the conversion was no good after Frank Ryan's fourth-period pass to end Buddy Dial.

Wake Forest was defeated 34–7 on 27 second-quarter points and scored only in the last minute after Buck Jolly's recovered fumble. Georgia Tech gave the Dukes their first reversal 13–0 on Jim Benson's blast and Fred Braselton's toss to Les Simerville. Duke tied Navy 6–6 for the third year in a row, as Tom Forrestal hit end Pete Jokanovich and then end Wayne McKee for a score, and Carlton scored all the points in another 7–6 win over Clemson.

Duke was on the way to the ACC title with a 13-point lead on North Carolina when Giles Gaca's second-period score gave the Tar Heels new life. After guard Fred Swearingen recovered a fumble, Jack Cummings found end Buddy Payne and Phil Blazer's kick sent Carolina ahead. UNC won 21–13 after another fumble recovery by tackle John Stallings, and Duke had fumbled the crown away.

Duke played number-four Oklahoma in the Orange Bowl. Notre Dame had ended Oklahoma's 47-game win streak on Dick Lynch's pitch from Bob Williams, but OU was still potent with linemen Bob Harrison, Bill Krisher, and ends Don Stiller and Ross Coyle. They took a 14–0 lead on Dave Baker's 94-yard theft of a George Harris pass, and Clendon Thomas scored after punter Andy Cottingham was downed trying to get away a high snap from center Ted Royall. The score was 14–7 at the half as captain Hal McElhaney ran over, and 21–14 after three quarters on touchdowns by Carl Dodd and George Dutrow.

Duke outgained, outdowned, and ran 25 more plays than Oklahoma, but lost 48–21 on 27 last-period points. Jakie Sandefer and Dodd scored after fumble recoveries by Dennit Morris, and Brewster Hobby had a 9-yard catch. Bennett Watts returned an interception 38 yards, then lateraled to Dick Carpenter who ran the last 30.

Earlier in the year, the Orange Bowl committee voted to terminate the ACC–Big Seven contract. They did not like runner-ups, so the Big Seven changed its no-repeat clause and sent its champion after that, while the ACC was free to go its own way.

Lining up on the left for Duke were ends Dave Hurm, Bert Lattimore, and Jim Bartal, tackles Tom Topping and Don Denne, guards Roy Hord, Jim Keyser, and Phil Scudieri, with centers Wade Byrd, Bill Hoch, Jim Culp, and Jimmy Davis. On the right were guards Mel Guy, Mike McGee, and Carol Jamison, tackles John Kersey, Bill Recinella, and Jim Swofford, and ends John Thompson and Doug Padgett. Halfbacks were Eddie Rushton, Bob Fetsko, Floyd Bell, Dick Cutler, Phil Dupler at full, and Bob Brodhead and Pryor Millner at quarter.

Clemson, North Carolina, and Maryland tied for third. Clemson lost to Duke and North Carolina as Jim Schuler's early score started a 26–0 win. Carolina lost to Maryland and Virginia 20–13. Maryland lost to Clemson and Duke. All lost to the Wolfpack.

Clemson scored in the 20–6 defeat of Virginia after end Ray Masneri blocked Al Cash's punt. Pat Whitaker's catch set up a UVa score, and Jim Bakhtiar's 2,434 yards rushing finished second to John Papit's career mark. Rudy Hayes and Sonny Quesenberry scored to beat South Carolina 13–0, and Rice went in front on King Hill's toss to Gene Jones only to lose 20–7. Ted Kershner gave Maryland a halftime lead, but Harvey White's 65-yard pass to Whitey Jordan sliced off six and 20 last-period points won it 26–7. Wake Forest was caught in the last 90 seconds on two Doug Cline scores 13–6. In Furman's 45–6 loss, White's 254 yards passing expunged Johnny Gramling's one-game mark of 227, and his 1,038 yards total offense broke the 1,010 mark of Bill Barnes, who got all of his overland.

North Carolina intercepted five passes to thwart Navy 13–7, one by Leo Russavage for 32 yards. In Miami's 20–13 defeat, Ron Marquette threw for a score, but Fran Curci's toss to John Varone and Bill Sandie's late score were not enough. Bobby Gordon and Carroll Young both scored twice in Tennessee's 35–0 win, as Joe Lukowski's recovery led to one score and a Stockton Adkins block aided another. South Carolina gave it away 28–6 on three fumbles: tackle Don Redding's grab brought an Ed Lipski score, a recovery by center Jim Jones resulted in a Giles Gaca score, and end Buddy Payne's recovery ended in a Jack Cummings pass to Emil DeCantis. Mac Turlington's catch put Carolina ahead, but Virginia won with 20 points in 18 minutes on two Reece Whitley passes to Fred Polzer and Carl Moser's quick-opener after Dave Graham fell on a fumble.

Howie Dare dived over twice for Maryland to match two plunges by Rod Osborne and Charley Milstead for Texas A&M. With Heisman recipient John David Crow at halfback and Jim Stanley and Charley Krueger at tackle, it was the only contest all year in which Bear Bryant's Aggies gave up two touchdowns. Jim Wright took over for a while, but Osborne lofted a late pass to John Tracey for a 21–13 A&M win. After the Wolfpack and Blue Devils chewed them up, Maryland started slowly against Wake Forest as John Fritsch sneaked in after Pete Barham drew a pass interference call, but won 27–0 with last-quarter scores by John Forbes, Bob Rusevlyan's completion to Dare, and a 61-yard pass play from Dickie Lewis to Gene Veradi.

Daley Goff's run gave North Carolina a lead, but two fourth-period scores won it for Maryland 21–7. After the game, the team hoisted Tommy Mont to its shoulders before 43,000 at Byrd Stadium and presented him to Queen Elizabeth II and Prince Philip.

Tennessee came away with a 16–0 win as Tommy Potts blocked a punt back through the end zone, and Tommy Bronson and Carl Smith added two second-half scores. A three-pointer by Fritsch put the Terps ahead at the half, but South Carolina moved in front on a long drive only to lose 10–6 on a longer drive by Maryland, and Tom Gunderman recovered three fumbles in the 16–6 win over Miami of Florida. Rusevlyan squirmed in to lead Virginia at halftime, then locked it up 12–0 in the final frame on a pass to Ben Scotti.

1958

A change took place in the scoring for the first time since 1912. A conversion was worth two points if the ball was run or thrown successfully over the goal. A kick was still one point, but the ball was centered from the three instead of the two.

Clemson won its second ACC title in three years with a 5-1-0 mark. New coach Dick Vorhis had Virginia going as they took the lead on John Barger's run and a Bob Williams conversion. Clemson pushed ahead 14–7 on scores by George Usry and Lowndes Shingler. Quarterback Reece Whitley threw to Sonny Randle and hit him again for eight points to put Virginia on top once more. A last-period Bill Mathis touchdown won it for Clemson 20–15. Randle ended the year as the kickoff return champion with 506 yards on 21 runbacks.

The North Carolina game was a thriller, as the lead in Clemson's newly enlarged stadium switched hands six times. Carolina scored first on Sonny Folckomer's pass to end John Schroeder, but tackle Jim Padgett ran in a blocked punt, and Harvey White's pass to Usry made it 8–6. The Tar Heels drove the length of the field and scored on quarterback Jack Cummings' pass to end Don Kemper, but Usry's dive made it 14–14 at the half. Fullback Doug Cline's score took it to 20–14. Another long drive tied it on Don Coker's touchdown, and Phil Blazer kicked Carolina to 21–20. Clemson won 26–21 with five minutes left, and Frank Howard had his 100th win.

Maryland was downed 8–0 on White's 50-yard pass to Wyatt Cox. Vanderbilt took the lead on Tom Moore's 9-yard run and Joe Bates' conversion, but with nine seconds left White's second score won it 12–7. South Carolina spotted Clemson six points, then spoiled its perfect mark 26–6 as each of the starting backs scored: John Saunders, Bobby Bunch, King Dixon, and Alex Hawkins. A two-point White-to-Cox pass was Wake Forest's undoing 14–12. Bobby Robinson cut it to 8–6, but Johnnie Mac Goff's quarterback sneak and Norm Snead's short run and failed pass never caught the Tigers.

Georgia Tech gave Clemson its second defeat in three games 13–0, on scores by Floyd Faucette and Fred Braselton. Clemson clinched the ACC title with a 13–6 win over North Carolina State on a pair of fourth-quarter touchdowns by Usry and Bobby Morgan.

Clemson closed with two strong wins. Charlie Horne's last-half scores turned back Boston College 34–12. John Amabile threw touchdowns to Jim Colclough and Alan Miller for BC. Mike Dukes scored in Furman's 36–19 defeat. Furman had second-half scores by Hicky Horton and Bill Canty's tosses to ends Ray Siminski and Tom Avery. Right after the game, Clemson accepted the invitation of Sugar Bowl president Claude Simons to play in New Orleans.

Fullback Jim Taylor was the only player on any of the three all–SEC teams, for national champion LSU was three teams in one: the "Go Team" or two-way starters, the "White Team" or offensive unit, and the "Chinese Bandits" on defense. Louisiana State won 7–0 on Billy Cannon's pass to Mickey Mangham after Paul Snyder's center snap hit the up-man on the leg and Duane Leopard recovered for LSU. Clemson marched 65 yards in the final quarter, but the Chinese Bandits held them on downs, and the LSU fans sailed their coolie hats into the air like a flotilla of flying saucers.

Clemson linemen were Bill Thomas, Jim Payne, Dave Olson, Lou Cordileone, and ends Ray Masneri and Jack Webb. Others who played were

Sam Anderson, Bob Chatlin, Sam Crout, Bob DeBardelaben, Doug Daigneault, Terry Eberhart, Rudy Hayes, Dave Lynn, Jim McCanless, Harold Olson, Sonny Quesenberry, Larry Wagner, and Emil Zager.

For the second time in three years Warren Giese was 7-3-0, and South Carolina finished second in the ACC with five wins and two losses. They opened with an 8–0 defeat of Duke on a keeper by Bobby Bunch, but Army mauled them 45–8. Maurice Hilliard kicked the first of his three extra points after Harry Walters and Steve Waldrop scored for 19–0 at the half. Heisman winner Pete Dawkins scored four times, once on Bob Anderson's pass, and Carolina didn't solve the Lonesome End formation with Bill Carpenter until it was too late.

Georgia was on the schedule again after Frank Sinkwich had his jaw broken in the 1941 game. A theft of a Charley Britt pass and Jimmy Duncan's recovery of a mishandled punt put them in business 16–0, but George Guisler's short run and a Don Soberdash two-point reception shaved it in half. Last-period scores on Bunch's quarterback sneak and Britt's 89-yard pass play to Guisler ended it 24–14, and Carolina had its first win over Georgia since 1904.

Wade Smith's score gave the Tar Heels a 6–0 win, but South Carolina blasted Clemson on Big Thursday. Buddy Mayfield's catch in their ball-control offense led to a Gamecock score and Giese's first win over the Tigers. Frank Howard tipped his hat to Giese after the first score, but three more touchdowns brought the remark, "My head got sunburned I was taking off my hat so much."

Maryland won again 10–6 and Furman lost 32–7, but the 28–14 homecoming defeat of Virginia was tougher. Runs by Bunch and John Dorsett put them ahead, but Arnold Dempsey's toss to Berry Jones and a Jim Roberson dash tied it before the Gamecocks pulled away.

The 12–7 win over North Carolina State was scary. An Alex Hawkins 36-yard run and John Saunders plunge gave them the lead, but the Pack scored on Frank Cackovic's throw to Randy Harrell. Moments later, Bob Pepe stole the ball in a pile-up, but a King Dixon interception denied State's last-minute bid. Wake Forest led briefly on Norm Snead's 72-yard pass play to Jerry Ball and a Neil MacLean conversion before losing in the last quarter 24–7.

Bunch, Dixon, and Hawkins were three-year men with ends Weems Baskin and Eddie Beall, tackles John Kompara and Don Rogers, guards Corky Gaines and Jimmy Merck, and centers Lawton Rogers and Dwight Keith. Two-year players were guard Jack Ashton, tackles Bill Jerry, Kirk

Left: **South Carolina's Alex Hawkins was never at a loss for words, but he let his deeds do his talking on the field.** *Right:* **King Dixon returned to South Carolina as its athletic director.**

Phares, and Ed Pitts, ends Jimmy Duncan, Buddy Mayfield, and Bucky Walker, Steve Satterfield, Stan Spears, and W. L. Strickland at quarter, and backs John Saunders, Phil Lavoie, and John Dorsett.

Others in South Carolina's swarming defense, known as "The White Cloud" because of their white home jerseys, were quarterbacks Buddy Bennett and Harvey Shiflet, fullbacks Bob Farmer and Dan South, halfbacks Joe Gomes, Jim Bowman, and Steve Kopian, and Jerry Frye, Doug Hatcher, and Jack Pitt at end. Linemen were centers Bobby Long and John Gordon, guards Jake Bodkin, Ken Derriso, and Wayne Shiflet, and tackles Sam Fewell and Lamar Hammett.

Duke's two ACC losses to South Carolina and Virginia, 15–12, on a Willis Williams field goal put them third. George Dutrow's two-point catch downed Ray Eliot's Illinois club, 15–13, and his fourth-quarter run overcame Baylor 12–7, after the Bears led on a Buddy Humphrey completion to Al Witcher and Art Beall conversion.

Field goals lost two of the next three. Monty Stickles made all the Irish points in a 9–7 win, and a Tommy Wells kick won for Georgia Tech 10–8 after a Marv Tibbetts score. Wray Carlton's PAT led Notre Dame, but Bob Cruickshank's two-point reception against Tech came up short. In between, the Wolfpack lost 20–13. Floyd Bell's 65-yard run matched a State score by Arnold Nelson, and a Bob Brodhead to Doug Padgett two-pointer put Duke ahead for good.

Louisiana State destroyed Duke 50–18. After Gaynell Kinchen grabbed a punt blocked by Emile Fournet, Merle Schexnaildre scored for LSU. Then J. W. Brodnax dived over, and Warren Rabb threw to Billy Hendrix after Larry Kahlden's recovered fumble for State's third score in seven minutes. Johnny Robinson and Billy Cannon scored on long runs, and Durel Matherne ran in after a Don Purvis punt return. Carlton went in twice for Duke and Tee Moorman once.

Dan Lee and Dave Burch scored on short runs in the 29–0 win over Wake Forest. A Don Klochak plunge put North Carolina ahead, but guard Mike McGee blocked the extra point to save a 7–6 win.

Duke's line had tackles Don Denne, Jim Gardner, John Kersey, and Jim Swofford, guards Ron Bostian, Art Browning, Carl Drye, Carol Jamison, and Ed Lyon, and centers Wade Byrd, Bill Hoch, and Ted Royall. Ends were Jim Bartal, Dwight Bumgarner, Bert Lattimore, and Bob Spada. Fullbacks were Butch Allie, Andy Cottingham, and Bob Crummie, Bob Fetsko and Bob Honeycutt at half, and George Harris, Dortch Langston, and captain Pryor Millner at quarter.

North Carolina won four and lost three and finished fourth. The Wolfpack won on opening day for the third straight year with a three-touchdown bulge before scores on Nelson Lowe's quarterback sneak and a Jack Cummings pass to Jim Schuler closed it to 21–14. The Clemson win hurt, but Don Coker's two-point run edged a Tom Maudlin sneak for Don Clark's Southern Cal Trojans 8–7, as USC and other western schools suffered through the player payoff scandal that signaled the death knell of the Pacific Coast Conference.

After stopping South Carolina 6–0, three long drives and Al Goldstein's interception shut out Maryland 27–0. Ed Lipski went over at the end of the first one, and completions from Cummings to John Schroeder and Danny Droze capped the other two. Cummings tossed to Schroeder and Goldstein and Wade Smith ran 62 yards to knock Wake Forest from the ACC lead. Jim Dalrymple ran over for the Deacs, and Moyer Smith dived in to complete the 26–7 licking.

Carolina shocked the Knoxville fans by beating Tennessee for the first time in a decade 21–7. Emil DeCantis set up a score as Don Klochak lumbered in twice, but Carl Smith's score cut the lead in two. A late pass from Cummings to Wade Smith clinched it, and the mother of a Tar Heel player added spice to the game by rushing on the field to offer premature congratulations to her son.

Jim Tatum got his 100th win by thrashing Virginia 42–0, then Carolina gave the South Bend crowd some uneasy moments. Cummings threw to Don Kemper, but Bob Wetoska's catch led to the first of Nick Pietrosante's two scores. Cummings came back with a toss to Wade Smith, but Red Mack's score put the Irish ahead 21–12 at the half. Klochak powered in twice for the lead, but a 34–24 win on runs by Mack and George Izo could not save Terry Brennan's job at Notre Dame, and Duke squeezed past the Tar Heels on a blocked extra point.

1959

With 23 lettermen back from the bruising squad that played LSU close in the Sugar Bowl, Clemson won back-to-back ACC titles with a 6-1-0 mark. The showdown with North Carolina came early, as Jim Hickey took over after the untimely death of Jim Tatum.

Clemson went in front on two touchdowns after recovering an opening kickoff fumble, and added a third after the second-half kickoff. Don Klochak went in for Carolina before the half, and two scores by Milam Wall made it close, but a Jack Cummings two-point pass to Bob Elliott was smothered for the difference 20–18.

Virginia was overwhelmed 47–0, but Georgia Tech put them in the loss column 16–6. Fred Braselton's quarterback sneak put the Wreck ahead, but Bill Mathis returned the second-half kickoff 99 yards for 7–6. A Johnny Welch scamper and Tommy Wells field goal swelled the lead to ten. Tech's defense of Jack Rudolph, Butch Carter, Hal Ericksen, Mike Nicholl, Toby Deese, Billy Shaw, and captain Maxie Baughan stopped an early fourth-period threat, and an interception by safety Jimmy Sides thwarted the last one.

Four shutouts followed. A Lon Armstrong field goal and Ron Scrudato's 60-yard interception sparked the 23–0 defeat of North Carolina State, and South Carolina went down 27–0 in the last Big Thurday game at the state fair on Harvey White's long passes to Mathis and Gary Barnes. Center Paul Snyder ran in an intercepted pass in the 19–0 win over Rice, and Duke lost when Ronnie Osborne fell on Joel Arrington's fumbled pitch-out in the second quarter, and Lowndes Shingler threw 30 yards to end Ed Bost for 6–0.

Maryland's Dale Betty outdueled the Tigers with three touchdown passes. His first to Hank Poniatowski followed a long pass to Ron Shaffer. Jim Joyce and Doug Cline swapped scores for 14–7 at the half, and a Betty to Gary Collins 49-yarder stretched it further. Clemson went in front for the first time in the final quarter 25–21 on short runs by George Usry and Doug Daigneault. Betty's second last-period pass to Collins was the clincher 28–25.

Clemson was in another free-for-all a week later with Wake Forest. Bobby Robinson's 69-yard interception put Wake ahead, but Clemson narrowed it to one on Daigneault's six-pointer. A pass from Norm Snead to Jerry Ball gave Wake a little breathing room, but Cline's 2-yard run and Sam Anderson's 2-point catch evened it, only to have a Neil MacLean field goal give Wake the lead at intermission. Snead's 11-yard pass to Bob Allen made it 24–14, but Ed Bost's fourth-quarter throw from Lowndes Shingler and a Cline touchdown put the Tigers on top for the first time 27–24. The Deacs replied with a Johnny Morris run, but Usry's 73-yard interception and 2-point run won for Clemson 33–31.

Furman managed a 3–0 lead on Shelly Sutton's field goal, but Clemson scored 28 points in each half on seven rushing touchdowns and Harry Pavilack's 26-yard interception for a 56–3 win.

Clemson met Abe Martin's seventh-place Texas Christian team in the first Bluebonnet Bowl in Houston. TCU had a solid line in tackles Bob Lilly and Don Floyd, guards Ramon Armstrong and Sherrill Headrick, and center Arvie Martin, but backs Marvin Lasater and Jack Spikes got nowhere against Clemson's equally good line.

The Tigers went ahead on Armstrong's three-pointer, but Don George directed TCU to a halftime lead on Jack Reding's toss to Harry Moreland. Clemson unleashed 20 last-period points and won 23–7 on completions from White to Barnes and Shingler to Tommy King, then went to its running game and scored on Scrudato's run.

In the Clemson line that brought them their 300th win were starters Lou Cordileone, Harold Olson, Dave Lynn, Sam Crout, and reserves Calvin West, Ron Andreo, Jimmy King, and Jack Veronee.

After losses to Clemson and Notre Dame 28–8, Jim Hickey shed Jim Tatum's shadow and took the Tar Heels to second in the ACC. The Irish had scores by Bob Scarpitto after Pat Heenan grabbed a fumble, Jim Crotty, Monty Stickles' blocked punt in the end zone, and Ray Ratkowski's interception. Moyer Smith scored late for UNC.

North Carolina State, which had been a hair shirt for three years, was beaten 20–12. A score by Ray Farris and two smashes by Ron Podwika put the Pack out front, but last-half touchdowns by Gib Carson and Bob Elliott gave North Carolina the victory.

The Tar Heel's reply to Steve Satterfield's quarterback sneak for South Carolina was a catch by Skip Clement, and after a Jack Cummings pass to end John Schroeder they scored on two short runs in a 19–6 win. An interception by end Al Goldstein put UNC ahead of Maryland, but Jim Joyce's run evened it. Then the Terps went to a spread formation and won 14–7 on Dale Betty's throw to Bob Gallagher. Neil MacLean scored all the Wake Forest points as he matched a pair of plunges by Don Klochak and Wade Smith's 37-yard run, but Bob Shupin's three conversions were the difference 21–19.

Tennessee handed North Carolina another bad defeat 29–7. An interception by Bill Majors set up one of the two scores by Glenn Glass. Marv Phillips scored on a pass from Gene Etter, and Etter scored once and kicked a 31-yard field goal. The Tar Heels lost three of five fumbles to Paul Inglett, Cotton Letner, and Bunny Orr. Elliott scored for North Carolina in the final quarter.

Miami beat Carolina one week later. After Skip Clement was flagged for interference on Larry Wilson, Fran Curci scored on a quarterback sneak. A Cummings to Goldstein pass tied it, but Jim Vollenweider ran in a pitch for 14–7. Virginia was beaten badly 41–0, but not even that prepared people for the Duke game.

None of the Carolina players had mentioned Jim Tatum since his death the previous July. Now Jim Hickey told his squad that this game was for coach Tatum. The 28–0 score at halftime shows how much his talk impressed the team. The score grew bigger as Klochak returned the last-half kickoff 93 yards. After a 25-yard dash by George Knox, the Tar Heels wanted an even 50 points and got them as Farris plowed straight ahead on the conversion.

"It was like being in a one-hour defensive scrimmage with the other team having the ball all the time," said Mike McGee, Duke's Outland Trophy winner as the year's best lineman.

Linemen for North Carolina were tackles Don Stallings and Earl Butler, guards Fred Mueller and Frank Riggs, with centers Rip Hawkins and Jim Davis. Reserves were Ben Gallagher, John Hegarty, Jim LeCompte, Ralph Steele, and John Stunda, with Mike Greenday, Jim Rice, Conrad Sloop, and Rabe Walton at the ends.

New coach Tom Nugent brought Maryland in third with 4-2-0. Quarterback Dick Novak threw for three touchdowns and Vinny Scott kicked three field goals in the 27–7 win over West Virginia, but 26–0 defeats by Texas and 29–0 by national champion Syracuse followed. Jack Collins went 86 yards for Texas, and Syracuse held them to 29 yards total offense. After Roger Davis blocked a punt Bob Yates kicked a field goal, and a few plays later Ger Schwedes threw to Fred Mautino. A fumble recovery by Dick Feidler brought a John Nichols score, and a hit on Dale Betty by center Bob Stem resulted in an end zone recovery by Gene Grabosky for Syracuse.

The Terps led Navy 14–0, scoring once after a Kurt Schwarz fumble recovery, but Joe Bellino won it 22–14 with a 59-yard punt return, and Joe Tranchini hit Jim TenBrook for the two-pointer. Tranchini scored twice, once after Bellino's 33-yard punt return.

After the Clemson shoot-out, Maryland beat Virginia 55–12, but North Carolina State scored in each period on Roman Gabriel's quarterback sneak, two tosses to Jim Tapp, and Ron Podwika's run. Maryland scored after a Pete Boinis fumble recovery, and then got one more when Joe Gardi blocked a punt by Collice Moore and Betty threw to Ev Cloud to win a wild one from the Wolfpack 33–28.

With Norm Snead throwing in a double Lonesome End formation, Wake Forest was in every game and tied for fourth. His throw to Bill Hull and a Nick Patella field goal put Florida State behind, but Fred Pickard and Bud Whitehead interceptions and Joe Majors' pass to Jim Daniel set them back 20–9. Snead's completion to Bob Allen and Bobby Robinson's end run won 22–20 with 1:56 remaining.

Snead's pass to Pete Manning scored first, but two scores by Al Pugh, Sam Shaffer's two-point run, and a Chuck Stephens field goal put Virginia Tech ahead at the half 18–7. But short runs by Winston Futch, Jerry Ball, and Charles Reiley won for Wake 27–18.

After Tom McClellan's run won for Andy Pilney's Tulane team 6–0, a Patella field goal and Bill Ruby catch beat Maryland 10–7. Snead and Roman Gabriel of North Carolina State swapped keepers, and Bernie Latusick's catch put State ahead, but Joe Bonecutter's touchdown and another Patella field goal gave Wake the win 17–14.

Wake beat Virginia 34–12, but Snead's ACC mark of 44 passes couldn't catch Duke. After Dan Gelbert blocked a conversion, Duke won going away 27–15. Wake won the battle for fourth with South Carolina 43–20, as Snead set ACC season marks in passing attempts and completions, passing yards, total offense, and touchdowns.

An early superstar at North Carolina State, Roman Gabriel went on to fame with the Los Angeles Rams.

South Carolina's number-four mark was also 4-3-0. They beat Duke 12–7, and Phil Lavoie had three touchdowns in the 30–0 win over Furman and three more in the 30–14 defeat of Georgia. Quarterback Jim Costen sneaked in, and Georgia scored on passes from Fran Tarkenton to Bill McKenny and Charley Britt to Bob Towns.

They downed Virginia 32–20 but lost to Miami 26–6, as Frank Bouffard ran over twice and Fran Curci hit Bob Rosbaugh and Bill Miller. Two Ken Norton scores beat North Carolina State 12–7.

Warren Giese's head-on style of play brought many injuries. By year's end center Jim Nemeth, guard Ken Derriso, ends Conley Taylor and Bob

Norm Snead directed the Wake Forest attack in 1958-1959-1960, and then toiled 15 years as a pro quarterback.

Drost, and halfbacks Steve Kopian and Mel Harris were out, and Jim Hunter became the top receiver with 60 yards.

1960

Duke's five wins and a loss brought a fourth title and second one outright. In the opener with South Carolina, lonesome end Tee Moorman had 11 catches in the 31–0 win. Quarterback Walt Rappold, halfback Gary Wilson, and Dave Burch at full shared the scoring in Maryland's 20–7 loss. Michigan let Moorman have the short passes while guarding him deeper and won 31–6. Dennis Fitzgerald scored twice, once on the arm of Dave Glinka. Dave Raimey also had two touchdowns, and John Halstead added the conversion. Mark Leggett scored for Duke, and Jack Strobel made the last one for Michigan.

Duke did not lose for a month. John Tinnell and Dean Wright scored in North Carolina State's 17–13 defeat, with Bill Reynolds adding a field goal. Clemson's Bill McGuirt scored in their 21–6 loss, and after center Bob

Caldwell's fumble recovery stopped one Duke threat, Wright's fourth-quarter score beat Georgia Tech 6–0.

A fight broke out before the Navy game when the Middies came to get their stolen goat mascot, Billy XV, and saw a big blue "D" painted on its side. Navy took it to the Blue Devils with a 10–0 halftime surge on Greg Mather's touchdown and field goal. In the last half, Joe Bellino was forced inside by ends Dave Unser, Pete Widener, Jack Bush, Tee Moorman, and tackles Art Gregory, Dwight Bumgarner, and Rod Kotchin so the line-backers could pick him up. Joe Wuchina recovered a Hal Spooner fumble to set up a Duke score, and Don Altman's punt return led to a score after Randy Clark put one out for Duke. A last-quarter fumble by Joe Matalavage brought a Reynolds three-pointer and 19–10 win over the Midshipmen.

Ed Chesnutt tallied on a pass from Gil Garner in Duke's 34–7 defeat of Wake Forest and its new coach Billy Hildebrand. North Carolina made it two in a row as Ray Farris somersaulted over the Duke line in the last two minutes and Bob Elliott converted for a 7–6 win. UCLA won 27–6 on scores by Bobby Smith, Almose Thompson, and Bill Kilmer's toss to Dan Vena. Kilmer was the total offense champion with 1,889 yards on 803 rushing and 1,086 from fluttery passes. In the Cotton Bowl against Arkansas, top punt returner Lance Alworth scored on a 49-yard punt return, but Unser blocked the extra point. Duke came down the field on passes from Altman to Moorman and end Bob Spada, with Moorman getting the touchdown. Captain Art Browning converted for 7–6, and Jerry McGee recovered a Razorback fumble on the kickoff to lock it up.

Duke linemen were Butch Allie, Paul Bengel, Jean Berry, Dave Bosson, Dave Condon, Dick Crain, Bob Gardner, Dick Havens, John Lomax, John Markas, Fred McCollum, and Ken Williams. Ends were Dan Gelbert and Zo Potts, with backs Dan Bridges and Bob Garda.

North Carolina State, which lost nine straight in a 1-9-0 season last year, was second with 4-1-1. They beat Frank Moseley's Virginia Tech team in the opener 29–14, as Jim D'Antonio and Al Taylor both scored twice and Warren Price and Don Vaught scored for VPI. After Jake Shaffer's field goal beat North Carolina 3–0, they took Virginia 26–7 on two Roman Gabriel sneaks, one coming after Roger Moore's interception, and Gabriel's two tosses to Claude Gibson and George Vollmar. Virginia scored on a pass from quarterback Gary Cuozzo to halfback Tony Uleha.

Maryland was overcome 13–10 after Gordon Bennett's end zone recovery of a blocked punt gave the Terps a fourth-quarter lead. Southern Mississippi led 7–6 on John Sklopan's dash and a Tommy Morrow conver-

A tense moment in the game holds the attention of North Carolina's Al Gold-stein (81), John Schroeder (88), Moyer Smith (23), and Ray Farris (12).

sion, but lost 20–13 on Gabriel's score and a pair of passes. Andin McLeod scored for USM on Morris Meador's pass, but Jim Fitzgerald blocked the conversion try. UCLA turned them back 7–0 under the lights in Los Angeles on a Bill Kilmer score.

Two conversions by Nick Maravich edged Wake Forest, 14–12, as Snead's extra point hit the left upright and his two-pointer failed. In a Saturday night game at Arizona State, Jack Stanton put State ahead on a 42-yard dash, but ASU evened it 15–15 at the half on touchdowns by Ossie McCarty and Jim Cosner's pass to Ray Young. It was tied again at 22 as Gabriel and Joe Zuger scored, but a Nolan Jones 24-yard field goal won for ASU 25–22. A chance to share in the title faded away as South Carolina tied them 8–8. Buddy Bennett dived over and then took the two-pointer from Billy Gambrell, and Gabriel threw 24 yards to Vollmar who lateraled to Jim Tapp for the last 35 and Jim D'Antonio ran in the two points.

State had centers Joe Bushofsky, Harry Puckett, and Kent Morton, guards Dick Reynolds, Graham Singleton, and Bill Hill, and Collice Moore, Bert Wilder, Alex Gilleskie, and Skip Matthews at tackle. Ends were Dennis Kroll, John Gill, and John Morris, with backs Tom Dellinger, Ron Wojcicki, Randy Harrell, and Sam Raneri.

Third-place Maryland beat West Virginia 31–8, with Bob Benke scoring for new WVU coach Gene Corum. Jim Saxton's punt return and Jerry Cook's 62-yard run headed another shutout by Texas 34–0. Clemson held a 10–0 lead, but a Rex Collins dash and Dale Betty's passes to Tom Brown and Gary Collins won it 19–17. Maryland came from behind twice to beat Wake Forest 14–13 on Dick Novak's two-point pass to Hank Poniatowski, and took South Carolina into camp 15–0.

Jim Kerr scored twice in Penn State's 28–9 win, once after a Jay Huffman interception, and Don Jonas ran back a punt 55 yards. Fumbles led to scores as Dick Hoak lost the ball in the end zone to Maryland's Joe Mona, and Bud Torris ran in for PSU after Dick Pae fell on one. Dan Piper got the first score and Vinny Scott kicked a field goal in North Carolina's 22–19 loss, and Virginia was beaten 44–12 as Tom Brown had an 89-yard kickoff return and Dennis Condie scored three times, once on a 91-yard kickoff runback after a lateral from Novak who ran it out from the end zone.

Clemson came in fourth. Mack Matthews ran in a 55-yard punt return and Virginia's Joe Kehoe scored in their 21–7 loss. A two-touchdown lead vanished as Jim Johnson went in, Terrell Dye threw for one score and caught another from Hank Lesesne, and a safety by Vanderbilt's George Smith brought a 22–20 win. North Carolina was beaten 24–0, and South Carolina lost its first-ever game at Clemson 12–2. Boston College scored all its points in the first half for a 25–14 win. John Janus ran back a 60-yard interception, Harry Crump dived over, and after long passes to John

Flanagan and Mike Tomeo, Joe Sikorski scored on a diving catch from George Van Cott. Furman's Tom Campbell scored on a 29-yard draw play and a pass from Bill Canty in their 42–14 loss, and Joe Anderson threw to Tommy King and Harry Pavilack's 31-yard run scored for Clemson.

1961

Duke won its second straight title and fifth overall. Dean Findley's two field goals kept South Carolina and its first year coach Marvin Bass in the game, but Dave Burch dived over and Bill Reynolds' conversion won it 7–6. New coach Bill Elias had ended Virginia's 28-game losing streak by beating William and Mary 21–6 the previous week, but Duke kayoed them 42–0 with four knockout blows: Gil Garner's long passes to Jack Wilson and Bill Futrell, a Walt Rappold to Mark Leggett 67-yard pass, and a 63-yard punt return by Jay Wilkinson, the son of Oklahoma coach Bud Wilkinson.

After a Charles Reiley field goal, Wake Forest was put away 23–3 with Stan Crisson getting the last score. But Georgia Tech pulled away in the last half on touchdowns by Stan "the Man" Gann after a Joe Auer catch, one by captain Chick Graning, and another following Dave Watterson's fumble recovery. Clemson handed Duke its only conference loss 17–7, and Wilkinson had a scintillating 82-yard punt runback in the 17–6 defeat of North Carolina State.

Duke lost the return match with Bump Elliott's Wolverines, as Michigan quarterback Dave Glinka threw touchdowns to Bob Brown and Bennie McRae, who scored three times, one on an interception 40 seconds after his scoring catch. Duke never crossed mid-field until the second half when Burch took it in twice from fullback.

Navy was stunned with 16 first-quarter points. Rappold hit Wilkinson on the 35 who went 77 yards to score on the third play, Rappold ran 45 yards, and Reynolds added a field goal. Leggett's plunge pushed it to 23–6 at the half, as Navy's Bruce Abel threw to John Hughes after getting a toss from Ray Klemick. Wilson's interception and a Greg Mather field goal made the final 30–9.

Bob Elliott's early field goal for North Carolina held off Duke until a pair of last-period three-pointers by Reynolds won 6–3, with the last one clearing the bar at the two-second mark.

Joe Kuharich brought Notre Dame to Durham but was welcomed with a 37–13 defeat. After Angelo Dabiero's 54-yard run on the fifth play, Duke jumped in front as Rappold hit Pete Widener and Crisson and Garner tossed to Zo Potts and Wilkinson. Mike Lind scored for the Irish, and Joe Perkowski converted. Because of a penalty at the gun on Walt Sweeney, Perkowski's field goal with George Sefcik holding had beaten Syracuse two weeks before 17–15.

Duke had tackles Dave Bosson, Dave Condon, Art Gregory, John Lomax, Fred McCollum, Chuck Walker, guards Rex Adams, Jean Berry, Jim Dalton, Dick Havens, Gene Kendall, Dan Litaker, John Markas, Barry Ramsey, and Paul Bengel, Jack Kruzelyak, and Ken Williams at center. Ends were Dan Gelbert and Dave Unser, Roy Bostock, John Tinnell, and Gary Wilson at full, Randy Clark at quarter, and Joel Arrington, Dan Bridges, Bob Hawn, and Bob Wyatt at half.

North Carolina came in second when Maryland dropped its last game to Virginia. Gib Carson's three touchdowns overtook a Mike Clark 83-yard opening kickoff runback for North Carolina State. Roman Gabriel's sneak and throw to Al Taylor regained the lead, but Bob Elliott pounded in for the win, 27–22. After Clemson's 27–0 breeze, Carolina beat Maryland 14–8 as fumble recoveries by center Joe Craver and halfback Lenny Beck led to both touchdowns.

South Carolina lost 17–0 on Tommy Pilcher's punt into a high wind, field goal, and Dave Sowell's errant toss. Miami won 10–0 on Billy Wilson's field goal and a George Mira pass to Larry Wilson.

Carolina squeaked by Tennessee 22–21 as Ray Farris threw to Ward Marslender with 15 seconds left and then hit Gib Carson for the two-pointer. Two Gary Cannon conversions tied it twice when Pat Augustine's fumble recovery led to a Jack Nichols touchdown, and Mike Lucci's interception equaled a second Farris score. The Vols then led 21–14 on Mallon Faircloth's pass to Mike Stratton.

Wendell Harris scored twice, once on a Jimmy Field pass, in a 30–0 LSU win, as tackle Billy Booth and guards Monk Guillot and Roy Winston never let UNC past their 38-yard line. Bo Campbell had a 54-yard touchdown run, and Lynn Amedee added a late score.

UNC lost the next two to Duke and Wake Forest 17–14 on Mickey Walker's field goal with 25 seconds to go. Alan White's run and Jim Tejeck's blocked punt put Wake ahead, but Carolina evened it twice, once after Jim LeCompte recovered a Bruce McConnell fumble.

Doug Thompson's fumble led to a Jim Addison score in the 24–0 win over Virginia, but Addison and Vic Esposito and Virginia's Ed Menzer were ejected for fighting after Farris was dropped hard.

Others in Carolina Blue were ends Conrad Sloop, George Knox, John Runco, and Steve Yates, with backs Joe Davies, John Flournoy, and Joe McLamb. Tackles were Ben Gallagher, John Hegarty, Tony Hennessey, and Steve Serenko, guards Duff Greene and Jack Tillery, and centers Gary Truver and Bob Zaback. Reserves were Joe Davenport, Sam Loflin, Jim Shumate, Jud Spainhour, and Henry Taylor.

Maryland was third with three wins and three losses. Dick Novak ran in for one score and threw to Jim Davidson for another to beat Bill Meek's Southern Methodist squad 14–6. Tom Sherwin's 30-yard run scored for SMU. Clemson stayed with the Terrapins before losing 24–21 on John Hannigan's late field goal.

Fine pass blocking by guard Tom Sankovich led to a catch by Gary Collins to lead Syracuse, but Heisman winner Ernie Davis went over and Dave Sarette threw to Walt Sweeney for a 13–7 halftime lead. Dick Shiner's 29-yard run tied it, and Hannigan converted to lead by one. After a 43-yard dash by Davis, Collins stopped Pete Brokaw before Davis put the Orangemen ahead again. Dennis Condie dived in for the Terps, and 6'3" Collins reached back and wrenched the two-point pass from John Humphreys for a 22–21 win.

Air Force lost 21–0 on touchdowns by Ernie Arizzi, Tom Brown, and Don Van Reenan. Billy Gambrell scored twice for South Carolina and John Caskey once in a 20–10 win, while tackles Jim Moss and Joe Prehodka held the Terps to 72 yards rushing and guard Ed "Punky" Holler's last-period interceptions stopped Maryland twice.

Dick Barlund's catch led to a 21–17 win for Maryland's first and only defeat of Penn State. Collins carried over Joe Blasenstein and Bob Kline for the final Terp score, and Roger Kochman, an Al Gursky and Galen Hall hook-up, and Don Jonas three-pointer scored for the Lions. Hannigan's toe won the next two games 10–7, as Joe Scarpati ran over late for North Carolina State and Donnie Frederick scored for Wake Forest. Brown took a Bill Ruby punt all the way against Wake after giving it to Novak who gave it back.

Brown's punt return led Virginia, but Carl Kuhn's two-point catch overtook the Terps 8–7. Murny Banner scored for Maryland, but Gary Cuozzo's pass to John Hepler and a 95-yard interception by Ted Rzempoluch in the final period gave Virginia a 28–16 upset.

Clemson was hot and cold and tied for third. They fell to Florida 21–17 as Lindy Infante scored three times, once on Larry Liberatore's pass and once after a Bob Hoover catch. North Carolina lost 27–0 on touchdowns

Among the records Gary Collins set at Maryland were 74 career receptions for 1,182 yards.

No one looked for the hot dog vendor when Jay Wilkinson was loose in the open field for Duke.

by Tommy King, Gary Barnes, Ron Scrudato, and Tommy Black. Jim Parker's toss to King led Wake Forest, but Mickey Walker's kick made it 7–3 at the half. Charles Reiley threw to Bill Ruby as Clemson sputtered, and Alan White's 59-yard run cooled them more. Scrudato's late score closed it 17–13.

The Tigers got up for Duke, then gave way to Auburn 24–14. Wendall Black scored after Bob Poole's catch, but Bobby Hunt hit Don Downs to set up two Don Machen touchdowns for a 14–7 halftime lead. A Woody Woodall field goal and Jimmy Burson score increased the margin, and Scrudato again made the final Clemson tally.

The punts of Eddie Werntz bottled up Tulane until Tom Emerson scored on a 67-yard run, but Clemson won 21–6 on scores by Scrudato, Joe Anderson, and Elmo Lam's punt return. South Carolina's Billy Gambrell and Bill McGuirt made it 7–7 at the half, then Lam ran in for the lead, but two fourth-quarter scores by Jim Costen gave the Gamecocks a 21–14 win. Bob King's Furman squad lost the neighborhood battle 35–6, and the Wolfpack lost 20–0 as Roman Gabriel was held to 35 yards in his last game, and Jim Rossi threw to Joe Young for the only completion not made by Gabriel all year.

1962

Duke won an unprecedented third straight ACC title and had the conference's first-ever 6-0-0 mark. Jay Wilkinson's 25-yard pass from Gil Garner drew first blood, but John McKay's national champion Southern Cal Trojans beat them 14–7 on passes from Pete Beathard to Willie Brown and Bill Nelsen to Hal Bedsole.

Duke had South Carolina all the way on runs by Bill Futrell, Mark Leggett, and Mike Curtis. A Dan Reeves quarterback sneak in the final minute and two-point pass to Ken Lester ended it 21–8. Florida scored on Tom Shannon's throw to Sam Holland, a 70-yard Larry Dupree run, Jim O'Donnell's short run, and three Jim Hall conversions. The last half was all Duke on runs by Bob Weidman and passes to lonesome end Stan Crisson as Curtis scored twice, Leggett once, and Garner hit Pete Widener for a 28–21 comeback. Marv Levy's California Bears scored on Larry Balliett's toss to Alan Nelson before going down 21–7, and Clemson was tamed 16–0.

After Steve Parker's fumble recovery, North Carolina State scored on Bill Kriger's pass to Jim Guin and Jim Rossi's 7-yard run, but lost 21–14 on Walt Rappold's scoring throws and Curtis run. Georgia Tech gave Duke its second defeat 20–9 as Jim Mendheim scored on a short run and Billy Lothridge got all the rest.

Bill Reynolds kicked a 38-yard field goal to beat Maryland 10–7. Bill Baird had a 52-yard interception and Futrell scored three touchdowns to

Top: Dan Reeves quarterbacked South Carolina, played for the Dallas Cowboys, then became head coach of the Denver Broncos. *Bottom:* Billy Lothridge ran, passed, punted, and place-kicked his way into the Georgia Tech record books in the early 1960s.

Tackle Art Gregory was a two-time winner of the Jacobs Blocking Trophy while at Duke.

vanquish Wake Forest 50–0. North Carolina's Junior Edge threw to Roger Smith and Bob Lacey, but a third Reynolds field goal with 49 seconds remaining took it 16–14.

Duke's all-senior line had ends Ed Chesnutt and Zo Potts, tackles Art Gregory and Dick Havens, guards Jean Berry and John Markas, and center Paul Bengel. Others were ends Dave Burdette, Bob Beasley, and Jim Scott, tackles John Lomax, Dan Lonon, Jim McCarthy, and Chuck Walker, guards Dave Condon, Fred Cromartie, Jim Dalton, Jim Fuqua, Bob Johnson, and centers Bob Davis and Ken Williams. Jerry Stoltz and Dave Uible were at quarter, Barry Ramsey at full, and Dan Bridges, Rich Harris, and Bob Hawn at half.

Clemson was second with 5-1-0. Billy Lothridge scored once and threw touchdowns to ends Billy Martin and Ted Davis, and Joe Auer after a toss to Johnny Gresham in a 26–9 Georgia Tech win. A Rod Rogers field goal and Jerry Taylor run scored for Clemson. Pat Crain scored in the 7–0 win over North Carolina State and got two more in the 24–7 defeat of Wake Forest. John Mackovic passed to Jim Tejeck for the Wake score, and Mack Matthews scored on an 88-yard return of a Steve Bozarth punt, while Wake's Donnie Frederick led the nation in kickoff returns with a 22.8-yard average.

Hal Davis returned the opening kickoff 98 yards against Georgia, but Larry Rakestraw's scoring strikes to Frank Lankewicz and Don Porterfield and a Carlton Guthrie run put the Tigers in a hole. Matthews scored for Clemson in a 24–16 Georgia victory, as Rogers and Bill McCullough knocked 40-yard plus field goals over the bar.

Defeats by Duke and Auburn followed. Joe Anderson's 37-yard pass to Oscar Thorsland put Clemson ahead of Auburn, but fullback Larry Rawson tied it after a Billy Edge fumble recovery. Clemson fumbled the kickoff and Edge was there to cover it, and in three plays Auburn had the lead. A pitch to Hal Davis tied it, but a Woody Woodall field goal won it for Shug Jordan's men 17–14.

The Tigers came together to win the last four. Two Charlie Dumas touchdowns, one following a Jim Eason fumble recovery on the second-half kickoff, and a Rogers three-pointer beat North Carolina 17–6, with fullback Ken Willard going over for Carolina. After a Brownie Cordell field goal for Furman, Clemson won 44–3, as Jimmy Bell tossed to Coleman Glaze for the final score.

Rogers won the last two games with field goals. The Terps led 14–0 on the strength of Ernie Arizzi's 68-yard interception, but Clemson caught them in the last minute. Illegal motion nullified a Tiger touchdown, so they settled for a 17–14 win. The South Carolina game also went down to the wire. A Rogers field goal broke a 7–7 tie, but Dean Findley's 36-yarder evened it at ten. A Dan Reeves run gave the Gamecocks the lead, but Elmo Lam knotted it on a lateral from Jim Parker. Rogers untied it 20–17 with 1:45 left and set an ACC season mark of seven field goals.

Clemson's line had center Ted Bunton, guards Jack Aaron and Walter Cox, tackles Dave Hynes and Don Chuy, and end Bob Poole. Others were guard Clark Gaston, ends Lou Fogle and Johnny Case, halfback Billy Ward, and Jimmy Howard, the coach's son, at full.

Maryland's third-place finish started with a 7–0 win over SMU and a 13–2 victory over Wake Forest, with Wilbert Faircloth tackling Dick Shiner behind the goal. Ken Ambrusko's 78-yard punt runback helped beat North Carolina State 14–6, with Bill Kriger scoring for the Pack. Shiner and Tom Brown combined for a 14–0 lead on North Carolina, but a Junior Edge pass to Ward Marslender and Willard dive closed the gap. Maryland wrapped it up in the fourth period on a run by Len Chiaverini and Shiner toss to Ernie Arizzi for a 31–13 win.

Brown's 98-yard runback of the opening kickoff started Maryland right against Miami, but George Mira's passes to Nick Ryder, Jack Sims, and Bill Sparks brought Miami from behind three times to beat the Terps 28–24. A Shiner to Brown pass set South Carolina back, but after Larry Gill's interception and a Dan Reeves score to Ken Lester, Dean Findley's three-pointer made it 11–10, only to have John Hannigan's second field goal squeeze by 13–11.

Pete Liske scored twice in a 23–7 Penn State win, once after Don Caum intercepted Jerry Osler. Another Caum larceny of one to Mike Simpson led to a Roger Kochman score, and Ron Coates added a field goal after Dave Robinson's recovered fumble. Jim Corcoran threw to Mike Funk in Maryland's T-formation spread with the ball going to the deep back, and Brown had a 100-yard interception to defeat Virginia 40–18, but the Cavaliers had a six-minute splurge on two Bob Freeman scoring runs and a Stuart Christhilf catch.

The Maryland line had tackles Dave Crossan and Roger Shoals, guards Fred Joyce and Walter Rock, and center Gene Feher. Others were tackles Lou Bury, Norm Hatfield, Gary Jankowski, Joe Frattaroli, guards John Boinis, Ray Gibson, Ray Ferrante, Olaf Drozdov, Chet Detko, and centers Ron Lewis and Jack Gilmore. Ends were Dan Piper, Joe Mona, Tom Rae, Harry Butsko, Ed Rog, and Dave Nardo. Backs were Murny Banner and Ken Smith at half, Ron Mace and Joe Hrezo at full, with Bob Burton and Don White at quarterback.

III. The Return
of Two-Platoon Football
(1963–1972)

1963

North Carolina and North Carolina State tied for the league crown with 6-1-0 marks, and for the first time the ACC played in two bowl games as these two schools represented the conference.

Max Chapman opened the season with a field goal, but Henry Massie returned the second-half kickoff 99 yards to put Virginia in front. The Tar Heels won 11–7 as Ken Willard plowed over and took the two-pointer from Gary Black, in for woozy Junior Edge. "It's not a good feeling," said coach Jim Hickey, "to have your quarterback on the bench beside you asking you what his name is."

Michigan State led 10–0 at halftime on Steve Juday's pass to Tom Krze-mienski, who lateraled to Sherm Lewis, and a Lou Bobich field goal. The Spartans won 31–0 in the last half, with Roger Lopes scoring on a 76-yard run. Edge, halfback Ronnie Jackson, and end John Atherton scored in the 21–0 defeat of Wake Forest. Jerry Fishman took Maryland's forces to a touchdown and Art Carney tacked on the conversion, but Edge and Bob Lacey scored for a 14–7 win, as Dave Braine continued to convert each time.

It was 10–10 at the half on Braine's field goal and Black's toss to Ron Tuthill, with Gus Andrews putting one over and Tony Kozarsky's 74-yard interception scoring for North Carolina State. Willard's 6-yard run and a pair of passes from Edge to tight end Joe Robinson won in the last half

Jim Hickey had a tough act to follow when Jim Tatum died unexpectedly, but in a few years he had the Tar Heels in the Gator Bowl.

31–10. Bill Edwards won the punting duel with South Carolina, as Willard scored on the fifth play for 7–0 after a Gamecock punt only went to the 34-yard line.

Fullback Marvin Hurst scored for Georgia in their 28–7 loss, but Jim Parker and Tommy Ray engineered an 11–7 Clemson victory. Frank Pearce kicked a field goal, and Lou Fogle took a two-point pass after Parker nosed in. In the 27–16 battle with Miami, Edge sneaked in, threw to Jackson, and Willard scored, but George Mira connected with Pete Spinelli and John Bennett. Don Cifra kicked a field goal before Black's toss to Tuthill nailed it down.

Because of President Kennedy's assassination, the Duke game was postponed to the following Thursday. Willard and Eddie Kesler crashed over for a 13–0 Carolina lead, but Duke countered on Scotty Glacken's 70-yard pass to Bill Futrell and Jay Wilkinson's 24-yard run, and led 14–13 on Steve Holloway's two extra points. Max Chapman reversed last year's score and ended the season as it began with a field goal and 16–14 win in the last 33 seconds. An invitation from Gator Bowl chairman Joe Sykora to spend the holidays in Jacksonville was accepted immediately after the game.

While the Tar Heels enjoyed themselves at a plush hotel in St. Augustine, the Air Force experienced the regimen of an Army base near Orlando, and it showed in the game. The two 220-pound packages of halfback Willard and fullback Kesler made quick work of the Air Force. Edge, Robinson, and Black all scored, and the game that was billed as a toss-up ended in a 35–0 runaway.

The Tar Heels lined up with centers Chris Hanburger, Glenn Ogburn, and Ed Stringer, guards Jim Alderman, Jerry Cabe, Richy Zarro, Clint Eudy, and Jay Malobicky, tackles Gene Sigmon and Cole Kortner, Vic Esposito, and John Hill. Ends were John Hammett and Frank Gallagher, with Roger Smith and Tom Ward at halfback. Reserves were Lee Baggett, Hank Barden, Frank Bowman, Tom Brooks, Bob Cowles, Don Constantin, Jim Eason, George Ellison, Henry Hodges, Curt Ish, Sandy Kinney, Jim Naughton, Ray Paulos, Jim Ray, Dana Wellman, Loren Wells, and Barry Westfall.

Because Riddick Stadium had only 19,000 seats, North Carolina State played most of its games away. At College Park, they beat Maryland 36–14. Tony Kozarsky, Mike Clark, and captain Joe Scarpati ran over, while the Terps' Dick Shiner tossed to Andy Martin and scored himself. Pie Vann's Southern Mississippi team was beaten in Hattiesburg 14–0, as Jim Rossi threw to Ray Barlow and Bob Faircloth. At Clemson, the Pack won 7–3 as Rossi found Barlow all alone on a 77-yard play. In Columbia, South Carolina lost 18–6 on Rossi's throw to Kozarsky, Don Montgomery's blocked punt and touchdown, and a Pete Falzarano straight-ahead carry.

After the loss at Chapel Hill, State returned home and gave Duke its first loss 21–7, as Mike Clark's 55-yard run set up one score, Rossi hit Scarpati for another, and Montgomery intercepted a lateral. They trailed Virginia at the half for the first time 7–2, as Tom Hodges threw to Stuart Christhilf and Tom Shuman gave up a safety, but won 15–9 with State's Dave Houtz going down for another safety. Virginia Tech's Bob Schweickert scored in their 13–7 loss, as he raced 59 yards to the one and then took it in.

Florida State handed the Pack its only shutout 14–0. After center Bill Daly covered a fumble, Dave Snyder and Maury Bibent ran the ball until Larry Brinkley dived in, and Ed Pritchett ran over when State gambled and lost late in the game. Ron Skosnik threw to Shelby Mansfield for the final score in a 42–0 win over Wake Forest, which ended its 18-game losing streak the previous week when Brian Piccolo's extra point beat South Carolina 20–19.

The Wolfpack was invited to play Mississippi State in the Liberty Bowl – the last Liberty Bowl game played in Philadelphia. End Bill McGuire blocked a Carolina punt and Tommy Inman picked up the rolling ball on the 11 and dashed in for a score. Later in the first period, Sonny Fisher faked a handoff to Ode Burrell and went in from the 3 behind guard Pat Watson and tackle Tommy Neville. Justin Canale kicked a field goal for coach Paul Davis before Rossi scored and threw to Barlow in a 16–12 Bulldog win.

The Pack line had tackles Bert Wilder, Chuck Wachtel, Steve Parker, Glenn Sasser, Rosie Amato, guards Bennett Williams, Bill Sullivan, Silas Snow, Jim Martin, and centers Oscar Overcash and Lou DeAngelis. Billy Hall was at end and Merrick Barnes at quarter. Reserves were Ron England, Golden Simpson, and Dave Stout.

Duke tied for third with 5-2-0. Mike Curtis scored twice in South Carolina's 22–14 loss, and got the other on a fourth-and-12 play. Marty Rosen and Carl Huggins scored for the Gamecocks, and Dan Reeves threw to Ronnie Lamb for two points. Jay Wilkinson's 64-yard scoring run got oohs-and-ahs from the fans, and Bob Dunphey ran in twice for all the Virginia points in their 30–8 loss.

Maryland used a spread, shotgun, straight-T, and I-formation and led 12–10 with 9:20 left. Said coach Tom Nugent, "We'll need all the tricks we can cook up," but Duke showed him a trick in return. Scotty Glacken handed the ball to a halfback who reversed to another halfback who gave it back to Glacken who threw to Stan Crisson for the go-ahead score and eventual 30–12 margin. In for Maryland was Darryl Hill, the first black to play ACC football.

In the 22–22 tie with California, Wilkinson scored twice on passes, Bill Futrell ran in, and Cal's Craig Morton threw twice to Jack Schraub. Morton's quarterback sneak, safety on Jim Pinson's snap through the end zone, two Tom Blanchfield extra points, and Jerry Mosher's late two-point catch for Cal made it end even.

Glacken's four scoring passes set a one-game ACC mark against Clemson. Crisson caught three and Wilkinson one, a 38-yard screen pass, and scored again on a crowd-pleasing 67-yard run. Clemson's Mack Matthews ran in twice, Tommy Ray threw a 68-yarder to Johnny Case, and Frank Pearce added a three-pointer in Duke's 35–30 win.

After the loss in Raleigh, Duke traveled to Atlanta and was beaten badly by Georgia Tech 30–6. Billy Lothridge kicked three field goals and topped the career mark of Auburn's Ed Dyas with an NCAA mark of 19. Lothridge also threw touchdowns to Johnny Gresham and Frank Sexton and kicked three extra points. Jim Mendheim also ran over, with Andy Lucas getting the Duke score.

Wilkinson scored three times against Wake Forest, once on a 72-yard punt return that delighted the home crowd in Durham. Fullback Dick Kraft and halfback Jim Luciano also went over in the 39–7 win, and Brian Piccolo carried one in for the Deacs.

Wayne Hardin's Middies came to town and led 14–6 on scores by Roger Staubach and Johnny Sai, with Biff Bracy going in for Duke. Then the second period erupted for 36 points – 19 of them by Duke. Glacken ran in, and Fred Marlin's field goal made it 17–12. The stadium rocked as Glacken's throw to Crisson put the Blue Devils up by two, only to have Nick Markoff's run and Dave Sjuggerud's 34-yard interception give Navy the lead once more. After a Chuck Drulis 44-yard catch, Wilkinson scored for 31–25 at the half. Staubach tossed to Pat Donnelly for a new Academy completion mark, and Sai got the last-half score, a 93-yard run for the longest one in Navy history, to make the final 38–25.

Duke had center Bob Davis, guards Bob Johnson and Fred Cromartie, and tackles Dan Lonon and captain Chuck Walker. Others were tackles Jim McCarthy, Bill Jones, Don Lynch, Jerry Francis, guards Jim Fuqua, Wes Grant, Dan Litaker, Earl Yates, and centers Ron Winslow, John McNabb, and Bill Thomas. Ends were Jim Scott, Dave Burdette, Bob Beasley, Al Matuza, Bill Simpson, Rod Stewart, and Steve Holloway. Jerry Stoltz and Bob Jamieson were at quarter, Alex Bell at full, and Bill Baird and John Gutekunst at half.

Clemson was also third with 5-2-0. Injuries to backs George Sutton, Jim Ruffner, and starting tackle John Boyette got them off to a bad start. They led Oklahoma 14–7 on Jim Parker's pass to Lou Fogle and Hal Davis run, with Jim Grisham scoring for OU. Oklahoma won in the last half on Lance Rentzel's 49-yard run, a Mike Ringer sneak after John Flynn blocked a Bob Fritz punt and Dave Voiles recovered it, a tackle-eligible pass to Ralph Neely, and a John Jarman field goal after Ron Harmon fell on a fumble for a 31–14 win. A heavy rain in Atlanta didn't bother Billy Lothridge, as he threw to Gary Williams, Ted Davis, and Billy Martin, kicked field goals of 40 and 36 yards, and converted three times for a 27–0 victory. They lost to North Carolina State and Duke, and in between tied Georgia at home 7–7 as Larry Rakestraw went over after Benny Boyd came up with a fumble, with Bob Swift going in for Clemson. It was almost five-for-five as Bill McCullough's 34-yard field goal try just missed in the last few minutes.

The season was half over and the Tigers still had not won a game, but they put it all together in a 35–0 win over Virginia. A 36–0 defeat of Wake Forest followed, as Pat Crain scored three times, Bob Swift once, and Billy Ward had a 24-yard scoring run. They gave North Carolina its only league loss and beat Maryland 21–6, with Tommy Ray tossing to Charlie Meadowcroft and the Terps scoring on an Ernie Arizzi 85-yard interception at the end of the game. In the finale with South Carolina, Jimmy Howard's run put the Tigers ahead, but Dan Reeves threw to Billy Nies and Charley Williams for a 14–7 halftime lead. Ten points on Hugh Mauldin's touchdown and Frank Pearce field goal after Carolina lost the ball on downs made it 17–14. After another fourth-down failure, Hal Davis ran in and Reeves tossed to Marty Rosen for a 24–20 final.

Clemson had center Ted Bunton, guards Billy Weaver and Tracy Childers, tackles Vic Aliffi and Jack Aaron, and Bob Poole at end. Others were Joe Balles, Joe Blackwood, Richard Cooper, Walter Cox, Clark Gaston, Wade Hall, Bill Hecht, Ricky Johnson, Bruce McClure, Johnny Palmer, and Butch Robbins. Ends were Ted Petoskey and Mike Troy, with backs Jimmy Bell, Charlie Dumas, and Ellis Dantzler.

1964

After a dozen years of one-platoon football with its two-way players, two-platoon football and unlimited substitution returned. The new rule increased the use of specialized players and allowed coaches to send in offensive and defensive platoons when the clock was stopped. "This is the nearest you could possibly come to what the coaches wanted," said Jack Curtice, the rules committee chairman of the American Football Coaches Association.

Earle Edwards brought North Carolina State a second outright ACC title and third overall with a 5-2-0 mark. Tony Golmont got State started with a 47-yard interception against North Carolina, Pete Falzarano added a 39-yard run, and Harold Deters kicked both extra points. Ken Willard scored two Tar Heel touchdowns, one on Danny Talbott's last-minute toss, but Ron Skosnik batted away the two-point pass to win 14–13. After Shelby Mansfield returned the Clemson kickoff 41 yards, Deters booted a 21-yard field goal, and the Wolfpack won a tough defensive struggle 9–0. Maryland took a 13–0 lead on Bo Hickey's 77-yard run on the first play and Bobby Collins' 39-yard run on a blocked punt, but failed the two-point play. Charlie Noggle had two second-half scores, one after a Bob Smith fumble recovery, and Gus Andrews kicked them to a 14–13 win.

National champion Alabama gave the Wolfpack its first defeat at Tuscaloosa 21–0. After Joe Namath threw to Tommy Tolleson and Ray Odgen, he went out with a twisted right knee, but Steve Sloan came on to score once and throw for another. Steve Bowman added a touchdown, and David Ray kicked three extra points. Deters put them ahead in Durham, but Duke led by ten at the half and erupted for 22 last-quarter points on scores by Sonny Odom, Dick Kraft, and John Gutekunst's 83-yard interception to bury the Pack 35–3.

The Red and White improved its league mark with a 24–15 win over Virginia on two Gary Rowe touchdowns, and then downed South Carolina 17–14. Bill Gentry caught a pass from Skosnik, with a Deters last-period field goal and Skosnik's 72-yard run providing the winning points. Skosnik tossed once to Wendell Coleman and twice to Rowe, but Virginia Tech put them back in the loss column 28–19. Quarterback Bob Schweickert had 1,000 yards rushing for the second time and scored twice, once on a 66-yard run. Fullback Sonny Utz and end Tommy Marvin also scored for the Hokies.

The Wolfpack would not win again in 1964 as Florida State's "magnificent seven" held them to six yards rushing. In the FSU front were nose guard Jack Shinholser, tackles Frank Pennie and Avery Sumner, ends Max Wettstein and George D'Allesandro, backed up by Dick Herman and Bill McDowell. Coleman got the Pack score, and Steve Tensi hit flanker Fred Biletnikoff twice to win 28–6.

Because of a Friday night loss to Wake Forest 27–13, State did not win the pennant until North Carolina beat Duke the next day. Noggle scored and Coleman caught one from Skosnik, but a John Mackovic score for Wake and three Brian Piccolo touchdowns and conversions gave him 111 points and 1,044 yards, and the ACC had the nation's top scorer and ground gainer for the first time.

The State line was manned by seniors: center Lou DeAngelis, guards Silas Snow and Bennett Williams, tackles Glenn Sasser and Steve Parker, and ends Ray Barlow and Billy Hall. Larry Brown was at wingback in State's wing-T offense. Others were centers Charles Bradburn, Dave Everett, and Ron Jackson, guards Jim Martin, Terry Jenkins, and Golden Simpson, and tackles Rosie Amato, Dave Ellis, and Dave Carter. At end was Will Mann, with backs Bill James, Page Ashby, Don DeArment, Jim Guin, Gale Tart, and punt returner Julian James.

Duke lost its last game to North Carolina and came in second at 3-2-1. The seesaw with South Carolina finished 9–9, as Larry Gill and Mike Curtis traded touchdowns, and after a Lide Huggins fumble recovery Jack McCathern's field goal with 90 seconds left matched one by Rod Stewart for Duke. Virginia was downed 30–0, as Scotty Glacken threw to Jim Scott for 65 yards and then hit Chuck Drulis after a John Carlo interception. Bill Simpson and Dave Burdette added more quick points, as Simpson stepped in front of a pass on the one and walked in and Burdette blocked a punt for a safety.

The Tulane game in New Orleans was postponed due to Hurricane Hilda, but Maryland was beaten 24–17. Phil Petry tossed to Chip Myrtle and Walt Marciniak for the Terps, but a Curtis score, one by Sonny Odom after a captured fumble by tackle Sonny Morris, and Glacken's pass to Drulis kept the Devils in front. Mark Caldwell and Bernardo Bramson added field goals. Two Caldwell field goals beat Army 6–0, but the season was in the red from now on.

Duke's five defeats began with Georgia Tech's 21–8 win, as Terry Haddock scored twice and Jeff Davis once. Duke's I-formation spread the defense and gained 371 yards, but all they could get was a Glacken to Drulis score. "We did everything as planned except cross the goal," moaned coach Bill Murray. A 16-yard run by John Gutekunst tied Wake Forest, but Brian Piccolo scored all the points in a 20–7 triumph for rookie coach Bill Tate.

The woes continued against Navy. Biff Bracy's touchdown was set up by Mike Shasby's 26-yard runback and Glacken threw to Dave Dunaway, but the Middies took them in tow 27–14. Roger Staubach, Jim Angel, and Danny Wong, the first Chinese to play football at the Academy, all scored, and Fred Marlin added two field goals.

North Carolina's 21–15 victory knocked the title from Duke's grasp. Ken Willard pounded over twice, Gary Black threw to Billy Axselle, and Eddie Kesler broke by three the one-game school mark of Charley Justice with 172 yards rushing. Caldwell made a field goal, and Glacken had two last-half passes to Drulis and Burdette.

Duke lost the make-up game with Tommy O'Boyle's Tulane team, 17–0, on two Carl Crowder touchdowns and Don Bright's 53-yarder, a field goal that eclipsed Carl Woodward's 1913 kick. Dave East took Tulane to the Duke five where they fumbled, but "The Posse," Tulane's defensive unit, had no trouble handcuffing the Devils.

Brian Piccolo had to be carried from the field in 1964 as Wake Forest beat Duke 20–7 for the first time in 13 years. His jersey was caked with mud, but it wasn't even raining.

Duke had center Bob Davis, guards Jim McCarthy and Fred Cromartie, and tackles Bill Jones and Dan Lonon. Others were centers Bill Thomas and Roger Hughes, guards Earl Yates, John McNabb, and Jerry Barringer, and tackles Dan Litaker, Jerry Francis, and Don Lynch. Ends were Al Matuza and Bruce Wiesley, with Bob Matheson, Kent Denton, Bob Jamieson, and John Johnson in the backfield.

Maryland was one of three teams tied for third at 4-3-0. In the opener, Oklahoma's Gomer Jones rushed in John Hammond for one play, a 90-yard pass to Lance Rentzel, which opened the door to a 13–3 win. In the 24–6 defeat of South Carolina, the Terps never trailed after a Howard Humphries catch put them ahead. After the losses to North Carolina State and Duke, they beat North Carolina 10–9 on Bernardo Bramson's field goal and Walt Marciniak plunge. Maryland's lead went to 14–0 after Ron Shillinglaw's 3-yard punt for Wake Forest, but two Brian Piccolo scores and John Mackovic's pass to Dick Cameron gave the Deacs a 21–17 victory. Penn State took the lead on two Tom Urbanik touchdowns, one after Frank Hershey's interception, and Gerry Sanker kicked a field goal to win 17–9. The PSU defense, led by guard Glenn Ressler, stopped the Terps with nine first-half points on a Bramson field goal and Bo Hickey score after John Kenny grabbed a bad pitch by Gary Wydman.

Behind guard Chick Krahling and tackles Larry Bagranoff and Matt Arbutina, Maryland led Navy 21–8 on Phil Petry's touchdown and his tosses to Bill Pettit and Dick Absher, with Roger Staubach throwing to Danny Wong and Tom Leiser taking a two-pointer from Phil Bassi for the Middie points. The unsinkable Staubach came back with two last-period passes to Jim Ryan and Cal Huey, but Ken Ambrusko returned Tom Williams' kickoff 101 yards for a 27–22 win. Guard Jerry Fishman, who had been flagged twice for penalties, made an obscene gesture toward the Midshipmen in the stands as he walked off. He later apologized, but the incident contributed to a break in football relations between the schools.

Backs Doug Klingerman, Ron Adams, and George Stem saw action and Ron Nalewak's interception scored in the 34–0 win over Clemson's toothless Tigers, Virginia was blanked in the finale 10–0, and Bramson's nine field goals were a new one-year ACC mark.

North Carolina was also third. They lost two games by one point, but downed Duffy Daugherty's Michigan State squad 21–15. Three short runs by Danny Talbott and Ken Willard were enough to win, but the Spartans scored 15 fourth-quarter points on a Clint Jones 42-yard run, Harry Ammon's two-point toss to Dick Gordon, and Steve Juday's 11-yard pass to

Gene Washington. Wake Forest was dispatched easily 23–0, as Talbott scored and threw to Ronnie Jackson, Willard blasted in, and Max Chapman added a field goal.

The Louisiana State game was 3–3 on Chapman and Doug Moreau field goals until Gawain Dibetta scored and Pat Screen hit Moreau for a 20–3 LSU win. Doug Senter got the South Carolina score in their 24–6 defeat, and Georgia had it all the way 24–8 on a Lynn Hughes pass to Don Porterfield, Bob Etter's field goal, and runs by Preston Ridlehuber and Bob Taylor. Clemson fell 29–0, and Bob Davis and Gary Black traded touchdowns until Virginia was victorious 31–27, but Carolina closed the door on Duke for the crown.

Wake Forest was the third team at 4-3-0, with losses coming from South Carolina 23–13 and Clemson 21–2. Joe Sepic made the safety against Clemson, but Butch Robbins blocked a punt for one score, Hal Davis ran in, and Tommy Ray tossed to Richard Cooper for the other. They beat Virginia 31–21, and Brian Piccolo had two scores and Wayne Wellborn three in the 38–21 defeat of Virginia Tech, with Eddie McKinney adding a field goal. Vanderbilt won 9–6 on three Dick Lemay field goals, and Memphis State had a 23–14 win on Bob Sherlag's 56-yard punt return and Billy Fletcher field goal, with Piccolo and John Mackovic scoring for the Deacs.

1965

Duke finished at the top of the league with a 4-2-0 record. Ken Chatham scored to put them ahead of Virginia, but Tom Hodges went over right guard to tie it for new coach George Blackburn. Jake Devonshire's 55-yard run and Scotty Glacken's 10-yard jaunt around left end won in the final quarter 21–7. South Carolina lost 20–15 on two Jay Calabrese scores, with Bob Harris catching a pass for Carolina and Jule Smith scoring in the last minute.

Glacken tossed four touchdowns, three to end Dave Dunaway in Rice's 41–21 loss. Doug Nicholson threw to Les Lehman and Chuck Latourette for the Owls, and Ron Cervenka held for Rich Parker's three conversions. Kickoff return leader Eric Crabtree scored for Pitt, and Joe Jones kicked John Michelosen's Panthers ahead 7–0. Fullback Page Wilson tied it as Duke went on to win 21–13, with Ken Lucas throwing to Mitch Zalesky for Pitt's last score.

The Blue Devils lost their first game 3–2, as a Frank Pearce field goal for Clemson edged Don Barfield's blocked end zone punt by nose guard Bob Foyle. Cyril Pinder's 80-yard run broke a 7–7 tie with Pete Elliott's Illinois club, and Fred Custardo threw to Ron Bess after Ken Kmiec's fumble recovery for a 21–7 lead at the half. A captured fumble by Ron Acks led to another Pinder score, and Todd Orvald tossed to end Chuck Drulis in a 28–14 defeat.

Duke scored ten second-quarter points on Orvald's completion to Mike Swomley and Mark Caldwell field goal to lead Georgia Tech 16–14. But Tech battled back a second time as Doc Harvin scored after Kim King hit Lenny Snow and Gary Williams, then clinched it a minute later on a Randall Edmunds interception and Bunky Henry conversion. Wingback Craig Baynham had three scoring catches in Tech's 35–23 win. The Wolfpack gave them a fourth straight loss 21–0, as Page Ashby, Shelby Mansfield, and Dan Golden all scored.

The month of defeats ended on a positive note. In the 40–7 win over Wake Forest, Calabrese and Frank Ryan scored twice, with Don Davis scoring for the Deacons. Calabrese had three more in North Carolina's 34–7 loss, and Danny Talbott scored for Carolina.

After the players carried coach Murray to the center of the field to shake hands with Carolina coach Jim Hickey, they sang a chorus of "For He's a Jolly Good Fellow." A long silence filled the locker room, and those outside thought the team was offering a post-game prayer as they always did. Then the players came out one-by-one with sad eyes, Sonny Odom, Rod Stewart, Chuck Stavins, Don Lynch, while coach Murray, a staunch foe of free substitution, told newsmen at a press meeting that he resigned to take a job as executive director of the American Football Coaches Association. Bill Murray had taken his last victory ride to mid-field.

In Duke's line were center Mike Murphy, guards John McNabb and Jerry Barringer, and tackles Bill Jones and Earl Yates. On defense were ends Roger Hayes and Bruce Wiesley, linebackers Bob Matheson, John Carlo, Roger Hughes, Dick Kraft, and deep men Art Vann, Sonny Morris, Mike Shasby, and John Gutekunst.

Others were centers Bucky Fondren and Don Ashby, guards Bob Astley, Robin Bodkin, and Rodger Parker, and tackles Ross Arnold, Mike Renneker, Bob Lasky, Mal Travelstead, and Ed Virgin. At end were Al Matuza, Bill Serravezza, Bob Adams, and Fred Zirkle, with backs Andy Lucas, Rick Reider, Jim Barrett, Don Brannon, Bob Dow, Jim Shackford, Andy Beath, Joe Bussey, Mark Telge, and Herb Goins.

South Carolina's new assistant coaches for Marvin Bass, Dick Bestwick,

North Carolina coach Jim Hickey and 1965 ACC player of the year quarterback Danny Talbott.

Jimmy Vickers, and Dick Weldon, helped tie Duke for the league title. In a Saturday night game with The Citadel at Johnson Hagood Stadium in Charleston, they beat Eddie Teague's charges 13–3. After Kroghie Andresen and Scott Townsend exchanged punts, Pat Green kicked it to 3–0.

Jete Rhodes and Jim Rogers couldn't get started, so Ted Wingard came in and scored twice. After the defeat by Duke, they beat North Carolina State 13–7 on two Jimmy Poole field goals and Ben Garnto's 74-yard run. But Doug Dickey's Tennessee Vols manhandled them 24–3 as Walt Chadwick ran in twice, Charlie Fulton threw to David Leake, and Leake added a field goal.

Wake Forest struck quickly in the third quarter to lead 7–3 on Joe Carazo's 30-yard run and Ken Hauswald's 56-yard pass to end Jimmy Dixon. South Carolina came back with two Ben Galloway runs and one by Ronnie Lamb after a Stan Juk interception. Guard Don Somma blocked a punt that linebacker Johnny Glass covered in the end zone, and Leroy Bailey's blocked punt led to another score in a 38–7 win. End J.R. Wilburn's nine catches set a school record.

Louisiana State won 21–7 as 66,000 screaming fans turned up the heat at Tiger Stadium in Baton Rouge and cheered the scores by Joe Labruzzo, Danny LeBlanc, and Nelson Stokley. Doug Senter tied it as Buster Brown's punt was blocked before Charles McClendon's Tigers put it away. "You have to beat more than a football team there. They have tremendous crowd support," commented coach Bass.

The Maryland game had plenty of first-period action as fullback Phil Branson scored, but Bobby Collins returned the kickoff 91 yards for Maryland. On the next kickoff Lou Stickel recovered a fumble, and Ernie Torain carried to the one where Fred Cooper went in. Mike Fair scored for Carolina, but the Terps won 27–14. After a 17–7 win over Virginia, Alabama downed Carolina 35–14 as Steve Sloan set up two scores and hit Dennis Homan for two more.

The Gameroosters took on more Tigers and beat Clemson 17–16 at home. Phil Rogers scored with 40 seconds left, but the holder stood up on the two-point try only to have his pass batted away.

Gamecock centers were Jon Linder and Bob Gunnels, guards Dan Legat, Wilbur Hodge, David Berry, John Ewing, and Randy Harbour, and tackles Steve Cox, Paul Phillips, Len Sears, Dennis Darling, Billy Nelson, and Bob Collins. Ends were John Breeden and Bill Dickens, son of Indiana coach Phil Dickens, with wingback Curtis Williams. On defense were backs Butch Reeves, Bobby Bryant, Jim Mulvihill, Dave Truby, and linebackers Jimmy Killen and Bob Cole. Others were Terry Harmon, Wayne Tucker, and Marcellus Gabryelski.

A share of the league crown was as close as Carolina came to the throne that season. Commissioner James H. Weaver ruled that two ineligible players had received financial aid without making an 800 score on the College Board Exams. This was a violation of ACC rules, so South Carolina had to forfeit all conference games in which the players participated. Due to the forfeit wins they received, North Carolina State and Clemson shared the conference title, while Duke slipped to second and South Carolina was last.

The Wolfpack beat Wake Forest 13–11, lost to North Carolina 10–7 on Danny Talbott's field goal, then lost to Florida 28–6 as Steve Spurrier tossed twice to Charlie Casey and set up two more by John Feiber. They beat Maryland 29–7 as Pete Sokalsky blocked an end zone punt, Page Ashby hit Harry Martell, and Bill Wyland and Charlie Noggle scored on short runs. They blanked Virginia 13–0 with a seven-man umbrella pass defense, and Harold Deters stopped Bill Peterson's Florida State squad 3–0 in the last game at Riddick Field. Gary Snook was intercepted seven times, twice for touchdowns by Gus Andrews and Art McMahon, in a 28–20 defeat of Jerry Burns' Iowa Hawkeyes. The South Carolina forfeit made them 5-2-0 and boosted them to the top of the ACC standings.

After beating North Carolina State 21–7 and Virginia 20–14, Clemson crossed the border on successive weekends and was beaten by Georgia Tech 38–6 and Georgie 23–9. Back at home for much of the year, a no-give defense and Frank Pearce field goals won the next two games, first over Duke and then Texas Christian 3–0.

Hugh Mauldin started the scoring to beat Wake Forest 26–13. Phil Rogers went 61 yards on a reverse, Tommy Ray added another, and Jim Addison tossed to Wayne Bell. Wake scored on Jon Wilson passes to Butch Henry and Mike Kelly. North Carolina won 17–13 on a Dave Riggs punt return, and Danny Talbott's field goal and score after Jack Davenport's interception. Maryland had a 6–0 win on Bernardo Bramson's field goals, with two Clemson drives halted by interception leader Bob Sullivan. The South Carolina forfeit gave them a 5-2-0 mark and a share of the ACC title.

1966

The ACC had three new coaches this year: Tom Harp at Duke, Lou Saban at Maryland, and Paul Dietzel at South Carolina. Said Frank Howard before the Virginia game, "I kinda feel like a June bride. I know something's gonna happen, but I don't know what." His fears were justified, as Bob Davis ran for three touchdowns, completed two more to halfback Frank Quayle, and had Virginia in front 35–18 in the third period. A Frank

Liberatore 66-yard punt return kept them in the ball game, and Jim Addison hooked up with Wayne Bell on a 75-yard pass to win 40–35 with four minutes left.

Clemson lost again in Atlanta to Georgia Tech 13–12 on Bunky Henry's conversion. Addison threw to Bo Ruffner at full and tight end Ed McGee, but Bill Eastman's interception with 1:30 left ended it. Alabama won 26–0 as Ken Stabler scored once, tossed to Dennis Homan and Ken Martin, and Steve Davis added a pair of field goals.

Clemson's 6-1-0 record won the title. After Addison's pass to Phil Rogers beat Duke 9–6 in the last three minutes, Southern Cal stomped them in Los Angeles 30–0. Mike Battle had a 74-yard punt return, Troy Winslow, Toby Page, and Rod Sherman scored, and Page threw to Bob Klein. They beat Wake Forest 23–21 in the last minute as guard James Tompkins and tackle Wilson Childers dropped Ken Erickson for a safety. Charlie Hook's run put Clemson ahead, but Wake tied it on Andy Heck's score and second Eddie Arrington catch, and Ken Hauswald converted to match three by Don Barfield.

Jacky Jackson scored twice, Buddy Gore once, and Rich Garick ran in a Tim Karrs pass to beat North Carolina 27–3. Two runs by Jackson and Gore overtook Alan Pastrana's score for Maryland, but the Terps closed it to 14–10 on Bernardo Bramson's field goal and then drove inside the ten twice, but interceptions by linebacker Jimmy Catoe and defensive back Kit Jackson ended both threats.

North Carolina State gave Clemson its only conference loss. Clemson led 14–7 as Jackson and Gore went over again, but three last-half field goals by Harold Deters outstripped them, and Don DeArment's 53-yard run in the fourth quarter clinched it 23–14.

South Carolina trailed 14–10 at the half on Mike Fair's run and Jimmy Poole's field goal and two Jackson scores for the Tigers. Addison threw to Phil Rogers and McGee, and offensive guard Harry Olszewski ran 22 yards with a backfield bobble for a 35–10 win.

Clemson had center Wayne Mulligan, guard Mike Facciolo, tackles Wayne Mass and Larry Keys, and Jay Cooper at full. On defense were nose guard Mac McElmurray, tackle Floyd Rogers, and ends Joey Branton and Butch Sursavage. Backs were Phil Marion, Lee Rayburn, Wayne Page, and Art Craig, with Billy Ware at linebacker.

Others were Ronnie Ducworth, Billy Ammons, Charlie Ellenburg, Jackie Lee Jackson, Mike Locklair, Dan Gunnells, Richie Luzzi, Ray Mullen, Joe Lhotsky, Riley McLane, Hoss Hostetler, George Burnett, Barry

Cockfield, Bucky Turpin, Jimmy Logan, Ted Katana, Bob Craig, Chuck Werner, Willie Cropp, Benny Michael, Stu Capian, Connie Wade.

North Carolina State was not at the top for the first time in four years but came in second with 5-2-0. They opened with a loss to Michigan State at East Lansing 28–10. After a Clint Jones run put MSU ahead of a Deters field goal at intermission, Bob Apisa scored, Jimmy Raye ran in after a Jess Phillips punt return, Frank Waters added another, and Dick Kenney barefooted four conversions. A Jim Donnan pass to Wendell Coleman scored in the last seconds.

The Wolfpack split the next two conference games. With five minutes left, Danny Talbott threw to Tom Lampman in the corner of the end zone to overtake a Don DeArment run and Bill Dodson field goal and give North Carolina a 10–7 win. Two Chick George field goals put Wake Forest out front, but DeArment brought State from behind twice on Don Donaldson's pass and a 35-yard run after Ken Erickson tossed a 66-yarder to Butch Henry for a 15–12 State win.

After three road trips, State was home to dedicate its new football facility, Carter Stadium. The years of work by athletic director Roy Clogston, coach Edwards, and Wolfpack alumni ended the Pack's heavy away-game schedule and gave them the advantage of a home-town crowd more often. The stadium was near the fairgrounds in Raleigh a few miles from the campus, had 45,600 seats, and cost 3.7 million dollars. Half was paid by the State alumni, especially two brothers, W.J. and Harry Carter, who were alumni and had a textile manufacturing business. As a result of their generosity, Carter Stadium was the name given at the dedication.

Jimmy Killen's catch and Bill Morrow interception for State were the first scores in the new stadium, and a 98-yard kickoff return by Bobby Bryant helped dedicate it. Passes from Mike Fair to Johnny Gregory and Tony Barchuk to Coleman and a DeArment run knotted it, but a Jimmy Poole field goal unlaced it 24–21. Ben Galloway's 43-yard run gave South Carolina its only win 31–21.

The Pack still could not win in their new stadium as Florida drew even on Wayne Barfield's three-pointer and Larry Smith's run. Steve Spurrier's toss to Richard Trapp on a stop-and-go pass won for Ray Graves' Gators 17–10. State had its biggest point-margin ever in a 33–7 win over Duke at Durham. The Wolfpack led 13–7 on two field goals by Deters and Harry Martell's catch from Donnan. DeArment's 61-yard run in the fourth quarter broke open the game. Two quick scores followed on Art McMahon's

Tackle Dennis Byrd was a two-time all–American at North Carolina State in 1966 and 1967.

interception and Leon Mason run after Benny Lemmons recovered a fumble on the kickoff.

The third time at home was the charm as State beat Virginia 42–21 on six short runs, with Gary Rowe and Settle Dockery getting the last two. Bob Davis threw twice to Ed Carrington, and Stan Kemp had an 11-yard run for the Cavaliers. A Deters field goal was the difference in a 24–21 victory over Maryland at home. The Pack took a 24–0 lead on a Greg Williams interception, Rowe's 83-yard punt runback, and DeArment's score after a blocked punt, but Alan Pastrana threw three last-period touchdown passes before 250-pound tackle Dennis Byrd led the charge that held the Terps.

Two field goals by Deters equalled a score by Milo McCarthy, but

George Sumrall kicked Southern Mississippi to a 7–6 victory. State closed the campaign with another win at home over Clemson.

Virginia tied for third at 3-3-0 with its best-ever record since joining the ACC. They were 10–10 with Wake Forest as Jon Wilson's pass to Butch Henry and Chick George field goal matched Frank Quayle's catch from Bob Davis and Braxton Hill field goal. Jimmy Johnson carried the attack for Wake, but Virginia made two fourth-quarter scores to win 24–10. After the defeat by Clemson, Duke downed them 27–8 as Jay Calabrese and Jake Devonshire scored and Bob Matheson added a pair of field goals. Then Jim Pittman's Tulane team beat them 20–6. Bobby Duhon scored on a 45-yard run after throwing to Nick Pizzolatto, Jim Trahan ran in after Chuck Loftin pounded in close, and Uwe Pontius kicked two field goals, with end Joe Hoppe grabbing a fumble near the goal and stepping in for the Cavaliers. In the 38–27 victory over Virginia Military Institute, all nine touchdowns came on passes. Davis threw four, and Kemp tossed one to Ken Poates. Hill Ellett left-handed four of them for coach Vito Ragazzo's Keydets, two to Bill McGowan, and one each to Jimmy Breckinridge and Frank Easterly.

Virginia lost its next three games. Virginia Tech beat them 24–7, as Tommy Francisco scored on three drives directed by Tommy Stafford, and Jon Utin added a field goal. After the loss to the Wolfpack, Georgia Tech edged them 14–13 as Bunky Henry converted after Larry Good threw to Steve Almond and Lenny Snow dived over.

Coach George Blackburn used a 4-3-4 defense to stop Maryland 41–17. Davis threw touchdowns to Jeff Anderson and Ed Carrington and set up two more by Kemp and fullback Carroll Jarvis. Quayle scored three times to down North Carolina 21–14 in the last game, with Dick Wesolowski and Danny Talbott scoring for the Tar Heels.

Maryland also tied for third. Joe Paterno took over for Rip Engle at Penn State and beat the Terps in his first contest 15–7. Jack White, a worthy successor to Milt Plum, Richie Lucas, Galen Hall, and Pete Liske, scored and put PSU ahead 8–7. A Tom Sherman field goal and two safeties by Mike Reid gave State the win.

Alan Pastrana ran for one touchdown and threw for three in the 34–7 win over Wake Forest, with Wake scoring after John Hetric recovered Barry Hickman's kickoff fumble. But Syracuse held them to minus 45 yards rushing and won 28–7 on four Jim Del Gaizo passes to Tom Coughlin, Terry Roe, Dick Towne, and Floyd Little.

Duke took them to the tape before Maryland won it. Pastrana passed for one touchdown, ran for another, and set up a third by Billy Lovett. His

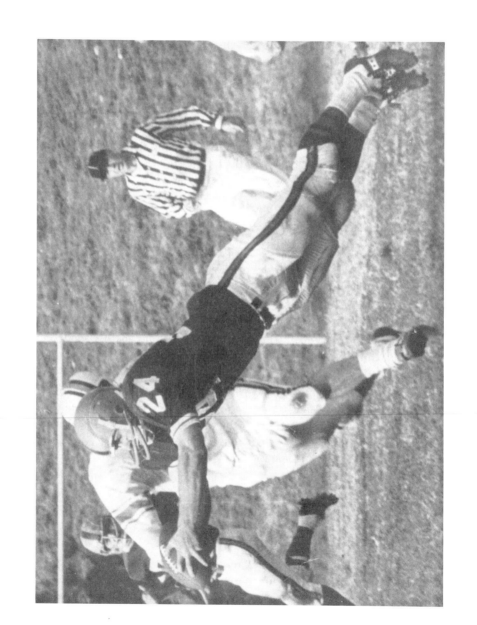

9-yard run with two minutes left put the Terps ahead, but Al Woodall closed it to 21–19 a minute later on a pass to Dave Dunaway. The onside kick failed, and Chilean soccer star Bernardo Bramson's three conversions were the margin of victory.

West Virginia was beaten 28–9 on Pastrana's passes to Ralph Donofrio and Rick Carlson and two Ernie Torain runs, with Garrett Ford and a Chuck Kinder field goal scoring for WVU. Johnny Glass blocked a punt for a safety, but a Pastrana pass to Bobby Collins and Billy Van Heusen's fingertip catch beat South Carolina 14–2.

Maryland lost its last four outings. Sun-Bowl bound Florida State put on a show as Frank Loner's field goal hit the crossbar and bounced over and everyone scored. Kim Hammond threw to Bill Cox, Gary Pajcic threw to Thurston Taylor, and Larry Green, Bill Moreman, Jim Mankins, and John Hurst ran over in a 45–21 win.

Lou Saban guided the Buffalo Bills to two straight championships in the American Football League, but he stayed only a year at Maryland. When he learned that Maryland was content with its ACC affiliation, he accepted the job to coach the Denver Broncos.

1967

Clemson claimed a second straight outright title and sixth overall with a perfect 6-0-0 mark. Speedsters Jacky Jackson and Buddy Gore led the 23–6 win over Wake Forest, but Georgia took a 17–3 lead on Jim McCullough's field goal and runs by Kirby Moore after interceptions by Happy Dicks and Jake Scott. Clemson made it a new game on Gore's run and Frank Liberatore's 52-yard punt return, but Kent Lawrence ran right end for a 24–17 Georgia win.

After a 10–0 loss to Georgia Tech and new coach Bud Carson on Kim King's run and Tommy Carmichael field goal, Frank Howard sat in the dressing room in Atlanta and cried. It would be even worse facing the folks he'd meet back home on College Avenue, but by then the pain could escape in a silly grin and empty remarks.

Jimmy Carter's 61-yard punt return in the second minute and three John Riley field goals next week were no comfort. Clemson clawed back

Opposite: **Gotcha! Frank Quayle is the career leader in all-purpose yards at Virginia with 4,981.**

26–21 as Jim Addison threw to Freddy Kelley and Phil Rogers and Jackson ran over. Runs by Al Giffin, Larry Blakeney, and Loran Carter's pass to Tim Christian gave Auburn a 43–21 win. When asked about losing to SEC teams Howard said, "Well, the SEC gets dedicated football players; the ACC gets dedicated students."

Duke lost 13–7, but Alabama beat Clemson 13–10 on two Steve Davis field goals to one by Steedlcy Candler. Ed Morgan and Gore scored close in. Gene Raburn threw to Dick Brewer before Davis' first field goal, and Ken Stabler left-handed one to Dennis Homan before the second, but Candler's last tries were short and wide. A late Tiger threat was thwarted by an Eddie Propst interception.

In the 17–0 shutout over new coach Bill Dooley's North Carolina team, Addison threw to Benny Michael, Billy Ware ran back a Jeff Beaver pass, and new kicker Art Craig made his first field goal. Maryland had its third coach in three years, Bob Ward, and its first winless season in 75 years. Clemson gave them a 28–7 loss as Jackson, Rick Medlin, and Charley Tolley ran in on short runs and Gore sprinted 38 yards to a score, with Paul Fitzpatrick completing one to Bill Gillespie for the Terrapin touchdown.

Addison's pass to Gore and a Jackson run overcame two Gerald Warren field goals for North Carolina State 14–6. Warren's pair of field goals broke by one the season mark of 16 set by Charlie Gogolak of Princeton in 1965. Along with his older brother Pete at Cornell, their soccer-style approach revolutionized field goal kicking and sent coaches to the soccer fields for good kickers.

Clemson clinched the crown with a fourth straight win in the season-ender with South Carolina. The Tigers took a 10–0 lead on Addison's pass to Ed McGee and a Craig three-pointer. It went to 23–0 on Gore's run and another by Addison after Ronnie Ducworth fell on Pat Watson's kickoff fumble. Two short runs by Mike Fair made the final 23–12. Gore finished with 1,045 yards rushing and became the first Tiger back to gain over 1,000 yards in a year.

Starting for Clemson were center Wayne Mulligan, guards Gary Arthur and Harry Olszewski, and tackles Wayne Mass and Larry Keys. The split end was Jimmy Abrams with Bo Ruffner at fullback. The defense had middle guard Randy Harvey, tackles Mike Locklair and John Cagle, and ends Butch Sursavage and Joey Blanton, with Jimmy Catoe at linebacker. Backs were Richie Luzzi, Kit Jackson, Lee Rayburn, sometime starter John Fulmer, and punter Sammy Cain.

Reserves were Billy Ammons, Charlie Ellenburg, Rich Garick, Jackie

Lee Jackson, Joe Lhotsky, James Tompkins, George Burnett, Riley McLane, Bucky Turpin, Wilson Childers, Hoss Hostetler, Ivan Southerland, Dan Gunnells, Randy Bell, Perry Waldrep, Wes Eidson, Grady Burgner, Connie Wade, Ronnie Kitchens, and Charlie Waters.

North Carolina State's defense helped bring them in second at 5-1-0. Linebacker Chuck Amato knew the defense was a special one, so he suggested that they put white polish on their shoes. Defensive coach Al Michaels didn't think much of the idea until they beat North Carolina the following day in Raleigh 13-7. It was 7-3 on Tommy Dempsey's touchdown for the Tar Heels, but Jim Donnan tossed to Harry Martell and Gerald Warren kicked another field goal, and putting white dye on their shoes became a Friday night ritual from then on. The game was also notable as part of a day-night twin bill that had Duke and Wake Forest and featured not only Hurricane Doria but Freddie Summers of the Deacons, the first black man to play quarterback at a major southern school.

Buffalo fell behind on another Warren field goal and Donnan to Martell pass, and two more scores followed an interception by cornerback Fred Combs and end Pete Sokalsky's recovered fumble. Buffalo scored on a Dennis Mason to Chuck Drankoski last-period completion, and tackle Dennis Byrd sacked Mick Murtha four times to put a 24-6 brand on coach Dick Urich and his Buffalo Bulls.

The Wolfpack traveled to Tallahassee and took a 10-0 lead on Florida State with Charlie Bowers scoring on a 49-yard run. The Seminoles tied it on a Gary Pajcic pass to Ron Sellers after Jack Klebe's short punt and scored again on Grant Guthrie's field goal after John Crowe covered a fumble. The White Shoes Gang held FSU to 36 yards rushing, linebacker Mike Hilka's interception led to a Tony Barchuk score, and Warren's second kick made it 20-10.

Visiting teams were given special shoes to wear when playing in the Astrodome, and the defensive unit quickly put white polish on them. Houston took a 6-0 halftime lead on Dick Woodall's pass to Bob Long, but two short runs by Bobby Hall and a Warren field goal made it 16-6. Ken Bailey led a drive for Houston but middle guard Terry Brookshire put a stop on it, and a field goal try by Ken Hebert was short. Jerry Drones intercepted late in the game, but the White Shoes Gang held and Houston lost the ball on downs.

Maryland's 3-0 lead at the half made the locker room of the offensive squad quiet as a tomb, but not for long. Each of the players in white shoes picked out a man on the offense and gave him a hard jab to jolt him into action. Nothing was said, just a good pop to the pads. The offense came out and scored on five of its first six possessions for a 31–9 win, with the last one a pass from Klebe to Don Donaldson, while the defense limited the Terps to a lone score on Chuck Drimal's pass to Rick Carlson.

Gold shoes didn't help Wake Forest's offensive line as Combs scored on a 71-yard punt return and Warren made three field goals in a 24–7 win. The Pack downed Duke 28–7 for its ninth straight homecoming win, with Frank Ryan getting the Blue Devil score.

Warren added three more field goals in the 30–8 victory over Virginia, Martell scored on a Donnan pass for the fourth game in a row, and Combs had an 85-yard punt runback for another. Settle Dockery ran in the last score, Stan Kemp tossed to Joe Hoppe for the Cavs, and the UP poll had North Carolina State in third place.

The White Shoes Gang had not yielded more than one touchdown in any contest or been scored on in the first quarter, but both streaks were ended by Penn State. After Tom Sherman threw to Don Abbey, he tossed to Ted Kwalick for a score, and Denny Onkotz ran 67 yards with an interception for a quick 13–0 lead. Joe Paterno put one split end, Jack Curry and Paul Johnson, on each side with Kwalick or Charlie Pittman, but the defense picked them up easily. The Pack chipped away with two Warren field goals, but defenders Mike McBath, Frank Spaziani, and Jim Litterelle held repeatedly, and Tim Montgomery's end-zone interception with 7:40 left killed another drive. Carolina kept coming and had a first down on the nine with 51 seconds remaining. On last down with 40 seconds to go, the Wolves went with what got them there, a blast by Barchuk up the middle. Onkotz and Jim Kates met him for no gain, and the crowd of 47,000 broke loose like a thunderclap. Four plays later punter Tom Cherry took an intentional safety for a 13–8 final.

Coach Paterno was carried from the field by his players, and a few fans snatched Confederate flags from the visitors and disappeared under the stands with them. Others tried to uproot the concrete-based goal posts but had no success, while most of them were reluctant to leave and milled around the stadium for hours.

The disappointment of the defeat showed when the Pack played for the ACC title in Clemson's Death Valley. Clemson wore orange shoes, but not even Warren's one-year field goal mark could help them cross the goal, while the Tigers scored twice to take it all.

State bounced back to beat Georgia in the Liberty Bowl 14–7. The Donnan-to-Martell combination clicked again, but Georgia took the kickoff and drove to a score by Ron Jenkins. Gary Yount held off the Dawgs with his punts, and Barchuk's last-period score put State ahead. Georgia drove deep again after the kickoff but was stopped by two goal-line stands, one on a tackle by Bill Morrow, and North Carolina State celebrated its first bowl-game win.

State lined up with centers Carey Metts and John McDuffie, guards Don Jones and Robby Evans, and tackles Marvin Tharp, Steve Warren, and Lloyd Spangler. At end were Wayne Lewis and Charlie Tope, with Leon Mason at halfback. In white shoes were end Mark Capuano, tackle Trent Holland, and safeties Art McMahon and Greg Williams. Others were Flake Campbell, Norm Cates, Art Hudson, Benny Lemmons, Dick Chapman, Bob Follweiller, Ron Carpenter, Don Jordan, Steve Diacont, Pete Bailey, Dickie Idol, and Jimmy Lisk.

South Carolina was third with 4-2-0. They beat Clay Stapleton's Iowa State team 34–3, with Vern Skripsky getting the State field goal. Behind 7–3, Ben Garnto scored after Gene Schwarting recovered a kickoff fumble to beat North Carolina 16–10. South Carolina ruined the dedication of Wallace Wade Stadium at Duke when Dave Lucas covered Bob Hepler's end-zone fumble and Warren Muir went over with 40 seconds left to snatch a 21–17 win. Bill Stanfill led the Georgia defense in a 21–0 win, and Florida State won 17–0 with T. K. Wetherell's interception setting up the final score.

Virginia came to Columbia for Carolina's homecoming game and took a 17–0 lead. The Gamecocks fought back with 15 points, but Frank Quayle's kickoff return made it 23–15. Muir's run cut it to two, and Jimmy Poole's field goal won 24–23 for Paul Dietzel who was coaching in a golf cart due to a practice-field injury.

South Carolina downed Maryland 31–0, but lost its last three games. Jack Dolbin's long runs led to a Ron Jurewicz score for Wake Forest, but Carolina tied it only to have Wake win 35–21 on two scores in the last three minutes, with Buz Leavitt going in for the final one. Alabama had a 17–0 win on Ken Stabler's toss to Dennis Homan, Tommy Wade plunge, and Steve Davis field goal, and Clemson won the state bragging rights for another year.

Virginia was fourth at 3-3-0. Army beat them 26–7 at Michie Stadium as Carl Woessner ran in, Van Evans scored twice, once on a punt return, and Nick Kurilko kicked two field goals for coach Tom Cahill. Gene Arnette scored four touchdowns and threw to Bob Serino to beat Buffalo 35–12, and Dave Wyncoop's last-quarter run slid by Wake Forest 14–12. Duke won 13–6 in the final period as Don Baglien dived over, and Russ Quay scored three times to give VMI an 18–13 lead, then held the Cavs at the two with 2:16 to go.

North Carolina lost 40–17 as a Pete Schmidt interception led to a score and Dennis Borchers ran back one for 79 yards. Tulane lost 14–10 on second-half scores by Quayle and Jeff Anderson, and Quayle scored twice in another last-half win over Maryland 12–7.

1968

North Carolina State lost eight offensive and nine defensive starters, but they won the title with a 6-1-0 mark. Wake Forest moved from city-owned Bowman Gray Stadium to its new 32,000 seat facility, Groves Stadium, and State helped them dedicate it in a 10–6 win. After a Gerald Warren field goal, all the scoring was at the end of the game, as Jack Klebe dived over with 1:53 to go and Lee Clymer went in at the gun for Wake. North Carolina lost 38–6 for State's biggest point total ever against the Tar Heels, as Gary Yount returned a punt 84 yards and Jack Whitley went 42 yards with a fumble recovery for 14–0 before the offense got in.

Two more away games brought two losses. Oklahoma won 28–14 on two Steve Owens touchdowns and two Bob Warmack passes to Eddie Hinton and Steve Zabel. Klebe threw to Jim Hardin and Bobby Hall for State. Chuck Hixson threw three touchdowns to Jerry Levias, scored once, and Mike Richardson ran over in Southern Methodist's 35–14 win. The Wolfpack scored on Klebe's 16-yard pass to George Botsko and 20-yarder from Darrell Moody to Jimmy Lisk.

State continued its quest for the crown with a 36–12 defeat of South Carolina. Whitley returned a punt 86 yards and Charlie Bowers scored three times behind the blocking of Robby Evans and Don Jordan at guard and center Carey Metts. Virginia was blanked 19–0 as end Mark Capuano and linebackers Paul Reid, Dickie Idol, and Steve Diacont held the Cavs to 166 yards total offense. Rick Carlson's field goal and Billy Lovett touchdown scored for Maryland, but Bowers scored three more times to tame the Terps 31–11.

The Clemson game was nip-and-tuck all the way. Hall raced 80 yards on the first play and Warren kicked a field goal, but Clemson took the lead as Billy Ammons sneaked over and threw to Jim Sursavage. Jim Barnette added a field goal, and Idol downed Ammons for a safety. The Wolfpack went in front 19–17 as Klebe left-handed a completion to Lisk, but with 53 seconds remaining Ray Yauger ran seven yards for the winning touchdown 24–19.

The State–Duke game was another nail-biter. Earle Mowry and Warren made field goals, and Hall and Bowers ran in for the Pack. Leo Hart threw to Jim Dearth, but State held its lead as Duke was thrown back twice at the 1-foot line and intercepted twice in key situations. Late in the contest Hart's 5-yard run trimmed it to 17–15, but tackles Ron Carpenter and Art Hudson stopped the two-point run. Hart finished with 2,238 yards passing and became the first ACC player to throw for 2,000 yards in one season.

The Pack was first in total defense for the third year in a row in the ACC, but their crown was slightly dented after Florida State capitalized on four errors to win 48–7. They trailed 14–7 at the half on Klebe's pass to Lisk, but Bill Gunter scored three times in the third quarter, Bill Cappleman tossed twice to Phil Abraira, and Walt Sumner ran 58 yards with a blocked field goal.

In addition to those mentioned, State's offense had tackles Marvin Tharp and Ed Nicholas, ends Wayne Lewis and Charlie Tope, and Settle Dockery in the fullback spot. On defense were guard Alan Solonoski and end Bob Follweiller. Others were Dick Chapman, Benny Lemmons, Lee Roy Hamilton, Harry Billger, and Pete Sowirka.

Clemson placed second with 4-1-1. The tie was in the first game with Wake Forest. Freddie Summers and Lee Clymer scored for Wake, while Jim Sursavage fell on an end-zone fumble and Charlie Waters ran in for Clemson. Summers scored again to break a 13–13 tie, but Benny Michael's 7-yard run scored with two minutes left. Mike Funderburk converted to match two by Chick George for 20–20.

Two more trips across the border brought two defeats. Mike Cavan threw to Kent Lawrence and Dennis Hughes, Donnie Hampton had another in Georgia's 31–13 win, but Richie Luzzi ran back a missed field goal 108 yards for Clemson. The next week Georgia Tech won 24–21. Larry Good tossed to John Weaver and Joel Stevenson, but Clemson countered with runs by Ray Yauger and Buddy Gore. A pair of last-quarter turnovers led to a Dennis James run and Weaver's pass to Stevenson. Clemson scored as Billy Ammons connected with Sursavage, but Johnny Duncan's three-pointer was the difference. "It's hell to go home without a win," moaned Frank Howard, but a check for $150,000 in his pocket made the trip a little easier.

Jim Barnette's field goal put Clemson ahead, but a Connie Frederick catch from Loran Carter and a Carter score gave Auburn the lead for good.

After Sonny Ferguson's interception, Dwight Hurston went 39 yards two plays later, and Buddy McClinton had a 53-yard interception. The Tigers scored on Michael's 5-yard run after Tom English threw to Jack Anderson for a final of 21–10.

Duke self-destructed on five fumbles in a 39–22 defeat, but Alabama struck quickly for 14–0 as Mike Dean's interception set up Scott Hunter's toss to Donnie Sutton. After Mike Hall forced a fumble, Joe Kelley led a drive that ended in a score by Buddy Seay. Clemson tied it on Gore's run and Ammons' pass to Yauger, but Hunter's fourth-quarter toss to George Ranager won it 21–14. On the sidelines directing the Tide attack in his hound's tooth hat which he wore for the first time this year was Bear Bryant.

After the Wolfpack lost, two Yauger runs beat Maryland 16–0. An Ammons run and Barnette field goal put North Carolina behind, but Gayle Bomar's pass to Tony Blanchard, the son of Army's Doc Blanchard, made it 10–7. Ammons threw to Waters and Yauger ran in, and Ken Borries scored for Carolina to make the final 24–14.

Clemson was unbeaten in conference play and had the inside track to the title until the last game. Anderson's 72-yard kickoff return set up Barnette's field goal, but South Carolina's 7–3 win on a Tyler Hellams 73-yard punt return made them runner-up.

Clemson had center Wayne Mulligan, guards Grady Burgner and Gary Arthur, and tackles Rich Garick and Joe Lhotsky. On defense were middle guard B. B. Elvington, tackles Mike Locklair and John Cagle, and ends Ronnie Ducworth and Ivan Southerland. Billy Ware and Jimmy Catoe were linebackers, with backs Gary Compton, Chuck Werner, and Lee Rayburn, and Sammy Cain to do the punting.

Reserves were Sonny Cassady, John Fulmer, Willie Cropp, Bob Craig, Jackie Lee Jackson, Ronnie Kitchens, James Tompkins, Wes Eidson, George Ducworth, Rick Medlin, Dave Thompson, Rick Eyler, Randy Harvey, Dave Kormanicki, John Shields, and Bill DePew.

Virginia's 25 lettermen brought them in third with a 3-2-0 record. Billy McKoy ran 78 yards to start the scoring for Jack Mollenkopf's Boilermakers after Chuck Kyle blocked a field goal. Leroy Keyes and Perry Williams scored on short runs, John Bullock and Stan Brown ran for longer ones, Bob Dillingham had a scoring catch, and a Jeff Jones field goal added to Purdue's 44–6 total.

VMI was beaten 47–0, Davidson 41–14, and UVa had its biggest point total against Duke 50–20. Jeff Anderson tallied three times and Dave Wyncoop two, with Phil Asack and Wes Chesson scoring for Duke. The Pack gave UVa its only shutout, but Navy was drydocked 24–0. Bob Rannigan intercepted Mike McNallen for 6–0, Ed Kihm's steal set up another touchdown, Gene Arnette connected with Joe Hoppe and Jeff Calamus, and Frank Quayle carried in the last one.

Virginia's 439.4 yards total offense continued to roll and was the ACC's first to average 400 yards per game. Arnette threw twice to Chuck Mooser, but Tommy Suggs tossed to Fred Zeigler and Rudy Holloman in South Carolina's 49–28 win. Quayle and Anderson both scored twice and Arnette and Clinch Heyward once in a 41–6 North Carolina loss, with Ricky Lanier going in for the Tar Heels.

A Bart Bookatz field goal put Tulane ahead, but it was lost under an avalanche of touchdowns as Virginia won 63–47. Arnette scored four times and threw to Bob Bischoff, Quayle scored three, and Al Sinesky ran in a fumble, with Warren Bankston, Wayne Francingues, Hal Sisk, and Jack Laborde scoring for Tulane. Alan Pastrana tossed to Billy Lovett and Rollie Merritt and Rick Carlson's field goal sent Maryland ahead, but the lead changed six times as Quayle's third touchdown won it 28–23 with four minutes remaining. Quayle had 2,695 yards rushing to pass Jim Bakhtiar's career mark.

The Gamecocks finished fourth at 4-3-0. They lost the first game to Duke 14–7 on two first-quarter scores by Wes Chesson and Henley Carter's pass from Leo Hart, and 25 solo tackles by linebacker Dick Biddle. Randy Yoakum and Tommy Suggs spearheaded a South Carolina drive as fullback Warren Muir, who came from West Point with coach Paul Dietzel, bull-dozed in from the one. Down 27–3 against North Carolina at the end of three, Yoakum and Suggs set up four touchdowns to overtake the Tar Heels 32–27. Dietzel was ecstatic as he cavorted on the sideline, "The greatest comeback of any team I've ever been associated with," he enthused.

South Carolina led Georgia 20–7 at the half on runs by Muir and Lynn Hodge and two Billy DuPre field goals. But they failed to live up to Dietzel's slogan "The fourth quarter is ours" and lost late as Brad Johnson scored twice for the Bulldogs and Jim McCullough kicked his third extra point in a 21–20 Georgia win.

The Gamecocks missed two late two-point plays and Dean Landolt's last-period interception won for Maryland 21–19, and four Bill Cappleman to Ron Sellers passes won for Florida State 35–28.

South Carolina closed with three wins in its last four games. After defeating Virginia, they overcame Wake Forest 34–21 as Pat Watson set a league record with four interceptions and Carolina's mighty mites, Suggs

Paul Dietzel coached South Carolina to the ACC title in 1969.

and Johnny Gregory, whose brother, Art, was a Duke tackle, connected on three touchdowns. A Suggs to Muir pass scored against Virginia Tech, but six-pointers by Terry Smoot and Ken Edwards and a Jack Simcsak field goal won for VPI 17–6, and Clemson succumbed in Death Valley by a touchdown to a field goal.

1969

Like Wallace Wade at Duke, Frank Howard at Clemson, and Earle Edwards at North Carolina State, Paul Dietzel upgraded South Carolina's football program and gave them respectability. His efforts led to a five-building complex for student athletes and a program of athletics that operated in the black. Now he gave them what he was hired to do: win a league title and a national reputation.

South Carolina's champions were only the third to take the title with a 6-0-0 mark and made the Chinese calendar's naming of 1969 as the "Year of the Rooster" a reality. A crowd of 42,791 gathered in Carolina Stadium for the Duke game to watch the Gamecocks take up where they left off. Rudy Holloman's 60-yard dash and Tommy Suggs' 48-yard run brought the crowd to its feet, but Duke came back on Leo Hart's passes to Marcel Courtillet and Wes Chesson. The game was knotted 10–10 and 20–20 as Dave Pugh, who was known to warm up by kicking footballs into the stands, and Billy DuPre made three-pointers. Carolina won on two successful fourth-down plays in the last four minutes as Fred Zeigler made his 100th career catch and Warren Muir crashed over to win 27–20.

North Carolina's Don Hartig kicked two field goals, but the Gamecocks won on two third-period scores by Muir and a Suggs-to-Zeigler pass. Dick Harris saved the 14–6 win on an interception with 0:22 remaining. Georgia brought them back to reality with a 41–16 win in Athens on runs by Julian Smiley and Craig Elrod. Muir and DuPre scored for Carolina, but Suggs threw four interceptions, and Randy Yoakum came in to toss to Billy Freeman.

North Carolina State led 10–0 on Mike Charron's field goal and Leon Mason run, but South Carolina moved ahead as Billy Ray Rice ran in and Jim Mitchell had a 72-yard punt return. Fourth-quarter scores by Muir and Wayne Lewis made it 21–16. Virginia Tech took a 16–14 lead on Gil Schwabe's pass to Jimmy Quinn with 1:13 to go, but the Gamecocks took it back 17–16 on DuPre's 47-yarder with nine seconds left. At home in the "Cockpit" before a fourth straight sellout crowd, Maryland lost 17–0 on a Suggs-to-Holloman pass, a smash by Muir, and another DuPre field goal.

Florida State had a 20–3 lead at the half on Paul Magalski's 33-yard run, Tom Bailey's pass to Mike Gray, and two Grant Guthrie field goals. Yoakum threw to Doug Hamrick for the Gamecocks, but John Montgomery's interception and another Magalski score pushed it to 34–9. "We did a lot of dumb things today, and I did most of them," groaned Dietzel. Carolina was superb before a capacity crowd of 62,868 in Knoxville, but three George Hunt field goals and Bobby Scott's pass to George McLeary gave Tennessee a 16–14 lead late in the game. More mistakes led to two quick scores as Scott threw to Gary Kreis and Ken DeLong for a 29–14 Vol victory.

Steve Bowden scored for Wake Forest, but Suggs tossed three touchdowns to down the Deacons 24–6. Executive director George Crumbley liked the wide-open brand of football Carolina played, and he invited them to the second annual Peach Bowl in Atlanta. The squad was told at practice before the Clemson game, and the shout was heard by alumni all over the South, for they had a team to be proud of and were off on their first bowl trip in 24 years.

South Carolina's bowl fever erupted for a school mark of 517 yards total offense and a second straight win over Clemson. The Gameroosters scored on their first three series, but the Tigers trimmed it to 17–13 at intermission after Charlie Mayer captured a blocked end zone punt and Tommy Kendrick tossed to Ray Yauger. Another Holloman score and second DuPre field goal made it 27–13.

The 20,000 Gamecock fans who sat in the Peach Bowl at Grant Field saw a defensive battle with West Virginia as Bob Gresham's run and DuPre field goal made it 7–3. The Carolina defense held the Mountaineers to three yards passing, but Eddie Williams led the ground attack and Jim Braxton scored late as WVU won 14–3.

Carolina's left had tackles Dave DeCamilla and Joe Regalis, guards Tony Fusaro and Richie Moye, centers Danny Dyches and Ken Ross, guards Chris Bank and Ken Wheat, tackles Rick Hipkins and Bill Boyte on the right, Tommy Simmons and Byron Sistare at full, flankers Tom Trevillian and Ken Walkup, and punter Bill Parker.

The defense on the left had ends Lynn Hodge and Jimmy Pope, tackles Jimmy Poston and Jake Wright, middle guards Don Buckner and Pat Kohout, tackles Rusty Ganas and George McCarthy, and ends Dave Lucas and Joe Wingard on the right. Linebackers were Benny Padgett, Mack Lee Tharpe, Greg Crabb, and Al Usher. Backs were Don Bailey at halfback, rover backs Bo Davies and Candler Boyd, and safeties Andy Chavous and Jimmy Nash.

North Carolina State was second at 3-2-1. They lost to Wake Forest at the gun 22–21 as Larry Russell, who had already thrown a touchdown to Don Kobos, tossed to Buz Leavitt for the two-point conversion. Mike Charron's field goal and Darrell Moody run beat North Carolina 10–3. Maryland went ahead on Dennis O'Hara's pass to Sonny Demczuk, but Jack Whitley's interception tied it. Charlie Bowers' run, Leon Mason's 74-yard dash, and Paul Sharp's two-pointer to Bob McLean won 24–7 over new coach Roy Lester's Terps.

Steve Schaap scored for Charley Tate's Miami Hurricanes, but State

Coach Earle Edwards of North Carolina State and his 1970 captain, Jack Whitley.

went ahead 13–10 only to lose 23–13 as Tom Sullivan ran in behind Vince Opalsky's block and Jim Huff kicked two more field goals. After the loss to South Carolina they defeated Virginia 31–0, but Duke tied them 25–25 with 2:24 to go on Bob Zwirko's second touchdown and Leo Hart's conversion pass to Jim Dearth.

State was outgunned by Houston's veer-T offense 34–13 as Jim Strong and Ted Heiskell both scored twice, once after a Charles Ford interception, Gary Mullins ran over once, and Carlos Lopez added two field goals. Bowers went 64 yards for the Wolfpack, and a 46-yard run by Dave Rogers set up a Moody touchdown.

State ran into another buzz saw a week later. Florida State won 33–22 as Phil Abraira returned a punt 92 yards, and tackle Frank Vohun scored on a 22-yard interception but drew a penalty for not giving up the ball. Bill Cappleman threw to Jim Tyson, Jim Jarrett ran in, and Grant Guthrie kicked two three-pointers.

Penn State completed two back-to-back 10-0-0 seasons with a 33–8 win over the Pack. Franco Harris led the Lions as Charlie Pittman had three scores, one on Charlie Burkhart's pass, Lydell Mitchell one, and Mike Reitz made two field goals. Fumble recoveries by Denny Onkotz and Gary Hull and a George Landis interception led to scores and held the Pack to 49 yards total offense. A 71-yard interception by Van Walker scored for the Wolfpack.

Clemson tied for third with 3-3-0. They beat Virginia 21–14 on two touchdowns in the last five minutes, and gave Frank Howard a nice going-away present in his final year with a 21–10 win over Georgia Tech. But the 30–0 beating by Georgia and a 51–0 win by Auburn were the worst losses while he was at the wheel. Georgia's Mike Cavan threw strikes to Dennis Hughes and Charles Whittemore, and Don Webb's punt return for Auburn set up a Pat Sullivan pass to Terry Beasley. Back-up Tommy Traylor added two touchdowns, and Mickey Zofko, in for injured Mike Currier, scored another.

After Wake Forest lost 28–14, Bear Bryant got his 100th win at Alabama 38–13, as Johnny Musso scored twice, Neb Hayden threw for one and Bubba Sawyer caught another. The Tigers clawed Maryland 40–0, but lost to Duke 34–27 on a John Cappellano run and Leo Hart's passes, and Don McCauley led North Carolina's 32–15 win.

Maryland was also third at 3-3-0. West Virginia won 31–7 on Ed Silverio's run and Mike Sherwood's pass to Oscar Patrick. They lost to the Wolfpack, and beat Wake Forest 19–14 as Al Thomas ran in after Gary Van Sickler's recovered fumble. George Jakowenko's two field goals put Syracuse ahead 6–3 until the last period when Rich Panczyszyn threw twice to Tony Gabriel for a 20–9 Orangemen win. After shutouts by South Carolina and Clemson, Miami of Ohio led 27–0 after Dick Adams returned the last-half kickoff 90 yards for coach Bill Mallory. Jeff Shugars tossed to Paul Fitzpatrick and Rollie Merritt, and Hank Barnes had a catch in the 34–21 loss.

Penn State's defense of Jack Ham, John Ebersole, Neal Smith, Mike Smith, and Pete Johnson stopped Maryland 48–0. Tom Miller's run gave them a 7–6 lead at the half over Jim Carrington's field goals, and Larry Marshall's run stretched it further. But Dave Wyncoop went over for Virginia,

One of the greatest to wear Carolina Blue was North Carolina halfback Don McCauley.

and Danny Fassio's two-point run evened the count. Charles Reilly fell on a fumble for the Terps, and a Greg Fries field goal won it 17–14 with 20 seconds to go.

North Carolina was the third team at 3-3-0. After losses to the Pack and the Gamecocks, they beat Bill Pace's Vanderbilt team 38–22. Dennis Painter threw to Bill Mathews and Dave Strong ran in and caught a pass from Mathews, but John Swofford tossed three touchdown passes and Don McCauley scored twice for the Tar Heels.

A Saulis Zemaitis run scored for Carolina and a Gary Baxter to Dave MacGhee pass scored for Air Force, but Denny Leuthauser's interception and Jim DeOrio run gave the Falcons a 20–10 victory. John Reaves started Florida's 52–2 win with a touchdown to Carlos Alvarez on the first play. After Tracy Lounsbury's field goal for Wake Forest, Don Hartig kicked three in Carolina's 23–3 win.

Lewis Jolley scored in the 12–0 win over Virginia. McCauley scored three times in VMI's 61–11 defeat, Tony Blanchard and Bucky Perry had touchdown catches, and Sam Cook ran in an interception.

Duke scored on Hart's pass to Wes Chesson and Dave Pugh field goal, but Ricky Lanier put Carolina ahead on tosses to Bob Schult and McCauley. After Ernie Jackson stole a pass, Hart faked tying his shoe. As the team waited left of the ball, Marcel Courtillet shoveled it to Chesson who turned left end 53 yards to win 17–13.

1970

In his second year as head coach, Cal Stoll took Wake Forest to its first league title with a 5-1-0 mark. They were picked to finish last and didn't look like champions as they dropped their first three games, but came on to win five league games in a row.

Nebraska's national champs had a 36–12 win at Lincoln as Joe Orduna scored twice and Johnny Rodgers went 61 yards with a Jerry Tagge pass. Jeff Kinney and Tagge also ran in for Bob Devaney's Cornhuskers. Wake scored on a Tracy Lounsbury field goal and Pat McHenry's block on a Jeff Hughes punt in the first half, and Jim McMahen threw to Gary Johnson for a touchdown in the last minute.

Defending league champ South Carolina poured it on with 507 yards total offense and a 43–7 win on two Tommy Suggs passes to Mike Haggard and two Chuck Mimms touchdowns. Billy Ray Rice and Jackie Brown also scored and Billy DuPre added three field goals.

The Deacons led Florida State 14–6 at intermission on Larry Hopkins and Larry Russell runs, but Art Monroe plunged over and Frank Fontes barefooted four field goals for a 19–14 FSU win.

Virginia lost four fumbles and was intercepted five times in a 27–7 defeat, and the veer-T offense put in after the third loss began to take off. Russell's quick hands and feet at quarterback took him to two touchdowns and a pitch to Ken Garrett for another. Lounsbury added two field goals, and Bill Troup ran over for the Cavs in the final minute. Russell had two more scores and threw to Gary Winrow and Dave Lindsay to beat Virginia Tech 28–9, with Jack Simcsak's field goal and Rich Matijevich run scoring for VPI.

Russell and Hopkins both scored twice to beat Clemson 36–20, and Hopkins ran for 230 yards against the Tigers. Don Kelley had a 67-yard punt return, Tommy Kendrick threw to Bobby Johnson, and Chuck Huntley scored on a short run for Clemson. North Carolina led 13–0 at the end of three quarters, but Russell went in on a sneak and Hopkins barreled over from fullback with three seconds to go, and Lounsbury added the extra point to pull it out 14–13.

Tennessee showed why it was in the top ten with a 41–7 win over Wake at Memphis. Junior Moore ran 61 yards to a score, but a barrage of touchdowns by Steve Wold, Bobby Scott, Les McClain, and Dennis Chadwick's pass to Bob Lassiter won for the Vols.

John Phillips fell on a fumble to stop Duke's first threat, but the Deacs downed the Blue Devils 28–14 to tie for the league lead. They shared the top spot for another week as Duke stopped South Carolina, and Wake won 16–13 over North Carolina State at the gun on Russell's two-handed basketball pass to Garrett.

Wake Forest was conference champion a week later as the Tar Heels outscored Duke, but in a night game at the Astrodome Bill Yeomans' Houston Cougars chewed up the Deacs 26–2 on short runs by Tommy Mozisek, Robert Newhouse, and Ted Heiskell. Houston's one-two passing combo of Riley Odoms and Elmo Wright was not to be outdone as Wright had a catch from Joel DeSpain on the way to his record-setting career mark of 34 touchdowns. McHenry closed the year as it began by blocking Mike Parrott's punt for a safety.

Wake Forest lined up with center Nick Vrhovac, guards Bill Bobbora and Ted Waite, tackles Vince Nedimyer and Gerald McGowan, end Dave Doda, and flanker Steve Bowden. Gone were Al Beard, Ed George, Larry Pons, and Roman Wszelaki to impede enemy maneuvers, but the defense still had tackles Win Headley, Dick Chulada, and Mike Magnot, flanked by Don Brown, Ernie Jakubovic, Frank Hawkins, Jim Pope, and linebackers Ed Bradley, Larry Causey, tackle leader Ed Stetz, and sophomore Mike Rose. Backs were Frank Fussell, Dick Bozoian, interception leader Terry Kuharchek, backed by Sammy Rothrock, Nick Arcaro, and Carlyle Pate, out last year with an injury. Others were Gary German, Archie Logan, Terry Bennett, Bill Gebert, Tom Martin, Tony Mangiaracina, Tommy Campbell, and Joe Theriault.

Duke tied for second with 5–2–0. After John Reaves threw to Mike Rich and Charles Hood, Tommy Durrance went over twice to put Florida out front 14–0. Two Dave Wright field goals narrowed it to eight, but a 67-yard punt return by Carlos Alvarez took it to 21–6. A pair of fourth-quarter scores on Leo Hart's pass to Dennis Satyshur and a 9-yard run by Steve Jones came up short 21–19.

Fred Zeigler left with his name etched in the South Carolina and ACC record books.

Maryland led 12–3 at the half on two Art Seymour scores, but a Hart-to-Jones pass and Wright's second field goal won it 13–12 with one second to go. The Blue Devils fell behind again at the half 7–3 on Larry Albert's pass to Dave Sullivan, but a score by Jones and Satyshur's late pass to Brad Evans downed Virginia 17–7.

Duke trailed 6–3 at the half as Ken Luttner ran in a blocked punt, but couldn't overcome the Ohio State onslaught as Rex Kern threw to Larry Zelina, John Brockington ran over, and Dick Galbos scored on a drive led by Ron Maciejowski in a 34–10 Buckeye win.

Duke got on track again with a 21–13 win over West Virginia. Mike Sherwood's keeper put the Mountaineers in front, but an end-around by Evans tied it and Jones blasted up the middle twice for the win. Mike Charron kicked two field goals for North Carolina State, but the Pack lost its punch when Don Bradley left with a knee injury. Interceptions by Rich Searl and Dick Biddle set up two three-pointers by Dave Pugh, and Wright's 53-yarder broke the ACC record of 49 yards set by State's Harold Deters in 1966. Tom Ussery's late score added to Duke's 22–6 margin and made them the first team to win 100 games since the ACC was formed in 1953.

Dan Phelan had a touchdown catch and Hart threw for one and scored one in Duke's 21–10 defeat of Clemson, but Don Kelley had a 102-yard interception and Eddie Seigler kicked a field goal for the Tigers. Ray Yauger ended with 2,439 yards rushing for Clemson and was second to Buddy Gore's career mark of 2,571 yards.

Bill Thompson raced 73 yards to a touchdown against Georgia Tech, but Jack Moore kicked a field goal and Eddie McAshen threw to Bruce Cunningham for his second score, and Stan Beavers went 75 yards with a late interception to clinch a 24–16 win for Tech.

In the ding-dong battle with South Carolina, Tommy Suggs hit Jim Mitchell twice, Hart threw two to Wes Chesson, and Bill Baker had another from Evans. Midway through the final quarter, Tommy Simmons put the Gameroosters in front 38–35 with his third score, but Art Bosetti's third touchdown won it 42–38 with two minutes to go. Don McCauley's five touchdowns beat Duke 59–34 to knock them from the top spot, but Chesson's 1,080 yards on receptions made him the first ACC player to gain 1,000 yards in a season. He broke Fred Zeigler's career record of 146 catches set the previous year, and his 164 career catches for 2,399 yards were both league marks.

North Carolina's defeat of Duke tied them for second with a 5-2-0 record. In the opener it was 10–10 at the half on a Cecil Bowens run and Bob Jones field goal for Kentucky, and Paul Miller pass to Lewis Jolley and Ken Craven field goal for the Tar Heels. Houston Hogg and Stan Forston found the Carolina defense tough in the second half, but Dave Hardt's punts kept Kentucky in it until another Craven field goal and Don McCauley's 48-yard dash won it 20–10. The defensive front of ends Bill Brafford and

Gene Brown, tackles Flip Ray and Bud Grissom, and guards Bill Richardson and Tom Cantrell charged quarterback Pat Korsnick all day to beat the Wolfpack 19–0, as McCauley scored and Miller tossed to Geof Hamlin and John Swofford, the younger brother of pop star, Oliver.

As UNC students unfurled a banner at College Park that said, "Tom – Say Hi to Your Mom," referring to basketballer Tom McMillen who left North Carolina for Maryland at his mother's insistence, the Tar Heels disposed of the Terps 53–20. After Al Thomas put Maryland in front, McCauley scored twice, Jolley caught a pass from Swofford after Tony Blanchard's captured fumble, and Ricky Lanier went 47 yards on Mike Mansfield's toss. The Terps scored late when Jeff Shugars threw to Bob Mahnic and Bob Tucker ran in.

The Tar Heels traveled to Nashville for their first game on synthetic turf and beat Vanderbilt 10–7. Danny Miller's pass to Karl Weiss and Bob Bayless extra point put the Commodores ahead, but Swofford threw to Jolley and Craven's field goal put it away.

McCauley's 48-yard run put South Carolina behind, but a Dick Harris 97-yard punt return and two Tommy Simmons' scores made it 21–7 at halftime. Ike Oglesby and McCauley evened the score, but the Gamecocks scored twice in the last six minutes and won 35–21 as Jackie Young hit Doug Hamrick and Billy Ray Rice ran 65 yards.

A trip to New Orleans brought a 24–17 loss to Tulane. Steve Barrios scored on a 74-yarder from Dave Abercrombie, but McCauley scored twice and Craven's field goal balanced one by Lee Gibson. Abercrombie scored the winning touchdown with 8:46 left, and Rick Kingrea knocked down a late Miller pass to secure the victory.

After Wake Forest won, Virginia lost 30–15. McCauley scored twice again next week, Oglesby had three, Tim Kirkpatrick ran in, and Bill Sigler caught another as Carolina beat VMI 62–13. Gary Shope threw to Steve Conlan and Buster Venable for VMI. McCauley scored three times to beat Clemson 42–7, Bill Taylor caught one, and Oscar Carter scored for rookie coach Hootie Ingram's Tigers.

The "Beat Dook Parade" lit up Chapel Hill, and well-planned attempts were made to steal Rameses, the Tar Heel mascot, and the Victory Bell, loaned to the winner of the Duke–Carolina contest. McCauley, who broke Charlie Justice's 1946 mark of 943 yards last year with 1,092 yards, now rushed for 1,720 yards to break O. J. Simpson's 1968 record of 1,709 yards, and set ACC records of 21 touchdowns and 126 points. Three times the crowd swept onto the field as he ran wild for 279 yards, and after the game they carried him across the field in a mad celebration. McCauley's three touchdowns gave the Tar Heels a 26–21 halftime lead in the Peach Bowl, but Bob Thomas scored three times, Monroe Eley twice, and J. D. Hill and Steve Holden once each as Arizona State won 48–26.

1971

Due to its high academic standards, recruiting good scholar-athletes had always been a problem in the ACC. In addition to the NCAA entrance requirements of a 1.6 grade-point average, the ACC also required an 800 Scholastic Aptitude Test score on the College Board exams. A provision was made by a 5–3 vote to admit athletes with a 1.75 GPA and 700 SAT score, but South Carolina thought the requirements were still too high and withdrew from the conference, and for the first time since 1953 the ACC started the season with seven teams.

North Carolina won its first outright title with a 6-0-0 mark. They stopped Richmond 28–0 and Illinois 27–0 in Bob Blackman's Big Ten debut. Maryland was beaten 35–14 as John Bunting added a last-quarter interception, and the Terps scored on Al Neville's toss to Dan Bungori after Don Ratliff's recovered fumble, and Art Seymour ran in after Tim Brant fell on one. Paul Miller threw two touchdowns to Lewis Jolley for the second straight week in a 27–7 win over North Carolina State, with Charley Young scoring for State.

Rookie coach Bennie Ellender of Tulane brought the four-game win streak to a halt 37–29. Mike Walker threw four scoring passes, two to Bob Marshall and Maxie LeBlanc, and Coleman Dupre ran from goal to goal with a kickoff return. Bob Thomas kicked three field goals for the Irish, and Cliff Brown, Notre Dame's first black signal caller, threw to Tom Gatewood, who broke Jim Seymour's career reception mark in a 16–0 win. Coach Ara Parseghian also used Pat Steenberge and Bill Etter in order to find a quarterback like John Huarte, Terry Hanratty, Joe Theismann, Tom Myers at Northwestern, and Jim Root at Miami of Ohio.

The Tar Heels returned home and began a five-game win streak as they bested Wake Forest 7–3 in the rain on early scores by Ted Leverenz and a Chuck Ramsey field goal. The Deacs plodded back in the mud late in the game but a pass was intercepted by Lou Angelo and another drive was stopped at the five with 25 seconds to go.

The William and Mary game was wild as John Gargano and Phil Mosser

Wake Forest's Chuck Ramsey shows the form that made him the top ACC punter for three years, 1971–1972–1973.

both scored twice for Lou Holtz's eleven, and John Cowell scored three times for Carolina. Mike Dodds kicked W&M in front after Dennis Cambal scored, but Jolley ran 13 yards and took the two-pointer from Miller to win 36–35 with two minutes remaining.

Ken Craven kicked four field goals, Bill Brafford blocked a Tony Anderson punt and fell on it for a score, and Terry Taylor's interception set up another score in Clemson's 26–13 defeat. Carolina continued its chase for the crown by beating Virginia 32–20, as Miller left-handed two tosses to Ken Taylor and Craven had three more field goals. Jolley scored three touchdowns against Duke, the last one coming after linebacker Jim Webster's interception, and Johnny Klise threw to Leverenz to beat the Blue Devils 38–0.

The team immediately accepted general manager George Olson's offer to play in the Gator Bowl. There Bill Dooley met Georgia's Vince Dooley, but brother Vince was victorious. After Andy Johnson threw to Lynn Hunnicutt for a first down, Jimmy Poulos caught Carolina on a blitz and scored to outdo Craven's field goal 7–3.

Lining up for the Tar Heels were center Bob Thornton, guards Ron Rusnak and Bob Walters, tackles Jerry Sain and Bob Pratt, Ike Oglesby and Tim Kirkpatrick as backs, and split end Earle Bethea.

Defenders were end Gene Brown, tackles Bud Grissom and Eric Hyman, linebacker Ricky Packard, and backs Rusty Culbreth, Rich Stilley, and Greg Ward. Others were John Anderson, Joe Bradshaw, Bill Chapman, Earl Chesson, Steve Early, Steve Hodgin, Billy Hite, Geof Hamlin, Phil Lamm, Mike Lemmons, Reid Lookabill, Jim Papai, Billy Newton, Mel Riddile, Bill Sigler, Pete Talty, Bill Taylor, Charlie Turco, Robbi Vandenbroek, and punter Nick Vidnovic.

Clemson finished two games back with a record of 4-2-0. Doug Kotar ran back a kickoff 98 yards on his first play for Kentucky, and Clemson's Smiley Sanders fell on an end-zone fumble after Buzz Burnam touched it, but Tom Kirk's second field goal won for John Ray's Wildcats 13–10. Jimmy Shirer punted Clemson into a hole all day as Rickey Lake scored in Georgia's 28–0 win, and Greg Horne's run and Cameron Bonifay field goal won for Georgia Tech 24–14. Wayne Baker grabbed a late fumble but Clemson couldn't move, and Hootie Ingram wondered what he wold say to the folks on College Avenue.

After three losses, Eddie Seigler's field goal beat Duke 3–0. Harrison Davis and Kent Merritt, Virginia's first black players, hooked up for a score, but Tommy Kendrick's pass to Don Kelley, and runs by Sanders and Heide Davis gave Clemson a 32–15 win and made them the second team to win 100 games since joining the ACC.

Heisman winner Pat Sullivan threw scores to Terry Beasley and Dick Schmalz, Sandy Cannon caught another, Terry Henley and Tommy Lowry ran in, Mike Flynn had a fumble recovery, and Gardner Jett kicked five extra points in Auburn's 35–13 win. Wake Forest led 6–0 for three periods on Larry Russell's pass to Kevin Byrnes, but Ricky Gilstrap scored to put Clemson ahead by one. The Deacs regained the lead 9–7 on Chuck Ramsey's field goal only to have a Seigler three-pointer take it 10–9 with 37 seconds remaining.

The Tigers faltered in the stretch but had enough claw left to beat Maryland. Kendrick's pass to Karl Andreas, a Gilstrap score and Seigler 48-yarder gave them a 17–0 halftime bulge, but Monte Hinkle's run and Jeff Shugars pass to Tom Miller made the final 20–14. Seigler's 47-yard field goal put Clemson ahead of the Pack, but three Mike Stultz touchdowns, one on Bruce Shaw's pass, and two Sam Harrell field goals caged the Tigers. Kendrick tossed to Wade Hughes and John McMakin, who caught another from Ken Pengitore, but Willie Burden bolted through the line and ran 81 yards to win for North Carolina State 31–23. Seigler put one over from 52 yards against South Carolina, Ben Anderson's interception set up a score, and Kendrick threw to McMakin in a 17–7 win to end his career as Clemson's top passer with 3,893 yards.

New coach Mike McGee stressed attitude and fundamentals and had Duke in a three-way tie for third. John Reaves threw to Joe Parker for Florida, but Dave Wright's four field goals won 12–6. Tommy Bell kicked two field goals and Glenn Morris threw late for South Carolina, but Ernie Jackson's interceptions of Jackie Young and Robbie Davis and 74-yard punt return led to Duke's 28–12 win. Ironically, the Gamecocks left the ACC because so many local athletes got away but did not want Jackson who was from Columbia.

Steve Jones had two touchdowns for the second week in a row to beat Virginia 28–0, but did not make the trip to Palo Alto due to an injury in a car accident. Chuck Munday backed up Stanford with his punts, and Jackson's 54-yard interception gave Duke all the points it needed. Willie Clayton and John Ricca stopped Don Bunce in close and Stanford was forced to settle for a Rod Garcia field goal and 9–3 loss. That night the team sang the Duke fight song as they rode the cable cars along the San Francisco streets.

Injuries forced Jackson to tailback where he and Bill Thompson scored twice and Rusty McDow once to beat the Wolfpack 41–13. Duke's 14–0 lead melted away as Fred Stuvek threw to Steve Ogden, then hit Andy Pease for his second score and conversion in a 15–14 Navy win. Tom Broderick's late steal nailed it down. Tom Lang's two runs and Jim Owings' catch won

Outland Trophy winner Mike McGee later held the coaching reins at Duke.

for Georgia Tech 21–0. Chris Potts scored on a pass from Bernie Galiffa and Brian Chiles added another for West Virginia in their 31–15 defeat, and Rich Searl's run ended the year that started so well as Wake Forest won 23–7.

Virginia also tied for third under new coach Don Lawrence. Larry Van Loan's catch set up Navy's first score in a 10–6 win, as John Sparaco's fumble recovery and two Gary Rhoads interceptions held Virginia to a pair of Billy Maxwell field goals. The Cavs found no mercy in Ann Arbor as Billy Taylor scored twice, Harry Banks three times, Dave Elliott had a kickoff return from the end zone, and Dana Coin hit all eight conversions in a 56–0

Michigan win. Dave and his older brother, defensive back Bruce Elliott, were the sons of former Michigan star Pete Elliott.

Steve Burger threw to Walt Overton, Doug Nettles returned a kickoff 95 yards, and Jamie O'Rourke's 10-yard run put Vanderbilt ahead 21–20. Dave Leffers added two on the conversion catch, but Larry Albert hit Bill Davis with 1:45 left to win for UVa 27–23. South Carolina won 34–14, as the "Carolina Bandits" stole three passes, recovered four fumbles, blocked a punt, and scored twice.

Kingsley Fink replaced Dick Atha after Grover Dailey's interception for Army and threw to Bob Hines and Ed Francis. Gary Topping and Tim Pfister stopped the Cavalier attack, but Bob McGrail ran in a stolen pass in a 14–9 Cadet victory. Two interceptions by linebacker Kevin Michaels led to a pair of passes from Albert to Bill Davis and Dave Sullivan in a 14–10 win over the Wolfpack. Don Strock and Dave Strock teamed up in a 6–0 Virginia Tech win as Don got the team in position for two field goals by brother Dave. A Maryland fumble led to Jim Lacey's catch, but the Terps replied on Carl Shelton's score and two Kambiz Behbahani field goals only to have Maxwell's three-pointer win 29–27 with 18 seconds to go.

Wake Forest was the last team to tie for third. Dave Fagg's Davidson Wildcats lost the battle of the little giants 27–7, and Junior Moore's 89-yard kickoff return put Wake ahead to stay in a 20–9 win over Virginia Tech. Chuck Foreman scored twice and John Hornibrook threw to Witt Beckman in Miami's 29–10 victory. Down 14–0, the Deacs beat Maryland 18–14. The Wolfpack won 21–14 but not before Chuck Ramsey missed a field goal and Bill Miller ran it back. Larry Russell left the bench and tackled him, but State was awarded a score. Larry Hopkins had another 230-yard rushing day in Tulsa's 51–21 loss, as school marks were set with 528 yards rushing and 32 first downs. Russell's four touchdowns led William and Mary, and Steve Regan threw to Ivan Stovall and Jack Hurley in W&M's 36–29 defeat. South Carolina took the final game 24–7, and Hopkins had 2,212 career yards to finish as Wake's leading rusher.

1972

In a surprise move, the NCAA announced that freshmen would be eligible to play football this year. The proposal was made by the ACC and Western Athletic Conference and passed by a vote of 94–67 over the objection of most major college football coaches.

Steve Jones is Duke's career rushing leader with 2,951 yards.

North Carolina repeated as league champ with another 6-0-0 mark. In the opener with Richmond, Tommy Bradley went in after Greg Ward's interception, and Johnny Klise ran in after another turnover. Andy Harris added a score, and Weldon Edwards scored twice on passes from Dave

Yount and Harry Knight in a 28–18 loss for Frank Jones' Spiders. Carolina led Maryland 17–3 on runs by Nick Vidnovic and Ellis Alexander field goal, but the Terps cut it to 24–20 on Bob Smith's punt return, Jamie Franklin dash, and two Steve Mike-Mayer field goals. Jimmy DeRatt's fumble recovery stopped a late threat as the Tar Heels outlasted the Terps 31–26.

Another donnybrook came one week later. The Wolfpack took a 19–10 halftime lead on runs by Stan Fritts, Charley Young, and a Mike Stultz punt return, but Carolina responded with two scores. Willie Burden took it in for 27–24, but Alexander's second field goal tied it. In the last minute, the Chapel Hill crowd erupted as Billy Hite's second score put Carolina ahead. The Pack tore down the field and with ten seconds left Bruce Shaw threw to Pat Kenney for the score. State went for the win as the fans stood in silence, but Terry Taylor broke up Dave Buckey's two-pointer to Roland Hooks for a 34–33 victory, and the afternoon sky was assaulted by the delirious shouts of the Tar Heel faithful.

Elmer Lippert ran for 116 yards behind John Hicks but Archie Griffin gained 239 yards in his first game to pass by ten Ollie Cline's 1945 mark at Ohio State. Griffin also set up touchdowns by Randy Keith, Harold Henson, Greg Hare, and a Blair Conway kick in a 29–14 win. Vidnovic hit Earle Bethea twice as linebackers Randy Gradishar and Vic Koegel closed off Carolina's ground game.

Back home again, Gary Knutson, Sonny Collins, and Arvie Carroll ran in for Kentucky in their 31–20 loss, and Wake Forest was blanked 21–0. Dick Oliver and Tim Kirkpatrick scored in Clemson's 26–10 loss, and Chris Kupec threw to Jimmy Jerome and Charlie Waddell scored to beat Virginia 23–3. Duke held Carolina scoreless until the last ten minutes when Mark DiCarlo and Phil Lamm intercepted two passes and Vidnovic threw to Ken Taylor twice for 14–0.

Carlester Crumpler tallied twice and Les Strayhorn once for East Carolina, but Ike Oglesby's three scores gained UNC a 42–19 win. After leading the Gators, Nat Moore's run tied it and Dave Bowden's pass to Lee McGriff and a John Williams field goal put Florida on top 17–14. Sammy Johnson vaulted Carolina ahead, but with three minutes to go a screen pass to Vince Kendrick set up a Willie Jackson score to leapfrog Florida in front 24–20. Johnson scored a third time with 1:41 left to give Carolina a 28–24 edge for good, as the Gators drove inside the ten but couldn't score.

North Carolina scored every way possible to beat Texas Tech in the Sun Bowl. Andre Tillman scored for the Red Raiders, and a penalty canceled a score by Don Rives for a 9–7 Tar Heel advantage at the half, but George

Coach Lou Holtz and co-captains Pat Kenney and Tom Siegfried accept North Carolina State's 1972 Peach Bowl trophy.

Smith rallied Tech with runs of 65 and 46 yards for a 21–9 lead. Carolina came back and went ahead 24–21, but after punter Dale Lydecker made a saving tackle on Lawrence Williams, Smith's third score and another Don Grimes extra point gave Texas Tech a 28–24 lead late in the game. Vidnovic hit Ted Leverenz for the go-ahead score with 1:54 left, and Bill Chapman and Ronnie Robinson dropped Joe Barnes for a safety as the "Cardiac Kids" won 32–28 to give Carolina 11 wins for the first time.

Carolina's line had center Bob Thornton, guards Ron Rusnak and Ken Huff, tackles Jerry Sain and Bob Pratt, and split end Pat Norton. Defensively, they had end Gene Brown, tackle Eric Hyman, linebackers Mike Mansfield, Steve Early, and Gary Cowan, and Lou Angelo, Tom Embrey, and Earl Chesson in the backfield.

Other lettermen were Deke Andrews, Kip Arnall, Dave Barrett, Joe Bradshaw, Andy Chacos, Phil Daly, Harper Donahoe, Ted Elkins, John Frerotte, Bill Hollingsworth, Ed Lamens, Mike Lemmons, Billy Newton, Don Shore, Mike Shuster, Ricky Sigmon, Pete Talty, Gary Ulicny, Robbi Vandenbroek, Bob Walters, and Bill Wicks.

Maryland's Randy White blocks a pass by Virginia's Scott Gardner.

Although the Wolfpack team gave interim coach Al Michaels a vote of confidence, they never dreamed of the success Lou Holtz would bring them, for his winning ways made them runner-up.

State opened against Maryland at home. They led 17–10 at the half on Bruce Shaw's passes to Willie Burden and Pat Kenney and a Ron Sewell field goal, but Mike Reitz tied it 24–24 after a second pass interference call. The Wolfpack was also home for Syracuse. They led again at the half 17–7 as Chuck Boniti's fumble recovery set up a Syracuse score, and Dave Buckey ran in and threw to Steve Lester for the Pack. Roger Praetorius and Brian Handleton scored for the Orangemen, but Roland Hooks scored twice and Stan Fritts and Gary Clements once each in a 43–20 second-half outburst.

A trip to Athens gave State its first defeat. After a 14–14 halftime deadlock on Pat Kenney and Harvey Willis catches, Horace King scored and threw to Johnny Ray for a 28–22 victory. Charley Young scored for the Pack, but five turnovers let the Dawgs have the ball for 20 of 30 minutes to defuse State's last-half heroics.

By now, the enthusiasm and optimism of their coach gave the team the confidence they needed to win. After holding Duke on an early goal line stand, middle guard Mike Daley's interception led to a second score by Fritts and 17–0 win. Wake Forest jumped to a 13–0 lead, but after a Holtz halftime speech, Fritts set a school record of five touchdowns in a 42–13 romp. East Carolina came to town, but the twin veer offense rolled to 24 last-half points and a 38–16 margin. South Carolina led at the half on Tom Zipperly's 98-yard kickoff return and Ron Parson touchdown, but State's homecoming crowd left happy as Dobby Grossman's pass to Tom Amrein did not match the Wolfpack's 28-point second-half splurge and a 42–24 victory. Scott Gardner threw to Ken Shelton and Chuck Belic for Virginia, but Fritts scored twice for the second straight week in a tight game as the Pack scored 21 last-half points to win 35–14.

John Hufnagel threw to John Cappelletti, Al Vitiello kicked three field goals, and Tom Shuman tossed to Dave Bland in a 37–22 Penn State win. Behind 23–0 at the half, Shaw and Kenney hooked up on a 98-yard score, but John Skorupan, Gregg Ducatte, and Dave Graf stopped any last-half bid and ended the Pack's five-game win streak. State put Clemson away with 35 first-half points to win 42–17 for a 4-1-1 league record. Burden and Young scored twice, and Fritts set a school mark with his 17th touchdown of the year.

In the Peach Bowl, two Frank Nester field goals and a Danny Buggs catch kept Bobby Bowden's West Virginia eleven in it at the half 14–13. Shaw sat out the game with a broken arm, but Buckey tossed to his brother, Don, Pat Hovance had another, and Fritts scored three times as State's second-half explosion won 49–13.

With a loss and a tie to the front-runners, Maryland's new coach Jerry Claiborne beat VMI 28–16. After Mike Cole's field goal, three interceptions led to touchdowns by Al Neville, Leroy Hughes, and Don Ratliff's pass from Bob Avellini. Bob Thalman's club came back on passes from Tom Schultze to Ronnie Norman and Ronnie Moore, but after Jim Santa grabbed a fumble, Lou Carter ran over to wrap it up. Art Seymour scored twice for the Terps, but Syracuse scored 16 points in three minutes on a Marty Januszkiewicz run, safety, and Dave King pass to Greg Allen to win 16–12.

Claiborne's no-nonsense approach, one-on-one counseling with his players, and weight-lifting and conditioning program began to pay off. The defense of linebacker Kevin Benson, backs Pat Ulam and Ken Schroy, and linemen Randy White and Dave Visaggio started to jell in a 23–0 shutout of Wake Forest and a 37–7 victory over Villanova. Duke had a 20–14 win, but on the way to a third-place finish and 3-2-1 record the Terps turned three interceptions into touchdowns to overcome a 20–0 deficit and sail by Virginia 24–23.

Penn State was too much in a 46–16 win. Steve Mike-Mayer's field goal tied it at ten, but after Randy Crowder came up with a fumble John Hufnagel tossed to Chuck Herd and Jim Scott to set up two John Cappelletti touchdowns. Hufnagel threw to Bob Rickenbach for another, and Walt Addie added one. Clemson was beaten 31–6, but Ed Carney completed three scoring passes in a 28–8 Miami win.

Duke was fourth at 3-3-0. Bob Albright tossed to Mark Landon and Mike Bomgardner after Ernie Clark's recovered fumble, but Paul Spivey and Joe LaBue scored behind the blocks of John Hannah, Buddy Brown, and Jim Krapf for a 14–12 Alabama lead. John Croyle halted Duke in the last half as Terry Davis, Steve Bisceglia, and Wilbur Jackson ran in for a 35–12 Bama win. A week later, Paul Taggeres ran over and Sonny Sixkiller tossed to Tom Scott as Washington won 14–6. After throwing to Reggie Ishman, Mike Boryla threw to Bill Scott and a Rod Garcia field goal gave Stanford a 10–6 victory.

Steve Jones scored three times and Hal Spears threw to Rich Brienza and Tom Chambers to beat Virginia 37–13, and George Allen, who transferred from UCLA when his dad took over as Redskin coach, scored for UVa. Winslow Stillman and Ed Newman led the defense in Clemson's 7–0 loss, and Mark Johnson guided the win over Maryland. Hugh Bayless and Roger Lanning traded field goals, but after Jack Forde's catch, Mel Parker sacked Al Glenny's two-point try to sink Rick Forzano's Navy crew 17–16. Johnson had two scores and Greg Garvin one to beat Georgia Tech 20–14, and Wake Forest got a second win 9–7 after firing its first-year coach. "Winning one like this makes it all worth while," said a slightly used Tom Harper.

IV. The ACC Is Number One Again (1973–1982)

1973

The third decade of ACC football started with North Carolina State taking the title with a 6-0-0 mark. Nine offensive starters who set 33 school records the previous year returned to beat East Carolina easily 57–8. Carl Summerell tossed to Stan Eure for ECU, but Lou Holtz cleared the bench as eight players scored, including Horace Whitaker and Roland Hooks. Harvey Willis and Don Buckey were two of seven who scored to down Virginia 43–23, and State scored 100 points as the defense had a safety for the second straight week.

State led Nebrasks at the end of three as Stan Fritts scored twice and Frosty Anderson's catch and Rich Sanger field goal made it 14–10, but a Dave Humm sneak, a toss to Brent Longwell, and a Tony Davis run gave Tom Osborne's Cornhuskers a 31–14 win. State trailed in another away game, as Gene Washington scored on an 86-yard punt return and end-around for Georgia. Fritts scored twice for the Pack, but Andy Reid ran 20 yards to make the final 31–12.

The largest crowd to date, 50,200, came to Carter Stadium to see State battle North Carolina. The Pack built a 21–3 bulge as Dave Buckey ran for one and threw to end Pat Hovance, and Fritts ran in at the end of a 99-yard drive after deep back Mike Stultz forced a fumble which linebacker Mike Daley covered. After Ellis Alexander's field goal, the Tar Heels bent their shaved heads to the task as Billy Paschall scored and tossed to Charlie

Waddell, who scored twice, but Willie Burden ran in for the equalizer, and Ron Sewell's four extra points were the margin of victory 28–26.

The Wolfpack led the Terps 17–0 as Dave Buckey ran over and threw to John Gargano, who followed Holtz from William and Mary, and Sewell added a field goal. Burden scored from ten yards out, but Maryland's whirlwind finish fell short 24–22, as Walter White caught a pass from Al Neville, Lou Carter ran in twice, and Steve Mike-Mayer made a field goal. Gordy Bengel caught the touchdown for the Tigers in Clemson's Death Valley before stumbling 29–6. Another trip to the Palmetto State saw Jay Lynn Hodgin score three times, Casper Carter twice, and Randy Spinks once for South Carolina, but Charley Young scored three times as the Pack's powerful offense churned out 556 yards total offense and a 56–35 victory.

Penn State ended the win streak a week later. Fritts scored twice, but Chris Bahr kicked a field goal and Bob Nagle ran in to make it 14–9 at the half. Gary Hayman's punt return put PSU ahead 22–14. Bruce Shaw ran in and Young's 69-yard dash tied it 29–29, but Heisman winner John Cappelletti's third touchdown won 35–29.

The Wolfpack finished with wins over Duke and Wake Forest. It was 7–3 going into the final period on Burden's score and Dave Malechek field goal, but Shaw ran in and threw to Mike Hardy for a 21–3 defeat of Duke. A fight emptied both benches as end Brian Krueger sacked Hal Spears hard and Spears kicked Krueger. Terry Karl ran in and Tom Lockridge returned a kickoff 98 yards as Wake lost 52–13, but Burden's 1,014 yards made him State's first back to gain 1,000 yards in a year. Shaw's 2,999 career passing yards edged Roman Gabriel's 2,951 yards as State's top passer, and the Pack's 40,480 fans was the first ACC team to average over 40,000.

State's first perfect ACC campaign earned them a trip to the Liberty Bowl against Don Fambrough's Kansas Jayhawks. Sewell and Mike Love exchanged field goals, but State broke a 10–10 deadlock with a relentless second-half ground game. "We felt all season long we could run against anybody," said Fritts who scored twice, Young once, and tackle Jim Henderson rambled 31 yards with an interception. Bob Miller ran in for Kansas and caught a pass from Dave Jaynes, who ended it 31–18 on a two-pointer to Bruce Adams.

State's movers up front were center Justus Everett, guards Bill Yoest and Bob Blanchard, tackles Al Sitterle and Rick Druschel, and flanker George Gantt. Defenders were end Craig Xander, tackles John Goeller and Randy Lail, linebackers Ken Sheesley and Mike Cowan, and backs Bobby Pilz, Eddie Poole, and Mike Devine.

Other Pack lettermen were Mike Adamczyk, Ron Banther, Howard Bradburn, Doug Carter, Joe Grasso, Jack Hall, Frank Haywood, T. J. Kennedy, Richard Lehr, Dan Meier, Joe Robinson, Sam Senneca, Tom Serfass, Kirby Shimp, Ralph Stringer, and Mark Wilks.

Maryland had its best season in 18 years and finished second at 5-1-0. In the opener with West Virginia, four field goals by Frank Nester and Steve Mike-Mayer tied it 6–6, but the Terps took the lead on a score after a bad center snap on a punt. With five minutes left, former Navy quarterback Ade Dillon connected with Dwayne Woods on a 75-yard touchdown pass, and Danny "Lightning" Buggs gathered in a punt, eluded the grasp of Leroy Hughes, and raced 69 yards for a 20–13 victory with eight seconds remaining.

After an Ellis Alexander field goal, Maryland stopped North Carolina 23–3 as Frank Russell outmaneuvered defender Russ Conley and caught a pass which led to the first score, scored the second on Al Neville's toss, and set up a third on another catch. Said Tar Heel coach Bill Dooley, "We haven't been handled like this in years," as tackle Randy White's 18 tackles were instrumental in keeping Carolina from crossing mid-field until late in the third quarter to end UNC's string of 15 straight ACC victories.

The game with Lou Ferry's Villanova Wildcats was a 9–3 field goal battle for three periods as Dennis Griggs made one and Mike-Mayer made three, including an ACC record 54-yarder. Maryland's defense shut down Bill Hatty and Bill Margetich, as UM won 31–3 with long-range salvos on Lou Carter's 61-yard run, Bob Smith's 56-yard punt return, and Mike Cielensky's 30-yard interception.

Randy White and Paul Vellano sacked the Syracuse quarterback seven times, as the Orangemen never got inside Maryland's 25-yard line. The offense rolled to a 38–0 win on Bob Avellini's 60-yard completion to Walter White, and Harry Walters recovered a blocked punt in the end zone. After Maryland lost to the Wolfpack on a missed field goal at the gun because of a high center snap, Wake Forest was held to one first down in a 37–0 loss, with Ken Roy, Ricky Jennings, and Alan Bloomingdale running in for the Terps. Duke had a 10–10 tie before losing 30–10 on three fourth-quarter touchdowns, including tackle Ken Scott's 15-yard interception.

Gary Hayman returned the opening kickoff 98 yards, and Penn State scored again within 84 seconds after Greg Buttle covered a fumble. Maryland stormed back on Roy's halfback option pass to Russell, Mike-Mayer's field goal, and then took the lead 16–12 on another halfback option pass from Carter to Walter White. State regained the lead on Tom Shuman's pass to Dan Natale and a Chris Bahr field goal, but Smith's punt return made it a new game 22–22.

The Lions won it 42–22 on 20 third-quarter points after Jim Bradley's interception, a Greg Murphy fumble recovery, and two Bahr field goals. "This is the best team we've played," said a sore John Cappelletti afterward. "I felt them when they hit."

Maryland closed with three wins. Ben Kinard ran 52 yards to a score on his first carry against Virginia to start a 33–0 win, and Jim Brechbiel blocked a punt for a safety. Carter scampered 50 yards on the fourth play and added two more touchdowns to beat Clemson 28–13. Tulane trailed 14–3 at halftime and drove inside the ten but lost the ball on a fumble, and the Terrapins marched 93 yards to turn the game around in a 42–9 win. "The hitting was unbelievable out there," declared defensive end Kevin Ward.

The Terps took their tough defense which led the ACC for the last two years in total defense and rushing defense to the Peach Bowl to play Georgia. After a scoreless first period, the Dawgs drew first blood on Andy Johnson's 62-yard screen pass to Jimmy Poulos. Maryland countered with a 68-yard completion from Carter to Walter White, and Mike-Mayer added a field goal with 1:31 left in the half. Georgia swept down the field and tied it at ten on Allan Leavitt's field goal with six seconds still on the clock.

Georgia took a 17–16 win after scoring on a Maryland miscue, while the Terps got inside the 20 twice but had to settle for two Mike-Mayer field goals. "We had a very satisfying season," said coach Jerry Claiborne, "but the ones we almost won, they hurt."

Clemson was third at 4-2-0 under new coach Jim "Red" Parker, newly moved from The Citadel. His old school gave him pause, as Billy Paine ran in to put coach Bobby Ross up by six. Two first-half runs by Smiley Sanders and Ken Pengitore gave Clemson the lead, but a Harry Lynch pass to Rod Lanning closed the gap, and two Bob Burgess conversions were all that separated them 14–12.

Jay Washington scored to put Clemson ahead at the half 7–3, but Georgia began its mastery of the top ACC teams as Ralph Page, Jerome Jackson, and Glynn Harrison ran over, and Gene Washington topped it off 31–14 with a 97-yard kickoff return. Georgia Tech took the lead on Rick Hill's run but a Craig Brantley catch tied it, and then moved ahead 16–14 on a Jim Stevens sneak and Cameron Bonifay field goal. Washington scored twice for the Tigers, but a Mark Fields catch and Greg Horne run won it 29–21. Randy Rhino was the stopper for coach Bill Fulcher, as Georgia

Randy Rhino made all–American three times as a defensive back at Georgia Tech by the time he turned in his pads in 1974.

Tech gave Red Parker the same treatment it gave Frank Howard and Hootie Ingram.

Facing Texas A&M for the first time, Emory Bellard's Aggies handed Clemson its third straight loss. Down 9–0, A&M turned it around on Bubba Bean's 78-yard run, took the lead on two runs by Ronnie Hubby, and then put it away 30–15 as David Walker came in at quarterback for Mike Jay and scored the final touchdown.

Virginia came to play and took a 13–0 lead on short runs by Scott Gardner and Bill Copeland, but Clemson went ahead 18–13 at the half as Dave Sasser and Ken Callicutt scored. Kent Merritt's run and Mike Lacika's end zone fumble recovery put the Cavs back on top 27–18, but last-quarter scores on Pengitore's second pass to Jim Lanzendoen made it close and a Sanders dash won it 32–27.

Clemson beat Duke 24–8, as Roger Neighborgall threw to Troy Slade for Duke with 16 seconds left. After besting Wake Forest 35–8 and North Carolina 37–29, Clemson came to South Carolina's newly-enlarged Williams-Brice Stadium. Martha Williams Brice, the widow of Tom Brice, a Gamecock player under Sol Metzger in the 20s, left a large sum to her nephews, Tom and Phil Edwards, who gave much of it to the Columbia school. Clemson lost 32–20, as quarterback Jeff Grantz scored twice and Randy Chastain once. "He's a super quarterback," said Gamecock center Darrell Austin, but the GROD (Get Rid of Dietzel) bumper stickers in the parking lot revealed the fan displeasure with Gamecock coach Paul Dietzel.

Virginia was fourth at 3-3-0. Ray Keys and Mike McGugan had touchdowns as VMI lost 16–0, but Missouri took it to them 31–7 on scores by Leroy Moss, Jim Smith, John Cherry's pass to Jim Sharp, and Greg Hill field goal. Vanderbilt won 39–22, but they downed Duke 7–3, outlasted North Carolina 44–40, and beat Wake Forest on two long passes to Mike Bennett and Harrison Davis 21–10. Charley Coffey's Virginia Tech team scored early as Phil Rogers threw to Ricky Scales, but Virginia scored on a Joe Jenkins field goal and Scott Gardner's pass to Jim Colleran. J. B. Barber's run put VPI ahead to stay, but Wayne Latimer's field goal and Davis catch made it 17–15. Another Latimer field goal and Eddie Joyce score ended it 27–15, and Artie Owens led West Virginia's 42–17 win.

1974

Maryland's 17 veteran starters took the Terps to their first undisputed title with a 6-0-0 mark. Temporary bleachers were set up by athletic director Jim Kehoe in the open end of Byrd Stadium to accommodate the crowd of 54,412 on hand for the Alabama game. Calvin Culliver scored twice, but Steve Mike-Mayer cut it to 14–9 as he buggy-whipped a third field goal after Ricky Jennings took the second-half kickoff back 61 yards. Richard Todd scored after Ben Kinard's fumble, and Lou Carter dived in for a 21–16 Bama win.

Maryland led 10–7 at the half a week later in Tampa as Tony Green's 74-yard dash scored for Florida, but Dave Posey tied it with a 49-yarder. After Wayne Fields intercepted for the Gators, Jimmy Fisher threw to Lee McGriff for the winning touchdown 17–10.

The Terps regrouped against North Carolina as Carter swept right end for 76 yards behind blocks by wingback John Schultz and fullback Alan Bloomingdale. Maryland led 24–0 in the rain before Billy Paschall hit Andy Chacos and Jimmy Jerome for a 24–12 final.

Maryland shut out the next three foes and added scoring defense to its league-leading laurels of total defense and rushing defense. Schultz scored twice to beat Syracuse 31–0, scored two more against Clemson, and Ken Roy scored twice in Clemson's 41–0 loss. The kicking game was superb, as Phil Waganheim averaged 46 yards on punts and Ken Schroy returned three punts for 84 yards. Bob Avellini hit Schultz on the first play against Wake Forest, halfback Jim Brechbiel's theft scored another, and end Bob Raba's catch made it 19–0 at the half. After Kim Hoover and Mark Manges scored in Wake's 47–0 loss, second-year Deacon coach Chuck Mills said about Wake Forest's 18 scoreless quarters and high academic requirements, "The obvious thing wrong with college athletics is that the policies are made by people not in the trenches."

Maryland was up for North Carolina State because a film clip showed the State players taunting Mike-Mayer after he missed last year's game-winning field goal try. John Huff's three-pointer put the Pack ahead, but Avellini's 30-yard spurt scored for Maryland, Mike-Mayer added a field goal after Bob Smith's interception, and Dave Buckey's pass to B. J. Lyttle evened it at ten. Mike-Mayer's field goal kicked Maryland ahead, and another Smith interception in the final quarter let Carter's 6-yard run extend it to 20–10.

Before 60,125 fans against Penn State in Beaver Stadium, Jeff Hite ran 79 yards with an interception, but Avellini tied it on a toss to tight end Walter White. After Tom Shuman passed to Dick Barvinchak, Hite stole a lateral from Jennings to Carter on the kickoff and raced 21 yards to another score. Avellini threw 66 yards to White on the first play after the kickoff for 21–14 at the half, and anyone who left a seat missed three touchdowns in 25 seconds. Last-quarter field goals by Chris Bahr and Mike-Mayer ended it 24–17.

Joe Brancato, Tony Black, and Tim Wilson all scored their first collegiate touchdowns in the 41–0 win over Villanova. Bob Corbett threw to Ben Fordham and Tony Benjamin scored in Duke's 56–13 loss. In

Virginia's 10–0 defeat, Carter ran for 213 yards to break Ray Poppelman's 1931 single-game mark, and finished as Maryland's top ground gainer with 2,392 career yards.

Other records also fell. Avellini had 1,648 passing yards to break Alan Pastrana's 1966 season mark of 1,499 yards and Dick Shiner's 1962 mark of 1,324 yards. End Frank Russell, Avellini's favorite target, held career marks with 100 receptions and 1,346 yards, and Mike-Mayer set an ACC career mark with 37 field goals. Randy White, with 12 sacks and 24 tackles in the backfield, won the Outland Trophy as the year's best interior lineman.

In the Liberty Bowl, Mike-Mayer made it 3–0 but with 2:38 to go Randy Wallace threw 11 yards to Larry Seivers. Ricky Townsend added the conversion, and Bill Battle's Tennessee Vols won 7–3.

Only Bart Purvis was missing from the Terp line of center Bob Lange, guards John Nash and John Vesce, and tackles Frank Romano and Stan Rogers. On defense were ends Leroy Hughes and Rod Sharpless, tackle Joe Campbell, guards Dave Visaggio and Paul Divito, linebackers Harry Walters and Kevin Benson, and Pat Ulam deep.

Others were center Gene Ochap, guard Ed Fulton, tackles Tom Schick, John Zernhelt, and Marion Koprowski, ends Rick Schmaltz and John Alkire, and back Dan DeCarlo. Defenders were ends Bill Evans and George Shihda, tackles Ralph Fisher, Richard DiCaprio, and Al LaHayne, guards Guy Dietz, Ernie Salley, and Derick Harris, and linebackers Jim Santa, Steve Zannoni, Chris Miller, and Brad Carr. Deep men were Mike Cielensky, Joe Younge, and Pete Zachary.

North Carolina State was the first of three teams that tied for second with 4-2-0. They took off like a rocket with a 33–15 win over Wake Forest. After John Huff's field goal gave them a halftime edge, Dave Buckey scored once and threw to B. J. Lyttle and Mike Hardy to rally the Wolfpack. Wake scored on a long pass from Mike McGlamry to Tom Fehring and Frank Harsh run. Duke lost 35–21 on two scoring strikes to Don Buckey, one from twin brother Dave and one on a halfback pass from Stan Fritts. Elijah Marshall caught another long scoring pass from Johnny Evans. Clemson led 10–9 at the half, but Fritts scored three times for a 31–10 win.

New coach Frank Maloney had Syracuse ahead 14–7 before State won in the last half 28–22. Ken Kinsey and Jim Donoghue ran over for the Orangemen, while Roland Hooks scored three times for the Pack. Ken Strayhorn and Mike Weaver ran over for East Carolina, and Jim Woody kicked Pat Dye's "Wild Dogs" in front 14–7. Mike Myrick added another touchdown, but for the third straight week State came from behind to win

24–20 and embellish the reputation of Lou Holtz as one of the best last-half coaches in the game. Virginia led 21–0 a week later as Scott Gardner threw to Jim Colleran and Ken Shelton and Mike Dowe ran over. Buckey cut the margin on a pass to Hooks and two-pointer to Pat Hovance. Then with 3:46 to go he sneaked in and Hooks ran the two-pointer for a 22–21 win.

State's suspect defense was found out for sure as they fell behind North Carolina on another 21–0 deficit. With Holtz looking at the ground as he paced the sidelines, tackle Rod Broadway had three sacks, one blocked pass, and one recovered fumble in a 33–14 win to end State's 14 straight ACC triumphs.

South Carolina was in the way as the Pack rebounded with a 42–27 win. Clarence Williams scored twice and Bobby Marino made two field goals for the Gamecocks, and Ralph Stringer's interception set up State's first score. Tommy London scored twice, and Ron Banther returned a fumble 84 yards for a Wolfpack record.

Penn State came to Raleigh confident of another win in the series, but was surprised with a 12–7 defeat. Mike Hartenstine blocked the conversion after Fritts scored, but it didn't matter as Fritts threw to Hovance for the insurance score. Middle guard Tom Higgins, linebacker Mike Daley, and an interception by safety Bob Divens helped stop the Lions seven times inside the eight and keep them out of the end zone until the last 43 seconds.

The Pack ended its schedule in Tempe against Arizona State. ASU scored on a Dennis Sproul to Morris Owens pass and closed it to 21–14 at the half for coach Frank Kush as Mike Haynes returned a kickoff 97 yards. Fritts and Hooks both scored twice, and Mike Hardy made another to take it 35–14. Fritts had 1,169 yards for the year to pass Willie Burden's mark, and his 2,542 career yards rushing passed Burden's 2,529 yards. Fritts also set school records with 256 points on 42 touchdowns, 41 of them overland.

The Wolfpack took its 9-2-0 record to the Astro-Bluebonnet Bowl and came away with a 31–31 tie against Houston. State led 17–10 at the end of three as Lennard Coplin's field goal and John Housman scored for Houston, but Marshall Johnson's run evened it early in the fourth quarter. Bubba McGallion's 73-yard pass to Eddie Foster and a second Housman score after Joe Rust's interception put Houston up 31–17. They were driving to another score as Reggie Cherry and Donnie McGraw tore through the tiring Wolfpack line when Clarence Cotton came up with a fumble. Seven plays and 86 yards later London ran in, but the two-point pass failed. Jay Sherrill tried an onside kick which twisted into the hands of Lou Alcamo. Buckey nosed in with 2:17 remaining, and as the Cougars dropped off for a pass, Fritts pounded up the middle for the tie.

Clemson also tied for second at 4-2-0. In the return match with Texas A&M, the Aggies blanked them 24–0 on two Skip Walker touchdowns, one by Bubba Bean, and a Bennie Haddox field goal.

Clemson was home for the first time in 44 games with Georgia Tech and took a 21–17 verdict. Bennie Cunningham scored twice on passes from Mark Fellers and Mike O'Cain and Ken Callicutt ran in for the Tigers, but a Danny Smith field goal, Adrian Rucker run, and Joel Porter's intercepted lateral scored for new coach Pepper Rodgers' Yellow Jackets. O'Cain came off the bench a week later with two last-half runs, one for 39 yards, to beat Georgia 28–24.

Duke battled all the way on Hal Spears tosses to Randy Cobb and Troy Slade but lost 17–13, as a late end zone pass was batted down. In a barn-burner with Tennessee, Fellers tossed twice to Cunningham, Callicutt threw to Rickey Bustle, Don Testerman went 68 yards to a score, and four Bob Burgess conversions kept Clemson in front. Mike Gayles ran in for the Vols, Stanley Morgan had a scoring catch, and after Morgan ran in twice, Condredge Holloway hit Larry Seivers on a two-pointer to win 29–28 with 1:31 left.

Clemson ended with four wins. After Wake Forest lost 21–9, North Carolina was outgunned 54–32 as Joey Walters had a catch, Virginia lost 28–9, and South Carolina went down 39–21 as Dennis Smith ran in an interception and Tony Mathews took one in.

North Carolina was the third team to tie for second at 4-2-0. After a 42–7 warmup over Bill Hess and Miami of Ohio, Wake Forest lost 31–0 as Charlie Williams scored and Mel Collins ran in a punt. UNC's defense faded after Maryland won due to slim recruiting when Bill Arnold died in 1971 after a tough workout. Chris Kupec threw for one and Jim Betterson scored twice but Pitt led 21–20 at the half on scores by Tony Dorsett, Bill Daniels, and Carl Farmer. Last-half touchdowns by Mike Voight and Dick Oliver won it 45–29, with Elliott Walker going 80 yards for Pitt in the final minute.

Georgia Tech tied it 14–14 after three on runs by Dave Sims and Jim Murray, then took a wild finish 29–28 on Jimmy Robinson's two-point catch with 36 seconds to go. South Carolina won 31–23 and Virginia lost 24–10, but Clemson's onslaught overwhelmed them. Another foot race followed as Army led on runs by Markus Hardy and Brad Dodrill, but Ray Stanford caught one of Kupec's four scoring passes to pull ahead. Leamon Hall threw to John Hodges and Scott Gilloghly scored twice for Army before being out-distanced 56–42.

Art Gore scored after Duke's Laniel Crawford blocked a punt, and Voight scored after Bobby Trott's steal, but Rich McInturff's conversion was blocked, and two Ellis Alexander PATs won it 14–13.

The Tar Heels torrid offense took them back to the Sun Bowl against Bob Tyler's Mississippi State Maroons. Walt Packer, Terry Vitrano, and two Vic Nickels field goals put MSU ahead 26–24. On fourth-and-one at mid-field with 1:23 remaining, the Tar Heels ran behind bread-and-butter blocker Mark Griffin. The Maroons smelled it out as Jimmy Webb, Sidney Key, and Harvey Hull held for no gain.

1975

Maryland's five wins brought a second consecutive title and tied the league record of 15 straight victories. Villanova lost again 41–0 under new coach Dick Bedesem, as Mark Manges completed four touchdown passes, two to end Vince Kinney. Larry Dick came in and tossed a 70-yarder to end Chuck White in the last quarter.

Stanley Morgan's 50-yard run and 70-yard punt return paced a 26–8 win for Tennessee. Tackle Joe Campbell dropped punter Craig Colquitt for a safety, but Manges suffered a shoulder separation.

After spotting North Carolina a score, fullback Tim Wilson barreled over after a John Schultz 92-yard kickoff return. Two Mike Sochko field goals made it 13–7 at intermission. Dick threw to Kim Hoover, Jamie Franklin ran in, and Steve Atkins made his first college score in a 34–7 win. Interceptions by back Ken Roy and tackle Ralph Fisher ended two Tar Heel drives. Sonny Collins scored to put Kentucky ahead, but Ricky Jennings tied it with a 93-yard kickoff runback. Sochko's kick gave Maryland the lead, but John Pierce knotted it at ten with eight seconds remaining.

Syracuse scored after Nick Marsella recovered a fumble and Mike Jones grabbed a loose ball in the end zone when Jim Donoghue was hit, but Maryland did not clinch the 24–7 win until the last quarter when guard Paul Divito fell on a Bob Mitch fumble. North Carolina State's 7–3 margin was short-lived as Jennings returned the kickoff 96 yards to put Maryland ahead for good. Atkins and Ted Brown ran in for 17–14 at the half, but the Pack wilted in the stretch as Scott Wade's second score for State ended it 37–22.

Dean Richards took over at wingback for Schultz in the 27–0 defeat of Wake Forest. A crowd of 58,973, the largest ever in Byrd Stadium, saw Penn State go in front on two Chris Bahr field goals, one on Ron Cuder's fumble recovery after a Jim Rosecrans hit, and another on Kurt Allerman's fumble recovery after a Greg Buttle hit. Woody Petchell's 36-yard sprint extended it to 12–0 with only 9:06 gone, but the Terps trimmed it to two on Sochko's field goal and run by Atkins. Sochko kicked Maryland ahead by one in the third quarter, but Bahr's field goal with 7:42 to go won it 15–13. Sochko's 42-yard try with 15 seconds left sailed wide right as long snapper Marion Koprowski hiked the ball low.

Cincinnati's Frank Jeter scored on a pass from Henry Miller, and two Dan Shepard field goals gave Tony Mason's Bearcats a 13–0 lead. The Terps pulled in front by one in the third quarter, but with 4:44 to go Jay Bonds put Cincinnati back on top. With 1:38 left, Dick threw to Franklin for his third score and a 21–19 win.

Another nail-biter followed as Clemson went in front, but Schultz returned the kickoff 92 yards to lead 7–6. Two Sochko field goals offset Mike O'Cain's second score to still lead by one. Ken Callicutt and Atkins traded touchdowns to put Clemson up by one as they made the two-pointer and Maryland didn't, but with eight seconds left Sochko's third field goal won it 22–20.

Maryland led 14–10 as Scott Gardner's run and Dan Hottowe field goal scored for Virginia, but it was 42–10 before the Cavs scored again. Virginia's Dave Sloan and Bill Copeland ran over, and Dan DeCarlo and Al Maddox ran in for a 62–24 Maryland final.

Maryland, which set an ACC mark of 802 yards total offense against Virginia, took its high-powered attack and tough defense to meet Florida in the Gator Bowl. The Gators were led by linebacker Sammy Green, tackle Darrell Carpenter, and halfback Henry Davis on defense, and center Robbie Moore, guard Gerald Loper, tackle Mike Williams, quarterback Don Gaffney, and Jimmy DuBose, whose 1,307 yards rushing was a SEC mark. Interceptions by deep backs Jim Brechbiel and Mike Cielensky and Kevin Benson at linebacker shut out Doug Dickey's Gators 13–0, while Maryland scored on a Dick to Hoover 19-yarder and a pair of Sochko field goals.

The Terps had center Gene Ochap, guards John Nash and Ed Fulton, and tackles Dave Conrad and Marion Koprowski, backed by center Jack Sharkey, guard Mike Yeates, and tight ends Bob Raba and Scott Murphy. On defense were guards Ernie Salley and Ted Klaube, ends Leroy Hughes and Bill Evans, with linebackers George Shihda, Mike Miller, and Brad Carr. Safeties were Joe Younge and Pete Zachary.

Others on defense were guards Bob Schwartz and Rich Cozzi, tackles Al LaHayne and Larry Seder, ends Dan Foster and Chip Garber, and backs Doug Harbert and Jon Claiborne, the coach's son.

Duke's 3-0-2 record made it the second team to complete its conference schedule unbeaten but not finish first. In Southern Cal's 35–7 triumph, Ricky Bell scored four touchdowns and his 256 yards rushing broke the USC mark of 251 yards set by C. R. Roberts in 1956. Mosi Tatupu and Art Gore ran in to complete the scoring. Chuck Williamson and Hal Spears scored against USC a week later, but two Jeff Grantz keepers took South Carolina to a 24–16 win.

Vince Fusco kicked a field goal for the second week in a row as Duke finally got in the win column 26–11. Larry Martinez went in twice, and Larry Upshaw had a scoring catch from Bob Corbett. Joe Jenkins kicked a field goal for Virginia, and Scott Gardner tossed to Dave Sloan and then for two points to Joe Sroba. Tony Dorsett and Bob Haygood ran in and Carson Long kicked both extra points in Pitt's 14–0 win, as Duke was held to 33 yards rushing.

Tony Pyne scored on Leamon Hall's pass, and Howard Williams had eight catches, but interceptions by Kirk May, Tom Knotts, and Rod Sensibaugh halted Army 21–10. Williamson and Mike Barney ran over and Carl McGee's 68-yard interception scored for Duke, and Mike Castelli made a field goal for Homer Smith's Cadets. Another Duke attempt was nipped by Al Stuhlmiller's end zone interception.

Willie Jordan had a hand in two scores and Don Testerman ran in for Clemson, but Mike Dunn ran over for Duke. Fusco's second kick cut it to 21–19 in the last quarter. After Rich Holliday's punt, Tony Benjamin ran 19 yards for a 25–21 win with 1:38 left.

Corbett threw to Ed Kornberger against Florida, Martinez ran in and Fusco added a kick, but Jimmy DuBose scored three times and Dave Posey's field goal gave the Gators a 24–16 win. Fusco kicked two more against Georgia Tech, but Dan Myers and Adrian Rucker ran in, Rudy Allen tossed to Steve Raible, and Don Bessillieu's field goal won it 21–6. Wake Forest had a 14–14 tie before Benjamin's four last-half scores beat the Deacs 42–14. North Carolina State gained a 21–21 tie on a two-point pass with 12 seconds to go, and North Carolina was 17–17 despite Duke's 471 yards total offense.

North Carolina State was third at 2-2-1. Pete Conaty kicked a field goal for East Carolina, and Mike Nail made two in State's 26–3 win. Dave Buckey tossed twice and scored once against Wake Forest, but Jerry McManus threw to Bill Millner twice and scored once in a 30–22 Wake win. Larry Brinson ran in early for Florida, but with three minutes remaining Buckey passed to Elijah Marshall and Johnny Evans ran in the two-pointer to edge the Gators 8–7.

The Wolfpack hit the road, but three first-quarter fumbles led to three Michigan State touchdowns by Levi Jackson. Charley Baggett ran in, and Hans Nielson added three field goals to give Denny Stolz's Spartans a 37–15 win. Buckey threw to Pat Hovance and Richard Carter ran in for State. Back home in Raleigh, three freshmen and one sophomore running back, Rickey Adams, took the field against Lee Corso's Hoosiers. Ted Brown, who didn't even make the trip to East Lansing, scored twice, and Scott Wade and Timmy Johnson once each as the Pack turned back Indiana 27–0.

A crowd of 50,500 showed up at Carter Stadium for the North Carolina game. Down 14–0, Brown's second score and two-pointer from Evans to Don Buckey put State ahead 21–14. UNC scored with 12 seconds left, but State nixed the two-pointer for a 21–20 win.

Brown scored four times to beat Clemson 45–7, passed Willie Burden's one-game mark of 198 yards with 227 yards rushing, and helped set a one-game school mark of 409 yards rushing. A Jeff Grantz score and two-pointer to Brian Nemeth gave South Carolina a 21–6 lead, but 22 last-period points on Buckey's pass to Ricky Knowles and Johnson's dive with nine seconds to go won it 28–21.

Penn State led 14–0 as Larry Suhey and John Andress ran in, but Brown bucked over twice and Jay Sherrill kicked a field goal to win 15–14 and beat PSU two years in a row. West Virginia reversed a Peach Bowl loss, as Dan Kendra threw to Scott MacDonald for the winning score and Bill McKenzie converted in a 13–10 win.

Dave Buckey finished as State's career passing leader with 4,286 yards, while Don, "The Other Buckey," as he called himself, ended as the career leader with 102 receptions for 1,735 yards.

After two years with no league wins, Wake Forest was fourth with 3-3-0. Dave Smith's Southern Methodist team won 14–7, but said SMU's Dave Headstream, "Wake Forest was a lot better than I thought." A late Gary Davis field goal won 19–17 for Jim Brakefield's Appalachian State squad, and Ellis Rainsberger's Kansas Staters took a 17–16 win. Mike Harris ran in and threw to L. P. Edwards for K-State, and Bob Hely and Bill Sinovic swapped field goals, but two Jerry McManus throws to John Zeglinski and

Clark Gaines came up a point short. Another field goal killed them, as Clemson won 16–14 on Willie Jordan's 34-yarder with no time left.

Virginia was crushed 66–21, and Zeglinski's three scores beat North Carolina 21–9. South Carolina led 21–0 as Tom Amrein, Kevin Long, and Clarence Williams ran in, but three Mike McGlamry tosses to Zeglinski couldn't catch Jim Carlen's club. Randy Chastain ran 53 yards to a score, Jeff Grantz tossed to Phil Logan, and Bobby Marino's field goal ended it 37–26. Jimmy Sharpe's Virginia Tech squad won 40–10, as Roscoe Coles had 1,045 yards rushing to break the one-year record of 1,036 yards set by Phil Rogers in 1973.

1976

Maryland won all five games, extended its conference winning string to 20, and became the second ACC team to win three titles in a row. They were also the first Terp team to win 11 games and finished the regular season in fourth place, but a loss in their fourth straight bowl game dropped them to eighth in the AP poll.

Milt Ruffin ran in for Jim Tait's Richmond Spiders, but Mark Manges threw strikes to Dean Richards and Chuck White for a 14–7 halftime lead. Linebacker Brad Carr was in on 24 tackles to aid a 31–7 final. Halfbacks Doug Harbert and Ken Roy had interceptions, and tackle Ralph Fisher had five tackles in the backfield in West Virginia's 24–3 loss under new coach Frank Cignetti.

Tom Schick, out last season with a fractured leg, moved from tackle to guard against Syracuse to replace injured Mike Yeates with John Zernhelt taking his tackle spot, and Neal Olkewicz took over beside linebacker Jim Fotta to replace injured Mike Miller. John Stanford ran in an interception, but Bob Avery ran in twice for Syracuse, Bill Hurley once, and Ray Farneski hit Mike Jones to trail by seven with four minutes left. Steve Atkins scored a third time to win 42–28 and gained 215 yards for a school record.

Punter Mike Sochko picked up a high center snap at the nine and ran in for a safety in a driving rain, but Tony Serge's score and Gus Fernandez's conversion put Villanova ahead 9–6. The Terps ran 11 straight plays inside tackle where the footing was better and scored twice in the third period for a 20–9 win. Larry Seder replaced injured defensive guard Ernie Salley and had 14 tackles.

Tim Wilson made the go-ahead score to spoil Bo Rein's debut at North

Center Billy Bryan became the third Duke player to win the Jacobs Blocking Trophy twice (1975–1976).

Carolina State 16–6, but Atkins left with an injury and was replaced by Al Maddox. A Manges to Wilson pass put Maryland in front of Wake Forest, but James McDougald tied it at halftime. Maddox left hurt, but George Scott's fourth-quarter score put the Terps on top again. Mike McGlamry threw to Bill Millner and then to Solomon Everett for the two-pointer with 1:29 left, but tackle Joe Campbell, who had 14 tackles for the second consecutive game, sacked the quarterback on the final play to preserve a 17–15 win.

John Douglas, starting at defensive end for the first time, had an interception and sack in his seven tackles, while end Bob Raba caught two scoring passes in a 30–3 win over Duke. Derrick Ramsey threw to Charlie Dickerson and Randy Brooks for Kentucky, but Maryland put away Fran Curci's Cats with a steady 24–14 win.

The Terps finished with three shutouts, as Vince Kinney had scoring catches in Cincinnati's 21–0 loss and again in Clemson's 20–0 defeat. Lloyd Burruss started in the secondary for Harbert who was injured, Don Dotter came in to throw for a score against Virginia, and Ed Loncar converted four times in the 28–0 victory.

Houston led 21–0 in the Cotton Bowl on early scores by Dyral Thomas and Alois Blackwell, one after Mark Mohr blocked a punt. Manges ran one in, but a Danny Davis toss to Don Bass stretched it to 27–7 at the half. Manges threw to Eric Sievers and Wilson ran in, but Robert Lavergne's catch set up Lennard Coplin's field goal for a 30–21 win. "We haven't seen a team that quick," said Manges later. "They really took it to us that first quarter."

The Terps also had center Gene Ochap, guard Ed Fulton, and tackle Dave Conrad, backed by linemen Ted Klaube, Kerwin Wyatt, Mike Simon, end Rick Schmaltz, and backs Mickey Dudish and Steve Koziol. Defenders were end Chip Garber, guard Bruce Palmer, and Jon Claiborne and Chris Ward deep. Others on defense were ends Joe Muffler, Jim Shaffer, Mickey Pelanda, and Keith Calta, tackles Ken Watson and Charlie Johnson, guard Marlin Van Horn, linebackers Dave Odell and Brian Matera, and halfback Jim Ford.

Senior linemen Mark Cantrell, Craig Funk, Tom Burkett, Mark Griffin, and defenders Chuck Austin, Bill Perdue, Roger Shonosky, Ronny Johnson, and Russ Conley made the Tar Heels second at 4-1-0. Led by Rob Carpenter, Miami of Ohio went ahead on Fred Johnson's field goal and a Tom Zwayer dive, but a second score by Mel Collins won 14–10 over Dick Crum's Redskins. A trip to Tampa saw a 24–21 win over Florida. Again it was 10–7 at the half on Tom Biddle's field goal and Brooks Williams' catch from Bernie Menapace and Wes Chandler's catch for Florida, but short runs by Jimmy Fisher and Willie Wilder and two for North Carolina kept them apart by three.

Johnny Pont's Northwestern Wildcats were shut out 12–0, as Mark Bailey and Scott Yelvington were held to 70 yards on seven catches and Greg Boykin got even less rushing, but it took Mike Voight's four touchdowns and one by Menapace to down Army 34–32. Two Mike Castelli field goals and Leamon Hall's air strikes to Jim Merriken, Clennie Brundidge, and Tom Kuchar kept the Cadets jumping at West Point. Hall's 28 of 55 for 385 yards were all onc-game academy records, as his attempts erased Joe Caldwell's 1959 mark, his completions passed Tom Blanda's 1960 mark, and his yards passing exceeded Kingsley Fink's 1973 record.

Missouri scored in each quarter as Joe Stewart ran 11 yards, Pete Woods nosed in, Curtis Brown went 52 yards, and Tim Gibbons' field goal won 24–3 for Al Onofrio's squad. North Carolina State went in front after Richard Wheeler's interception, and then took a 21–0 lead on two second-period drives of 98 and 97 yards before Matt Kupec threw to Wayne Tucker and Voight's run ended it 21–13.

The Tar Heels got on target with a 12–0 win over East Carolina, as three Biddle field goals, the last with two minutes left after Walker Lee's catch, and Jeff Arnold's 49-yarder held off a last-period Mike Weaver run and Pete Conaty field goal. Biddle's four field goals kicked Wake Forest into submission 34–14, Voight took it in twice, and Del Powell set a school mark with a 98-yard kickoff return after James McDougald's first score for the Deacs.

Voight's 84-yard sprint sparked a 21–7 lead over Clemson at the half, as Tracy Perry ran in for the Tigers, and Steve Fuller closed it to seven at the end of three on a pass to Anthony King. Jimmy Russell kicked a field goal and Harold Goggins ran over for Clemson, but another touchdown by Voight ended it 27–23. Voight scored three more times and Billy Johnson added one in Virginia's 31–6 loss, with Ray Keys running in for the Cavaliers.

In the annual set-to with Duke, Tony Benjamin and Mike Dunn ran over for the Blue Devils, but Voight scored three times for a 21–19 halftime lead. Vince Fusco and Biddle swapped field goals and Voight and Dunn both scored a fourth touchdown, but with 37 seconds left Kupec threw to Johnson and Voight added to his 261 yards rushing with a two-point run to win another thriller 39–38.

Voight's 254 points and 3,971 yards gained were career tops at Carolina, but he missed the Peach Bowl due to an ankle injury in practice. After Jim Ramey's fumble recovery, Rod Stewart ran in the first of three last-half scores for a 21–0 Kentucky win.

Safety Bill Armstrong was Wake Forest's first consensus all–American in 1976.

Captain Bill Armstrong, the first consensus all–American at Wake Forest, brought them in third at 3-3-0. Virginia Tech won 23–6 with Moses Foster scoring on a Mitch Barnes toss. Paul Engle added three field goals, and Al Zyskowski's catch scored for Wake.

Bob Hely's two field goals edged North Carolina State 20–18, but Wake lost a close game at Nashville one week later. James McDougald ran 62 yards to a score, but a pair of Greg Martin field goals, touchdown runs by Adolph Groves and Dave Johnson, and Mike Wright's last-period score won for Fred Pancoast's Vanderbilt squad 27–24.

After Wake Forest downed Kansas State 13–0, Michigan runs by Rick Leach, Harlan Huckleby, and Rob Lytle, and a Bob Wood field goal beat the Deacs 31–0. McDougald had a record-setting 249 yards rushing in his first start against Clemson, and Harold Goggins and Jerry Butler's catch scored for the Tigers, but George Ervin's run and Hely's two field goals won it 20–14. McDougald and Ervin scored to lead Virginia at the half, but Andy

Hitt threw to Skip Browning and Andre Grier, and two Joe Jenkins field goals outstripped one by Hely in an 18–17 win for new coach Dick Bestwick's Cavs.

Mike McGlamry threw to Steve Young for another 14–0 lead at the half, but Mike Dunn's run and toss to Tom Hall for Duke never caught the Deacs. Jerry McManus and Jim Mach ran in for a 38–17 win, and Urban Eriksson's field goal beat South Carolina 10–7.

1977

The ACC celebrated its Silver Anniversary by having four of its teams participate in a bowl game. The first team to go bowling was conference champion North Carolina with a 5-1-0 record. Joe Bryant put Kentucky ahead at the half in the opener, but Matt Kupec's toss to Mike Finn gave the Tar Heels a last-quarter lead. After Fred Williams recovered a dropped punt, Derrick Ramsey went over on the fourth straight carry for a 10–7 win. Fullback Billy Johnson started the scoring in a 31–0 shutout of Richmond, as Bob Allen was downed in the end zone by linebacker Ricky Barden, and P. J. Gay came in and threw to split end Del Powell for a score.

Tailback Amos Lawrence scored on a 53-yard run to lead Northwestern 27–7 at the half, then threw to tight end Brooks Williams for a last-half score. Scott Stranski tossed to Todd Sheets and Sam Poulos converted for NU, and Clyde Christensen hit split end Walker Lee in a 41–7 final. Another 10–7 loss took place as Phil Farris ran over against Texas Tech, but Mark Johnson came in for injured Rod Allison and tied it on a third-quarter run, then Bill Adams kicked the Red Raiders home with a fourth-period field goal.

Carolina began its run for the title by beating Wake Forest 24–3. After Bob Hely's first-quarter field goal for Wake, safety Alan Caldwell ran 72 yards with a fumble recovery to put Carolina ahead for good, with Doug Paschal adding a fourth-quarter score. Against North Carolina State, linebacker Buddy Curry ran in a 31-yard interception and Bob Loomis scored before Johnny Evans threw to Lin Dawson and Ted Brown for State in a 27–14 Tar Heel win.

South Carolina was beaten 17–0, and Tom Biddle added a third field goal after Ken Mack's fumble recovery to down Maryland 16–7. Tracy Perry's score put Clemson ahead, but Lawrence ran 59 yards to put Carolina up 10–7 at the half. Lester Brown ran in for the Tigers, but

Biddle's second field goal tied it 13–13. Virginia's Joe Mark threw to Tom Champion and Mike Newhall and Russ Henderson converted in their 35–14 loss, but Lawrence had 286 yards rushing to set a school mark. Scott Wolcott kicked a field goal for Duke, but Biddle made three in a 16–3 win to even the series 30-30-4.

UNC's number one scoring defense of 7.4 points per game had the Liberty Bowl under control until Nebraska's Randy Garcia came in for Tom Sorley in the last period. Monte Anthony, I. M. Hipp, and Dodie Donnell carried the attack, but Curtis Craig's diving end zone catch ignited the Huskers. After Bill Mabry captured a fumble Dan Pensick grabbed one for UN, and Garcia tossed to Tim Smith for a 21–17 win as Billy Todd converted all three times.

UNC had center Scott Davison, guards Mike Salzano and John Rushing, tackles Steve Junkmann and Bobby Hukill, and flanker Mel Collins, backed by center Phil Ragazzo, guards Lowell Eakin and Don Lucas, tackles Ron Wooten and Hannon Fry, and end Jim Rouse.

On defense were nose guard Dave Simmons, tackles Rod Broadway and Dee Hardison, ends Ken Sheets and T. K. McDaniels, linebackers Bobby Gay and Rick Downs, and Bernie Menapace and Bobby Cale deep. Behind them were nose guard Bob Duncan, tackles Bunn Rhames and Donnell Thompson, ends Stan Lancaster and Lawrence Taylor, linebackers Steve Taylor and Ron Dowdy, Steve Streater, Frank Winters, Jay Faulkner, and Max McGee deep, and punter Johnny Elam.

Others were Jim Andrews, Mike Argo, Terence Burrell, Carey Casey, Billy Dunn, Jeff Grey, Carl Hackley, Rich Kleinman, Rolo Lassiter, Van Lippencott, Mitchell Strickland, and Rick Van Hoy.

Clemson at 4-1-1 was the second team to go to a bowl. After Rex Varn's 93-yard interception in the opener, Larry Dick tossed to Chuck White and Jim Hagan to win for Maryland 21–14. Georgia fell behind, but Jeff Pyburn threw to Jessie Murray and then to Pay Norris for a score with six seconds left, but the two-pointer was batted away for a 7–6 win. Pat Moriarty and Rodney Lee ran in for Georgia Tech, but Clemson had another double win over the border by giving Tech the biggest beating yet in the series 31–14.

Steve Fuller ran over and tossed to Rick Weddington to lead Virginia Tech 14–0, and Warren Ratchford's 68-yard run and Dwight Clark's catch made it 28–7 at the half, with Dennis Scott scoring for VPI. Obed Ariri's field goal and a Roscoe Coles run ended it 31–13. Ariri's three-pointers helped beat Virginia 31–0 and Duke 17–11, and Willie Underwood's 75-yard punt return set up Fuller's pass to Jerry Butler that overcame North

Carolina State 7–3, with Ariri arching four more skyward to defeat Wake Forest 26–0.

A record crowd of 54,189 was in Death Valley on a chilly day to see Notre Dame. The Irish wore green numerals and scored on a Jerome Heavens burst and Dave Reeve conversion, but Ariri's field goal and Fuller's rollout made it 10–7 at the half. Lester Brown ran in for a 17–7 lead as head linesman Bill Cummings backed into Ted Burgmcicr and kept him from making the tackle. Irish coach Dan Devine screamed and was flagged for unsportsmanlike conduct. A complaint on a clipping call brought another penalty, but after Mike Calhoun's fumble recovery Joe Montana made two fourth-period scores to win 21–17 and advance his reputation as one of the best comeback quarterbacks to play the game. Devine didn't let up on the official: "The linesman is a disgrace to football," he said.

After Clemson beat South Carolina 31–27 on Fuller's pass to Butler with 49 seconds to go, the Tigers were in the Gator Bowl with Pitt. Matt Cavanaugh threw three scoring passes to Elliott Walker and one to Gordon Jones as he broke between Steve Ryan and Bubba Brown. Bob Jury made two interceptions and Mark Schubert had two field goals for Jackie Sherrill's Panthers, while Ariri kicked a Gator Bowl record 49-yard field goal in the 34–3 loss.

North Carolina State tied for third with a 4-2-0 record and was the third team to play in a bowl. East Carolina went ahead in the first game as Leander Green sped 82 yards to a score and back-up Tommy Southerland ran for one and threw for two to make the crowd of 49,200 in the 90-degree heat at Raleigh even more uncomfortable. State's two last-period scores fell short 28–23 as a Rickey Adams catch was downed at the two with no time left.

The Pack put together two shutouts as Virginia was stopped twice inside the ten, and Syracuse did not cross mid-field until late in the fourth quarter. Ted Brown and Timmy Johnson scored to beat Virginia 14–0, Brown had three more in the 38–0 win over Syracuse, one on a 95-yard run for a school mark, and Billy Ray Vickers had over 100 yards rushing for the second straight game.

State's string of scoreless quarters went to ten before Wake Forest scored twice in the last half in a 41–14 loss. Al Maddox ran over and Ed Loncar kicked a field goal in each half for Maryland, but Brown scored twice, Jay Sherrill made a field goal, and Johnny Evans took it in with 27 seconds left for a 24–20 victory.

The Wolfpack invaded the Tiger lair in Alabama and came away with

North Carolina State punter, passer, and runner Johnny Evans capped his career with an MVP award in the 1977 Peach Bowl.

a 17–15 win over Auburn. Evans ran in and James Butler went 36 yards with a punt blocked by Jeff Easter, but a 23-yard run by Joe Cribbs and Sherrill's three-pointer made it 17–6 at the half. Jorge Portella kicked a fourth-quarter field goal for coach Dick Barfield, and John Crane connected on a 55-yarder to Byron Franklin, but Crane's two-point pass failed in a bid to tie the game.

State was flying high with five straight wins, but they lost three fumbles and two interceptions while bowing to the Tar Heels. A pair of 7–3 games followed as Clemson took the first one, and a Britt Parrish field goal scored for South Carolina. Brown ran in after Woodrow Wilson intercepted Ron Bass, and another steal by Richard Carter with 2:44 to go stopped a late Gamerooster rally.

After being dormant for two games, State's offensive might exploded against Penn State's defensive muscle. Jimmy Cefalo's catch led Sherrill's field goal at intermission, but Brown and Vickers scored for the Pack. Matt Suhey went in for the Lions, and Chuck Fusina's pass to Scott Fitzkee in the final minute won 21–17, but Brown's 251 yards rushing outdid his own school mark.

The offensive show continued as Evans tossed to Lin Dawson, but Scott Wolcott's field goal gave Duke a 17–14 halftime bulge. The wild third quarter saw Evans unload a 73-yard bomb to Elijah Marshall and Jon Hall run in a punt blocked by Marion Gale, but Duke went ahead 32–31 on Mike Dunn's tosses to Stan Broadie and Glenn Sandefur, only to see Brown's second score take it 37–32.

In the Peach Bowl, the Pack met Iowa State and Dexter Green, who had 1,074 yards and 1,240 yards rushing in each of the last two years, but Randy Hall's 77-yarder from Evans sparked State's 21–0 halftime lead. Terry Rubley was 10 of 12 in the first half, but Earle Bruce went with John Quinn who ran over in the fourth quarter and tossed to Greg Meckstroth to make the final 24–14.

Maryland tied for third and was the fourth team with eight wins in a bowl game. West Virginia led on Dave Riley and Cedric Thomas catches, but the Terps cut it to 24–16 as Ken Hatton was downed for a safety. Ed Loncar tied Penn State's Matt Bahr 3–3, but Chuck Fusina hit Jimmy Cefalo and Mike Guman and Tony Capozzoli tossed another to win 27–9, as PSU partisans paraded a bedsheet message around the stadium, "The Beast of the East is Back."

Syracuse was beaten 24–10, and Wake Forest's Tom Smith scored in their 35–7 defeat. Duke lost 31–13, and Ed Gall had 17 tackles as Villanova's Mike Chenet scored in a 19–13 loss. Richmond's Dave Taylor threw to Jesse Williams and Ken Tweedy, Larry Braun ran in a blocked punt, and a Dick Adams three-pointer came up short 27–24. After Virginia lost 28–0, an invitation to the first Hall of Fame game touched off a locker room celebration. In Birmingham, Marion Barber ran over and Paul Rogind converted for Minnesota, but two George Scott scores, one after Wendell Avery's fumble, won it 17–7.

1978

Second-year coach Charley Pell took Clemson to its first ACC title in more than a decade with a 6-0-0 record. In the 58–3 win over The Citadel, back-up Billy Lott had 139 yards passing against Art Baker's Bulldogs, and a student in a tiger uniform matched the team's points with push-ups—287 in all. Georgia won 12–0 a week later, as Rex Robinson kicked two first-half field goals and Jeff Pyburn threw to Carmon Prince. Lester Brown and Marvin Sims both scored twice in Villanova's 31–0 loss, and Steve Fuller's 75-yard run on the second play led to a 38–7 win over Virginia Tech, with Larry Fallen getting the VPI score on a 100-yard kickoff runback.

Brown and Fuller both scored twice in Virginia's 30–14 loss, and two fumble recoveries by linebacker Randy Scott led to Duke's 28–8 defeat. Safety Rex Varn ran in a 94-yard interception, and linebacker Bubba Brown was in on 17 tackles as the Wolfpack lost 33–10. Wake Forest under new coach John Mackovic went down 51–6, but the Tar Heels came to Death Valley ready for Tiger meat. Two Obed Ariri field goals outpointed one by Jeff Hayes to lead 6–3 at the half, but a Doug Paschal dive seesawed North Carolina back on top 9–6, only to have Brown's fourth-period score win it 13–9.

When Clemson met Maryland in November both were tied at the top. Maryland led 14–7 at the half as Al Maddox ran in and Mike Carney covered a blocked David Sims punt over the goal line. No sooner did Fuller tie it on an 87-yard pass to Jerry Butler than Steve Atkins put Maryland ahead with a 98-yard scoring scamper. Fuller came back with another third-period score on a 62-yarder to Dwight Clark for a 21–21 knot. Brown's fourth-period run put Clemson up by seven, but Ed Loncar's field goal closed it 28–24.

The Tigers took a 21–0 lead over South Carolina, then pushed it further as Tracy Perry scored for Clemson and Johnnie Wright for the Gamecocks, and Brown's third score made the final 41–23.

Charley Pell left for Florida, and Danny Ford took over in the Gator Bowl against Ohio State. Bob Atha kicked a field goal after Art Schlichter hit Ron Barwig and Doug Donley, but Fuller ran in for a 7–3 lead. Schlichter scored on a keeper, but end Steve Gibbs blocked Vlade Janakievski's extra point, and Ariri made it 10–9. Cliff Austin and Schlichter scored, but tackle Jim Stuckey stopped Schlichter's two-point run to keep it 17–15.

Nose guard Charlie Bauman's late interception by the Buckeye bench brought Woody Hayes after him. Ken Fritz tried to restrain his coach but was also punched. After meeting with OSU president Harold Enarson, athletic director Hugh Hindman announced Woody's retirement, and Clemson climbed to sixth in the final AP poll.

Clemson's 5,134 yards total offense made it the only Tiger team over 5,000 yards for one year, and its 427.8 yards per game made it the only one over a 400-yard average. Fuller ended his career with 6,096 yards total offense and 4,359 yards passing, and Brown had 17 touchdowns for the year, all Clemson records.

Clemson had center Jeff Bostic, guards Chris Dolce and Joe Bostic, tackles Billy Hudson and Steve Kenney, and Anthony King at end. Others were linemen Pat Fitzpatrick, John Murray, Ron West, Mark Thornton, ends Cliff Bray, Eric Young, Ed Abreu, and backs Harold Goggins, Warren Ratchford, Paul Williams, and J. D. Haglan.

On defense were nose guard Rich Tuten, tackle Toney Williams, end Jonathan Brooks, and Willie Jordan, Steve Ryan, and Bubba Rollins deep. Others were linemen Chip Pruett, Steve Durham, Chuck Rose, and Jeff Bryant, ends Dave Reed, Bob Goldberg, Bill Smith, and Rick Wyatt, and backs Willie Underwood, Eddie Gaethers, Perry Tuttle, Ogden Hansford, Al Latimer, Gary Webb, Jeff Soowal, and Jack Cain.

Maryland's 5-1-0 record was second. In the 31–7 opening win over Tulane, Tim O'Hare left-handed a touchdown to Eric Sievers and Lloyd Burruss returned a punt all the way. The Terps mishandled a kickoff and trailed Vince Gibson's Louisville squad, but a record crowd saw Maryland's wide tackle six defense and wide ends come to life late in the game. After Dean Richards evened it 17–17, Neal Olkewicz recovered a fumble on a hit by Charlie Johnson and Brian Matera, and Al Maddox ran in for a 24–17 win with 1:36 remaining.

The North Carolina game was also settled in the final period. Clyde Christensen completed to Wayne Tucker for a 20–15 Carolina lead, but after O'Hare threw 28 yards to Gary Ellis on second-and-28, Steve Atkins scored his second touchdown for a 21–20 victory.

Kentucky lost 20–3, but the Wolfpack provided the most exciting 25 seconds of the year. Scott Smith's run closed it to 10–7, but Atkins spread the lead to ten with a 98-yard kickoff runback. On the next kickoff Todd Benson knocked the ball from the receiver back into the end zone where Steve Trimble fell on it. The Terps now led 24–7 and went on to win 31–7. Maryland moved on to play their final game with Syracuse in Archbold Stadium which would be replaced next season with the Carrier Dome. After trailing 6–3, the Terps checked Joe Morris, SU's only freshman to run for 1,000 yards, and Dave Jacobs added a field goal in the 24–9 win. Seven

Opposite: **Rain didn't slow the passing arm of Clemson's Steve Fuller.**

turnovers beat Wake Forest 39–0, and Duke lost 27–0 as Ed Loncar had four field goals and Atkins scored five times in two games.

Number-five Maryland took its 12-game winning streak to play number-two Penn State, which had the nation's longest win streak of 16 games. A record crowd of 78,019 saw the Lions give up only a field goal in a 27–3 win, as Chuck Fusina threw a 63-yarder to Tom Donovan, Booker Moore ran in, and Matt Bahr added two field goals. But it was the defense of ends Larry Kubin and Joe Lally, backs Pete Harris and Don Bassett, middle guard Greg Jones, and linebackers Lance Mehl and Paul Suhey that Joe Paterno praised, especially Matt Millen and Bruce Clark at tackle. "They just whipped us," said Jerry Claiborne as his team had 32 yards rushing and suffered ten quarterback sacks and five interceptions.

Maddox scored twice to beat Virginia 17–7, but Maryland did not go ahead until the third period when Loncar made a field goal after Brad Senft recovered a fumble. O'Hare established a school total offense mark of 324 yards on 222 passing and 102 running.

Athletic director Carl James accepted the invitation of Jimmy Rogers, Jr., to play in the Sun Bowl, but they got whipped again. Texas won the toss but allowed the Terps to take the side with the wind which was gusting to 45 miles per hour. Dale Castro tried to punt into it, but after three possessions Texas was in front 21–0. Johnny "Lam" Jones ran in and caught a pass from Mark McBath, who got his job back after Randy McEachern replaced him, and A. J. "Jam" Jones scored the first of his two touchdowns. McBath also ran in, Johnny "Ham" Jones scored the last one, and Russell Erxleben converted each time. Texas had four interceptions and five sacks as guard Jim Yarbrough, tackle Steve McMichael, end Dwight Jefferson, linebacker Lance Taylor, and backs Ricky Churchman and Glenn Blackford kept the pressure on all afternoon to win 42–0.

North Carolina State was third at 4-2-0. Sam Harrell's 71-yard sprint for East Carolina and Scott Smith's score for State started the season, Billy Ray Washington added a 46-yard touchdown catch, but Nathan Ritter's five field goals stole the show in a 29–13 win.

Ted Brown's run and a Ritter field goal made it 10–0 against Syracuse, but Tim Wilson threw to Art Monk and a Dave Jacobs kick tied it at ten. Billy Ray Vickers boosted it to 17–10, but three more kicks by Jacobs turned it around 19–17. Ritter put the Pack up by one, and another Vickers touchdown gave State a 27–19 win.

Brown's three scores beat West Virginia 29–15, back-up Todd Baker threw 85 yards to Buster Ray in Wake Forest's 34–10 defeat, and in North

North Carolina State's Ted Brown, the ACC record holder in scoring, touch-downs, and yardage, gained more yards on the ground than many quarter-backs did through the air.

Carolina's 34–7 loss Brown became the sixth player in NCAA history with Ed Marinaro, Archie Griffin, Tony Dorsett, Earl Campbell, and Terry Miller to gain 4,000 yards rushing.

After interceptions by Ronnie Lee and Mike Nail and a safety by Kyle Wescoe and 14 tackles by Bill Cowher stopped South Carolina 22–13, the Pack met Penn State before 77,443 fans in Beaver Stadium. Matt Bahr's four field goals kicked PSU ahead, but the game was in doubt until Matt Suhey's late punt return won it 19–10.

Duke lost 24–10, Brown threw his first scoring pass to Fred Sherrill against Virginia, but Curtis Rein, the coach's brother, nipped the Cavs 24–21 on a punt return. Brown hung up his cleats as State's season leader with 1,350 yards rushing, and the ACC's top rusher with 4,602 yards, 49 touchdowns, and 312 points.

The Pack had the Tangerine Bowl all the way as Ritter kicked three field goals, one after Bubba Green's interception, and John Isley threw to Lee Jukes. Pitt ended it 30–17 as Mark Schubert made a field goal after Lindsay Delaney's toss to Ray "Rooster" Jones, and Fred Jacobs and Russ Carter scored late in the game.

North Carolina was fourth with 3-3-0. Ted Sutton and Bill Lamm's field goal scored for East Carolina in their 14–10 loss, and a third score by Fred Jacobs on Rick Trocano's pass gave Pitt a 20–16 win. Dick Crum lost 7–3 to his old team, Miami of Ohio, as flanker Don Treadwell hit Mark Mattison on a reverse to win for Tom Reed. Two Jeff Hayes field goals beat Dave Webber's pass to Eddie Wright and Wayne McMillan's run for Wake Forest 34–29.

Willie Scott scored for South Carolina, and Skip Ramsey had touchdown passes to Tim Gillespie and Horace Smith but could not overcome three Chuck Sharpe passes 24–22. Jesse Williams scored twice, James Short once, and Jeff Nixon ran in an interception as Richmond won 27–18. Dan Hottowe and Tommy Vigorito ran over, and Joe Mark threw to Jim Thelling in Virginia's 38–20 defeat.

Duke led 9–3 on three Scott McKinney field goals to one by Hayes, but the Tar Heels scored with 2:46 left, and Amos Lawrence ran 11 yards up the middle at 0:13 to pull it out 16–15.

1979

Georgia Tech joined the ACC this year, but 5-1-0 North Carolina State, with Outland winner Jim Ritcher at center, took the title. A crowd of 53,400 was on hand to see the facility renamed Carter-Finley Stadium at halftime, thanks to the gift of a field house by A. E. Finley. Down 17–13, State held East Carolina to minus eight yards rushing in the last half and won 34–20.

Greg Taylor scored for Virginia, but State led 31–7 at the half on three Scott Smith scores. Tommy Vigorito ran over twice and Todd Kirtley threw to Ted Marchibroda, but the Pack escaped with a 31–27 win. Billy Ray Vickers and Dwight Sullivan scored against West Virginia and Oliver Luck and Cedric Thomas ran over for WVU, but Smith scored three times for a 38–14 North Carolina State victory.

Jay Venuto tossed two touchdowns for Wake Forest and Smith ran in twice for the Pack, but the game was in doubt until Nathan Ritter's field goal won it 17–14 with 5:13 left. Mike Quick's catch led Auburn, but the crushing

Coach Pepper Rodgers sends in signals from third base for Georgia Tech.

ground game of Joe Cribbs and James Brooks and runs by Charles Thomas and Joe Sullivan overwhelmed the Pack 44–31.

State squeezed out a 7–0 win over Maryland, but the 54,200 fans at the North Carolina game broke the attendance mark set in the season opener. The Tar Heels took a 35–21 win, and Matt Kupec ended as North Carolina's career passing leader with 3,840 yards.

Center Jim Ritcher of North Carolina State, Outland Trophy winner in 1979.

After Smith's pass to Quick put the Pack ahead 13–3, Clemson rallied to tie the score, but Ritter's third field goal untied it 16–13 with 4:47 left. Billy Lott raced 39 yards to the four, but four tries on first-and-goal by Tracy Perry came up a yard short.

Another tough battle saw Smith match two scores by Spencer Clark of South Carolina, but George Rogers hammered away for 221 yards and a

Jay Venuto guided the 1979 Wake Forest team to its first bowl game in three decades, then set school marks the next year with 2,624 yards passing and 21 touchdowns.

touchdown. Wayne McLean and Chuckie Canady ran over for State, but Eddie Leopard's early field goal decided it 30–28. A field goal also won for Penn State 9–7. Smith went in to send the Raleigh crowd into ecstasy with a one-point lead and 1:18 to go. But Dayle Tate tossed to Terry Rakowsky, and Herb Menhardt's third field goal, a 54-yarder, stunned the fans to silence as they watched its arc graze the right upright and sail through to win.

Duke was done in 28–7, as Smith scored twice and McLean and Rickey Adams got the other two. Safety Eric Williams made three interceptions, with Stan Driskell tossing to Joel Patten for Duke.

State lined up with guards Chuck Stone and Chris Dieterich, tackles Todd Eckerson and Chris Koehne, and ends Lin Dawson and Lee Jukes. Behind them were center Frank Sisto, guards Earnest Butler and Doug Howard, tackles Chris Carr and Terry Moore, ends Curtis Rein and Todd Baker, and backs Eddie Jackson, Andre Marks, and Darnell Johnson. John Isley punted and Todd Auten kicked off.

Defenders were middle guard John Stanton, tackles Simon Gupton and Brian O'Doherty, ends David Horning and Joe Hannah, and linebackers Bob Abraham and Dann Lute. Halfbacks were Ronnie Lee and Donnie Le-Grande, with Woodrow Wilson and Mike Nail at safety. Backing them were middle guard Dennis Owens, tackles Bubba Green and Herman Bethel, ends Dave Shelton and Rick Etheridge, and linebackers Neal Musser and Marion Gale. Louie Meadows and Ken Perry were halfbacks, with Jeff Culler at safety.

Others were linemen Barry Amatucci, Ricky Bunch, Jim Butler, Martin Cornelson, Dave Fillippelli, Mark Freeman, Richard Learn, Rich Grube, Chuck Long, Bobby Martin, Jeff Nyce, Phil Piurkoski, Bill Powell, linebackers Don Ritter and Greg Steele, and deep men Nat Brown, Hillery Honeycutt, Ralph Sandello, and Perry Williams. Receivers were Steve Jones, Randy Phelps, Cleve Roberson, and Dee Whitley, with backs Sam Key, Larmount Lawson, and Calvin Warren.

Clemson was one of three teams to tie for second with 4-2-0. Danny Ford downed Furman 21–0 for his first regular-season win as players dehydrated in the 80-degree heat, but Maryland beat them 19–0 on Wayne Wingfield's 31-yard run and four Dale Castro field goals, one after Ralph Lary's interception. Georgia lost 12–7, as Buck Belue scored with nine seconds left but their onside kick failed. Virginia was beaten 17–7 on two Lester Brown touchdowns, Billy Lott tossed two scoring passes to Perry Tuttle to overcome Virginia Tech 21–0 in spite of the strong wind in Lane Stadium at Blacksburg, and Duke lost 28–10 on two Chuck McSwain touchdowns, with Greg Rhett's run and Scott McKinney's kick scoring for Duke.

McSwain scored two more against Wake Forest, as the Tigers pressured Jay Venuto in a 31–0 victory. "Every time I wanted to throw, all I saw was orange," lamented Venuto who was intercepted three times, once by Jeff Davis for a score. North Carolina lost 19–10, as Obed Ariri made four field goals, three after turnovers.

Notre Dame took a 10–0 lead on a Chuck Male field goal and Vagas Ferguson run, but Clemson struck back as Lott turned right end behind Mark Clifford's block and went 26 yards to score. The Tigers tied it on Ariri's field goal after Chuck Rose recovered a fumbled punt by Ty Dickerson. Ariri sent two more over the bar, and two late interceptions by Terry Kinard saved the 16–10 win.

Clemson closed the season in Columbia with a defeat by South Carolina. Ariri and Eddie Leopard battled each other with field goals, but Garry Harper threw to Ben Cornett for a 10–6 halftime lead. Another three-pointer by each of them finished it 13–9.

The Tigers made their third straight bowl appearance against Baylor in the Peach Bowl. Brown's run put Clemson in front, but Mike Brannan threw to Bo Taylor and Robert "Radar" Holt to lead 14–7 at the half. Ariri and Bob Bledsoe kicked field goals, but after Mickey Elam's 63-yarder to Walter Abercrombie, he threw to Ray Cockrell to make it 24–10. The crowd of 57,731 came to its feet when Andy Headen blocked Ron Stowe's punt and Jim Robinson recovered on the one. McSwain took it in and Lott threw a two-pointer to Jeff McCall with 20 seconds left for 24–18. Clemson grabbed the onside kick, but Doak Field's interception iced the game for Grant Teaff's Bears. Lott was sacked nine times—four by Andrew Melontree, as Mike Singletary, Lester Ward, Joe Campbell, Howard Fields, and Vann McElroy got to him all day.

Maryland was also in a second-place tie. Fumble recoveries by Tom Jensen and Tommy Fitzpatrick, and an Anthony Griggs interception led to three Villanova scores. Sam Johnson's punt return set up the first Maryland score, but Spencer Prescott evened it. Dale Castro and Chuck Bushbeck exchanged field goals, and Willie Sydnor's catch from Pat O'Brien gave Villanova a 17–10 halftime lead. The Terps tied it, but Bushbeck kicked Villanova in front with 6:39 left. After Mike Tice hit Mike Lewis, Charlie Wysocki scored his third touchdown with 54 seconds to go in a 24–20 win.

Donald Ray King scored in Emory Bellard's Mississippi State wishbone, but after Castro's fifth field goal James Jones went 92 yards on a kickoff return for a 35–14 win. Kentucky punter Randy Jenkins left with a broken leg, but Chris Poulton came in and kept Maryland backed up with his punts until late in the contest. Mike Shutt and Chris Jones guided Kentucky to a 14–7 win, as Tice threw to his brother, John, for the Terp score, and Andy Molls broke up a late pass and Larry Carter intercepted another to nail it down. "Their line didn't have quick feet," said Kentucky's Kevin Kearns, "so we'd fake one way and go another." Then Penn State won

Bill Ard started at offensive guard for three years at Wake Forest and then took over the same job for the Green Bay Packers.

27–7, as Bob Milkovich tossed the Terp touchdown, North Carolina State won, and Wake Forest gave them their fourth straight loss 25–17.

A 27–0 win over Duke turned the season around, and Castro's field goal with 1:21 left beat North Carolina 17–14. Stu Stram's pass to Mark Wilson scored for Louisville, but last-quarter runs won it 28–7, and Dick Bestwick, who axed the alumni game at Virginia, lost again 17–7, with Quentin Murray scoring for the Cavs.

Wake Forest was the third team to tie for second, and their three wins in three starts were the best since 1951. Jay Venuto's toss to James McDougald beat Appalachian State 30–23, and Georgia took a 21–13 halftime lead on Scott Woerner's interception, an Ed Guthrie run, and Norris Brown's catch, but Wake drove to a 22–21 win behind guard Bill Ard's charge. Nose guard Jim Parker picked up a handful of Athens turf when it was over and carried it home, and Venuto's 28 of 33 for 334 yards overcame East Carolina 23–20.

Virginia Tech scored on a Cy Lawrence dash and a Sidney Snell pass to Steve Casey, but Wake won 19–14 on Ronchie Johnson's late run. North Carolina's Amos Lawrence was held to 34 yards rushing as linebacker coach Dennis Haglan shouted "Close in on him," and Venuto unloaded to Al Kirby on a blitz to put Wake in front. After a safety, Donnie Jackson's fumble recovery clinched it 24–19. Joe Cribbs and James Brooks took Auburn to a 38–20 halftime bulge, but Wake charged back to lead 42–38, then won on a great defensive effort. Auburn marched to the 3-yard line where Carlos Bradley recovered a Charlie Trotman fumble with five minutes left, and Larry Ingram intercepted a pass in the final minute to hold the Tigers.

Duke's Cedric Jones scored on a 97-yard kickoff return on a soggy field and Craig Browning's 80-yard pass play, but the Deacs won 17–14 on a Frank Harnisch field goal with 17 seconds showing. South Carolina led on two Garry Harper tosses to Zion McKinney, and three Gamecock interceptions set up scores by George Rogers, Spencer Clark, and Percy Reeves. Venuto threw to Mike Mullen and Wayne Baumgardner at the close of each half in a 35–14 loss, and McDougald became Wake's career rushing leader with 3,910 yards.

In Orlando's Tangerine Bowl, Dave Woodley scored twice and Jerry Murphree once, and Don Barthel kicked two field goals in Charles McClendon's last game at Louisiana State. Benjy Thibodeaux nabbed Venuto's third interception and Lyman White got the third sack, and Steve Ensminger ran in a keeper for a 34–10 win.

1980

Fresh from a 17–15 Gator Bowl victory over Bo Schembechler's Michigan Wolverines, North Carolina won the conference title with a 6-0-0 record. Their terrific tailback tandem of Amos Lawrence and Kelvin Bryant were off to the races as they scored five times to beat Furman 35–13. Tim Tanguay made two field goals and Kevin Quinlan ran 94 yards with a recovered fumble for Dick Sheridan's Paladins. Jesse Garcia kicked Texas

Left: **"Famous Amos" Lawrence gained over 100 yards 25 different times while at North Carolina.** *Right:* **Kelvin Bryant scored 15 touchdowns in the first three games for North Carolina in 1981 before a knee injury knocked him out for over a month.**

Tech ahead, but a Jeff Hayes field goal tied it and Rod Elkins threw to Bryant for a 9–3 win.

After Joe Wilkins intercepted for Maryland, the Terps lost five fumbles to Carolina's linebacking corps of Lawrence Taylor and Calvin Daniels. Dale Castro's 50-yarder and Chris Havener's five catches were too little for the Terps, as Lawrence, Bryant, and Hayes did it again 17–3. The talented trio took the Tar Heels to a 17–0 lead over first-year coach Bill Curry and Georgia Tech, then Elkins hit Jon Richardson and Vic Harrison, and Joel Peeples was caught for a safety in the 33–0 shutout. Del Powell's catch scored against Wake Forest in a 27–9 win, with Wake scoring on a Phil Denfield field goal and Jay Venuto's toss to Kenny Duckett.

Steve Streater scored on a fake punt against North Carolina State, with Ron Laraway making the Pack score in a 28–8 loss. Ed Emory took over at East Carolina, but his team couldn't stop Lawrence and Bryant as both gained over 100 yards in a 31–3 triumph.

Oklahoma's wishbone was just as potent without Billy Sims, as J. C.

Quarterbacks thought twice when they looked into the linebacker eyes of North Carolina's Lawrence Taylor.

Watts scored three times, Dave Overstreet twice, Darrell Shepard once, and Michael Keeling converted five times for Barry Switzer's Sooners in a 41–7 win. In Clemson's Death Valley, the crowd roar rocked the stadium as Homer Jordan and Wilbur Bullard scored late, but four shots from the one in the last minute could not crack Carolina's defense of nose guard Paul

Davis, tackle Donnell Thompson, and Taylor at linebacker in a 24–19 Tar Heel win.

Two Hayes field goals led one by Virginia's Wayne Morrison, but Lawrence and Bryant put it away in the last half 26–3. Ben Bennett threw twice to Cedric Jones and scored once for Duke, but Lawrence and Bryant both scored twice and Billy Johnson once in a 44–21 win. "Famous Amos" joined Tony Dorsett as the only players to rush for 1,000 yards in each of their four years, and Lawrence became North Carolina's career rushing leader with 4,391 yards.

In the Bluebonnet Bowl, Herkie Walls ran 42 yards to the one where Mike Luck took it in for Texas. Lawrence scored after Mike Chatham's catch, and Mark Smith's sprint set up Bryant's go-ahead touchdown. Hayes added a last-half field goal after John Goodson fumbled a punt to win 16–7, and Carolina finished in tenth place.

The Tar Heels lined up with center Rick Donnally, guards Ron Spruill and Ron Wooten, tackles Mike Marr and Dave Drechsler, and end Shelton Robinson. Backing them were center Bill Lippincott, guards Steve McGrew and Clay Hassard, tackles Mark Sugg and Brian Blados, end Doug Sickels, and backs Walt Sturdivant and Dan Bunn.

On defense were tackle Harry Stanback, linebackers Darrell Nicholson and Lee Shaffer, supported by Jack Parry at nose guard, tackles John Brugos and Darryl Lucas, and linebackers Chris Ward, Jeff Pierce, Mike Wilcher, and Kris Keeney. Deep men were Tyress Bratton, Greg Poole, and Bill Jackson, backed by Dave Singleton, Sammy Johnson, Willie Harris, Larry Winters, and Rocky White.

Others were Alan Burrus, Ron DeMarco, Travis Freeman, Butch Griffin, Jimbo Harrell, Mike McCormick, and Bill Sheppard.

Maryland was 5-1-0 and placed second. On the opening kickoff to Villanova, Sam Johnson smacked Dave Martin and Howard Eubanks grabbed the ball in mid-air. Charlie Wysocki scored on the fifth play, and Chuck Bushbeck kicked a second-period field goal after John Kreider intercepted. Villanova's three down linemen, Howie Long, Paul Phillipy, and Joe Makoid, were tough in the last half and the game ended 7–3. Mike Lewis caught a 46-yard scoring pass from Mike Tice for the first points against Vanderbilt, and Tice tossed to Eric Sievers for the last one in a 31–6 final. After Mike Woodard's second field goal trimmed it to 14–6, Wayne Wingfield took it in after Johnson returned the kickoff 97 yards for the longest non-scoring kickoff return in ACC history.

West Virginia hosted Maryland with a new coach, Don Nehlen, and a new 50,000-seat stadium, but the Terps won 14–11. Wysocki ran in twice, with WVU scoring on Steve Sinclair's field goal and Oliver Luck's pass to Billy Evans and two-pointer to Dave Johnson.

Dan Marino tossed twice to Dwight Collins and once to Willie Collier in a 38–9 Pitt victory. Randy McMillan ran over, and Pat McQuaide covered an end-zone fumble for Pitt's last score. Dale Castro and Dave Trout traded three-pointers, and Chris Havener's catch made it 24–9 after three periods. Mike Muller ran back an interception 44 yards to the Pitt one when time ran out.

Maryland returned home after three road games to tie Herb Menhardt's field goal for Penn State with one by Castro. Wysocki put the Terps in front, but Booker Moore's 55-yard run evened it again. The Lions took a 24–10 win on a Todd Blackledge toss to Kenny Jackson and a Jonathan Williams connection to Mike Meade.

After three losses to top ten teams, the Terps took an 11–10 win from Wake Forest. Castro and Wingfield combined to give Maryland a 9–0 halftime lead, but Wayne McMillan's run and Phil Denfield's field goal put the Deacs ahead by one at the end of three. Lightning knocked out the scoreboard in the fourth quarter, and a Castro punt rolled dead at the two in a driving rain. Linebacker coach John Devlin called for a blitz, and Mark Wilson dropped Jay Venuto in the end zone for the winning points.

Ben Bennett was on target with a touchdown to Marvin Brown, and Greg Boone's halfback pass to John Brinkman gave Duke a 14–0 first-quarter lead. Brent Dewitz came in to direct a comeback as Wysocki carried 50 times for an ACC mark and scored twice to tie it. Castro's kick cut the knot 17–14, and Lloyd Burruss, Joe Wilkins, and Mike Muller intercepted to slow Duke's aerial attack.

Maryland ended with three impressive wins. Ed Gall came up with a fumble to start the scoring against North Carolina State, and Wilson had a quick score by stealing a pass behind the goal. The Pack's 24–0 shutout halted their scoring streak at 112 games, third to Oklahoma's 123 games and Notre Dame's 131 games. After beating Clemson 34–7, the locker room went wild as John Shelton and Herb Hinely were hoisted aloft to extend their invitation to the Tangerine Bowl from the shoulders of the team. Tim Whittie scored in Virginia's 31–0 loss, and Wysocki's 1,359 yards rushing broke Maryland's single-season record of 1,261 yards set by Steve Atkins in 1978 and his 334 carries were an ACC high for one year.

Castro kicked three field goals in the Tangerine Bowl, but Wayne Peace threw to Cris Collinsworth and James Jones ran in to give Florida a 14–9 lead. After Roger Sibbald fumbled the last-half kickoff, Wysocki scored and Castro's fourth field goal made it 20–14. The Gators regained the lead 28–20 as Peace wedged in and hit Collinsworth again. After Sonny Gilliam forced a fumble, Johnell Brown ended it 35–20 as Brian Clark converted each time.

North Carolina State finished third at 3-3-0. Rookie coach Monte Kiffin promoted Pack football with youthful enthusiasm, as he donned a Lone Ranger outfit complete with mask and big palomino. Then he rode across the campus to the student union and invited students to the annual spring football scrimmage. Later in the season, he arrived in a helicopter and fought a few good-natured rounds with former heavyweight champion Joe Frazier.

The season started with Eddie Jackson and Wayne McLean both scoring twice to beat William and Mary 42–0. Virginia scored on Tommy Vigorito's run and catch from Todd Kirtley, but Tol Avery threw to Mike Quick and Dwight Sullivan's run tied it. Avery's run and two Nathan Ritter field goals closed it 27–13, and Vigorito ended second in career rushing at Virginia with 2,913 yards.

State lost three of its next four games. Jay Venuto's toss to Wayne Baumgardner and Phil Denfield's field goals gave Wake a 13–0 halftime lead, but Avery's third-period run cut it to six. Venuto tossed to Kenny Duckett and Baumgardner for a 27–7 win, and Venuto ended as Wake's top passer with 5,251 career yards. South Carolina gave State its second straight defeat 30–10, as George Rogers scored three times and went on to win the Heisman.

Before their third loss, the Pack took a disputed win from Appalachian State 17–14. After Todd Baker's catch won it, Steve Brown and Rick Beasley connected but the catch was ruled out of the end zone, and a Mark French field goal failed with 33 ticks to go. The uproar didn't end at the gun, as the TV showed for a week that Beasley was two steps inside on the controversial call.

State's defensive work beat Clemson 24–20. Rich Hendley was downed in the end zone by Darryl Harris on an attempted punt, and Jim Butler ran in a punt blocked by Vaughan Johnson for the win.

Kevin Baugh's catch set up a quick score by Booker Moore for Penn State, and Todd Blackledge threw to Kenny Jackson and Brad Scovil in a 21–13 win after the Pack narrowed it to one. Avery tossed touchdowns to Quick, McLean, and Lin Dawson to beat Duke, but the defense was tough again as Neal Musser and Dave Shelton intercepted and Perry Williams

Clemson's Danny Ford tells it like it is on the sideline.

recovered a fumble. Ben Bennett tossed twice to Chris Castor, and Ron Frederick threw to Brent Clinkscale in Duke's 38–21 loss. In the finale, Anthony Collins returned the opening kickoff 97 yards and Ted Sutton's run gave East Carolina an early lead, but Avery's run and Ritter's field goal made it 14–10 at halftime, and second-half runs by Jackson, McLean, and Andre Marks won for the Wolfpack 36–14.

1981

With 53 lettermen back, including all 11 offensive starters, Clemson's six wins swept the ACC and finished first nationally. Danny Ford, at 34, became the youngest coach to gain the title, and Tiger paws were painted everywhere in Pickens County.

Homer Jordan quarterbacked Clemson's 1981 national champions.

When Villanova gave up football this year, Clemson athletic director Bill McLellan asked coach Tom Sasser at Wofford to be a replacement. Don Hairston kicked Wofford in front, but Nigerian Donald Igwebuike evened it with a 52-yarder on his first college try. Homer Jordan and Perry Tuttle hooked up for 80 yards to put Clemson ahead, Frank Magwood caught another from Jordan, and Wofford's Barry Thompson threw to Dirk Derrick in their 45–10 loss.

Playing inside on artificial turf in a night game were all firsts for Clemson, but the seniors did not let the Superdome's instant replay and the sights of New Orleans in the long afternoon distract them from the game. Tulane

Linebacker Jeff Davis set a school mark with 175 tackles in Clemson's 1981 championship season.

led on Vince Manalla's field goal and a safety as punter Dale Hatcher fell on a bad center snap. Clemson caught them before the half when Cliff Austin scored after Joe Glenn's fumble recovery. Bob Paulling kicked it to 13–5, and linebacker Jeff Davis led defenders with 20 tackles.

When defending national champ Georgia came to Death Valley, they were cresting a 15-game winning streak. The team wanted to wear their special pants, but Ford wanted to save them for South Carolina. He did an about-face when Ray Brown echoed the sentiment of the players for the Georgia game, "You bring your silver ones and we'll bring our orange ones and see what happens."

The first half saw Jeff Suttle grab a Herschel Walker fumble and 62,446 fans rise as one when Jordan tossed to Tuttle for six after Tim Childers intercepted. Igwebuike made it ten when middle guard William Perry, who alternated with William Devane, recovered another Walker fumble. Kevin Butler's field goal after Buck Belue threw to Lindsay Scott and one by Igwebuike ended it 13–3. "This is the best I've ever felt after a football game," said defensive tackle Dan Benish, and Tiger fans celebrated far into the night.

A crowd of 57,453 came to Commonwealth Stadium in Lexington to see Clemson take on Kentucky. Tom Griggs booted Youkay ahead, but

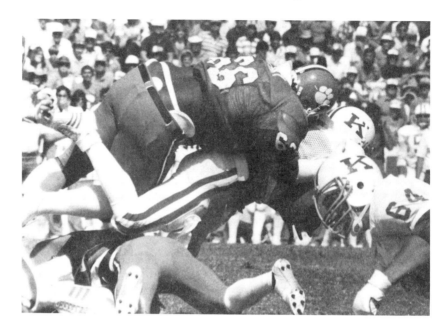

Clemson's William Perry about to deflate a Kentucky player with 310 pounds pressure.

Kevin Mack's third-quarter dash put Clemson ahead for keeps. Jordan scored after Andy Headen at end recovered Rich Abraham's fumble, and Chuck McSwain got another in a 21–3 conquest. Linebacker Danny Triplett spoke bluntly about Kentucky's five turnovers, "The harder you hit them, the harder it is for them not to fumble," and Clemson cracked the top ten for the first time.

The Tigers now turned their attention to conference rivals. Jeff McCall scored in the homecoming game, but the rugged defense resented the field goals they had given up and shut out Virginia 27–0. "Our goal was to keep them from scoring," stated defensive end Bill Smith as Clemson moved up to sixth. Executive director Mickey Holmes remembered the Tigers' earlier visit to New Orleans and considered inviting them to the Sugar Bowl. "When they came down here for the Tulane game, the Clemson people brought a bunch of $2 bills with Tiger paws on them," he mused, "and for the next week after that the Clemson fans were the talk of the town."

Duke coach Red Wilson was glad to see Clemson come to Durham because their high ranking would draw big, but the Tigers came to avenge Duke's victory in Death Valley a year ago. "They made some derogatory comments about us after last year's game," said offensive tackle Lee Nanney. It showed in the score, as Brendon Crite ran in to start a 38–10 win, but Ben Bennett ended 18 quarters of not yielding a touchdown with a toss to Cedric Jones. The Tigers jumped to fourth place, then chewed up North Carolina State 17–7. The defense surrendered its first score on the ground as Larmount Lawson put State ahead, but got no more even with five turnovers.

Clemson climbed to the heady atmosphere of number three and prepared for Wake Forest. Gary Schofield's pass to Kenny Duckett kept Wake in it for a quarter, but 35 points and a Deac score by Carlos Cunningham gave Clemson an insurmountable 49–14 halftime lead. Mike Gasque's pass and scores by Duke Holloman and Craig Crawford made the total 82–24, and Clemson crept to number two.

The 82 points broke a 27-year-old ACC mark, and the 756-yard total offense and 12 touchdowns were single-game Clemson records. Tiger mascot Ricky Capps kept pace with push-ups on each score, but didn't get up after 382 as it was probably a record too.

It was a big football weekend in tobaccoland as Penn State was in Raleigh to play the Wolfpack, and 28 miles away in Chapel Hill 53,611 fans filed into Kenan Stadium to see Clemson battle North Carolina for the conference crown. With the standing room only crowd were representatives from eight bowl events who were scouting these teams for a bowl game at the end of the season.

The war in the trenches lasted into the second quarter when Brooks Barwick booted a field goal after gimpy Rod Elkins got the Tar Heels close. Clemson came back on McCall's score at the end of an 81-yard march, but Carolina cut it to 7–5 when Danny Barlow blocked a punt out of the end zone. Igwebuike doubled the score with a second-half field goal but Barwick trimmed it to 10–8 when Kelvin Bryant was stopped by Davis, who had arms like Popeye and was named "the Judge" for taking charge. Clemson kept the lid on as Scott Stankavage came in but Perry dropped him for a big loss, and Perry and Davis forced Stankavage into a bad lateral to Alan Burrus which Davis covered. On the sideline, Dick Crum could not conceal his disappointment at losing a share of the league title.

Clemson's seniors beat Maryland for the first time 21–7, as Jordan threw two touchdowns to Tuttle and one to Jerry Gaillard, and the fans pelted the field with oranges in anticipation of an Orange Bowl trip. In the game at Columbia, Johnnie Wright's run had the South Carolina crowd jumping. They were still thinking upset when Paulling missed a conversion

for the first time after Rod McSwain blocked a Chris Norman punt covered by Johnny Rembert. But Paulling silenced them with a field goal and Jordan ran over for 15–7 after Hollis Hall intercepted. Gordon Beckham's pass to Horace Smith cut it to two, but two McSwain scores ended it 29–13. The Tiger Rag was heard all the way home, and Clemson moved into first place as the only unbeaten team when Penn State beat Pitt.

Director George Dostal's sign hung in the training room all summer: "Tigers 11–0. In the Orange Bowl vs. Nebraska." Now it had come true. Clemson was in the Orange Bowl with Nebraska and its Outland winner center Dave Rimington. But before they left for Miami, Pepsi-Cola vice-president Mark Avant toasted them with special cans of orange soda covered with purple Tiger paws.

Igwebuike's field goal opened the scoring after Mark Mauer's fumble, but Mike Rozier's halfback pass to Anthony Steels put the Huskers ahead, and Kevin Seibel converted. Igwebuike trimmed it to one after Jeff Krezci broke up a pass and Jeff Stockstill was interfered with. Jordan led Clemson down the field when Nebraska had to punt after the kickoff, but Sammy Sims tipped one pass and Ric Lindquist intercepted for a touchback. After Phil Bates fumbled, Austin ran in to bring the score to 12–7 and put the Tigers in front for good.

In the last half, Tuttle got behind Allen Lyday for 19–7 to end as Clemson's top receiver with 2,534 career yards, and Igwebuike added three when Billy Davis returned a Grant Campbell punt 47 yards. Mauer tossed to Jamie Williams after the kickoff, but again Nebraska had to punt. Roger Craig high-stepped over for 22–15 after Irving Fryar's fair catch, and no one doubted who was numero uno.

The Tigers lined up with center Tony Berryhill, guards James Farr and Brian Clark, tackle Brad Fisher, and Bubba Diggs at end. Tackle Jeff Bryant led the defense with 19 tackles for losses and eight sacks, and Terry Kinard and Anthony Rose were deep. Others were Kendall Alley, Vernie Anthony, Dave Bounds, Nick Bowman, Gary Brown, Ken Brown, Lockie Brown, Roy Brown, Brian Butcher, Dean Day, Randy Cheek, Pete Demery, Joe Ellis, Rich Hendley, Randy Learn, Otis Lindsey, Bob Mayberry, Eldridge Milton, Anthony Parete, Ed Pickett, Mark Richardson, and Scott Williams.

North Carolina came in second at 5-1-0. Former lineman Ken Saylor reported two suspicious observers at practice, but it did not matter as Kelvin

Opposite: **The New York Giants liked the pass-stealing talent of Clemson's Terry Kinard and drafted him in the first round.**

Gary Schofield ended in 1983 with 44 touchdown passes to set a career mark for Wake Forest quarterbacks.

Bryant's six scores set an ACC record in the 56–0 win over East Carolina. Bryant had five more to beat Miami of Ohio 49–7, as John Appold hit Bailie Morlidge and Mike Kiebach converted for Miami. Bryant added four more in the 56–14 Boston College loss, with Dennis Scala tossing to Brian Brennan and Doug Guyer throwing to Brian Krystoforski for Jack Bicknell's Eagles.

Rod Elkins scored once and Tyrone Anthony twice as Georgia Tech was beaten 28–7, but Bryant was lost with an injured knee. Ronny Cone ran in for the Ramblin' Wreck, and Mike Kelley ended as Tech's passing leader with 5,219 career yards. Gary Schofield tossed to Bill Ruffner and Phil Denfield kicked a field goal for Wake Forest, but Elkins threw two touchdowns to Shelton Robinson and Greg Poole ran in a 66-yard interception in a 48–10 triumph.

North Carolina State led 10–0 on Tol Avery's pass to Rufus Friday and Todd Auten's field goal, but failed to collar the last-half onside kickoff. Alan Burrus ran over ten plays later, and Walter Black blocked a punt and had an interception in the 21–10 Tar Heel win. "There have been other disappointments," sobbed a tearful Monte Kiffin, "but not like this one." Jim Seawright's 12 solo tackles led South Carolina's 31–13 win. Gordon Beckham hit DeWayne Chivers, Kent Hagood, and Todd Berry, Ken

Stafford ran in, and Mark Fleetwood added a field goal for the Gamecocks. Scott Stankavage tossed to Larry Griffin for one Tar Heel score, and Jeff Hayes added another with a 79-yard run on a fake punt.

Bill Pugh's catch put Maryland ahead, but Scott Stankavage hit Anthony in the last minute for a 17–10 win. Gordon Whitehead threw to Greg Taylor and Henry Johnson for Virginia, but the Tar Heels tied it, then won it 17–14 on a Brooks Barwick field goal, and Duke lost 31–10 with Ron Sally throwing for the Duke score.

The Gator Bowl started sunny but turned into the fog bowl. It was 7–3 as Brad Taylor threw to Derek Holloway for Arkansas, but Gary Anderson lost a punt in the fog and the ball hit Mike Harris. Larry James covered it and Bryant took it in, but Bruce Lahay's field goal tied it at ten. Ethan Horton scored twice in the last half, but Lou Holtz's club had the fans stomping with a last-minute comeback. After Jessie Clark ran in, Ed Jackson fell on the onside kick and Taylor tossed to Darryl Mason before they ran out of gas 31–27. North Carolina's ninth-place finish made it the first time two ACC teams ended in the top ten.

Maryland came in third at 4-2-0. Vanderbilt beat them 23–17 in the opener as Whit Taylor tossed two scoring passes and Mike Woodard kicked three field goals. Boomer Esiason got his first start as both quarterbacks were injured, but the Terps lost 17–13 to West Virginia with 3:52 left in the game. Oliver Luck ran in for the win after Rich Hollins recovered a punt fumbled by Lendell Jones and Jon Simmons was flagged for pass interference.

North Carolina State was handled easily 34–9, as Mike Lewis scored on a reverse and caught a pass from Esiason. Boomer also tossed a touchdown to John Tice, John Nash ran one in, and Jess Atkinson kicked two field goals for the second straight week.

Maryland led Syracuse on Esiason's passes to Lewis and Russ Davis, with Atkinson and Gary Anderson making the three-pointers. But the 17–3 lead vanished on two Dave Warner tosses to Villanova transfer Willie Sydnor and two-point hookup to Marty Chalk for a 17–17 tie with 16 seconds to go. Maryland also led Florida, but Kyle Knight downed Esiason for a safety to take an 8–7 lead. An option pass from fullback James Jones to quarterback Wayne Peace widened it to 15–7, and the Gators went on to a 15–10 verdict.

In the Wake Forest free-for-all, the Deacons drove deep on the first possession but Bill McFadden returned an interception 97 yards for Maryland's initial score. Joe Brkovich was on the end of six completions,

With Ben Bennett at the controls at the start of the 1980s, Duke fans felt they had a chance to win any game at any time.

as the Terps never trailed but the score was tied at 17–17, 24–24 and 31–31 with a 45–33 final. The Deacs had 556 yards passing for a school mark, and Gary Schofield threw for an ACC record of 504 yards, with 161 going to Tommy Gregg.

Ben Bennett's toss to Cedric Jones put Duke ahead, but Tim Quander tied it with a 92-yard kickoff runback. Charlie Wysocki went in twice, Atkinson kicked a field goal, and Mike Atkinson's score for Duke made the halftime 24–14. Another Bennett-to-Jones connection ended it 24–21, as Scott McKinney's last-second field goal was wide. Linebacker Darnell Dailey had 18 tackles against Tulane in a losing cause, but Mike McKay completed two touchdown passes to Marvin Lewis and Reggie Reginelli for a 14–7 conquest. Wysocki scored four times in Virginia's 48–7 loss to become Maryland's leading career rusher with 3,317 yards, and Esiason's 122 completions broke Dick Shiner's 1962 season mark by one.

1982

Clemson repeated as conference champion with six more wins but was shaky at the start. After Homer Jordan's score against Georgia in the first game, Stan Dooley carried in a punt blocked by Dale Carver, and Kevin Butler's two field goals won it 13–7. The Tigers took a 14–0 lead over Boston College, but Troy Stradford's run and a Doug Flutie pass to John Schoen tied it. Field goals by Kevin Snow and Donald Igwebuike made it a 17–17 final.

Clemson had four turnovers in its first six possessions, and the Western Carolina Cats of Bob Waters had a 10–9 halftime lead on Ronnie Mixon's passes and a Dean Biasucci field goal. Option quarterback Mike Eppley came in and guided the Tigers to a 21–10 win. "It's similar to running a fast break," said Eppley about the option play. Eppley was Clemson's point guard on the basketball team and the only two-sport starter in the NCAA's Division I.

Clemson president Bill Atchley benched Jordan pending an investigation into a 1982 Chevrolet Monte Carlo bought by Jordan. Eppley led the Tigers to a 24–6 win over Kentucky, now coached by Jerry Claiborne, with George Adams tossing to Rob Mangas for the Youkay score. Rookie coach George Welsh and Virginia lost 48–0, as Chuck McSwain whizzed 82 yards down the sideline for a score.

No one slept with Ben Bennett throwing as his toss to Chris Castor and a Joel Blunk run were early points for Duke, but Cliff Austin had three scores and 260 yards rushing to break Don King's 1952 record of 234 yards. Johnny Rembert ran in an interception, and Anthony Parete connected with K. D. Dunn and Frank Magwood in a 49–14 win.

The nation's only two-sport starter in 1982 was football quarterback and basketball guard Mike Eppley.

Austin and Jeff McCall both scored twice in the 38–29 defeat of North Carolina State. Joe McIntosh ran in twice for the Pack, Tol Avery threw to Dave Davis and Stan Davis for two State scores, and Mike Cofer and Igwebuike added field goals, with Igwebuike's sailing over from 55 yards away. Another rip-roaring battle took place as Brooks Barwick kicked two field goals for North Carolina and Bob Paulling kicked two for the Tigers. An Eppley-to-Magwood pass put Clemson ahead at the half, but a Scott Stankavage toss to Arnold Franklin tied it. Paulling put it away 16–13 with another kick, and Ray Brown covered a fumble to thwart a Tar Heel threat.

Clemson and Maryland were both unbeaten in conference play, and 51,750 filled Byrd Stadium to see which team would take over first place. The Tigers went in front after two short punts by Alan Sadler, but Rick Badanjek scored for the Terps. Kevin Mack ran in and Paulling's field goal gave Clemson a 24–7 lead early in the last quarter. The Terps quickly closed it to 24–22 on a Boomer Esiason toss to Greg Hill and another score by Badanjek. Dale Hatcher was the only player besides Ray Guy and Russell Erxleben to kick a ball into the overhead gondola at the Superdome, but the wind bit off his punt. John Tice's 11th catch set a Terrapin record, but safety Terry Kinard knocked the ball loose and cornerback Reggie Pleasant fell on it. Linebacker Danny Triplett sacked Boomer and Billy Davis intercepted him to nail it down.

After a 24–6 win over South Carolina and coach Richard Bell, Clemson downed Wake Forest at the Mirage Bowl in Tokyo. The game was named for a car built by Mitsubishi Motors which displays two behind each end zone and rings the stadium with its red and white corporate banners. Wake's Gary Schofield threw to Tim Ryan on an 85-yarder, but Clemson had the 80,000 fans yelling "Dewhence, Dewhence" as they made a late goal line stand to turn back the Deacs 21–17.

The Tigers' Tokyo trip took the sting out of no post-season games for violations of the NCAA code, but Clemson's nine wins in a row put them eighth. Jordan's 3,643 yards was third among Clemson's career passers, and Kinard set a school mark with 17 career interceptions. Steve Griffin's 19.1-yard average led in kickoff returns, end Ed Pickett led the team in tackles for losses with ten, and tackle Jim Scott was the sack leader with six.

Clemson starters were center Cary Massaro, guards James Farr and Brian Butcher, tackles Gary Brown and Bob Mayberry, and ends Jeff Stockstill and Bubba Diggs. On defense were middle guards William Perry and William Devane, tackles Dan Benish, Jim Robinson, and Vernie Anthony, Andy Headen and Joe Glenn at end, linebackers Otis Lindsey and Mark Richardson, halfbacks Ty Davis, Ron Watson, and Van Arrington, with Tim Childers and Jeff Suttle deep.

Others who saw action were Kendall Alley, Rick Bailey, Roy Brown, Rich Butler, Andy Cheatham, Brendon Crite, Rich Donaldson, Stacey

Maryland's Rick Badanjek steps out of the grasp of the Wolfpack's Mark Franklin.

Driver, Terrence Flagler, Bob Frierson, Rich Hendley, Alex Hudson, Reid Ingle, Randy Learn, Rod McSwain, Dave Noelte, Steve Reese, Chuckie Richardson, Sonny Sealy, Dale Swing, Jeff Wells, Braxton Williams, Scott Williams, and Jim Wurst.

Maryland's two-point loss to Clemson dropped them to second with

5-1-0. A crowd of 84,597 was in Beaver Stadium to see Penn State get off to a good start on the way to the national title, but before it was over the Terps made the first step a rocky one. Massimo Manca kicked a field goal after Roger Jackson blocked a punt on the fourth play, but Jess Atkinson evened it before the quarter was over. Manca made another three-pointer after Harry Hamilton's interception, and Todd Blackledge threw to Curt Warner after Greg Gattuso fell on a fumble for 13–3. Willie Joyner went over for the Terrapins, but Blackledge tossed to Kenny Jackson to make the halftime 20–10. Boomer Esiason and Russ Davis hooked up on a 50-yarder after Lendell Jones intercepted, but Manca's kick kept the Lions in front 23–17. Maryland led by one on Esiason's 60-yarder to Davis, but Blackledge connected on two game-winning blows to Gregg Garrity and Jackson to put the Terps on the ropes 36–24. Mike McCloskey's catches kept the Terps off balance, and another Joyner run and Manca's fourth field goal ended it 39–31.

Maryland lost another tough one in Morgantown on Mountaineer Field a week later. The Terps scored first as Jeff Hostetler was assessed two points for intentionally grounding a pass in the end zone. Two Paul Woodside field goals put West Virginia ahead, but Esiason's pass to Davis made it 9–6 at the half. Woodside kicked it into a tie, and Atkinson's kick opened it to three again. Hostetler threw to Rich Hollins and Woodside's fourth three-pointer gave WVU a 19–12 lead. Rick Badanjek crashed over for his first college touchdown with 1:39 left, but Darryl Talley and Ed Hughes rushed Boomer on the conversion. His pass to Ron Fazio failed for a 19–18 defeat, and the fans whooped and hollered long after the game was over.

Bobby Ross made his coaching debut at home with a 23–6 win over North Carolina State, as the Terps held State to zero yards rushing and tackle Mark Duda was the ACC defensive player of the week. Syracuse lost in the Carrier Dome 26–3, as John Nash and Dave D'Addio scored to give Maryland a 20–0 lead at halftime for the second straight week, and Atkinson topped last week's three field goals with four more. The Orangemen crossed mid-field once in each half, as guard Mike Corvino, the ACC defensive player of the week, stopped them the first time with a sack and recovered fumble, but Russ Carpentieri made a field goal on the second try. Syracuse gained only 23 yards on the ground, and Jim Gross picked off Todd Norley's last-period pass to smother another attempt.

Greg Hill and Darryl Emerson had scoring catches in the 38–0 win over the Indiana State Sycamores under Dennis Raetz, but Wake Forest made a game of it before losing 52–31. The teams went up and down the field for 983 yards total offense, as Mike Ramseur scored four times for coach Al Groh, Nash had three for Maryland, and guard Ron Solt was the ACC's offensive lineman of the week. The offensive fireworks had the hometown crowd cheering for the third consecutive week as Duke lost 49–22. Tim Quander ran back the kickoff 74 yards to set up Esiason's touchdown toss to Hill, and Jones had two of his four interceptions in the opening period to run the score to 29–0. John Tice added another, while Duke's Joel Blunk ran in and Ben Bennett threw to Jim Long in the loss.

The anticipated defensive struggle with North Carolina went out the window as Rod Elkins and Esiason came out throwing. Two catches by Kelvin Bryant and Mark Smith against one by Davis and Atkinson's field goal gave the Tar Heels a 14–10 halftime margin. A Brooks Barwick field goal expanded it further, but D'Addio ran in for a 17–17 tie. Another Elkins-to-Bryant connection put the Terps behind for the third time, but Joyner scored twice on runs of 49 and 84 yards to win it 31–24 and set a single-game school mark of 240 yards rushing. The College Park crowd was treated to another great game when Miami of Florida, led by quarterback Jim Kelly and middle guard Tony Chickillo, came to town. Badanjek's score led two Jeff Davis field goals, but Keith Griffin ran in to double the count on the Terps. A third Davis field goal swelled it to 17–7, but Badanjek blasted in and Esiason's two-point throw to Mike Lewis cut it to two. Atkinson had the fans reeling on a 38-yarder to win 18–17 with 2:14 left, but they watched in horror as Howard Schnellenberger's Hurricanes swept down the field and Davis missed a 40-yard attempt with 12 seconds remaining.

Virginia made second-half scores on a Wayne Schuchts pass to Kevin Riccio and a Quentin Walker run, but the Terps won it 45–14. Joyner's 1,039 yards put him in the 1,000-yard club, and UM was offered a trip to Hawaii.

Maryland met Washington in the first Aloha Bowl in Honolulu on Christmas Day. Esiason threw to D'Addio and Tice to trail 7–6 and 14–12, but Nash ran over and the two-pointer to Tice put the Terps ahead for the first time 20–14. The Huskies tied it on Tim Cowan's third scoring pass to Anthony Allen with six seconds to go, and Chuck Nelson converted to give Don James a 21–20 present.

North Carolina was third at 3-3-0. They lost the opener 7–6 to Foge Fazio's Pitt Panthers, as Snuffy Everett converted after Dan Marino's pass to Bryan Thomas matched field goals by Brooks Barwick and Rob Rogers. Ricky Anderson's field goal and a Whit Taylor toss to Norman Jordan kept George MacIntyre's Vanderbilt squad in it for thirty minutes, but Carolina won in the last half 34–10.

James Jones was pulled from blocking duty to start the scoring against Ed Cavanaugh's Army team, but by halftime it was 41–0 on runs by Vic Harrison, Bobby Ratliff, Ethan Horton, and a Scott Stankavage pass to Horton. Tyrone Anthony scored twice, once on an 83-yard run, and Bob McKinley ran over behind the blocking of all-conference guards Dave Drechsler and Ron Spruill to complete the 62–8 rout. Army finally scored at the end on Bill Lampley's run and Bryan Allem's two-point pass to Bill Stewart, while the swarming Carolina defense dumped quarterback Rich Laughlin for minus 32 yards. Another game that was even until the coin toss was the 41–0 defeat of Georgia Tech, as the Tar Heel defenders did a number on quarterback Jim Bob Taylor for minus 37 yards.

Anthony's 40-yard run and one by Wake Forest's Mike Ramseur tied it at intermission, but Stankavage threw twice to Mark Smith and Barwick added a field goal in the 24–7 win, while the defense dropped Gary Schofield for minus 24 yards. Stankavage was hot in the Wolfpack's 41–9 loss with passes to Kelvin Bryant, another to Harrison, and two more to Smith. State scored on a punt blocked out of the end zone and Dee Dee Hoggard's interception, while the front five of nose guard Steve Fortson, tackles Bill Fuller and Jack Parry, and outside linebackers, or ends, Aaron Jackson and Mike Wilcher contained Tol Avery at quarter with minus 28 yards.

The Tar Heels lost to Maryland and Clemson, but they took no prisoners from Virginia as Gordon Whitehead scored once and threw for another but was thrown for minus 45 yards in a 27–14 defeat. Runs by Bryant and Horton outpointed Mike Grayson's run and John Tolish's field goal for Duke at the half, but Greg Boone's run and Barwick's field goal tied it 17–17 after three periods. Carolina often had eight players in pass coverage, leaving little work for linemen Robert Oxendine, Tim Bumgarner, Tee Moorman, Jr., Phil Ebinger, and Ted Million, but Ben Bennett threw for 273 yards, including the winning toss to Carl Franks for a 23–17 conquest.

Denny Stolz brought Bowling Green to Chapel Hill, but they went away with a 33–14 loss. Barwick's two field goals trailed a Dayne Palsgrove pass to Shawn Potts and a Gehad Youssef conversion at the half, but he added two more for a school record and an Eddie Colson catch from Stankavage put the Tar Heels in front to stay. Potts scored again on a pass from Steve Swan, but Stankavage hit Earl Winfield and Horton ran in to end the scoring.

The Tar Heels took on number-eight Texas in the Sun Bowl and won

26–10. Texas led at the half on a Ronnie Mullins end zone recovery and a Raul Allegre field goal, but another Rogers field goal and two by Barwick put Carolina in front. Wilcher added a score on a recovered fumble in the end zone, as Carolina's lunch-bucket defense, which was second nationally with 236.5 yards per game in total defense, held Darryl Clark and Mike Luck to 88 yards rushing and quarterback Todd Dodge to minus 28 yards.

Duke earned a third-place tie by beating North Carolina, but they slumped badly after three early wins. Ben Bennett and Chris Castor connected on an 88-yarder, Greg Boone had a 100-yard kickoff return, and John Tolish kicked the extra point that defeated Tennessee 25–24. Emmett Tilley was a standout on defense with 12 solo tackles. Wins over South Carolina 30–17 and Virginia 51–17 followed, but Navy led 27–0 at the end of the third on Napoleon McCallum's run, Marco Pagnanelli's tosses to Ken Heine and Chris Weiler, and two Steve Young field goals. Bennett threw to Castor, Chuck Herring, and Glenn Tillery, but Steve Peters covered a fumble to halt the Blue Devil heroics 27–21. Bennett threw twice to Castor, and Joel Blunk ran in for a 21–7 lead over Virginia Tech at the half. Mark Cox completed to Tony McKee to trim off seven, and Todd Greenwood's 49-yarder to Allan Thomas and two-pointer to Mike Shaw with 33 seconds left handed Duke another setback 22–21. Big defeats by Clemson and Maryland completed the October tumble.

Duke bounced back to beat Georgia Tech 38–21 and Wake Forest 46–26. Marvin Young scored twice to keep Wake in it at the half, but Castor set an ACC record with 283 yards on catches. Duke led North Carolina State 10–0 at the half, but Ken Loney intercepted and Andre Marks ran in at the end of an 80-yard drive to turn the game around. A fumble recovery kept the momentum on State's side, and Tol Avery threw to Dave Davis for the lead. Mike Miller went 30 yards to sew it up, and Bennett's toss to Mark Militello in the last minute ended it 21–16. Duke was second nationally in passing offense after Bennett's 25 of 34 against UNC, and its 304.5 yards made it the first ACC team to average 300 yards passing for a year.

The Wolfpack started slowly, but Tol Avery had two last-half scoring strikes and Joe McIntosh ran in twice to beat Furman 26–0. Linebackers Vaughan Johnson and Andy Hendel made 23 stops to lead the defense. Jeff Heath kicked two field goals and Greg Stewart threw to Ricky Nichols to gain East Carolina a 13–13 halftime tie. Kevin Ingram's score kept it even after three, but two Ricky Wall catches and Mike Cofer's field goal put State ahead. Tony Baker scored and Stewart's two-pointer to Carlton Nelson made it 33–26, but Perry Williams intercepted for a North Carolina State win.

After beating Wake Forest 30–0, State lost to the leading ACC teams, but overcame Virginia 16–13 with a tough last-half defense. Wayne Schuchts threw to Nick Merrick, and two Wayne Morrison field goals overshadowed one by Cofer for 13–3 at halftime. Andre Marks leaped over for a score and Mike Miller ran in for the lead after Jeff Byrd's 53-yard punt return. Billy Smith's catch gave UVa a first down on the 16, but State held with 1:10 to go for the win.

Mark Fleetwood's kick gave the Gamecocks a lead, but 21 last-period points, capped by Don Wilson's pass theft, won for the Pack 33–3. An early November freeze didn't slow Penn State's climb to the title, as 84,437 fans cheered the 54–0 drubbing. Curt Warner, Tony Mumford, and Jonathan Williams each ran in twice. A fumble recovery by Dave Paffenroth led to one score, and Brian McCann's recovery led to a field goal. Scott Radecic scored on a 32-yard interception. State beat Duke for a third-place tie, but the warm weather was no help as Miami thrashed them 41–3. Albert Bentley and Speedy Neal ran over, Kyle Vanderwende hit speedster Rocky Belk twice, Jeff Davis added a field goal, and Vinny Testaverde came in to toss to Andy Baratta. Eric Williams ended with 16 career interceptions to tie the school mark set by Art Rooney in the late 1930s.

V. A Third National Champion (1983–1991)

1983

With talented receivers to catch Boomer Esiason's passes and an explosive backfield, Maryland was ACC champion with six wins. They started by scoring first and last at Dudley Field in Nashville to beat Vanderbilt 21–14. Dave D'Addio ran in after Scott Tye blocked a punt and Bobby DePaul advanced it, but Vandy took a 14–7 halftime lead on two Kurt Page passes to Phil Roach. After Rick Badanjek's run tied it, Lendell Jones intercepted on the six with 3:24 left. One minute and 94 yards later Boomer left-handed a toss to tight end Bill Rogers on the fourth play. Vanderbilt came back but Clarence Baldwin's last-play interception saved it.

West Virginia ruined the first night game at Byrd Stadium as 54,715 fans looked on. Maryland jumped to a 10–0 margin on Jess Atkinson's first field goal and Esiason's first pass to Greg Hill, but WVU tied it on Paul Woodside's kick and Jeff Hostetler's pass to Rich Hollins. The Mountaineers took a commanding lead on Hostetler's completion to Rob Bennett and runs by Tom Gray and Ron Wolfley. After Esiason tossed to Hill again, Atkinson's second kick and Tommy Neal's two-point run ended the long night 31–21.

With Esiason sidelined by a shoulder separation the previous week, Frank Reich directed the win over Pitt. Marc Bailey dived in for a 7–3 Pitt lead, but linebacker Doug Cox blocked a punt by Tony Recchia, took it on the hop and rambled 49 yards to put the Terps ahead at the half. "Please, nobody catch me," he mumbled as he outdistanced everyone to the goal. After another Atkinson three-pointer put Maryland out front 13–7, special teams man Bob Gunderman blocked Eric Schubert's field goal try. The Panthers drove deep again, but linebackers Brian Baker and Chuck Faucette spoiled a John Congemi pitch to Darnell Stone on a hit and fumble recovery to banish the crowd anxiety and save it with 1:14 to go.

While Alan Sadler's punts kept Virginia in a hole, Badanjek punched in twice and Atkinson made three field goals to beat the Cavs 23–3 and drop them to 4-1-0. Kenny Stadlin made Virginia's points, and Malcolm Pittman gave a kickoff a 91-yard ride before Steve Burke pushed him out at the six. Maryland held, and guard Tyrone Furman was named the ACC defensive player of the week.

Two field goals by Atkinson, D'Addio's first score, and Sean Sullivan's pass from Esiason put Maryland ahead of Syracuse 20–3. Badanjek ran 25 yards to a score, and linebacker Eric Wilson was the ACC player of the week. Todd Norley's pass to Brent Ziegler and Don McAulay's field goals scored for Syracuse in a 34–13 loss.

Gary Schofield threw to Duane Owens for Wake Forest, but the Terps led 7–6 at the half on D'Addio's run. After Ramon Paredes kicked off, the last-half explosion began with two Topper Clemons scores for a 19–7 lead. Esiason replied with two tosses to Hill only to have Tim Ryan's 55-yarder keep the Deacs in front after three periods 26–21. Badanjek slammed over for a 29–26 lead, but Wake cashed in a fumble to forge ahead 33–29 on another Schofield to Ryan connection. The 479 yards total offense for Maryland and 476 for Wake Forest had the fans yelling at the scoring display, but Boomer tossed to Sullivan for a 36–33 win with 1:15 to go.

After Ken Harper scored for Duke in their 38–3 defeat, the Terps took on unbeaten and third-ranked North Carolina for the ACC title. The wind gave Maryland a first-quarter advantage on Willie Joyner's run and Atkinson's field goal, but the Tar Heels swept to a 17–10 halftime lead as Scott Stankavage threw to Mark Smith and Larry Griffin and Brooks Barwick put one over. Maryland took the last-half kickoff and went ahead 18–17 on Esiason's pass to Badanjek and two-pointer to Chris Knight. After Atkinson kicked a field goal and recovered the kickoff, Esiason's toss to Sullivan made it 28–17 after three periods. Barwick made another field goal and Tyrone Anthony ran over to close it to 28–26 with 22 seconds left. The fans stood motionless on the two-point try, but linebacker Jim Gross rushed Stankavage so his pass went wide, then they let go with a shout heard all the way to Washington.

Maryland met the nation's number-three team for the second straight week, but couldn't hold the Auburn Tigers at Jordan-Hare Stadium. Atkinson started things with a field goal, but Auburn led 14–3 at the half on Randy Campbell's toss to Chris Woods and a run by Tommie Agee, who started for Greg Pratt after he died of heat stroke in a pre-season drill. Two Esiason passes put Maryland in front after three periods, but Pat Dye's wishbone of Bo Jackson, Lionel James, and Agee crunched to a 28–17 lead. After Esiason's toss to Russ Davis made it 28–23, Lewis Colbert punted to the 1-yard line. Quency Williams blindsided Esiason on third down and Donnie Humphrey recovered the ball for a 35–23 win, and 75,600 fans cheered as Maryland took the long walk to the showers.

Clemson was the first ACC team to draw 500,000 fans for one year but was still ineligible for the title. A crowd of 80,000 showed up to release 310,000 balloons four at a time as the team ran down the hill onto the field at the east end of Death Valley. An alumni group prepared them at 7 AM, breaking the record of 300,424 balloons loosed on July 4 at Itasca, Illinois. Maryland was the last victim in Clemson's 7-0-0 season as they fell behind 28–7 at the half. Before it ended, Kevin Mack ran in three times and Mike Eppley threw three touchdowns in the 52–27 thrashing.

Esiason's pass to Sullivan and a two-point run by Vic Kronberg started it off against the Wolfpack at Raleigh. Two field goals by Atkinson, Neal's run, and another two points on Knight's catch closed it 29–6. State scored on Tim Esposito's completion to Tim Foster. Moments later the Disney Characters led by Mickey Mouse appeared on the Maryland sideline, and John Lord and Herb Hinely added to the locker room celebration with a bowl invitation.

The Tangerine Bowl was renamed the Florida Citrus Bowl this year, and Tennessee took a 10–9 halftime lead on Alan Cockrell's pass to Lenny Taylor and a Fuad Reveiz field goal. A fourth kick by Atkinson gave the Terps a brief lead, but Sam Henderson's run put the Vols on top again 16–12. Badanjek went in to regain the lead 20–16 after three periods. Johnnie Jones made the last two scores, one after Alvin Toles intercepted, and Atkinson's record-setting fifth boot, including a 48-yarder, made the final 30–23.

Esiason's 6,184 yards passing on 461 of 850 attempts and 42 regular-season scoring passes were all Maryland career records.

The Terps lined up with center Kevin Glover, guards Ron Solt and Shawn Benson, tackles Harry Venezia and Greg Harraka, and ends Ron Fazio and Eric Holder. On defense were guard Greg Thompson, tackles Pete Koch and Jim Joyce, backed by Jeff Holinka, Tony Edwards, Tom McHale, and Bruce Mesner, and ends Scott Schankweiler and Kevin

Donas. Linebackers were Steve Kelly and Terry Burke, with backs Joe Kraus and Al Covington, supported by Gil Hoffman.

Others were Joe Brkovich, Al Blount, Steve Burdelski, Vernon Carter, Chris Igus, Chris Marino, Joe Niederhelman, Chris Renaldo, Eddie Schultz, Spencer Scriber, Jeff Schmitt, Dan Sileo, and Jon Simmons.

North Carolina came in second at 4-2-0. Bill Bradshaw threw for South Carolina's score to Tom Dendy and then to Quinton Lewis in their 24–8 loss, and Danny Sparkman tossed to Smokey Jordan in Memphis State's 24–10 loss with Don Glosson adding the field goal.

The Tar Heels won big against Tim Rose and Miami of Ohio in their new Fred C. Yager Stadium, as Kevin Anthony tossed for one and Bill Humes ran for one in a 48–17 win. Miami scored on Mike Kiebach's field goal, a Todd Rollins pass to Glen Hirschfeld and Tom Graham's run. Scott Stankavage tossed a score to Mark Smith for the second straight week and hit Dave Truitt for another to beat Jimmye Laycock and William and Mary 51–20. James Jones and Ray Littlejohn ran in, and W&M scored on Stan Yagiello's pass to Jeff Sanders, a Mike Clemons run and two Brian Morris field goals.

Georgia Tech led 14–0 on Robert Lavette's 58-yard sprint and John Dewberry's pass to Darrell Norton, but Stankavage ran in and Dewberry threw to Ken Whisenhunt for 21–7 at the half. A Brooks Barwick field goal and a Stankavage pass to Larry Griffin for the third week in a row and one to Earl Winfield put North Carolina in front 24–21. Runs by Tyrone Anthony and Ethan Horton won it 38–21. Three backs gained 100 yards for the first time in Carolina history as Anthony had 157, Horton had 116, and Eddie Colson had 119 in Wake Forest's 30–10 loss. Wake scored on Harry Newsome's field goal and a Gary Schofield pass to Duane Owens.

North Carolina made it seven in a row with a 42–14 win over the Wolfpack, but losses to Maryland, Clemson 16–3, and Virginia followed. Kenny Stadlin made a field goal but trailed 14–3 when Wayne Schuchts threw to Bill Griggs and Howard Petty two minutes later for a 17–14 win. Safety Lester Lyles made 17 tackles and linebacker Charlie McDaniel had 20 to curb a Carolina comeback.

Stankavage threw to Arnold Franklin, but Ben Bennett tied it for Duke on a toss to Joel Blunk. Bill Sheppard ran in an interception, and Ken Harper kicked it to 14–10 at the half. Duke led 17–14 as Bennett threw to Scott Russell and 24–17 as Doug Green's catch set up Mike Grayson's run. Anthony's 54-yard run tied it, then Carolina won it 34–27 on a Stankavage run, two Barwick field goals and another by Harper. Stankavage had 3,363

Robert Lavette owns the Georgia Tech records for season touchdowns (19), season scoring (114), career touchdowns (46), and career scoring (276).

career passing yards to overtake the 2,707 yards of Rod Elkins set last year.

Bennett set an ACC season record of 3,086 passing yards and national marks in completions (820), attempts (1,375), and yards (9,614) to break Jim McMahon's career mark of 9,536 yards. After the game Dick Crum

North Carolina was a contender for a decade while Dick Crum was coach.

knocked on Duke's dressing room. Steve Sloan asked for quiet as Crum walked up to Bennett with the ball and said, "Our kids wanted to give you the game ball. You had four great football seasons." It doesn't get any better than this.

The Tar Heels were in a post-season game for the fifth year in a row, but they lost to Bobby Bowden's Florida State squad in the Peach Bowl's 20-degree temperature. Weegie Thompson started his first game in place of injured Kelly Lowrey and scored on an Eric Thomas pass. Roosevelt Snipes scored on the second series, and it was 21–0 at the half as Thomas ran over after Pete Panton recovered a fumble. Thomas went in again and Phil Hall made the extra points, with Barwick adding a field goal in the 28–3 loss.

In its first season of conference play, Georgia Tech came in third at 3-2-0. In the first game at Legion Field in Birmingham before 77,143 fans, the Alabama squad under new coach Ray Perkins wore hound's-tooth decals on their helmets. It was in memory of Bear Bryant who died after his 323rd victory last season made him the winningest coach in college football. After Emanuel King hit Stu Rogers and Randy Edwards covered the ball, Walter Lewis threw to Joe Carter for 7–0. Van Tiffin made three points when Tech's Jack Westbrook intercepted but fumbled on the runback.

Another Tiffin field goal and score by Stan Gay when Todd Roper blocked a punt made it 20–0, and Robert Lavette ran in for a 20–7 final.

Tech traded touchdowns as Ronny Cone ran in, but Stan Jennings ran 48 yards for Furman to tie it. The teams battled away for two quarters before Lavette scored, but Bobby Lamb tossed to Chas Fox for the tie. Gary Keller nabbed a deflected pass late in the game, and Keven Esval booted Furman to a 17–14 win.

After defeats by Clemson 41–14 and North Carolina, the Ramblin' Wreck downed the Wolfpack 20–10. The defense took over in the last half as linebackers Rob Horton had 16 tackles, Ted Roof had 11, and Dante Jones had 10, with Lavette's run clinching it.

Tech led Auburn 10–7 at the half, but 17 last-period points including an Al Del Greco field goal won for the Tigers 31–13. A crowd of 94,768 watched in rainy Knoxville as Tennessee handed Tech a 37–3 beating. After Fuad Reveiz and Ron Rice field goals, Alan Cockrell's 55-yard completion to Clyde Duncan gave the Vols a 13–3 halftime lead. The fans peeked from parkas and umbrellas to see Reveiz kick one more, Johnnie Jones run in, Cockrell's 50-yarder to Lenny Taylor, and Tony Robinson's pass to Laron Brown.

A Gary Wilkins catch led Duke at the half, and Keith Glanton ran in to make it 26–14 after Cory Collier returned the last-half kickoff 95 yards, but Julius Grantham's second score gave Duke a 27–26 lead after three. Ben Bennett threw no scoring passes, but Harry Ward's end zone tackle and Ken Harper's kick ended it 32–26.

Derek Jenkins and Barry Word ran in to tie it for Virginia, but Tech overcame the Cavs 31–27, then took a 49–33 slugfest from Wake Forest. Georgia defensive coordinator Erk Russell sent his unit on the field by butting his bald head against their helmets, and the game was even at 6–6 on John Lastinger's score and 17–17 as Barry Young went in and Kevin Butler put one through. Catches by Kevin Harris and Lavette and another Butler kick made it 27–24 for Georgia. John Dewberry's pass to Daryl Wise took them across mid-field, but Tony Flack intercepted on the 36 with 1:22 left.

1984

Maryland lost its first two games but was ACC champion again with a 6-0-0 record. Frank Reich threw to Greg Hill on the first possession, but Syracuse evened it on Jaime Covington's run. Don McAulay made three field goals to win it 23–7, with the last one coming after Tim Pidgeon covered Don Brown's fumble. Reich tossed to Al Blount, Jess Atkinson kicked a pair of three pointers, and two Kurt Page passes to Chuck Scott for Vanderbilt knotted it 14–14, but three Ricky Anderson field goals won for the Commodores 23–14.

Keeta Covington parked a punt return on the 12 where Blount took it in, and Maryland had a score on its first series for the third consecutive week. West Virginia went ahead 14–10 on Kevin White's 28-yard scramble and completion to Pat Randolph, but Rick Badanjek hammered home for the lead. Paul Woodside's kick tied it, but Atkinson's second kick won it 20–17. Wake Forest led on Doug Illing's field goal, then tied it 17–17 at the half as Foy White threw to James Brim and Tommy Gregg, with Atkinson's kick and Reich's passes to Blount and Ferrell Edmunds scoring for the Terps. Badanjek ran in twice and Tommy Neal once in a 38–17 win, and linebacker Chuck Faucette was the ACC player of the week.

The largest crowd ever to see Maryland play, 85,486, was at Penn State to see Atkinson kick the Terps ahead. Doug Strang hit Rocky Washington and Tony Mumford, scored once and tossed to Herb Bellamy for two points, and Nick Gancitano added a field goal to lead 25–11. Stan Gelbaugh threw to Eric Holder and Blount ran in with 1:39 left to make it 25–24, but the two-pointer sailed harmlessly overhead as the fans cheered. Maryland couldn't get off a last-second field goal, and the cheers filled Happy Valley again.

Doug Burmeister made the last score in the 44–21 defeat of North Carolina State, and Azizuddin Abdur-Ra'oof had a touchdown catch in Duke's 43–7 loss. Bill Rogers had a scoring catch from Reich who returned from his injury. Ethan Horton's run and three Kenny Miller field goals gave North Carolina a 16–10 third-period lead, but Badanjek added three runs to his catch for a 34–23 win, and Carolina scored late on Wes Sweetser's pass to Eric Streater.

Greg Cox kicked a 48-yarder and Bernie Kosar tossed to tight ends Willie Smith and Charles Henry to put Miami out front 31–0. Reich started the second half and threw to Hill on the third play and squeezed in for another. His toss to Blount and a field goal by Cox made it 34–21 after three quarters. Neal's run and Hill's second catch tied it, and Atkinson kicked the Terps ahead by one. Miami fumbled the kickoff, and Badanjek powered over for a 42–34 lead. Kosar threw to Eddie Brown with one minute left, but Keeta Covington smothered Mel Bratton's two-point run to keep it 42–40. Joe Kraus returned the onside kick to the one, and Maryland had

Kenny Flowers made Clemson's offense run-run-run in the mid–1980s.

the greatest comeback in major college football. New coach Jimmy Johnson couldn't believe the turnaround, while a jubilant Bobby Ross shouted "No practice tonight" to cancel his halftime threat.

In Baltimore's Memorial Stadium, Clemson's 17 second-quarter points started with Shelton Boyer's catch, but Atkinson kicked it to a 17–17 halftime tie. A Kenny Flowers 48-yard run put Clemson ahead again, but the Terps rallied for the third week in a row on 17 points of their own to lead 34–23 after three periods. Blount ran in twice and Neal's second scoring run made the final 41–23.

For the first time ever, Maryland and Virginia played for the ACC title. Don Majkowski and Steve Morse went over for Virginia, but Atkinson kicked Maryland to a 24–14 halftime lead and became their all-time scorer with 308 points. A 65-yard run by Badanjek and one of 72 yards by Blount brought a 45–34 win, and the Terps were rematched with Tennessee in the Sun Bowl. Tim McGee's catch crowned a 21–0 halftime lead for the Vols, but Maryland led by one on another great comeback. Pete Panuska took the kickoff all the way back to lead 27–22, but Badanjek turned right end for a 28–27 win with 2:28 left, and Al Covington covered a fumble to save it.

Maryland had center Kevin Glover, guards Len Lynch and Greg Harraka, and tackles Jeff Holinka and Tony Edwards, supported by center Brian Conroy, guards George Colton and Carl Bond, and John Maarleveld, tackles Bill Hughes and John Sorna, ends Larry Miles and Jim Milling, back Stephon Scriber, and punter Darryl Wright.

On defense were guards Bruce Mesner and Neal Sampson, tackles Ted Chapman and Scott Tye, ends Scott Schankweiler and Kevin Donas, linebacker Richie Petitbon, backed by guards Bob Klein, Greg Thompson, Bob Arnold, and Tom Parker, tackles Dave Amend and Duane Dunham, ends O'Brien Alston, Steve Kelly, Terry Burke, and Sean Scott, linebackers Jon Sabrowski, Kevin Walker, Bobby DePaul, Doug Dragan, and Pat D'Atri, with Joe Bailey, Gil Hoffman, and Lewis Askew deep.

Others who suited up were Jeff Furman, Greg Harrell, Chris Igus, Terry Ridgely, Dan Swingle, and Barry Waseleski.

Virginia's four wins last year were their best start since 1952, and they continued with a second-place finish of 3-1-2 for their best ACC record to date. They were outclassed in the opener 55–0, but Clemson was still on probation so it didn't count. They got going with a 35–7 defeat of VMI as Kevin Ferguson threw twice to John Ford and once to Jon Muha, with Jim Daly throwing to James Wright for VMI. Todd Solomon kicked three field goals for coach Gary Tranquill in Navy's 21–9 loss, but Virginia Tech, led by Outland winner Bruce Smith, was another matter. Virginia had a 13–6 halftime lead on Kenny Stadlin's record-setting boot of 56 yards, but VPI scored on a Bob Thomas interception and Eddie Hunter run. VPI's Don

Georgia Tech's Pat Swilling readies his battle-scarred helmet for another enemy charge.

Wade made three field goals but Mark Cox threw no touchdown passes, while Don Majkowski had one in a 26–23 Virginia win.

After Ken Harper's field goal and Mike Peacock's run scored for Duke in their 38–10 loss, Virginia played Georgia Tech to a 20–20 draw. Tech's Pat Swilling and Ted Roof had 12 tackles and Anthony Harrison 10 in the knock-down game, with Robert Lavette's fourth-quarter run putting Tech ahead 17–13. A Majkowski-to-Ford aerial for the second straight week gave Virginia the lead again, but Ralph Malone intercepted at the four and David Bell capped a Ramblin' Wreck march on a game-tying field goal with 3:33 to go.

Danny Nolan's field goal sent Wake Forest ahead in the homecoming game, but Barry Word and Howard Petty both ran over twice for a 28–9 win. A Geno Zimmerlink catch and runs by Steve Morse and Antonio Rice put West Virginia behind, but Tony Reda threw to Gary Mullen for WVU, and Bob Sweeney's end zone interception saved another touchdown to win 27–7. The band played "Auld Lang Syne" after every score and the theme from "Jaws" before each kickoff to the delight of the picnickers in the open end of Scott Stadium. They got a workout in North Carolina State's 45–0 beating as Word and Majkowski both ran in twice and Keith Vanderbeek scored once.

Kevin Anthony and Eric Streater exchanged scoring passes to put North Carolina ahead, but Stadlin's kick made it 14–3 at the half. Morse ran in and Majkowski scored one and hit Ford for the lead, but Anthony tossed to Arnold Franklin to trim it to three. After Kenny Miller kicked it to 24–24 with seven seconds to go, Virginia was invited to its first bowl game as George Welsh was given a giant chocolate chip cookie with the Peach Bowl logo on it, and he accepted by devouring it amid the cheers of the team.

Jim Everett threw touchdowns for Purdue to Jeff Price, Marty Scott, and Steve Griffin, and Mike Rendina added a field goal to give Leon Burtnett's team a 24–14 halftime lead. Virginia closed the gap, tied it on Stadlin's first fourth-quarter kick, then won it 27–24 after Ray Daly intercepted with 4:56 left on the clock.

North Carolina was the third-place team with 3-2-1. Eddie Colson ran in twice and Mark Maye threw to Eric Streater to lead Navy, but Bob Misch completed to Ken Heine and two Todd Solomon field goals made it 21–12 at halftime. Rob Rogers added a field goal, but Bill Byrne came in and tossed to Rich Clouse and Chris Weiler to put the Middies ahead 25–24. Ethan Horton went in to regain the lead 30–25, but Navy won it 33–30 on Byrne's throw to Tony Hollinger and Napoleon McCallum's two-point run.

Heisman winner Doug Flutie staked Boston College to a 28–0 halftime lead with passes to Troy Stradford, Kelvin Martin, and Scott Gieselman. His tosses to Steve Williams and Gieselman put him at six to break Kenny Smith's 1977 school mark. Kevin Snow kicked a field goal, and Shawn Halloran threw to Jim Browne for BC's last score, with Horton getting all three Carolina scores.

The Tar Heels got in gear as Anthony ran over and tossed to Streater, but Mike Norseth brought Kansas back with two scores to Robert Mimbs and Skip Peete. Dodge Schwartzburg added a kick for Mike Gottfried's

Bill Curry gets set to send in placekicker David Bell for Georgia Tech.

squad, but Kenny Miller put two through the uprights and a Rob Rogers 45-yarder won for North Carolina 23–17.

Donald Igwebuike sent Clemson ahead, but two more by Miller gave Carolina a 6–3 lead. Mike Eppley's 76-yard pass to Terrance Roulhac highlighted Clemson's 17 last-quarter points for a 20–12 win. Miller kicked Carolina in front by three at the half again, but Ken Grantham's tackle and Tony Scott's fumble recovery gave Wake Forest new life. The Tar Heels lost in the last period for the second straight Saturday, as Foy White threw to David Chambers and Stuart Stogner fell on a muffed end zone punt to win it 14–3. Wake's Rory Holt was the ACC defensive back of the week.

Ronnie Burgess reacts to the news that his 17th interception for Wake Forest tied the ACC career mark.

Carolina came back to beat the Pack 28–21 as Miller made two more and Bill Humes ran in three times, with State scoring on Tim Esposito's tosses to Ralph Britt and Ricky Wall and Mike Miller's run.

Anthony completed to Horton and both ran in against Memphis State, but State scored as Enis Jackson ran over and Jeff Womack and Derrick Burroughs both carried in blocked kicks. Don Glosson added two field goals, but Miller's third kick won it 30–27 with 4:34 left to beat Rey Dempsey who took over at Memphis State when Rex Dockery died in a private plane crash the previous December.

Georgia Tech lost 24–17 as Anthony threw twice to Horton and once to Eric Lewis and Miller added a field goal. David Bell made one for Tech, and Robert Lavette ran in twice to become their top rusher with 4,066 career yards. Carl Carr's 96-yard scamper with a fumble led Duke 7–6 at the half, but Steve Slayden threw to Gary Frederick and Ken Harper made three field goals for Duke. Horton ran in and Miller kicked Carolina to a 17–15 win with a 36-yarder.

Wake Forest's fourth-place finish with 3-3-0 was its best in years. Don Wade's conversion gave Virginia Tech a 21–20 win, and John Settle ran in twice for Appalachian State, but the Deacs won 17–13 as Steve Lambert stopped one threat and Gary Baldinger was the ACC defensive lineman of the week. Haywood Jeffires scored on passes from Tim Esposito and Bob Guidice for the Wolfpack, but after Reggie McCummings intercepted Wake went ahead to win 24–15.

Dal Shealy's Richmond club fought back from a two-touchdown deficit on runs by Greg Grooms and Bob Bleier's passes to Leland Melvin, with John Henry's catch, Glenn Bensley's run, and a field goal by Brendan Tobin scoring for Richmond in their 29–16 loss.

Mike Ramseur's four touchdowns beat William and Mary 34–21, but Clemson won 37–14 as Duane Owens and Wes Stauffer scored for Wake. The Deacs won the state title by beating Duke 20–16, and Kevin Wieczorek's catch scored in the 24–7 loss to Georgia Tech, with Mike Harrington catching a touchdown for the last Tech score.

1985

Maryland's 19 seniors took them to a 6-0-0 record and third straight ACC title. They lost again to Penn State before 50,750 sweltering fans in Byrd Stadium, as PSU's blaster and blowtorch pair, D. J. Dozier and Steve Smith, led them to three scores in 18 minutes. Mike Zordich went in on an interception and Massimo Manca kicked a field goal, and after John Shaffer tossed to Mike Timpson he completed to Bob Williams for 17–0. Maryland replied with a Ramon Paredes field goal and two blasts by Rick Badanjek to go in front 18–17 on a two-pointer to Chris Knight. Manca's second kick won it 20–18 with 38 seconds left, and the fans shook their heads at Joe Paterno's 17 straight wins over the Terps.

Tommy Neal and Al Blount ran over and Paredes added a field goal, but Shawn Halloran threw twice to Kelvin Martin as Boston College trailed 17–13 after three periods. After Stan Gelbaugh threw to Eric Holder, Scott Tye fell on the kickoff and Badanjek ran in for a 31–13 win. West Virginia suffered its first shutout in three years as Neal went in twice and Gelbaugh connected with Azizuddin Abdur-Ra'oof and Sean Sullivan for a 28–0 triumph. Maryland met another hammer-and-tongs pair in Michigan's Bob Perryman and Jamie Morris. Michigan led 10–0 at the half on Mike Gillette's field goal and Eric Kattus' pass from Jim Harbaugh, the son of Western Michigan coach Jack Harbaugh. After Tom Wilcher's fumble and recovery on the two, Harbaugh tossed another score to Kattus behind the pass blocking of John Vitale, Clay Miller, and 6'7", 290-pound Jumbo Elliott, and Gillette's second kick made it a 20–0 final. Michigan's Mike Mallory had an end zone interception and Jeff Akers made five stops in the rough game, but two of their players, Mike Husar and Mark Hammerstein, younger brother of defensive tackle Mike Hammerstein, were hospitalized with serious injuries.

Blount's score with 3:27 left broke a tie with the Wolfpack, then Gelbaugh ran in to end it 31–17. Dan Plocki's two kicks led a field goal by Wake Forest's Doug Illing, but Gelbaugh hit Abdur-Ra'oof twice to wrap it up 26–3. Ken Harper's three-pointer and Steve Slayden's pass to Doug Green scored for Duke, but Badanjek ran in twice and Plocki's kick made it 17–10 at the end of three. A safety on Eric Sanders and three scoring passes ended it 40–10. Kenny Miller's three-pointer and Jon Hall's pass to Eric Streater scored for North Carolina, but Badanjek went in three times the hard way to make it 43 touchdowns in 44 games for a 28–10 win.

Gelbaugh passed to Ferrell Edmunds and Plocki added a pair of field goals, but Mel Bratton leaped over and Vinny Testaverde tossed to Mike Irvin to tie it 13–13 for Miami. Badanjek ran in and the score went to 22–13 as Jeff Feagles dropped an attempted punt and Greg Cox kicked the ball in the end zone for a safety. Brett Perriman's 74-yard punt return and Cox's field goal gave Miami a one-point lead, and another Bratton leap made the final 29–22.

Maryland invaded Death Valley and fell behind 10–0 on David Treadwell's three-pointer and score as Donnell Woolford blocked Darryl Wright's punt and Terence Mack tipped it to Perry Williams who took it in. The Terps came right back as Blount ran over and Gelbaugh tossed to Holder to lead 14–10. Clemson responded on a Kenny Flowers run and another by Stacey Driver after Gene Beasley got his hand on a punt for a 24–17 halftime lead. Gelbaugh threw to Edmunds to tie it, but Tracy Johnson's run put Clemson ahead. Maryland pulled even as Gelbaugh and Edmunds connected once more, then won it 34–31 on Plocki's field goal with three seconds left.

The Terps beat Virginia to complete another unbeaten ACC season. Down 23–7 at the half on two scores by Badanjek and one by Blount, Howard Petty scored again and Majkowski squirmed over to trim it to two. The Terps struck back quickly on Gelbaugh's pass to Edmunds and another Plocki three-pointer to finish it 33–21.

The Terps were in a bowl game for the fourth year in a row and 11th in 13 seasons, beating Syracuse in the second and last Cherry Bowl in the Pontiac Silverdome. With the temperature 70 degrees inside and 18 outside, Dick MacPherson's Orangemen took a 10–6 lead on Don McAulay's three-pointer and Bob Drummond's run. Scott Schankweiler stripped the ball from Scott Schwedes and Tye took it in and Keeta Covington belted the ball from Don McPherson to highlight 22 second-quarter points for a 28–10 halftime lead. Another Gelbaugh pass padded the score, but McPherson ran in for a 35–18 final after tossing to Mike Siano and Roland Grimes.

Maryland starters were center Dave Amend, guards Len Lynch and Jeff Holinka, and tackles Tony Edwards and John Maarleveld. Backing them were center John Rugg, guards George Colton and Carl Bond, tackles John Sorna, Bill Hughes, and Ben Jefferson, ends Larry Miles, Jim Milling, and Vernon Joines, and backs Dan Henning, Ken Vierra, Stephon Scriber, Keith Bullock, and Rich Shure.

Starting on defense were guards Bruce Mesner and Bob Arnold, tackle Ted Chapman, end O'Brien Alston, linebackers Richie Petitbon and Chuck Faucette, dividing the time with Terry Burke and Steve Kelly, Al Covington at safety, with halfbacks Don Brown and Lewis Askew. Behind them were guards Tom Parker and Bob Klein, tackles Duane Dunham, Wayne Brunson, and Warren Powers, end Sean Scott, Jon Sabrowski, Kevin Walker, Pat D'Atri, and Matt D'Amico at linebacker, with backs Joe Bailey, Chad Sydnor, and J. B. Brown.

Others were linemen Rob Sterling, Rich Nelson, Joe Giuliano, Jason Edwards, ends John Bonato and Dolph Tokarczyk, linebackers Jim Wilson and Nick Marchetti, and backs Carl Morton and Leon Bray.

Georgia Tech placed second with a 5-1-0 record. Erik Kramer put North Carolina State ahead on a pass to Haywood Jeffires, but John Dewberry tossed twice to Gary Lee and once to Tim Manion for a 21–7 halftime lead. The "Black Watch" defense of coordinator Doug Lindsey, with its black stripes on the middle of the helmet and black GT on the sides instead of white, took over as Reggie Rutland blocked a punt for a score and end Pat Swilling had seven sacks. Kramer came up long enough to throw to Phil Brothers and Kelly Hollodick added a field goal in the Wolfpack's 28–18 loss.

Barry Word bolted 79 yards to a touchdown for a 7–3 Virginia lead, but Dewberry connected with Manion, and Majkowski ran in to retake the lead after one quarter. Kenny Stadlin kicked a field goal and Majkowski threw to Geno Zimmerlink for the Cavs, but Tom Palmer's second field goal ended the scoring flurry at 24–13. The defense on both sides kept the second half scoreless, and UVa end Sean Scott was the ACC defensive player of the week. The Wreck beat Clemson for the first time in three trips to Death Valley, with Malcolm King going in and David Treadwell kicking it to 7–3 at the half. Noseguard Ivery Lee, linebacker Ted Roof, and cornerback Mike Travis forced Clemson into four turnovers, and Jerry Mays threw to Dewberry in a 14–3 win. North Carolina went under 31–0, with roverback Cleve Pounds leading the Tech defense.

October 13 marked Georgia Tech's centennial celebration, but Western Carolina almost spoiled homecoming with a 17–17 tie after three frames. Dave Mayfield ran in and Kirk Roach kicked a field goal for WCU to trail 17–10 at the half. Willie Perkins threw to Vince Nowell for the knot, but Mays ran 28 yards to undo it 24–17.

Three defensive struggles followed as Tech led Auburn 14–7 at the half, but Chris Knapp's kick closed it to four. Auburn's Pat Washington completed only two passes to Freddy Weygand and Jeff Parks, while their down linemen, Gerald Williams, Harold Hallman, Tracy Rocker, and Alex Dudchock cut off Tech at the pass. Heisman winner Bo Jackson raced 76 yards to the winning score, 17–14, and became the leading Tiger rusher with 3,750 career yards. Two field goals, one by Palmer and one by David Bell, led Tennessee in the fourth quarter, but Carlos Reveiz booted two 50-yard plus kicks to tie it 6–6, the last one coming with four seconds to go after Darryl Dickey's pass to Eric Swanson set it up. Duke lost 9–0 on a field made soggy by three days of rain, with cornerback Sammy Lilly coming up with an interception and recovered fumble to stop receivers Doug Green and Chuck Herring on the wet turf.

The dormant offense exploded with 32 last-quarter points to beat Buddy Nix's UT–Chattanooga squad 35–7. Holder Wayne Koontz put UTC ahead with a pass to Byron Holmes on a botched field goal try, but Bell made it 7–3 in the third, with Chuck Easley getting the last score. A Topper Clemons run and Doug Illing's kick got Wake Forest on the boards, but King and Cory Collier both scored twice and Charles Mack once in a 41–10 win. Bell kicked Tech in front of Georgia in the skirmish for the state title,

Jerry Mays continued to make jersey number 20 the most prolific ground gainer in Georgia Tech history.

but Steve Crumley's field goal tied it. The Wreck's Nate Kelsey ran in for the lead, but a Davis Jacobs kick made it 10–6 at the half. Lars Tate went over for the Dawgs and Jacobs kicked one more, but Lee returned the kickoff 95 yards to put Tech ahead. Bell made it a 20–16 final, and Jim Anderson's late fumble recovery secured it.

Georgia Tech was the underdog in the All–American Bowl with the Michigan State Spartans of George Perles due to suspensions of Dewberry, Lee, Mack, and Toby Pearson. MSU scored on two Dave Yarema passes to Mark Ingram and Chris Caudell's two conversions, but Todd Rampley's sneak made it 14–7 going into the last stanza. Bell cut the lead to four, and King went in with 1:50 left for a 17–14 win after Swilling fell on Lorenzo White's fumble, and the New Year's Eve celebrations started early in Birmingham.

Clemson's 4-3-0 record tied for third. Todd Greenwood put Virginia Tech ahead in the opener, and Tom Taricani kicked it to 10–3 at the end of the third. Kenny Flowers ran over and Randy Anderson threw to Ray Williams for the lead, but Greenwood tossed to Steve Johnson to tie it. David Treadwell missed a last-second field goal, but Morgan Roane was flagged for roughing the kicker, and Treadwell's second chance won it 20–17 with no time showing.

Anderson's pass to Jim Riggs and Treadwell's field goal led Georgia 10–3 after three periods. James Jackson ran in to tie it at ten, but Treadwell kicked Clemson ahead again. Pete Anderson pounced on Keith Henderson's end zone fumble, and Steve Crumley's second kick gave Georgia a 20–13 win. John Little intercepted to preserve it, and Keith Williams had 17 tackles in a losing cause.

Defeats by Georgia Tech and Kentucky gave Danny Ford three losses in a row for the first time. Four Joe Worley field goals and a Brian Williams punt return outweighed a score for Clemson, and Kevin Dooley came in for Bill Ransdell who was injured on the first play and connected with Mark Logan for a 26–7 Youkay win.

Virginia's Don Majkowski threw touchdowns to Quanah Bullock and Joel Dempsey, but Treadwell sent two over for Clemson. Kenny Stadlin's field goal and a Terrance Roulhac run made it 17–13 at the half for the Cavs. Roulhac scored again on a pass off a Ray Williams reverse to go ahead, but Kevin Morgan ran in to take it back. Flowers won it 27–24 on a late run to keep the homecoming crowd festive, and Kenny Danforth's interception saved it. UVa's Russ Swan was in on 18 tackles to win ACC back of the week honors. Jenny Bussey, daughter of ex–Clemson back Charlie Bussey, was the homecoming queen at Tigerama. Her sister, Pam, was queen in 1979, making Bussey the first father with two Clemson homecoming queens.

Duke took the opening kickoff and drove to the six, but lost the ball on Steve Berlin's hit and a Henry Walls recovery. Clemson then went all the

Terrence Flagler danced away from Howard Woods and then gained 1,258 yards for a one-year record at Clemson.

way, with Flowers going the final 46 yards. Flowers scored on another run of 50 yards, with Terrence Flagler racing 27 yards to make it 21–0. Tracy Smith ran in for Duke and Ken Harper kicked one over in a 21–9 final. North Carolina State was beaten 39–10 in the reciprocating Textile Bowl with the Pack, as Flowers went 40 yards to score, Stacey Driver had a 29-yarder, and Flagler contributed a 47-yard scurry. State scored on Kelly Hollodick's field goal and John Heinle's pass to Haywood Jeffires. Wake Forest lost 26–10, as Flowers had a 52-yard scoring run, and Roulhac caught the first scoring pass thrown by Rodney Williams.

Jon Hall tossed a touchdown to Arnold Franklin in his first starting assignment for North Carolina, and Bill Humes ran in for the second time to tie the game in the last minute. Lee Gliarmis tacked on the extra point for a 21–20 win with ten seconds to go. After the Tigers lost to Maryland in the last seconds, they faced South Carolina before a record crowd of 75,026 in Williams-Bryce Stadium. The upper deck rolled as they stomped when Kent Hagood scored twice to put the Gamecocks up 14–3, and Joe Morrison had a new slogan, "If it ain't swaying, we ain't playing." Flowers went in twice for the lead, but Scott Hagler made a 54-yarder for South Carolina. Treadwell added another kick after George Hyder drew a penalty to make it 24–17, and Mike Hold's errant toss ended it.

Lou Holtz replaced Gerry Faust at Notre Dame, and John Gutekunst took over for Minnesota against Clemson in the Independence Bowl. Rickey Foggie's pass to Mel Anderson put Minnesota ahead, but a Keith Jennings catch gave Clemson a 13–10 lead. Chip Lohmiller's second kick tied it after Craig Otto's catch, and Valdez Baylor leaped over for a 20–13 Gopher win after Gary Couch caught a pass, and Donovan Small broke up two late passes to protect it. A. J. Johnson had seven stops in the secondary, and Flowers passed Cliff Austin's 1982 mark of 1,064 yards rushing with 1,200 yards.

Virginia was also third at 4-3-0. Howard Petty ran in twice and Keith Vanderbeek once, and Kenny Stadlin made four field goals to down VMI 40–15. Scott Urch had two sacks, and a Trent Bridges run and Al Comer's pass to Steve Pancham scored for the Keydets.

Navy ruined homecoming 17–13, and Shawn Lewis had a scoring catch to beat Duke 37–14, with Steve Slayden going in and tossing to Jason Cooper for Duke. Todd Greenwood hit Terrence Howell and Eddie Hunter ran in once and Maurice Williams twice for Virginia Tech in their 28–10 win. Chris Warren's punt return set up Stadlin's first field goal, and Charlie McDaniel, Scott Lageman, and Ryan Jackson intercepted to best Wake Forest 20–18. Wake scored on two Mike Elkins passes to Greg Scales and Doug Illing's kick, and West Virginia's Mike Timko threw to John Gray in a 27–7 loss.

North Carolina State led big on Bryan Carter's field goal, a Vince Evans run, and Erik Kramer's passes to Frank Harris and Haywood Jeffires. The Cavs replied with 19 last-half points to none for the Pack but lost 23–22 as the two-point throw failed in the last minute. After Kevin Gould's fumble recovery, Barry Word ran in behind ACC lineman of the week Jim Dombrowski to subdue North Carolina 24–22. Word's season mark of 1,224

Wake Forest's Mike Elkins led the ACC in 1986 with 205 pass completions, 17 touchdown passes, and 254.1 yards passing per game.

yards rushing passed by ten John Papit's 1949 school record, but he was mousetrapped by scholastic requirements and missed the last game with Maryland.

1986

Seven returning starters on offense and eight on defense took Clemson to the title with a 5-1-1 record. Virginia Tech began to scuttle opening day when Vic Jones blocked a Bill Spiers punt and Mitch Dove fell on it for a score. Terrence Flagler tied it, but Chris Kinzer kicked Tech ahead and Erik Chapman's pass to Maurice Williams inflated the score to 17–7. Kenny Flowers ran in to trim it to three, but Kinzer's second field goal closed it 20–14.

Georgia's James Jackson tossed a 32-yard touchdown to Keith Henderson to highlight a 21–21 halftime tie, and Jackson tied it in the third on a 78-yarder to Fred Lane. David Treadwell's field goal won it 31–28 with no time left, and the Clemson seniors left Sanford Stadium with their first win. Linebacker Norman Haynes had 14 tackles, halfback Donnell Woolford had ten, and tackle Ray Chavous was the ACC lineman of the week with 12 and a recovered fumble. For only the third time in the seasons when Clemson has played both Georgia and Georgia Tech on the road, they swept both clubs. Tracy Johnson made his first score after Terrance Roulhac returned the opening kickoff 81 yards, and Treadwell added a pair of field goals. David Bell kicked one for Tech as Rusty Seyle's kickoffs gave the Ramblin' Wreck poor field position, and Chris Lancaster ran ten yards for the last score in a 27–3 Clemson win.

Coach Tom Moore had Kip Allen throwing for The Citadel, but Jim Earle, Dorian Mariable, Otis Moore, and Perry Williams broke up passes, and Gene Beasley intercepted two, nipped two more, and had eight stops to win ACC back of the week honors as Clemson won 24–0. Virginia's Scott Secules hit John Ford twice and Jeff Gaffney made a field goal in a 31–17 loss, and defensive back Delton Hall and offensive guard John Phillips were ACC weekly players.

Duke managed only a Doug Peterson field goal in a 35–3 loss, and tackle Michael Dean Perry made two sacks and was ACC lineman of the week. Next week it was Clemson that made the field goal, as North Carolina State won 27–3. Linebacker Duane Walker had 12 tackles and middle guard Tony Stephens 11, but Erik Kramer threw two touchdowns and Mike Cofer kicked two field goals in the win.

Darryl McGill ran in twice and Wilson Hoyle kicked two field goals for Wake Forest, but Flagler set a single-game school mark of 274 all-purpose yards on dashes of 88 and 50 yards and had two catches from Rodney Williams to score four times in a 28–20 win.

Athletic director Bobby Robinson announced the suspension of Roulhac, Rodney Curtis, and Keith Jennings for the North Carolina game, but the Tigers breezed to a 38–10 win. A Mark Maye pass to Eric Streater and a Lee Gliarmis kick scored for the Tar Heels, but receptions by tight end Jim Riggs and wideout Ray Williams set up two touchdowns each by Flowers and Flagler. Tommy Neal went over twice and Maryland's Dan Plocki kicked it to 17–14, but Clemson drove 92 yards to tie it on Treadwell's field goal with 0:10 left.

The Tigers played another tie before a record crowd of 82,500 in Memorial Stadium. South Carolina took a 21–18 halftime lead on Harold Green's run, a Brad Edwards theft of Todd Schonhar's pass, and a Todd Ellis 72-yarder to Sterling Sharpe. Safety James Lott and linebacker Vince Taylor combined for 14 tackles, and the fans cheered as Treadwell tied it with 2:20 to go. They cheered again as the Gamecocks' Scott Hagler missed a kick with 25 seconds left.

A record crowd of 80,104 in the Gator Bowl saw Clemson score more points in the first half than Stanford did in the last half in a 27–21 game. Ray Williams scored on a reverse after Reggie Harris knocked the ball loose on a kickoff return, and Henry Carter led defenders with 13 tackles. Brad Muster ran in once, and Greg Ennis, who replaced injured John Paye, threw twice to Muster and Dave Sweeney converted three times for Jack Elway's Cardinal. Perry made his debut as a blocking back near the goal, and tackle Jeff Nunamacher stood out on offense. Flowers had 2,914 rushing yards to pass Buddy Gore's school mark of 2,571 career yards.

Clemson starters were center Jeff Bak, guard Pat Williams, and tackles Ty Granger and Frank Deluliis. Behind them were centers Dave Spry, Eric Nix, and Hank Phillips, guards John Jansen, Pat McKenny, and Mark Inge, tackle Stacy Long, ends Dan Pearman, Jim Coley, Jerome Williams, Gary Cooper, Ricardo Hooper, and backs Randy Anderson, Steve Griffin, Wes McFadden, and Chris Morocco.

Defenders were tackle Dwayne Meadows, end Terence Mack, and safety A. J. Johnson. In relief were middle guards Mark Drag and Brian Raber, tackles Rich McCullough and J. C. Harper, ends Wayne Harps and Clay Gilstrap, linebackers Scott Enzor and Mike Jollay, and backs Kevin Brady, Crosby Broadwater, Chip Davis, Rusty Charpia, Geoff Ciniero, Tyler Grimes, Matt Riggs, and Rich Smith.

North Carolina placed second with 5-2-0. Kip Allen threw to Dayle Rust and Warren McGuire and Greg Davis converted twice for The Citadel, but Derrick Donald stole two passes and Derrick Fenner and Bill Humes both ran in twice for a 45–14 win. Linebacker Mitch Wike had two interceptions and a fumble recovery to defeat Kansas 20–0 and spoil Bob Valesente's first game as Jayhawk coach.

After Jon Hall's touchdown to Eric Streater, Florida State's defensive backfield of Deion Sanders, Eric Williams, Greg Newell, and Stan Shiver held Carolina to a 10–10 tie. The Tar Heels put a clamp on Sammie Smith, but while Chip Ferguson and Danny McManus battled for the top spot, Peter Tom Willis threw to Ron Lewis and Herb Gainer for the two-point pass. FSU's Felton Hayes blocked a punt for a safety. The Seminoles had oval decals on their helmets in honor of teammate Pablo Lopez who was shot to death last week. Lee Gliarmis tied it with a last-period field goal, but the Seminole fans groaned when Derek Schmidt missed a kick with eight seconds left.

Georgia Tech overcame a 14–3 halftime deficit to go in front by three on two Rick Strom passes to Jerry Mays. Another David Bell field goal swelled it to six, but Hall hit Eric Lewis to tie it with 58 seconds to go. After two illegal procedure penalties, Kenan Stadium shook as Gliarmis kicked a 31-yard conversion for a 21–20 win, then shook again as Bell's 55-yard attempt fell short.

Hall threw touchdowns to John Keller, Randy Marriott, Quint Smith, and Lewis against Wake Forest, but Mike Elkins tossed to Chip Rives after Ronnie Grinton recovered a fumble. Wake scored on a Wilson Hoyle field goal, but Carolina had a three-touchdown lead when the Deacs closed it to seven on a James Brim catch and Mark Young's run, but a second Gliarmis field goal made it 40–30.

Ralph Britt's fumble recovery in the end zone put the Wolfpack ahead, but Lewis tied it with an 84-yard punt return. Short runs by Eric Starr and State's Bobby Crumpler evened it 14–14 at the half. Frank Harris ran in for State, but Mark Maye's toss to Marriott tied it. Steve Salley's 45-yard run put the Pack ahead, but Maye threw to Lewis for a 28–28 knot. Erik Kramer's pass to Nasrallah Worthen and Mike Cofer's fifth conversion made it 35–28 with 1:01 left, but Maye needed only 53 seconds to go the length of the field. He tossed to Smith for a score, but Dave Truitt's two-point catch was ruled dead when his knee touched the turf at the seven to bring down the hopes of the Tar Heel faithful 35–34.

The week of practice after the loss was a long one, but the ride home from Baton Rouge was even longer as Bill Arnsparger's Louisiana State team led 13–0 at the half on two David Browndyke field goals and Mickey Guidry's pass to Rogie Magee. LSU gave up only a Gliarmis three-pointer in the final period as runs by Sam Martin, Harvey Williams, and Eddie Fuller set up two Tom Hodson tosses to Wendell Davis and another Browndyke kick in a 30–3 win.

Carolina came back to lead Maryland 20–0, but Jim Milling's three scoring passes, two for 77 and 88 yards, from Dan Henning, Jr., son of Atlanta Falcons coach Dan Henning, put the Terrapins ahead. Gliarmis won it 32–30 on a late field goal after a time out, but Terp coach Bobby Ross grabbed referee Donald Safrit and yelled that North Carolina had used all its time outs. Although the scoreboard showed none remained, ACC supervisor of officials Bradley Faircloth said the Tar Heels still had one time out left.

Fenner set a one-game ACC mark of 328 yards rushing against Virginia to give Dick Crum his 100th career win. James Thompson and Brad Lopp had good averages up the middle, and Dan Vooletich, who started in place of Dan Burmeister, intercepted twice in the 27–7 win. The Duke game had heads going back and forth as Fenner ran 32 yards to score and Maye completed an 82-yarder to Marriott, but Steve Slayden ran in and threw 29 yards to Stan Monk for Duke. Tracy Smith went 24 yards to put Duke ahead, but Starr's 67-yard dash and a Gliarmis field goal gave Carolina a 24–21 halftime lead. Starr's 57-yard scoring sprint started the second half and Kenny Miller kicked a 50-yard field goal, but Slayden tossed twice to Doug Green for a 35–34 Duke lead. Maye found Lewis for 51 yards with 2:24 to go and hit Streater for two points and a 42–35 win.

Carolina's front four of Tim Goad, Ron Burton, Reuben Davis, and Carlton Bailey suffered as the Tar Heels lost five fumbles to Larry Smith's Arizona Wildcats in the Aloha Bowl. The score went to 30–0 as Dave Adams ran in, Al Jenkins threw to Jon Horton, Art Greathouse went over, Gary Coston kicked two field goals and Jeff Valder added a 52-yarder. The line of Jeff Garnica, Pat Crowley, Steve Steinbacher, Harris Barton, and Creighton Incorminias shook loose Torin Dorn on a 58-yard scoring run, and Maye threw one and ran for one after Norris Davis blocked a punt for a 30–21 final.

North Carolina State also tied for second at 5-2-0. A crowd of 58,650, the largest ever to watch a football game in the state of North Carolina, gathered in Raleigh to watch Dick Sheridan in his first game as State's new mentor. Art Baker's run-and-shoot for East Carolina, with Charlie Libretto throwing to halfbacks Jarrod Moody and Ron Jones in the slots between the tackles and ends went in front 10–0 on Chuck Berleth's three-pointer and a score by the lone deep back Anthony Simpson. Erik Kramer tossed to Nasrallah Worthen and ran in himself for a 13–10 third-period lead, and

Left: **Offensive tackle Harris Barton was an all–American at North Carolina and then won a pair of Super Bowl rings with the San Francisco 49ers.** *Right:* **Naz Worthen holds the receiving records at North Carolina State for one game (187 yards), season (856 yards), and career (2,247 yards).**

Derrick Taylor stole two passes to spark State's last-quarter outburst for a 38–10 win.

Pitt led 14–3 in the third as Craig Heyward and Charles Gladman ran over, but Kramer threw to Haywood Jeffires and to Worthen on the two-pointer. Mike Cofer's second field goal tied it after punter John Rasp bobbled the ball, but the Carter-Finley crowd relaxed only when Jeff Van Horne's field goal try failed at the gun.

Wake Forest's 24–7 halftime lead featured Dexter Victor's 53-yard scoring interception, but the Pack scored three times in its next three possessions to go ahead 28–24. The Deacs regained the lead early in the last period on a Mike Elkins pass to James Brim, whose 15 catches were a one-game Deacon mark, but Kramer dived in for 35–31. A Chip Rives catch with 2:38 to go made it 38–35, but Kramer threw to Danny Peebles for the last score to win it 42–38.

State staged a comeback for the fourth straight game to snap Maryland's string of ACC successes again. State trailed 13–7 at the end of three, but 21 last-quarter points for the second game in a row won for the Wolfpack

28–16. Mal Crite scored twice for State, and Dan Henning threw for 2,725 yards to overtake Stan Gelbaugh's one-year mark of 2,475 yards set at Maryland last year.

The Pack tallied 21 points again but none in the last period as Georgia Tech scored on eight of its first nine possessions in a 59–21 shocker. Jerry Mays ran 79 yards on the third play, then hit Toby Pearson for another, Darrell Gast threw to Robert Massey, and Gary Lee returned a kickoff 99 yards to keep it going. After beating the top ACC teams, State bested South Carolina 23–22 on a "Hail Mary" pass to Peebles as time ran out. Todd Ellis went on to set a one-year Gamecock record with 3,020 yards passing.

After Derrick Taylor's 88-yard interception tied Virginia, Frank Stevens covered the onside kick and Cofer made it 10–7 for State at the half. Don Majkowski put UVa in front for good, and Cofer and Jeff Gaffney traded field goals to end it 20–16. Mike Pettine intercepted twice at the goal inside 1:11 to save it.

Homecoming dawned wet and cold, but Bobby Crumpler warmed it with two touchdowns, one after Mark Smith blocked a punt. Duke's Tracy Smith trimmed the lead in two at 14–7, but Pat Teague's fumble recovery set up Todd Varn's catch for the Pack. Three Cofer field goals and Steve Slayden's pass to Stan Monk closed it 29–15.

After sidewinder Kirk Roach barefooted four field goals for Western Carolina in a 31–18 loss, the Wolfpack was invited to play Virginia Tech in the Peach Bowl. Brian Bullock covered a blocked end zone punt to tie the Hokies, but Steve Johnson's last-quarter catch put VPI up 22–21. Cofer sent State ahead by two, but Chris Kinzer's late kick won for Tech 25–24. Kramer eclipsed Tim Esposito's season mark of 2,096 yards passing with 2,510 and his career mark of 3,847 yards with 4,602 to become State's top passer.

Georgia Tech was next with 3-3-0. Ken Goldsmith went in for Furman, but Tech's 17–7 lead evaporated as Keith Moore tossed to Larry Grady and Mike Wood kicked it to 17–17 with 29 seconds to go. After beating Virginia 28–14, losing to Clemson, being edged by North Carolina, and destroying the Wolfpack, Tech faced Auburn. Behind the Tiger line of Ben Tamburello, Steve Wilson, Yann Cowart, Jim Thompson, and Stacy Scarcls, Jeff Burger tossed to Lawyer Tillman and Walter Reeves and Reggie Ware ran in for a 24–3 halftime lead. Brent Fullwood added a third-period run for a 31–10 Auburn win.

David Bell's conversion led Tennessee 14–13, but the front five of Travis Moody, Kyle Ambrose, Steve Mullen, Paul Jurgensen, and Willis

Paul Kiser out in front of Mike Ramseur was a chief reason why Wake Forest led the ACC in scoring in 1986.

Crockett held off a late Vol drive led by Jeff Francis. Riccardo Ingram stopped Charles Wilson on third down, and on the next play Carlos Reveiz slipped on the wet astroturf and hooked a field goal try. Tech linemen Mitch Waters, Tyrone Sorrells, Eric Bearden, Dean Weaver, and John Davis paved the way for 398 yards total offense against Duke. John Porter's scoring interception keyed a 34–6 homecoming win, while Andre Thomas led the defense.

Jerry Mays went over twice and Gast threw to Massey and Bug Isom as Eddie Williamson's VMI squad was defeated 52–6, with Dave Brown throwing to Mark Stock for the Keydet score. Tech led Wake Forest 21–10 as Wake's Paul Mann was sidelined, but linemen Frank Carmines, Tim Morrison, Paul Kiser, Mike Rice, and Gregg Harris took the Deacs to a

24–21 win. Wilson Hoyle's field goal decided it, but Scott Roberts, Steve Lambert, Ernie Purnsley, and A. J. Greene on defense saved it. A Nathaniel Lewis catch scored for Georgia and Lars Tate's third tally won for the Dawgs 31–24, but the game was saddened by the traffic deaths of assistant athletic director Jim Luck and campus security officer Gary Beringause.

1987

Clemson successfully defended its league title with a 6-1-0 mark. Western Carolina lost the opener 43–0, as Wes McFadden and Terry Allen both ran over twice. Jesse Hatcher blocked a punt to set up a touchdown, and Randy Anderson saw action at quarterback. McFadden gained 226 yards behind blocks by guard John Phillips and fullback Chris Lancaster to defeat Virginia Tech 22–10, and VPI's Jon Jeffries returned a Rusty Seyle kickoff 92 yards in the mud at Blacksburg. John Johnson at end led defenders with nine tackles.

James Lott and Gene Beasley caught James Jackson in the end zone, and Georgia lost two years in a row in the final seconds on David Treadwell's field goal 21–20. Norman Haynes led the defense with 12 tackles. Donnell Woolford ran in a 78-yard punt return, Joe Henderson scored on a 95-yard kickoff return, and linebacker Henry Carter's seven stops led in the 33–12 win over Georgia Tech. Richard Hills threw to Greg Lester and Rick Strom tossed to Steve Davenport for the Tech scores, and for the first time since 1902–1903 the Tigers beat Georgia and Georgia Tech two straight years.

Jim Earle's 12 tackles led Clemson's defense in a 38–21 win over Virginia at homecoming. Jim Coley's catch led Duke at halftime, but Roger Boone tied it 10–10 after three. Anthony Dilweg kept Duke in it until the final 15 minutes, but the Tigers took a 17–10 win. The Wolfpack had Clemson's number again as they piled up a 30–0 halftime lead, but Rodney Williams put the ball in the air 46 times in the last half for an NCAA mark. Keith Jennings caught six passes, but Ricardo Hooper's catch with 3:56 left came up short 30–28. Linebacker Dorian Mariable had 15 stops, tackle Michael Dean Perry had 13, and middle guard Tony Stephens had 11.

After Woolford returned a Martin Bailey punt for six points, Wake Forest took a 17–10 halftime lead on two Mike Elkins tosses to Ricky Proehl, but three scores by Allen and Henderson won for the Tigers 31–17. Gary Cooper's catch and Treadwell's field goal tied a Torin Dorn run and Kenny

Miller's kick for North Carolina, but Treadwell won it 13–10 with 32 seconds left to cap a 67-yard drive. Tracy Johnson had 37 of those yards behind tight end Dan Pearman, and linebacker Vince Taylor's ten stops led the defense.

Arlington Nunn and Doug Brewster were the stoppers against Maryland, and Chris Morocco added a score in Clemson's 45–16 win. After losing to South Carolina 20–7, Clemson met Penn State in the Citrus Bowl. Matt Knizner threw to Mike Alexander and Eric Etze kicked a field goal, but Johnson scored three times to win 35–10 and finish tenth nationally. Safety Rich Smith had seven tackles and 300-pound tackle Jeff Nunamacher was a power on offense.

Clemson starters were tackle Ty Granger, guard Eric Harmon, center Jeff Bak, and tackle Ray Chavous on defense. Backups were centers Hank Phillips and Dave Spry, guard Pat Williams, tackle Frank Deluliis, ends Joey Haynes, Chip Davis and Doug Thomas, with backs Keith Ingram and Chinedu Ohan. Defenders were middle guards Mark Drag and Angelo Fox, tackles Vance Hammond, Rich McCullough, J. C. Harper, and Otis Moore, Stacy Fields, Chuck O'Brien, and Duane Walker at linebacker, and backs Crosby Broadwater, Rusty Charpia, Tyler Grimes, Wayne Harps, Jerome Henderson, and Matt Riggs.

Virginia graduated 88.9 percent of its football team and won the College Football Association achievement award for the second straight year, then came back to place second with a 5-2-0 record. Georgia beat them in the opener for both teams 30–22 on two last-period sprints by Rodney Hampton and Lars Tate. Four third-quarter turnovers by Sean Scott, Dave Griggs, and Keith McMeans could only produce two Mark Interlied field goals as Maryland won 21–19.

The Cavs beat Virginia Tech as Scott Secules tossed to Keith Mattioli and scored on an option play. Earnie Jones went in for 14–7, and Erik Chapman threw to Steve Johnson to trim it to 14–13 for Frank Beamer's squad, but Jeff Lageman, Chris Stearns, and Elton Oliver snuffed out the two-point run. Ray Savage made seven stops in the 42–17 win over Duke, and VMI's John Parrott, Arturo Johnson, and Joe France gained only 59 yards in their 30–0 defeat.

Two trips to the Palmetto state were disastrous as Clemson won going away after Bruce McGonnigal's catch and Marcus Wilson's run scored for

Opposite: Clemson's Michael Dean Perry sacks South Carolina's Todd Ellis while Brian Chaney looks for the pass that never came.

the Cavs, and UVa end Craig Fielder died of cancer in the team's hotel room on the day before South Carolina handed them a 58–10 beating. Harold Green, Greg Welch, and Ryan Bethea ran in, and Pat Hinton scored on an interception. Collin Mackie made two field goals, and Sterling Sharpe added two 59-yard scoring plays on a Todd Ellis pass and a return of Fred Carter's punt.

Ricky Proehl scored three Wake Forest touchdowns, but interceptions by McMeans, Savage, and Kevin Cook turned back the Deacs 35–21. Virginia won its first road game of the year, as Tim Finkelston caught the go-ahead score that beat Georgia Tech 23–14.

North Carolina led by ten with 4:44 left, but 16 solo stops by Phil Thomas and two long drives pulled it out 20–17. Virginia led the Wolfpack on a Durwin Greggs run and two John Ford scores, but State narrowed it to 24–17 at the half on Shane Montgomery's passes to Bobby Harrell and Todd Fisher and a Bryan Carter kick. Finkelston's catch and Interlied's second field goal doubled the score, but Kent Winstead fell on a fumble to start a State rally. Another Montgomery-to-Harrell connection and Bobby Crumpler's run made it 34–31, but McMeans intercepted behind the goal to end it. His nine steals led the nation and missed the league mark by one.

Virginia met LaVell Edwards' Brigham Young team in the All–American Bowl and fell behind on Leonard Chitty's field goal, but runs by Secules and Kevin Morgan put them ahead at the half 14–3. Fred Whittingham ran in and caught a Sean Covey pass, but Secules threw to Ford and to Wilson on a fake kick conversion to win 22–16.

After almost a decade at Virginia Tech, Bill Dooley was back in the ACC to take Wake Forest to third with a 4-3-0 mark. Todd Middleton's block of a Jeff Olivo punt set up the first score and Jimmie Simmons intercepted to set up the second against Richmond. Darryl McGill skipped 45 yards over center on a rain-soaked field after Ralph Godic covered a fumble and Wilson Hoyle kicked it to 24–0. A James DuBose end zone interception secured the shutout.

Mark Young scored twice to beat the Wolfpack 21–3, but Bjorn Nittmo kicked four field goals to give Sparky Woods' Appalachian State squad a 12–6 halftime lead. A. J. Greene broke through to block a Tony Cox punt, and Warren Belin took it in to put Wake in front. Hoyle's third kick made it 16–12, and Mark Agientas fell on a fumble to run out the clock when Marvin Mitchell sacked Todd Payton. Two Keith Walker field goals for Army trailed 10–6 after three periods, but Mark Mooney replaced injured Tory Crawford for Jim Young's Cadets and went in for the lead. Ricky Proehl's catch won it 17–13, and Ernie Purnsley's 29 tackles tied a Wake record. Clarence Carter's run and Quint Smith's pass from Mark Maye scored for North Carolina, but Mike Elkins threw to McGill and Hoyle was five-for-five in the 22–14 win. Tackle Kelly Vaughan was the ACC defensive lineman of the week, and the Deacons were 5-0-0 for the first time since Elmer Barbour captained the 1944 eleven.

Maryland and first-year coach Joe Krivak won next week 14–0. David Whitley's hit at the one averted one threat, but Dean Green intercepted to set up Mike Anderson's run, and the Terps tallied on the next series for the win. Losses to the top league teams looked like it might be four as Duke led 14–0 at homecoming, but Tony Mosley covered a punt blocked by Warren Smith for one score and a Tony Rogers run tied it. Hoyle kicked the Deacs ahead, but a catch by Duke's Keith Daniel gave new mentor Steve Spurrier a 21–17 halftime lead. Greene intercepted and Young ran in to put Wake ahead, but Stan Monk cut it to three and Terry Smith sacked Steve Slayden on the last series for a 30–27 win. The Deacs were state champs, but Harold Green and Collin Mackie scored all the points as South Carolina blanked Wake 30–0. Carl Nesbit started in the 33–6 win over Georgia Tech on a defense that stole seven passes, with Greene nabbing four as both tied one-game ACC marks.

North Carolina State also tied for third at 4-3-0. The Pack led on Mike Kavulik's catch after Sterling Quash covered a fumble, but East Carolina won 32–14 despite Fred Stone's 17 stops and 16 by Ray Agnew. ECU's Willie Lewis added a last-half score. Pitt's Craig Heyward ran in twice after Ezekial Gadson's interception and Henry Tuten's reverse. Izel Jenkins blocked an extra point after Sal Genilla tossed to Hosea Heard and Reggie Williams, and holder Bill Osborn ran 15 yards on a muffed field goal try for a 34–0 win.

Preston Poag's first start took State to a 28–0 first-quarter lead over Maryland. Chris Williams added a second-half score, and Bren Lowery scored twice in the Terps' 42–14 loss. Ray Frost and Clayton Henry both had seven stops to beat Georgia Tech 17–0, with a Scott Auer hit and a John Adleta recovery setting up a State score.

Poag threw to Danny Peebles and Chris Corders, but a bad snap sailed over punter Craig Salmon's head for a score and three Kenny Miller field goals gave the Tar Heels a 17–14 win. South Carolina ran it up 48–0, with Keith Bing and Kevin Jones adding late scores. Bobby Crumpler scored after Chris Johnson's recovery, but Jeff Morgan ran in and hit George Searcy to put Mike Ayers' East Tennessee State team ahead. ETSU's Rick

Steve Spurrier revived Duke's sagging football fortunes in the 1980s, first as an offensive coach then as head coach.

Harris ran in an interception, and State's Lenny Schultz was downed for a safety in their 29–14 loss.

Rodney Dickerson's blocked punt return and a Randy Jones run scored for Duke, but Shane Montgomery hit Mack Jones and Todd Varn and had 468 yards passing for a Wolfpack record. Steve Slayden's three touchdowns to Clarkston Hines put Duke in front by one, but Bryan Carter's third field goal won it 47–45 with 29 seconds left.

1988

Clemson's 6-1-0 record took the title and made it the third school to capture three straight conference crowns. Joe Henderson went over twice in the rain to beat Virginia Tech 40–7, with Rich Fox scoring for VPI. Ed McDaniel led defenders with nine stops, John Johnson had eight, Levon Kirkland and Vince Taylor both had seven, and Reggie Harris, Tyrone Mouzon, and Chuck O'Brien each had six. The weather was still wet as Jesse Hatcher covered a bad pitch by Furman quarterback Pat Baynes and Terry Allen ran in. Chris Gardocki kicked two field goals and Glen Connally

Clarkston Hines is Duke's career scoring leader with 234 points.

kicked the Furman points in a 23–3 win. Rich Smith led defenders with 14 tackles. Both replacements went in at quarterback: Chris Morocco for Clemson and Frankie DeBusk for Jimmy Satterfield's Paladins.

Rain did not dampen the spirit of 84,576 fans at the Florida State game. Chip Davis started an end-around and then tossed a 61-yarder to Gary Cooper, but FSU's Chip Ferguson threw to Dexter Carter on a blitz for the tie. Rodney Williams ran in for a 14–7 Clemson lead, but Deion Sanders tied it on a 76-yard interception to start the last half. Dayne Williams ran over to put the Seminoles ahead, but Tracy Johnson tied it with 2:32 left. FSU lined up to punt, but Williams handed the ball to Leroy Butler between his legs. Butler sprinted 78 yards down the sideline to set up a Richie Andrews field goal for a 24–21 win with 32 seconds to go.

Clemson hit the road for the first time to play Georgia Tech in newly named and remodeled Bobby Dodd Stadium. Keith Jennings had a scoring catch, and linebacker Doug Brewster ran in a 68-yard interception. Henderson scored his first touchdown on artificial turf after snapper Scott Beville covered a punt dropped by Gerald Chamblin to end it 30–13. Middle guard Mark Drag led the defense with 11 stops, tackle Rich McCullough had nine, and end Jim Coley and guard Eric Harmon led the blocking in the offensive line.

Clemson took a defensive struggle from Virginia under sunny skies at Charlottesville. Gardocki's third-period field goal put the Tigers out front, but Shawn Moore arched an alley-oop to 6'5" Herman Moore for the lead. Davis lined up with no coverage, and Williams hit him after changing the play at the line of scrimmage with 1:52 remaining. Rusty Seyle converted for a 10–7 final.

After Donnell Woolford's punt return set up the first score against Duke, DeChane Cameron took a pitch and completed to Cooper for another. Safety Gene Beasley intercepted to set up a score, but Quint McCracken returned the kickoff 96 yards. A Clarkston Hines catch made it 28–14 at the half, and Doug Peterson added a field goal in Clemson's 49–17 homecoming win. Linebacker Dorian Mariable and halfback Arlington Nunn also intercepted, and Dexter Davis at half broke up four passes by Anthony Dilweg and Ken Hull.

North Carolina State made it three in a row with a 10–3 win, but Wake Forest fell a week later. The Demon Deacons tied it on a Mike Elkins pass to David Jarvis, but tight end Steve Gerrald's recovery led to a field goal, and Ricardo Hooper's catch made it 17–7 at halftime. Wes McFadden's 11 knockdown blocks and a score led the offense. Elkins tossed twice to Ricky Proehl in a 38–21 Wake loss, and halfback James Lott led defenders with ten tackles.

The halftime score was 17–7 again next week as Ken Martin ran in for North Carolina. A Charlie James score and Todd Burnett's late pass to John Keller gave Clemson a 37–14 win, and guard Jeb Flesch led the offense with nine knockdown blocks. Maryland took a 14–3 halftime lead on Neil O'Donnell's throw to Ricky Johnson, but Allen ran in twice and Jerome Henderson blocked a punt to set up Cooper's second score. James added a score in the 49–25 Terp loss, and center Jeff Bak led with ten blocks. A record crowd of 84,867 was in Death Valley as South Carolina junked its pro-style offense for the run-and-shoot but lost the state squabble 29–10. Todd Ellis threw to Robert Brooks and Ron Rabune had seven solo stops for the Gamecocks, but Clemson had a date with Oklahoma.

After Hatcher sacked Jamelle Holieway in the Florida Citrus Bowl,

R. D. Lashar's first field goal put Barry Switzer's Sooners ahead, but Gardocki kicked two to tie it. Tackle Vance Hammond's 11 stops helped hold the OU wishbone of Leon Perry, Mike Gaddis, and Anthony Stafford to 91 yards rushing, and Allen went over to give Clemson a 13–6 win. The Tigers finished ninth, and Williams hung up his jersey as their top career passer with 4,647 yards.

Besides starting tackles Frank Deluliis and Jeff Nunamacher, others on offense were center Hank Phillips, guards Dave Puckett, Mark Inge, Curtis Whitley, Pat Williams, and tackles Ty Granger, Bruce Bratton, and Stacy Long. Receivers were Stacy Fields, Rodney Fletcher, Trey Howell, Chinedu Ohan, Robbie Spector, Doug Thomas, Richard Tucker, Fernandez West, and backs Reggie Damps, Cameron Gibson, Tony Kennedy, Chris Lancaster, and Reggie Lawrence.

Defensive backups were middle guards David Davis, Angelo Fox, and Merv Green, tackles Ray Chavous, J. C. Harper, Otis Moore, and Danny Sizer, end Wayne Harps, and William Bell, Mitch Belton, and Tyler Grimes deep. Punters were Blake Campbell and Jon Foster.

Virginia celebrated its 100th year of football with a 5-2-0 ACC record and second-place finish again. Mark Interlied's field goal kicked things off, but Alan Williams went in for William and Mary. Shawn Moore rifled one to Bruce McGonnigal to go ahead, but Steve Christie's kick and Jon Brosnahan's pass to Harry Mehre put W&M up 17–10 at the half. Marcus Wilson tallied on the first two series, and UVa gave up only two more field goals in a 31–23 win.

Scott Stadium bulged with a record crowd of 45,000, but Penn State took an easy 42–14 win. Sam Gash and Gary Brown ran in and Tom Bill threw to Mike Timpson on the first three possessions for a 21–0 first-quarter lead. There was no letup when John Greene, Leroy Thompson, Sean Redman, and John Gerak carried the ball, or when David Jakob, Odell Wilson, O. J. McDuffie, and Dave Daniels caught it, with Shawn Moore going in twice for the Cavaliers.

Tom Palmer's field goal with 47 seconds to go gave Georgia Tech the lead, but a Tyrone Lewis runback and two Derek Dooley catches positioned the ball for a 17–16 win on Interlied's kick with nine seconds left. The first half went to Duke as Anthony Dilweg tossed to Keith Ewell, Walter Jones, and Clarkston Hines. Runs by Roger Boone and Virginia's Durwin Greggs made it 31–7. Moore tossed to Tim Finkelston twice and ran in the second time with 0:29 left, but Duke covered the onside kick for a 38–34 win.

As part of Virginia's football centennial, Charles Mackall, who captained Greasy Neale's 1926 team, and Hunter Faulconer and William Byrd from Earl Abell's 1929 squad were introduced to the halftime crowd at homecoming against Clemson. Don Bryant put the Cavs ahead in the first-ever game with Louisville, but Jay Gruden threw to Calvin Dixson and Deon Booker and to Eric Broomfield on a two-pointer to go ahead. Moore ran in and hit McGonnigal twice for 28–14, but Gruden tossed to Chad Fortune and Klaus Wilmsmeyer converted to close it to 28–21. Latrell Ware went over, and Ron Bell kicked Louisville to a 30–28 win with ten seconds showing.

A Preston Hicks recovery led to a score as Wake Forest lost 34–14, and a Dave Griggs tackle after a big gain saved a score in Virginia Tech's 16–10 loss. VPI was blanked after Chris Kinzer's field goal and Will Furrer's first-half pass to Brian McCall.

After a 19–14 defeat of North Carolina State, the Cavs took a 27–24 win from North Carolina. Moore ran over and completed to John Ford for the second, and Joel Dempsey dropped a catch at the goal and Finkelston fell on it for the third. Clint Gwaltney's field goal and three Tar Heel touchdowns in six minutes tied it, but Interlied's second kick with 6:11 left provided the victory.

Virginia led Maryland 16–14 on Nikki Fisher's run and Johnnie Wilson's catch, but Dan Plocki's last-quarter kick put the Terps ahead by one. Moore ran in to regain the lead, but Ricky Johnson went over with 1:09 left to trim it to 24–23. Keith McMeans and Jason Wallace broke up Scott Zolak's two-point pass for the win, and the Cavaliers snapped a 16-game losing streak to the Terps.

North Carolina State finished third at 4-2-1. Preston Poag scored three times, once after a Fernandus Vinson interception, to beat Western Carolina 45–6. Fred Stone intercepted Todd Cottrell to set up Anthony Barbour's second score, and Steve Salley ran in after Chris Hartsell intercepted. Mark Fowble added a field goal and Clay Cox kicked two for WCU. The Pack spotted Wake Forest a pair of Wilson Hoyle field goals, but Poag ran over and hit Danny Peebles on a post pattern to win it 14–6. Fowble was injured on a blocked field goal by A. J. Greene and lost for the year.

Maryland zipped to a 14–0 lead on Bren Lowery's run and Mike Beasley's draw play, but State scored as Nasrallah Worthen caught the seventh pass on a 69-yard drive. The Terps came back on Neil O'Donnell's 72-yarder to Beasley and Dan Plocki's field goal for 23–7 at the half. Shane Montgomery came in to lead two marches that ended in a pair of Damon

Hartman field goals and then found Worthen who streaked 76 yards to score. State chipped away with two kicks by Hartman for the tie and then the lead, but O'Donnell completed to Dean Green with 1:12 to go for a 30–26 Terrapin win.

The defense tightened up as Jesse Campbell stepped in front of a Todd Rampley pass and returned it 64 yards against Georgia Tech. Mal Crite added another, and Lee Williamson came in to direct the Tech attack. Two Tom Palmer field goals ended it 14–6.

Tailback Tyrone Jackson scored the first of his three touchdowns after Dubie Picquet blocked a punt, and Chris Williams made three more in the 49–0 win over East Tennessee State. The Pack's no-huddle offense rolled on with a 48–3 defeat of North Carolina, the most lopsided win in the history of the series. Clint Gwaltney made the Tar Heel score for new coach Mack Brown, and Michael Brooks and Dexter Royal intercepted to set up the last two scores.

After the Wolfpack feasted the third straight time on Tiger meat, a Todd Ellis toss to Eddie Miller secured South Carolina's 23–7 win. Virginia's win ended the Pack's title hopes, but Hartman's field goal on the final play tied Duke 43–43. Charles Davenport's second straight start took State to a 14–3 win over Pitt. Scott Kaplan scored for Pitt, and Barry Anderson's recovered fumble and Joe Johnson's interception thwarted late Panther threats.

State's season ended in the rain-soaked Peach Bowl. Davenport pushed in after Lee Knight fell on a fumble, but George Murphy made three points for Hayden Fry's Hawkeyes. Montgomery hit Peebles on a 75-yarder and Jackson skipped 30 yards through the steady rain for his second score to put State up 28–3. Iowa came back on two Chuck Hartlieb passes to Deven Harberts, but the one to Sean Smith at the 0:08 mark fell short in a 28–23 final.

Wake Forest's 4-3-0 slate finished fourth. They opened with a 31–11 win over Villanova, back in the football business after a four-year layoff. The scoreboard read 31–0 before Tom Withka put Andy Talley's team on the plus side. Kirk Schulz threw to Robert Brady, then to Pete Lombardi for two points, but interceptions by Kelly Vaughan, James DuBose, and Levern Belin sealed the victory.

Another good defensive effort stopped Jim Heacock's Illinois State squad 35–0. After Mike Elkins tossed to Ricky Proehl on a 69-yarder, Wake's Dave Braxton snared a Pat Williams pass in the end zone. Steve Brown's catch keyed a Deacon drive for the next score, and backups Gregg Long and Phil Barnhill were both three-for-three. ISU's Mike McCabe was kept busy punting, and a field goal try by Rick Seitz was smothered because of a bad snap.

After the Wolfpack beat the Deacs in the mud and rain, Wake stepped into Michigan Stadium before 102,776 people and led on a Wilson Hoyle field goal. Mike Hooten's 14 tackles could not stop two scores by Tony Boles and Mike Gillette's field goal in a 19–9 Michigan win. Wake's Tony Rogers dived in to close the scoring.

The 100th anniversary of the first college football game in the state of North Carolina was celebrated when the Tar Heels met Wake Forest. Hamp Greene kicked Carolina ahead, but by halftime Wake was out front 35–9. Mike Benefield and Reggie Clark scored for Carolina, but the festivities were all Wake's in a 42–24 win. Maryland led 17–6 on Barry Johnson's catch, then fattened it to 24–12 on Irvin Smith's 86-yard interception, but 345 yards passing by Elkins and a plunge by Rogers with 1:22 left won it 27–24.

After Wake lost to the top ACC teams, Duke's Anthony Dilweg threw to Walter Jones and Keith Ewell, but Mark Young went over twice and Bob Niedbala scored in Wake's 35–16 win. Georgia Tech lost 28–24 as nose guard Mike Smith's late interception clinched it. Anthony Williams had three scores against Appalachian State, but Bjorn Nittmo left-footed two field goals and Bobby Fuller hit Ritchie Melchor, Kevin Armstrong, and Joe Briggs for a 34–34 tie. ASU's Mark Moore blocked Martin Bailey's punt to set up a score with two minutes left, and Gary Dandridge intercepted to end it.

Elkins threw for 7,304 yards to pass Gary Schofield's record of 7,205 yards to become Wake's leading career passer, and A. J. Greene's 17 interceptions tied the career mark of Ronnie Burgess.

Maryland was also fourth at 4-3-0. After beating Louisville 27–16, West Virginia's Undra Johnson ran in and Major Harris threw to Keith Winn. WVU's best team ever won 55–24 on runs by Anthony Brown, Craig Taylor, and Reggie Rembert, Bo Orlando's interception, and two Charlie Baumann field goals. The Wolfpack slipped in the last 72 seconds, but runs by Bob Drummond, Mike Owens, and two Kevin Greene field goals gave Syracuse a 20–9 win. Todd Rampley tossed to T. J. Edwards and Tom Covington for Georgia Tech's points, but Ricky Johnson's run and two Dan Plocki field goals won it 13–8.

Wake Forest won with 82 seconds left, but Maryland beat Duke 34–24 as a Vernon Joines catch scored early. Mark Allen sacked Neil O'Donnell to lead 16–14, but O'Donnell hit Barry Johnson to start the comeback.

Dennis Spinelli scored twice against North Carolina, but Ken Martin went over three times for the Tar Heels. Todd Burnett and James Thompson ran in and Clint Gwaltney added a field goal for Carolina, but the Terps kept pace as O'Donnell hit Mike Beasley and David Carr. With its defensive line graduated, Carolina was in a track meet every game, and the Terps took this one as Plocki tied it, then won it 41–38 on two late field goals.

Blaine Rose made his second straight start at end, but a Henry Adkins field goal and Lance Lonergan's bomb to John Greene put Penn State ahead. The Lions went on to a 17–10 win, then Clemson won and Virginia squeezed past with 69 seconds left on the clock.

1989

Virginia's 6-1-0 record took them to the top of the ACC for the first time. They were anything but champions in the Kickoff Classic against Notre Dame in the Meadowlands at East Rutherford, however. The Irish scored on their first six possessions as Ricky Watters, Anthony Johnson, Rodney Culver, and Tony Rice all ran in. Rice also had 147 yards passing, with 121 going to Raghib Ismail. After Billy Hackett missed two extra points, Craig Hentrich took over and added a field goal. Shawn Moore threw to Derek Dooley and Bruce McGonnigal in a 36–13 final. Virginia came back with a 14–6 win over Penn State as last year's blitz was held to a pair of Ray Tarasi field goals. Herman Moore's catches scored for UVa, while passes by Tom Bill and Tony Sacca to Terry Smith and Todd Young and runs by Blair Thomas and Gerry Collins were ineffective.

Georgia Tech's ten points were matched by Shawn Moore's run and a Jake McInerney field goal for Virginia. Terry Kirby ran over for a 17–10 win, and Yusef Jackson, Jesse Jackson's son, led with seven solo tackles. In the battle between the eventual league co-champions, Virginia took a 21–10 halftime lead. Dave Brown came in for Billy Ray and threw three touchdown passes for Duke, but Moore had 295 yards on 14 of 15 completions for a 49–28 triumph.

William and Mary lost 24–12 in spite of 251 yards on Chris Hakel's tosses to Ray Kingsfield, Robert Green, Alan Williams, Mark Compher, and Matt Shiffler, but two timely interceptions by Tony Covington turned the tide. In the annual loss to Clemson, Matt Blundin stepped in for Moore who was injured and passed for 248 yards and linebacker Ray Savage made 17 tackles in the 34–20 defeat. North Carolina's Aaron Staples went over twice and Randy Jordan donated two points when he stepped back into the end zone to down the ball on a kickoff, but UNC lost 50–17 as it struggled through a second straight 1-10-0 season. Phil Barnhill threw for 282 yards and three touchdowns to Ricky Proehl and Bobby Jones, but Moore had 280 yards passing in Wake Forest's 47–28 loss.

Browning Nagle threw to Anthony Cummings and Ron Bell kicked Louisville in front with 3:31 left, but McInerney's field goal as time expired gave Virginia a 16–15 homecoming win. Three Damon Hartman field goals scored for North Carolina State, but a Jason Wallace interception and the Moore-to-Moore combination sealed it 20–9. Virginia Tech trailed 24–0 at the half but fought back on Rodd Wooten's pass to Myron Richardson and a Marcus Mickel dash followed by Phil Bryant's two-point catch. Rich Fox went in and Mickey Thomas added a field goal, but UVa hung on for a 32–25 win on a second score by Durwin Greggs and 16 tackles by Phil Thomas.

Don Bryant's run closed the regular season with a 48–21 win at Maryland for the first time since 1971. They had ten wins for the first time and met Illinois in the Florida Citrus Bowl. Jeff George tossed to Steve Williams for the Illini, but a Tim Finkelston catch tied it. Dan Donovan's reception and a Doug Higgins field goal put Illinois up 17–7 at the half. A Howard Griffith run and Mike Bellamy's catch made the final 31–21 for the Illini. End Chris Slade, who replaced Don Reynolds when he was injured in the fifth game, had 11 tackles and a sack to win game MVP honors.

Virginia starters were center Tim Morris, guards Roy Brown and Trevor Ryals, tackles Ray Roberts and Tim O'Connor, who came in for Paul Collins when he was hurt against Clemson, and backs Marcus Wilson and Nikki Fisher. The defense had nose guard Ron Carey, tackles Chris Stearns, Joe Hall, and Billy Keys, deep men Keith McMeans and Tyrone Lewis, and linebacker Elton Toliver.

Backups were centers Lenny Pritchard and Tim Samec, guard Rip Leonard, and tackle Chris Borsari. Ends were Mark Cooke, Terry Tomlin, Johnnie Wilson, Dave Ware, and backs Alvin Snead and Gary Steele. Defenders were nose guard Matt Quigley, tackle Ken Miles, ends Tim Moss, James Pearson, Benson Goodwyn, John Runyon, linebackers Matt Woods and Mike Smith, and backs Greg Jeffries, Buddy Omohundro, Dave Brown, and Scott Griese, son of Miami Dolphins' Bob Griese. Letterman Chip Cathey was hurt and did not play. Ed Garno and Myron Martin were punters, and Mike Husted kicked off.

Duke's 6-1-0 record gave it a share of the league title and its best back-to-back seasons in over a quarter-century. Harold Green and Collin Mackie scored all of South Carolina's points in the opener until Mike Dingle ran in after Erik Anderson blocked a Bud Zuberer punt. Billy Ray threw to Clarkston Hines to close it to 27–21, but Dave Pitchko covered the onside kick to end it.

Ira Adler kicked three field goals for Northwestern, but Ray tossed twice to Walter Jones and two Roger Boone scores gave Duke the lead. Tim O'Brien threw to Rich Buchanan and Bob Griswold on a two-pointer and Bob Christian ran over twice for Francis Peay's Wildcats, but Chris Brown dived in for a 41–31 Blue Devil win.

Randy Gardner kicked two field goals against Tennessee, but three Reggie Cobb runs and one by Greg Amsler won it 28–6. Sterling Henton's passes to Von Reeves, the running of Chuck Webb, and a Thomas Woods punt return and Carl Pickens kickoff return set up Tennessee touchdowns, and Greg Burke kicked four extra points.

After losing to Virginia in the title chase, Duke was in it again with a 21–17 defeat of Clemson. A sunny day in Durham was even brighter as Ray and Hines had three scoring strikes and Randy Cuthbert went over twice against Army. Ben Barnett scored twice after Mike Mayweather and Calvin Cass carried it close, and Keith Havenstrite added a field goal for the Cadets. Bryan McWilliams ran in and threw to Bob Horn, but the last-period scores came up short in a 35–29 Duke win. A Dan DeArmas field goal for Maryland and Bren Lowery's 67-yard run on the first play of the last half cut Duke's lead to 22–10, but scoring catches by Dave Colonna and Marc Mays gave them breathing room. Wyatt Smith hijacked a pass to give Duke a 46–25 win and end a 17-year hex held by the Terps.

Duke led Georgia Tech 17–3 at the half, but Jerry Mays went 59 yards and Shawn Jones threw to Emmett Merchant to narrow it to 24–17. The Yellow Jackets were driving when Anthony Allen grabbed a fumble after a hit by Derrick Jackson. Cuthbert outran Thomas Balkcom 60 yards to the goal to add to his Duke mark of 234 yards rushing and finish off the pesky Jackets. A new rule since 1988 let Ken Swilling go 99 yards with an interception on the conversion attempt for a 30–19 final, but Ray was lost with an injury. Dave Brown took over against Wake Forest and threw a 76-yarder to Hines on the first play and hit him again on a 97-yarder for the longest play in Duke history. Wake pulled to within three points twice, but Duke kept the Deacons at arm's length for a 52–35 win.

Keith Ewell scored on a catch against North Carolina State, but Hines had two to break Elmo Wright's career mark in a 35–26 homecoming win.

Hines caught three more against North Carolina to set an ACC season mark of 17 and NCAA career mark of 38, and Brown had 479 yards passing for a one-game school record. Linebacker John Howell's sack on fourth down from the one preserved a shutout, as Duke stonewalled the Tar Heels for a 41–0 victory.

Duke's one-year school mark of 5,519 yards total offense ran dry against Texas Tech in the All–American Bowl. Jamie Gill hit Travis Price and Bart Talkington on the two-pointer and Jim Gray ran in three times before Duke scored. Anthony Lynn went in and Lin Elliott converted five times for Spike Dykes in a 49–21 win.

Duke starters included center Carey Metts, guards Brett Tulacro and Pete Petroff, and tackles Chip Nitowski and Chris Port. The defense had nose guard Scott Youmans, tackle Preston Anderson, and ends John McDonald and Tom Corpus. Linebackers were Mark Allen, Darrell Spells, George Edwards, and Randy Sally, with safety Erwin Sampson and cornerbacks Quint McCracken and Rodney Dickerson.

Backups on a team that graduated 24 of 25 were long snapper Stuart Albright, guards Bobby Highsmith and Kevin Patterson, and tackles Al Hagaman and Brandon Moore. Ends were Aaron Shaw, Andy Anderson, Darryl Clements, Keith Daniel, and Greg Downs, with running backs Randy Jones, Mike Verona, and conversion holder Steve Prince. On defense were nose guard Gregg McConnell, tackles Kedrick Eily and Doug Kley, and Tom Rhoads, Tim Curran, and Doug Atkinson at end. Linebackers were Marcus Dyer, Kurt Ligos, Chris Rising, and Chris Treston, with backs Mike Boland, Scott Brittingham, Keith DuBose, Rodney Hooks, Todd Hoyle, Mike Urso, Eric Volk, and Fonda Williams.

Clemson came in third at 5-2-0. Mitch Belton blocked Bruce Leicht's punt and Tony Mauney recovered for the final score in a 30–0 defeat of Furman. Florida State was stunned with two Terry Allen touchdowns and a Wayne Simmons 73-yard interception, a Tiger theft ranking with a Jimmy Quarles 90-yarder in 1951 and a James Hough 76-yarder in 1945. Allen's 73-yard dash made it 28–10 at the half, with Dexter Carter and Bill Mason kick scoring for FSU. Tackles Henry Ostazewski and Eric Hayes and nose guard Odell Haggins held Clemson to a pair of Chris Gardocki field goals, but a Paul Moore run and a Casey Weldon toss to Chris Parker fell short 34–23.

Three touchdowns in 32 seconds sealed Virginia Tech's fate 27–7. After Allen threw a 66-yard strike to Gary Cooper, Marcus Mickel returned the kickoff 90 yards for the VPI score, and Levon Kirkland's 47-yard interception ended the third quarter. Robert O'Neal and Eric Geter also intercepted, and Kirkland made seven stops on defense and Kenzil Jackson had six. Two Wes McFadden runs and one by Joe Henderson beat Maryland 31–7, and nose guard Rob Bodine had his best day with eight stops. The defeat by Duke set them back, but a win over Virginia put them in the hunt again.

Gardocki and Georgia Tech's Scott Sisson dueled each other with field goals until Jerry Mays caught a Shawn Jones pass and ran over for a 23–6 halftime lead. The shocked homecoming crowd saw Jones throw to Bobby Rodriguez for 30–6. DeChane Cameron ran in for Clemson, but Doug Brewster's 19 tackles could not hold off a 30–14 defeat. The Textile Bowl jinx ended as Dexter Davis made ten tackles, Ed McDaniel made nine, and Ashley Sheppard made five on special teams to turn back North Carolina State 30–10.

Clemson continued to win big. Wake Forest lost 44–10 as the Tigers scored on their first seven possessions, and Jon Kubu got in to kick the final conversion. Reggie Lawrence ran in for the second week in a row to overcome North Carolina 35–3, and Chester McGlockton had his sixth sack in the 45–0 rout of South Carolina.

Clemson's seniors were the first to win four bowl games in a row. West Virginia went ahead in the Gator Bowl on a Major Harris pass to James Jett, but the Tigers led 10–7 at the half. Harris dumped off repeatedly to Rico Tyler and Greg Dykes, but it usually ended in a Greg Hertzog punt. The last quarter belonged to Clemson as Vince Taylor's recovery choked off a drive, McGlockton had another sack for a score, and Gardocki's second kick made it 27–7.

Georgia Tech's strong finish brought them in fourth at 4-3-0. Stefan Scotton scored after Marco Coleman's recovery to put Tech ahead, but six opening-game turnovers won for the Wolfpack 38–28. Ken Swilling's 95-yard interception narrowed it to three at one time, but Barry Anderson's recovery set up the final score by the Pack. Eric Thomas had 19 tackles and Jerrelle Williams 18 in the loss to Virginia, and Calvin Tiggle led with 15 in the 21–10 loss to South Carolina. The Gamecocks went through Tech like Hurricane Hugo went through South Carolina two days before, as Mike Dingle's run, two Collin Mackie field goals, and George Rush's reception after Dale Campbell stole a pass made it 21–7 at intermission.

After three losses in three games, Georgia Tech finally got in the win column against Maryland. A Terry Pettis catch closed it to 14–7 at the half, but the Terp advantage went to 21–7 after recovering Willie Clay's muffed punt. Ten tackles by Mike Thomas kept Maryland afloat, but Shawn Jones tossed to Tom Covington and Scotton for the tie. After Jay Martin's recovery, Jones threw to Covington for the lead, and a Terrapin field goal ended it 28–24.

The Ramblin' Wreck was riding high as Ken Wilson's interception helped dump Clemson and North Carolina trailed 10–0 at the half. Then Mike Benefield scored after Doxie Jordan intercepted, and the Tar Heels went ahead as Larry Whiteside blocked a Scott Aldredge punt and Cliff Baskerville recovered the ball in the end zone. After Scott Barron's catch, Jones scrambled up the middle on a broken play, picked up a block by Dave Stegall, and ran 30 yards untouched to pull it out 17–14 with 51 seconds remaining.

After the loss to Duke, Tech came back to stomp Dale Strahm's Western Carolina team 34–7. Another score was averted when Tech's Jeff Howard coughed up the ball on a hit by Larry Inman. Strahm took over when Bob Waters died of amyotrophic lateral sclerosis (Lou Gehrig's disease), but WCU's only score was a 68-yard run by Ricky Gardin when Brett Baker blocked a field goal try. In Wake Forest's 43–14 loss, Tech added a safety when Travis Johns covered a loose ball in the end zone. T. J. Edwards ran in for the last Georgia Tech touchdown on a drive directed by Lee Williamson, and Tony Rogers and Ricky Proehl scored late for the Deacons. Proehl topped Wayne Baumgardner's 2,431 career yards with 2,949 yards on 188 catches (one behind the ACC mark of Duke's Clarkston Hines) to become Wake's leading receiver, and Wilson Hoyle ended as the leading Deacon scorer with 230 career points. Phil Barnhill finished with 2,454 yards passing for a one-year mark at Wake Forest.

Two Brian Lowe field goals sent Boston College ahead at the half, but Swilling's 72-yard abduction of a Mike Powers pass made it 7–6. BC's front five of Chris Gildea, Pete Gray, Jim Biestek, Ivan Caesar, and Kevin Pearson put on a rush to stymie the Tech attack, and catches by Mark Chmura, Ray Hilvert, and Mike Sanders set up two more kicks by Lowe to lead 12–7. Scott Sisson's field goal trimmed it to two, and Brent Goolsby's catch led to another Sisson kick and a 13–12 win with 42 seconds left on the clock.

The Yellow Jackets finished off Georgia in the finale. Rodney Hampton went in twice on drives led by Greg Talley for 14–13 at halftime, but Jerry Mays ran over to put Tech ahead. Scotton scored after Sean Smith deflected a pass to Willie Burks, and a Mays catch boosted it further. Georgia's Preston Jones threw to Sean Hummings and to Art Marshall for two points and a 33–22 final.

Mays ended the season with 1,349 yards rushing, a mark second to

Eddie Lee Ivery's 1,562 yards in 1978, and his career record of 3,699 yards was second to Robert Lavette's 4,066 yards.

North Carolina State's fourth-place tie at 4-3-0 opened with six straight wins. After downing Maryland 10–6 and Georgia Tech, State checkmated a John Henry Mills catch for Wake Forest to take a 27–17 win. North Carolina was crushed for the second straight year, as interceptions by Billy Ray Haynes, Bobby Houston, and Eddie Cashion led to scores by Chris Corders, Bobby Jurgens, and Preston Poag, with an Al Byrd catch setting up Corders' score. Derrick Debnam's end-zone tackle added a safety for a 40–6 win. Randy Perine ran over for Kent State, but two Damon Hartman field goals and Shawn Montgomery's pass to Todd Harrison put NCSU ahead. Pat Young threw to Shawn Barnes and Mark Cunningham after Reggie Cook blocked a punt for a KSU lead, but Joe Johnson ran in a 60-yard interception and Aubrey Shaw's 48-yard scoring run took it 42–22. Phil Ironside tossed to Kenny Donaldson and Wade Johnson went in for Boots Donnelly's Middle Tennessee State team, but runs by Greg Manior and Brian Roxburgh won for the Wolfpack 35–14.

After State lost to the top ACC teams, South Carolina's Todd Ellis left with an injury, but the passes of backup Dick DeMasi and Darren Parker's punts could not stem a 20–10 Gamecock loss. A Bo Campbell recovery and Roger Brown's pass theft led to Virginia Tech's 25–23 win, and State met Dick Tomey's Arizona team in the first Copper Bowl in Tucson. Elijah Austin, Mike Jones, and Ray Agnew led the Pack's front three, but Ron Veal hit Olatide Ogunfiditimi and Scott Geyer's 85-yard interception scored for Arizona. Gary Coston added a field goal to win 17–10, as linebacker twins Chris and Kevin Singleton stopped three late drives by the Pack.

Montgomery ended as State's leading passer with 5,298 career yards. His 2,632 yards passing were a season record for the Wolfpack, and his 73 attempts against Duke were a one-game NCAA mark.

1990

Georgia Tech was ACC champ for the first time with a 6-0-1 record. Bobby Ross added the national title for good measure and became the only coach to win the ACC crown at different schools.

North Carolina State opened the season with a Damon Hartman field goal. The Pack scored again as Tech started inside its ten but fumbled. Fernandus Vinson scooped up the ball and dashed 11 yards to make it 10–0.

Bobby Ross continued the national championship tradition at Georgia Tech.

Another Hartman kick and Shawn Jones pass to Greg Lester made the halftime 13–7. Two last-period scores on a Jones pass to William Bell and Jeff Wright's run took it 21–13. Safety Ken Swilling made 12 tackles, and tackle Jerimiah McClary and end Marlon Williams both made 11. Behind the running of Jim Roberts and Robert Shamsid-Deen, Vince Carelli directed Tennessee–Chattanooga to three Rodney Allen field goals and a 17–9 halftime deficit. The punting of Pumpy Tudors kept UTC in it until Stefan Scotton scored and another touchdown by Bell broke the game open early in the third quarter. Stan Nix, the coach's son, led UTC in the last half, but Scott Sisson's third field goal and a Jeff Howard completion to Derek Goshay closed the scoring at 44–9.

South Carolina's Bobby Fuller, who followed Sparky Woods to Columbia from Appalachian State, guided the Gamecocks to only two Collin

Mackie field goals, as linebacker Jerrelle Williams, end Marco Coleman, and safety Kevin Peebles led a relentless defense to a 27–6 win. The defense set a school record of 11 quarterback sacks on Maryland's Scott Zolak and Jim Sandwisch in a 31–3 win and ran its string of not allowing a touchdown to 14 quarters.

Clemson fell behind 14–0 as Jones tossed to Emmett Merchant and Lester, with the second score coming after tackle Coleman Rudolph's recovery on a Chris Simmons hit. Chris Gardocki's four field goals slimmed it to 14–12, but T. J. Edwards ran in to make it 21–12. The string of no-touchdown quarters ended as DeChane Cameron's late score cut it to 21–19. A short punt by Scott Aldredge put Gardocki at bat again, but the roar in Bobby Dodd Stadium told downtown Atlanta that his kick was short and Tech won.

The tie with North Carolina was the only blemish on Georgia Tech's championship season. Doxie Jordan's recovery and Cookie Massey's interception set up two Clint Gwaltney field goals, but Tech led 10–6 as the last period started. Carolina took the lead after Scott McAlister punted and Reggie Clark's recovery got it back, then stopped Tech on the next series at the one on a tackle by Eric Gash. Tech kept coming as a Tom Covington catch brought another Sisson three-pointer and 13–13 tie with 1:01 remaining. Duke trailed 17–14 at the half and an 85-yard kickoff return by Tech's Kevin Tisdel made it 31–24 after three. The margin went to 48–31 on 17 last-period Yellow Jacket points and a Duke score after Travis Pearson intercepted for rookie coach Barry Wilson.

A record crowd of 49,700 overflowed Scott Stadium to see one of the most historic games in ACC grid annals. Millions more on CBS-TV watched unbeaten Georgia Tech take on 7-0-0 Virginia which had been voted number one for the past three weeks. The Cavs led 13–0 on Shawn Moore's run and two Jake McInerney field goals, but a Jones 23-yard scramble sliced it to six. Moore pushed over for 21–7, but Jones threw to Jerry Gilchrist and a third run by Moore made it 28–14 at halftime. Gilchrist went in again on a flanker reverse after linebacker Calvin Tiggle's recovery, and Merchant's reception tied it at 28. Herman Moore's 63-yard pass play untied it quickly, but Tiggle's interception infused Tech with new life.

Momentum forsook the Wahoo camp and put zing into the Yellow Jackets. Bell knotted it to end the third quarter, and Sisson's field goal sent Tech ahead for the first time 38–35. The crown slipped away as the Cavs were called for illegal procedure and a touchdown pass to Aaron Mundy was nullified because only six men were on the offensive line. Then Tiggle batted down a pass, and McInerney's kick tied it with 2:34 left. Virginia failed to hold, and Sisson kicked home a 41–38 win with seven seconds remaining.

Georgia Tech climbed into the top ten for the first time and was voted seventh. They battled Virginia Tech for three quarters only to see it end scoreless as Keith Holmes blocked a field goal try by VPI's Brian Reaves. Will Furrer's passes to Tony Kennedy and Nick Cullen set up a Mickey Thomas three-pointer, but Sisson kicked it to a tie three minutes later. After Simmons fell on a muffed handoff, Sisson's kick won it for the second straight week with eight seconds left. Tech had a 6–3 win and rose to fourth.

A 42–7 win over Wake Forest gave Georgia Tech its first ACC championship. Bell went in and Jones tossed to Bobby Rodriguez, and Carl Lawson's plunge and flanker reverse by Rodriguez made it 28–0 at the half. Cornerback Willie Clay covered a loose ball to stop a Wake score, and offensive guard Jim Lavin captured an endzone fumble for more Tech points. Bryan Baxter took over in the last quarter for starting nose guard Kevin Battle, Jim Gallagher and Rich Kimsey stepped in at tackle, Tom Johnson and Bill Weaver labored at end or outside linebacker, and Darrell Swilling and Erick Fry finished up at linebacker. After Keith West came in and threw a 69-yarder to Todd Dixon for Wake, a Mike Williams 83-yard interception completed the scoring, and the Wreck crept up to third.

Georgia jumped to a 9–0 lead on Doobie Hearst's run and a John Kasay field goal, but a second-quarter splurge gave Tech a 23–12 halftime lead. After UGa's Larry Ware lost the ball in a crowd, Jones threw to Jim Mac-Kendree and Rodriguez again to go in front further. Georgia's Greg Talley replaced Joe Dupree and threw to Andre Hastings, and Mack Strong ran in the two-pointer. Kasay's third field goal and one by Sisson ended it 40–23, and the Ramblin' Wreck finished the regular season in second place.

Shamu the whale's Sea World blimp floated over the Florida Citrus Bowl as Mimi Mann interpreted for Nebraska's hearing-impaired Kenny Walker, but Georgia Tech rolled to a 21–0 lead. Tom Haase replaced Mike Grant and hit Johnny Mitchell, and Derek Brown ran 50 yards for the Cornhuskers. After Jay Martin nailed a fumble, Sisson kicked it to 24–14 at the half. Holmes blocked a field goal try by Greg Barrios, but Jones connected with Gilchrist and then went in on a bootleg. William Washington's score still separated them by ten. Nebraska came back on catches by Nate Turner and Omar Soto, but a pair of sacks by safety Thomas Balkcom slowed the Husker attack. Bell added two fourth-quarter touchdown runs for a 45–21 victory.

After Eric "Public" Bieniemy "Number one" scored the winning touchdown for coach Jim McCartney that beat Notre Dame 10–9, the AP voted Colorado number one, while the UPI had Georgia Tech in the top spot. After NBC-TV reported that Colorado was national champion, Georgia folks deluged NBC's switchboard with the other half of the story, and Tom Brokaw duly amended it the next day.

"It's settled now," said Bobby Ross. "What did Colorado beat Nebraska by, 15 points? We beat them by 24." Said Nebraska's Reggie Cooper, "They're the nation's only unbeaten team." Coach Tom Osborne agreed, "Anytime you go undefeated you've got an argument."

Georgia Tech starters were Billy Chubb and Veryl Miller at center, guard Joe Siffri, and tackles Mike Mooney and Darryl Jenkins. Backups were deep snapper Stacy Parker, guards Mark Hutto and Scott Gold, tackles Russ Freeman and Woodie Milam, ends Brent Goolsby, Terry Pettis, Anthony Rice, Keenan Walker, and backs Jim Reese, Derrick Hamilton, and Paul Bowman. On defense were Orion Cox at end, linebackers Steve Pharr and Scott Travis, and backs Angelo Rush, Curley Day, Eric Bellamy, Marcus Coleman, Darrell Ray, punt returner Jason McGill, and Alan Waters who kicked off.

After three weeks in Camelot, Virginia's veteran team ended second with 5-2-0. The Kansas sun sizzled at 94 degrees by game time with Glen Mason's Jayhawks, and by the last quarter Virginia was hotter than the 130-degree temperature of the artificial turf in Memorial Stadium. Kansas linebacker coach Bob Fello stationed Curtis Moore in the middle and loaded the perimeter, but instead of going wide Virginia went north and south. Terry Kirby started the scoring, and Shawn Moore threw to Bruce McGonnigal and pushed in himself. After Joe Hall recovered a Chip Hilleary fumble on a hit by tackle Dave Ware, a Moore to Brian Satola pass put it 31–0 at the half. Rickie Peete's recovery of a fumble by Tony "Quick" Sands set up a Jake McInerney field goal, and Moore's third scoring pass to Herman Moore made the margin 38–3. Another touchdown toss sailed over Terry Tomlin's head, but a Greg Jeffries interception set up Nikki Fisher's score. Jerrod Washington dived in twice to complete the scoring, and Dan Eichloff's field goal and a Roger Robben run for Kansas made the final 59–10.

A week later Virginia ended the three-decade torment with a first-ever defeat of Clemson after 29 straight losses. DeChane Cameron scrambled 25 yards for a Clemson lead, but two McInerney field goals, one after James Pearson's recovery on a Chris Slade hit, made it 7–6 at the half. The Cavs went ahead as Gary Steele and Dave Sweeney pounded over center, Derek Dooley, Vince Dooley's son, worked the sideline, Tomlin raced 23 yards on a reverse, and Kirby leaped the last few yards for a score. Jason Wallace, whose blown coverage last year gave Clemson a late win, redeemed himself on a weaving 79-yard punt return to set up the score that clinched it. He dipped in and out behind blocks by Randy Foley and Tyrone Lewis on his runback, and an alley-oop to Moore ended it 20–7.

Said defensive coordinator Frank Spaziani afterward, "Clemson's game is to run at you. They're not used to playing catch-up." A record crowd of 46,800 cheered the Tigers' dilemma: "No one beats Virginia thirty times in a row!"

The new goal posts were in place when George Chaump, who replaced Elliott Uzelak over the winter, brought Navy to town, but Moore threw four touchdowns and scored once for a 35–0 halftime lead. Navy's only bright spot during this time was an interception by Darrell Graham. B. J. Mason's flanker reverse and Frank Schenk's conversion scored for Navy, but Alvin Snead added one for UVa. After three sacks and interceptions by Keith McMeans, Buddy Omohundro, and Greg McClellan, Alton Grizzard threw to Bob Holmberg to make the final 56–14. The Cavaliers rounded out the top ten by taking over tenth in the Associated Press writers' poll.

McMeans hauled in a theft to tie Pat Chester's school mark of 16, Leroy Gallman fumbled the ball away, and Gene Toliver fell on yet another fumble as seven Duke turnovers were turned into five Cavalier touchdowns. Dave Brown ran in an option pitch from Matt Blundin for a 59–0 final, and Duke's frustration became evident when Duane Marks got into an altercation with Virginia punter Ed Garno. The Cavaliers climbed to seventh, but coach Tom O'Brien thought there was room for improvement in the offensive line.

Moore outlegged J. D. Gibbs, the son of Washington Redskins coach Joe Gibbs, to the goal with a touchdown catch, but William and Mary trailed only 27–21 at the half on the running of Tyrone Shelton and three Dan Mueller conversions. Mark Dixon recovered the onside kickoff after Tony Covington's fiery halftime speech, and backfield coach Ken Mack beamed as Kirby and Fisher led a 29-point third-period outbreak. "That just kills the defense," said W&M linebacker Brad Uhl. W&M's Robert Green scored three times and Chris Hakel tossed to Michael Locke to make the final 63–35, and Virginia moved up to fourth. Watching his son, Bill, center the ball on punts was Kentucky coach Bill Curry, who came over from Lexington since his Wildcats were idle that Saturday.

Eight sacks of North Carolina State's Terry Jordan and ten tackles by

P. J. Killian took UVa to a 31–0 win. Shawn Moore's first touchdown went to Steele on the first series when he raced past Billy Ray Haynes and Tyler Lawrence, and Herman Moore caught the second on his back when Joe Johnson tipped the ball into the air. Moore speared another toss behind Sebastian Savage for an 83-yard score, and George Welsh was so enthused that he ran out to high-five him on his return to the bench. When Michigan State bumped Gary Moeller's Michigan team from the top spot 28–27, the Cavaliers stepped into the hallowed precincts of number one.

McInerney's three field goals put Virginia ahead, but Wake Forest was not impressed by its illustrious visitor and led 14–9 on Phil Barnhill's toss to Darrell France and a Tony Rogers run after Aubrey Hollifield's recovered fumble. The Cavs put it in cruise when nose guard Mike Smith was hurt just before the half to lead 28–14. Then they won it 49–14 as tackle Robbie Lingerfelt left with a broken ankle, and backs Lamont Scales and George Coghill were swamped with 258 yards passing. The euphoria of the throne room cast a spell over Charlottesville until Georgia Tech kicked them out only seven seconds before the witching hour.

It was a tough week for Virginia, but the Moores took advantage of a Tar Heel blitz to go ahead 7–0. Clint Gwaltney's field goal cut it to four, but Fisher ran in after Moore outjumped the coverage by Doxie Jordan as help from Rondell Jones arrived too late. Kirby's touchdown catch made it 21–3 at the half. Linebackers Tommy Thigpen and Dwight Hollier held UVa to a last-half field goal, but five sacks on Todd Burnett, two each by tackles Hall and Marcus Washington and another by Killian at linebacker, benched him. Backup Chuckie Burnette came in and directed North Carolina to a late score by Mike Faulkerson for a 24–10 final.

For the third straight week, Virginia won the first half but slumped after intermission. Fisher ran in twice to lead Maryland 14–0, but Troy Jackson scored to cut it in half. Dooley's catch from Satola on a flanker reverse opened it to 21–7, and the Cavs lapsed into the lotus land which stole away their aggressiveness.

The second half started with a recovery by Rick Fleece when Moore fumbled on a sack by Glenn Page, and four plays later Scott Zolak's pass to Barry Johnson trimmed it to 21–14. A 59-yard end run by Mark Mason tied it soon after. Wallace made the gap seven again on a 60-yard punt return, but a Gene Thomas catch evened it at 28. After Scott Rosen intercepted, Marcus Badgett's 71-yard pass play set up Mason's go-ahead score to start the last period.

In the final minutes, Moore hurt his right thumb when he was downed by Louis Johnson, and Dan DeArmas took a safety to make it 35–30. Derek Steele sacked Blundin to end the game, and Maryland athletic director Andy Geiger congratulated everyone who crossed his path. "I feel great," yelled Maryland linebacker Jack Bradford. "This is a memory I'll have for the rest of my life."

The largest crowd ever to watch a football game in Virginia, 54,157, was in Blacksburg, but the Cavs didn't even win the first half this week. Mark Poindexter went in for Virginia Tech, Will Furrer threw to Nick Cullen, Mickey Thomas made a field goal, and a Greg Daniels catch made it 24–0. The Cavs got six points when Kirby ran in before the half after John Rivers and Tyrone Drakeford were caught holding, and when Moore beat Damien Russell on a 66-yard bomb it looked like UVa was back in it. Moore's scoring catch in his 10th straight game tied last year's mark set by Houston's Emanual Hazard, most of them on David Klingler's tosses for coach John Jenkins. But Rusty Pendleton recovered a bad exchange to nix it, and Vaughn Hebron's run and Poindexter's catch closed it 38–13. VPI played errorless ball, while Virginia's six turnovers underlined the hoary maxim of Hurry Up Yost that football games are lost and not won. UVa eschewed a trip to the Fiesta Bowl when Arizona voted against a holiday for Martin Luther King, and accepted an invitation to play Tennessee in the Sugar Bowl.

Virginia rolled to a 16–0 lead over Tennessee but again ran out of steam in the last half. Greg Burke's field goal trimmed away three, Tony Thompson ran in, and Andy Kelly's pass to Carl Pickens cut it to 19–17. McInerney's third field goal made it 22–17 and forced the Vols to go for a touchdown in order to win. In the last minute Kelly completed to Alvin Harper, Greg Amsler took it to the one, and Thompson went in with 31 seconds to go for a 23–22 win. "Masterful," said coach Johnny Majors. "Every tick of the clock counted, and there was no room for a mistake."

But Virginia's point-a-minute offense had sputtered, and the defense that had been found out by William and Mary sent its followers into the night broken-hearted and tearful again.

Danny Ford was forced to resign due to charges of questionable recruiting practices, but new coach Ken Hatfield led Clemson to a second-place tie at 5-2-0. Arlington Nunn's 55-yard interception started the scoring parade to make it a long day for Long Beach State and George Allen. Doug Thomas added a 98-yard kickoff return, and Rodney Blunt, Howard Hall, Jimmy McLees, and Ronald Williams all scored. Derrick Witherspoon,

Larry Ryans, Rudy Harris, and Paul Caputo fattened their averages in the 59–0 rout.

After the 30th time was the charm for Virginia, Clemson led the Terps on a Chris Gardocki field goal. Scott Zolak's pass to Gene Thomas put Maryland ahead, but the joy lasted just as long as it took Thomas to race 98 yards with another kickoff return. Troy Jackson ran in for a 14–10 Terp lead at the half, but Frank Namath centered the ball over Zolak's head from the shotgun for a safety to slice it to two. The Maryland lead went to 17–12 on a Dan DeArmas field goal, but DeChane Cameron's toss to Harris gave Clemson an 18–17 first-ever win in Baltimore's Memorial Stadium.

Williams ran in three times against Appalachian State, Ryans had a scoring catch, and Witherspoon streaked 81 yards on another score in the 48–0 win. Moaned App State coach Jerry Moore, "Our defense held them and Gardocki kicks a 57-yard field goal. We force a third-and-long and Cameron hits Ryans with a 40-yard TD." Leroy Gallman returned a kickoff 78 yards for the Duke score in a 26–7 Tiger win at homecoming, and Ray Goff's Georgia Dawgs got only a John Kasay field goal in a 34–3 loss as Clemson pushed on to the total defense title of 216.9 yards per game.

Georgia Tech won by two as Gardocki had four field goals and a fifth hit the crossbar from 53 yards out, but his kick put the Tigers ahead of North Carolina State. Ex-signal-caller Charles Davenport, now at split end, scored on a catch and a reverse for the Pack, but Dexter Davis went 52 yards with a fumble to cut it to 14–10. Cameron threw to Terry Smith for a Tiger lead, but a Damon Hartman field goal tied it. After Hall ran in for a 24–17 lead, Shane Scott recoverd the kickoff, and the Tigers left town victorious. Nunn ran in a pass theft on the second play to begin the 24–6 defeat of Wake Forest for Clemson's 500th win. Wake was held to two first-half field goals by Dave Behrmann, and Richard Moncrief came in to finish up at quarterback for the Tigers.

Clemson closed the season with a 20–3 win over the Tar Heels and a 24–15 defeat of South Carolina. The Gamecocks cut the lead to 17–15 in the last quarter but failed the two-pointer, and Tony Kennedy ran in for the insurance Clemson needed. The Tigers then met John Mackovic's Fighting Illini in the Hall of Fame Bowl in Tampa. Illinois was led by Howard Griffith, who gained 263 yards against Northwestern to break Jim Grabowski's one-game record of 239 yards. Before the game Griffith met Red Grange whose career record of 31 touchdowns he broke by one, but in the game Griffith gained only 59 yards. Cameron tossed scores to Hall and Thomas, Nunn ran in a Jason Verduzco interception, and Gardocki had three field goals in a 30–0 win. Steve Feagin's late run was stopped to secure the shutout, and the Tigers were 10-2-0 for the fourth consecutive year to become the ACC's winningest seniors.

Maryland finished fourth at 4-3-0. Virginia Tech led on a Mickey Thomas field goal, but Scott Zolak put the Terps ahead on a toss to Frank Wycheck. VPI countered with a Will Furrer pass, but Dan DeArmas kicked it to a tie at the half. Two more kicks tied it again, but Zolak's 51-yard strike to Gene Thomas with 61 seconds to go gave Maryland a 20–13 win. Zolak's throw to Barry Johnson held up until the last quarter against West Virginia, but a Brad Carroll field goal and Darren Studstill pass to Jon Jones sent the Mountaineers ahead. After Jim Gray's sack of Zolak was cancelled by a penalty, another Zolak-to-Thomas bomb of 59 yards down the middle won it 14–10 with 2:27 showing on the clock.

After a one-point loss to Clemson, Maryland beat North Carolina State by one point as Lubo Zizakovic blocked State's first conversion try. The Wolfpack struck first with a Charles Davenport pass to Bobby Jurgens, but a DeArmas three-pointer halved the score. Aubrey Shaw ran in after a David Merritt theft to make it 12–3 for the Pack, but the Terps replied with a touchdown by Troy Jackson to trim it to two. After a Mike Thomas fumble recovery, DeArmas sent one through for a 13–12 win with 11 seconds left.

Michigan's perennial powerhouse was pushed by the Terps before the Wolverine legions took their toll. An interception by Martin Davis and a DeArmas field goal made it 7–3 after one. Elvis Grbac cranked up and threw to Desmond Howard and Jon Vaughn ran in for Michigan, but Andre Vaughn's score cut it to 21–10 at the half. Darren Colvin's dash pared it to four, but a Jarrod Bunch catch and J. D. Carlson field goal swelled it to 31–17. Another Vaughn tally and Ken Sollom toss to Kevin Owen ended it 45–17.

Four early scores led to Wake Forest's 41–13 loss, and four Bret Boehly catches helped beat Duke, but a DeArmas missile won it 23–20 with 50 seconds left. Three Clint Gwaltney field goals scored for a resurgent North Carolina team, but DeArmas put the Terps ahead at intermission 10–9. The Tar Heels owned the last half as Natrone Means scored twice, Thomas Smith ran in an interception 24 yards, and another Gwaltney kick won going away 34–10.

Leonard Humphries scored on a 74-yard interception for Penn State, but the Zolak-to-Johnson connection tied it. DeArmas toed the Terps ahead, but a Craig Fayak field goal tied it after Mike Hopson dropped a punt and Matt Baggett recovered. Again Maryland ran out of petrol in the second half as Tony Sacca threw to Dave Daniels and Leroy Thompson ran ten yards for a 24–10 victory.

After getting the last half right against Virginia, Maryland met Louisiana Tech in the Independence Bowl at Shreveport. Jackson ran in twice for a Terp lead, but Mike Richardson went in to cut it in half. After Myron Baker intercepted, Jason Davis took it in for a 14–14 halftime tie, but the replay showed he stepped out of bounds. Louisiana Tech still led 21–20 after Richardson and Jackson ran over again, but Eddie Brown reversed to Davis on the kickoff for a 63-yard return. Gene Johnson tossed to Bobby Slaughter, and a Chris Boniol field goal made the spread 31–20. Maryland scored on a Mark Mason swing pass, and then went ahead as Zolak threw to Johnson on fourth-and-12 with 52 seconds left. After Lorenzo Baker's kickoff return, Boniol kicked it to a 34–34 knot for coach Joe Raymond Peace as the gun sounded.

Although North Carolina finished 3-3-1, 3-4-0 North Carolina State was pitted against Southern Mississippi in the All–American Bowl. Jeff Bower took over as USM coach when Curley Hallman left to replace Mike Archer at Louisiana State, and Brett Favre's toss to Mark Montgomery gave him a lead, but Jim Taylor failed to convert. Terry Jordan scored on an option play, and Mark Fowble's kick made it 7–6. Gary Downs went over the top for the Wolfpack, but another Favre-to-Montgomery hookup and a two-point pass to Mike Welch tied it. Fowble uncoupled it with a field goal for 17–14 at the half. Tony Smith scored after a sack by James Singleton and a punt blocked by Pat Wynn, but a Bobby Jurgens catch put State ahead again. Greg Manior increased the lead to ten in the last quarter, but Favre completed to Welch to end the game at 31–27.

The ACC won three of five bowl games, lost one in the final minute, and had one tied at the gun. It also won almost 53 percent of its non-conference games in the 1980s and 28 of 36 this year for the best percentage among major conferences. With the addition of Florida State for the 1991 season, the ACC looks to be even stronger in the future.

1991

Clemson was back with a 6-1-0 mark to take the title. Appalachian State was shut out in the opener 34–0, as Ronald Williams scored on the second series, and Paul Caputo and Derrick Witherspoon ran in to make it 24–0 at the half. Nelson Welch unlimbered his leg with a pair of field goals, and

Richard Moncrief added a pass to Terry Smith. Tiger punter Chuck Lynch got off to a good start with three punts inside the 20, and tackles Kelvin Hankins and Les Hall led the blocking on offense. Temple took the lead on a Trent Thompson to Bryant Garvin toss, but a Larry Ryans end-around tied it, and a DeChane Cameron pass to Dwayne Bryant put Clemson ahead. Rudy Harris bucked over in the second half, and Jeff Sauve came in to convert for 37–7 over Jerry Berndt's Owls.

National champ Georgia Tech went in front on a Shawn Jones run, but Welch cut it to 7–3 by halftime. The two teams knocked heads until Robert O'Neal's punt return set up the winning tally to take it 9–7 with 2:06 remaining. Middle guard Rob Bodine and linebacker Ed McDaniel again led in tackles and were instrumental in blanking Tech for three quarters. A road trip ended the victory string with a 27–12 Georgia win. Welch tied Kamon Parkman's three-pointer with less than a minute left in the half, but Eric Zeier came back with a 59-yarder to Art Marshall and another to Andre Hastings to lead at intermission. The teams traded field goals in the third period before another Zeier-to-Hastings pass widened the gap. A pair of touchdown passes kept the spread the same until a late Garrison Hearst plunge and Todd Peterson conversion locked it up. Linebacker Kenzil Jackson had his best day with ten tackles. The temporary setback leveled off in the 20–20 tie with Virginia, but it took 59 minutes to do it. Matt Blundin completed to Aaron Mundy and Mike Husted kicked the Cavaliers to ten first-period points, and they continued to lead by ten until a late touchdown and field goal knotted it. The Cavs drove into field goal range and were about to make it two in a row, but linebacker Wayne Simmons got his hand on the ball to gain the tie.

The Tigers had four ACC player of the week selections against Virginia. Tight end Tyrone Gibson was the offensive lineman with 12 knockdown blocks, while tackle Chester McGlockton was defensive lineman with ten tackles. Punt returner Darnell Stephens was the rookie of the week, and O'Neal was the defensive back of the week.

Clemson wore purple jerseys for the first time since 1939 and turned back previously unbeaten North Carolina State 29–19. Geoff Bender threw to Charles Davenport to cut the margin in two at 14–7, but Welch tied a school record with five field goals to maintain the lead. Bodine was again the ACC defensive lineman of the week with ten stops, while roverback Tyron Mouzon and linebacker Levon Kirkland both had eight. Rodney Blunt ran in twice and Doug Bolin once to lead Wake Forest 28–0 at the half, with Wake getting ten on a Mike Green field goal and a Keith West completion to Todd Dixon. Jeb Flesch keyed the offensive line with 12 knockdown blocks.

A driving rain as thick as coast guard weather kept the North Carolina game at 7–6 until two last-quarter scores won for Clemson 21–6. Jason Stanicek led two Carolina drives that ended in Clint Gwaltney field goals, but Brentson Buckner, Chuck O'Brien, and McGlockton all had sacks to stymie the Tar Heel attack. A Jim Sandwisch 56-yarder to Jason Kremus gave Maryland a brief lead, but it was all Clemson from then on, including an 89-yard punt return by Stephens for a 40–7 win. South Carolina scored first-half points on a Robert Brooks catch and a Marty Simpson field goal, but the Tigers topped last week's total in a 41–24 triumph. Rob DeBoer and Wright Mitchell added fourth-quarter touchdowns for the Gamecocks.

Ken Hatfield had to go a long way to get his 100th career victory, as Duke led 14–7 at the end of the third period on a pair of passes from Dave Brown to Brad Breedlove. Another catch by Chris Brown scored for the Blue Devils, but 26 last-quarter points won for Clemson 33–21 in the 16th annual Coca-Cola Bowl in Tokyo.

Clemson suffered its second defeat at the hands of California in the Florida Citrus Bowl. The Bears began with a pitch from Mike Pawlawski to Russell White around right end. White gave the ball to Sean Dawkins who tossed it back to Pawlawski. Pawlawski threw to White down the right sideline, and two plays later Greg Zomalt scored from the one. Doug Brien kicked a field goal after Buckner was ejected for punching, and Brian Treggs made it 17–0 with a 72-yard punt return. A block by Darryl Brown paved the way, and Matt Clizbe led the sideline celebration. Welch added a first-quarter field goal and Cameron went 62 yards on a scramble, but by halftime Cal had a 24–10 margin. Guard Eric Mahlum set up a Cal field goal on a fumbleroosky, and defensive MVP Mack Travis at nose guard led a defense that held the Tigers to one last-half field goal. Cal threw passes on 29 of its first 35 plays behind blocks by senior center Steve Gordon and four-year starter Troy Auzenne at tackle, and Bruce Snyder's Bears climbed to number eight with a 37–13 win.

In addition to those mentioned, Clemson starters were center Mike Brown, guard Stacy Seegars, and tackle Bruce Bratton. Others were center Curtis Whitley, guard John Harris, ends Jason Davis, Steve Derriso, Mike Samnik, and backs Lance Easton, Rich Cassidy, Howard Hall, Tony Kennedy, and Jimmy McLees.

Defensive starters were linebacker Ashley Sheppard, with Eric Geter and Tony Mauney at the corners. Others were David Davis at nose guard, and tackles Arthur Bussie, Pierre Wilson, Al Richard, Warren Forney, Mark Owens. Linebackers were Tim Jones, Michael Barber, Darren Calhoun, Lewis Usher, Rod Adams, Shane Scott, and backs Norris Brown, James Trapp, David Joye, Butch Fewster, Dave Goudelock, Stacy Lewis, Roger Hutchins.

North Carolina State's number-two finish started with a bang. Interceptions by starting backs Ricky Turner, Sebastian Savage, Dewayne Washington, Mike Reid, and Billy Ray Haynes at linebacker turned back Virginia Tech 7–0, and Terry Jordan completed to Shad Santee to start the 47–0 rout of Pete Cordelli's Kent State club. Greg Manior bulled straight ahead to put Wake Forest in the hole, as Mike Green's field goal gave the Deacs their only points in a 30–3 loss. A catch by Joey Jauch scored for North Carolina, but their 24–7 defeat marked the first time the Pack had beaten them four years in a row. Jordan and Haynes left hurt, but Geoff Bender threw to Eddie Goines and Charles Davenport, and linebacker Gregg Giannamore came in to shore up the defense. A Mark Thomas hit led to a David Merritt interception, and Savage sped 99 yards down the sideline with another stolen pass to sew it up.

After a Reggie Lawrence scoring catch, the defense continued to turn in big plays on a Tyler Lawrence theft and Turner's fumble recovery for a 20–7 lead over Georgia Tech. But Tech went ahead on a 52-yard burst over center by David Hendrix and Willie Clay's interception, only to have Bender's bootleg gain a 28–21 triumph. Another come-from-behind win saw Marshall go ahead 14–3 as Michael Payton threw to Brian Dowler and Orlando Hatchett dived in. After Keith Battle's kickoff return, Bender completed to Robert Hinton, Chris Williams, and Ledel George before Aubrey Shaw went in with 60 seconds left. Savage grabbed the onside kick on the hop, and State was still in business as the crowd went wild. William King intercepted to give their joy a roller-coaster ride, but a penalty gave the Pack one more chance. Bender lofted a pass to Davenport who leaped high in the end zone to bring it down, and Damon Hartman's third-quarter field goal was the margin of victory 15–14.

Clemson's win made them the favorite to take the title, but State bounced back to beat South Carolina 38–21. Bender tossed to Todd Harrison and Ray Griffis to make it 28–7, with Brandon Bennett going over for the Gamecock score. Bobby Fuller threw touchdowns to Eddie Miller and Leroy Jeter to close the gap to seven, but ten fourth-quarter points put the game out of reach. A 91-yard catch-and-run from Matt Blundin to Tyrone Davis touched off Virginia's 42–10 win over State. Blundin threw two scoring tosses to Larry Holmes and Gary Steele went over for 35–3 before Bender left with an injury and Terry Harvey took over. The homecoming fans finally had something to cheer about with a score by Gary Downs, but Alvin Snead scored so the spread stayed the same.

The Duke game had the crowd on its feet from start to finish. Randy Gardner kicked Duke ahead, but Anthony Barbour's 46-yard run put State in front. Dave Brown threw to Stan Dorsey and Marc Mays, and Downs ran in for 24–14 after three periods. State began its comeback as Damien Covington recovered a fumble to thwart a Duke drive, and seconds later Brad Breedlove bobbled a Tim Kilpatrick punt and Lee Knight fell on it in the end zone to make it 24–21. Duke spread it to ten again on Brown's pass to Walter Jones, but State stayed close with a field goal by Hartman at the 1:56 mark. Savage captured the onside kick and Harvey sneaked in, then threw to Hinton for two and a 32–31 lead. Mark Fowble kicked off with 14 seconds showing, and Breedlove zigged and zagged to the State 19 where Fowble wrestled him out of bounds with no time left.

The Pack beat Maryland 20–17 on Barbour's 75-yard dash, runs by Chris Cotton, and Hartman's late field goal, then took on East Carolina in the Peach Bowl. Jeff Blake threw to Cedric Van Buren and Hunter Gallimore behind Tom Scott's pass blocking, and Anthony Brennan kicked ECU to a 17–14 halftime lead. State forged ahead as they doubled the score, but Blake ran over and threw to Dion Johnson and Luke Fisher for a 37–34 win to deny State its first ten-win season, while the once-beaten Pirates of Bill Lewis ended in the top ten for the first time with a ninth-place finish.

Georgia Tech was also second with 5-2-0. They lost the Kickoff Classic to Penn State 34–22 as Tony Sacca threw five touchdown passes. Three of them came in the last half after Tyoka Jackson's recovery, Matt Baggett's interception, and another fumble recovery by Rich McKenzie. Richie Anderson caught the final one, but 19 fourth-period points on a Shawn Jones run and Jeff Howard's tosses to Jason McGill and Greg Lester started too late in the stretch.

Rodney Wilkerson ran over twice to beat Boston College 30–14, but Virginia pushed in front by seven on a scoring pass to Tyrone Davis. Jimy Lincoln's run set up a score by Wilkerson, and his 23-yard scamper put Tech up 21–14. Bobby Goodman threw to Aaron Mundy for the tie, but Scott Sisson's last-second kick edged the Cavs again 24–21. After back-to-back maulings by the Tigers and Wolfpack, Tech got on track with a 34–10 defeat of Maryland. It was only 10–3 at the half, but Jones threw three quick strikes to Ali Harris, McGill, and Keenan Walker to put the game away.

South Carolina's shotgun, aided by Darren Parker's fake punt and pass to Frank Adams and a Norman Greene fumble recovery, took them to a 20–0 halftime lead. Jones tossed to Anthony Rice and Emmett Merchant to narrow it to six, but a Marty Simpson three-pointer made the final 23–14. Tech's sloppy play ended with wins over North Carolina 35–14 and Duke 17–6. Michael Smith ran over to lead upset-minded Furman, but Jason Ensley's steal tied it. Sisson and Andrew Burr made it ten each at the end of three, but Andre Worrell intercepted and Carl Tremble ran in to put Furman in front. Jones threw to Lester but was downed on the two-point run, and Tech still trailed by one. Then Hugh Swilling lost the ball on a hit by Marlon Williams and Coleman Rudolph recovered, and Sisson kicked home a 19–17 win with 21 seconds showing.

Georgia Tech beat Wake Forest 27–3, but ran afoul of Georgia 18–15. LeMonte Tillis and Shannon Mitchell shook Garrison Hearst free for 69 yards and Frank Harvey added another for a 15–7 halftime lead, but Tech tied it before Kamon Parkman's third-quarter kick won it, and the Ramblin' Wreck faced Stanford in the Aloha Bowl. Two Tommy Vardell touchdowns and an Aaron Mills field goal gave Dennis Green's Cardinal a 17–10 halftime lead, but Jones ran in to pull within one and Lincoln's two-point dash won it 18–17 with 14 seconds remaining on the clock.

Jones ended as Tech's career passing leader with 6,044 yards and 36 touchdowns, while Marco Coleman was the career leader in sacks with 28 and Willie Clay in interceptions with 16.

Virginia also finished over .500 at 4-2-1. Four turnovers gave Maryland the opener 17–6, but in spite of ten penalties and a blocked punt Bobby Goodman guided the Cavs to a 17–10 win over Navy in his first start. After losing to Georgia Tech on a late field goal, Matt Blundin returned from an infected elbow to lead Virginia to triumphs over Duke 34–3 and Kansas 31–19, but another field goal in the final seconds gained Clemson a tie. Blundin's two touchdowns to Brian Satola overcame North Carolina 14–9, and the Cavs ended on a roll with big wins over Wake Forest 48–7, VMI 42–0, North Carolina State, and Virginia Tech 38–0 for the state title, then squared off against Oklahoma in the Gator Bowl.

Blundin set an NCAA record by not throwing an interception in 224 regular-season attempts, but OU's Cale Gundy upstaged him with two touchdowns to Joey Mickey and 329 yards passing to overtake Monte Deere's 1962 school mark. Blundin threw his first interception to Darnell Walker, and Mike Gaddis ran in three times to complete the 48–14 spanking by coach Gary Gibbs' Oklahomans.

The ACC took a beating in the bowl games, but Florida State, which was not yet eligible for the title, upheld the league honor with a 10–2 triumph over R. C. Slocum's Texas Aggies. A&M led on Quentin Coryatt's sack of Casey Weldon, but Weldon came back with a score for the lead. Gerry Thomas added three more, and Terrell Buckley intercepted in the end zone to add to his total of 12 for the year that led everyone. Florida State's fourth-place finish has already added muscle to the ACC's growing stature.

Although the pact with the Florida Citrus Bowl was not renewed, the ACC beat Oklahoma and Nebraska in its four appearances in Orlando and has long been known as a leader in student-athlete achievement. As Frank Howard once remarked, "Folks used to ask if Clemson was a fruit or vegetable, but not any more." Perhaps a paraphrase of the great Tiger coach may be a fitting way to close this chronicle of ACC football: Folks used to think of the ACC as a basketball conference, but not any more. The ACC can take its place beside those schools that seek to maintain high standards whether in the classroom, on the hardwood court, or on the gridiron.

ACC Records

Rushing Leaders

Annual Leaders

Year	Player, School	Yards
1953	Chet Hanulak, Mary.	953
1954	Ron Waller, Mary.	587
1955	Joel Wells, Clem.	782
1956	Bill Barnes, WF	1010
1957	Jim Bakhtiar, Virg.	822
1958	John Saunders, SC	653
1959	Jim Joyce, Mary.	567
1960	Fred Shepherd, Virg.	653
1961	Alan White, WF	586
1962	Len Chiaverini, Mary.	602
1963	Ken Willard, NC	648
1964	Brian Piccolo, WF	1044
1965	Hugh Mauldin, Clem.	664
1966	Buddy Gore, Clem.	750
1967	Buddy Gore, Clem.	1045
1968	Frank Quayle, Virg.	1213
1969	Don McCauley, NC	1092
1970	Don McCauley, NC	1720
1971	Larry Hopkins, WF	1228
1972	Steve Jones, Duke	1236
1973	Willie Burden, NCS	1014
1974	Stan Fritts, NCS	1169
1975	Mike Voight, NC	1250
1976	Mike Voight, NC	1407
1977	Amos Lawrence, NC	1211
1978	Ted Brown, NCS	1350

285

Year	Player, School	Yards
1979	Charlie Wysocki, Mary.	1140
1980	Charlie Wysocki, Mary.	1359
1981	Joe McIntosh, NCS	1190
1982	Robert Lavette, GT	1208
1983	Ethan Horton, NC	1107
1984	Ethan Horton, NC	1247
1985	Barry Word, Virg.	1224
1986	Derrick Fenner, NC	1250
1987	Terry Allen, Clem.	868
1988	Ken Martin, NC	1146
1989	Jerry Mays, GT	1349
1990	Terry Kirby, Virg.	1020

Career Leaders

Player, School	Years	Yards
Ted Brown, NCS	1975–78	4602
Amos Lawrence, NC	1977–80	4391
Robert Lavette, GT	1981–84	4066
Mike Voight, NC	1973–76	3971
James McDougald, WF	1976–79	3811
Jerry Mays, GT	1985–89	3699
Joe McIntosh, NCS	1981–84	3642
Mike Ramseur, WF	1982–85	3325
Charlie Wysocki, Mary.	1978–81	3317
Kelvin Bryant, NC	1980–82	3267
Don McCauley, NC	1968–70	3172
Ethan Horton, NC	1981–84	3074
Steve Atkins, Mary.	1975–78	2971
Steve Jones, Duke	1970–72	2951
Tommy Vigorito, Virg.	1977–80	2913
Kenny Flowers, Clem.	1983–86	2699
Frank Quayle, Virg.	1966–68	2695
Terry Allen, Clem.	1987–89	2620
Buddy Gore, Clem.	1966–68	2571
Stan Fritts, NCS	1972–74	2542
Willie Burden, NCS	1971–73	2529
Tyrone Anthony, NC	1980–83	2516
Topper Clemons, WF	1982–85	2479
Mike Grayson, Duke	1980–83	2441
Ray Yauger, Clem.	1968–70	2439

Top Single Game Yards

Derrick Fenner, NC vs Virg. 1986	328
Ken Martin, NC vs Duke 1988	291
Amos Lawrence, NC vs Virg. 1977	286
Don McCauley, NC vs Duke 1970	279
Mike Voight, NC vs Duke 1976	261
Cliff Austin, Clem. vs. Duke 1982	260
Natrone Means, NC vs Duke 1990	256
Ted Brown, NCS vs Penn St. 1977	251
James McDougald, WF vs Clem. 1976	249
Kelvin Bryant, NC vs Duke 1981	247

Passing Leaders

Annual Leaders

Year	Player, School	Comp/Att	TD	Yards
1953	Johnny Gramling, SC	68/133	8	1045
1954	Mackie Prickett, SC	68/116	1	682
1955	Nick Consoles, WF	66/123	6	767
1956	Nelson Yarbrough, Virg.	43/91	2	626
1957	Harvey White, Clem.	46/95	11	841
1958	Arnold Dempsey, Virg.	74/152	2	697
1959	Norm Snead, WF	85/191	12	1361
1960	Norm Snead, WF	123/259	10	1676
1961	Roman Gabriel, NCS	99/186	8	937
1962	Dick Shiner, Mary.	121/203	4	1324
1963	Dick Shiner, Mary.	108/222	10	1165
1964	Scotty Glacken, Duke	104/192	7	1178
1965	Tom Hodges, Virg.	103/196	4	1299
1966	Bob Davis, Virg.	107/222	10	1461
1967	Jim Addison, Clem.	82/174	5	924
1968	Leo Hart, Duke	162/301	11	2238
1969	Leo Hart, Duke	145/268	5	1642
1970	Leo Hart, Duke	180/308	7	2236
1971	Paul Miller, NC	75/146	9	1041
1972	Bob Avellini, Mary.	98/170	7	1251
1973	Scott Gardner, Virg.	99/234	10	1687
1974	Bob Avellini, Mary.	112/189	7	1648
1975	Scott Gardner, Virg.	133/272	5	1547
1976	Andy Hitt, Virg.	98/220	7	1222
1977	Mike McGlamry, WF	133/252	2	1532
1978	Tim O'Hare, Mary.	105/192	4	1368

Year	Player, School	Comp/Att	TD	Yards
1979	Matt Kupec, NC	123/227	18	1587
1980	Jay Venuto, WF	214/413	21	2624
1981	Homer Jordan, Clem.	96/174	8	1496
1982	Ben Bennett, Duke	236/374	20	3033
1983	Mike Eppley, Clem.	99/166	13	1410
1984	Frank Reich, Mary.	108/169	9	1446
1985	John Dewberry, GT	110/193	10	1557
1986	Mark Maye, NC	110/176	10	1401
1987	Scott Secules, Virg.	174/296	12	2311
1988	Anthony Dilweg, Duke	287/484	24	3824
1989	Dave Brown, Duke	104/163	14	1479
1990	Shawn Moore, Virg.	144/241	21	2262

Career Leaders

Player, School	Comp/Att	TD	Yards	Years
Ben Bennett, Duke	820/1375	55	9614	1980–83
Steve Slayden, Duke	699/1204	48	8004	1984–87
Mike Elkins, WF	609/1109	43	7304	1985–88
Gary Schofield, WF	640/1113	44	7205	1981–83
Shawn Moore, Virg.	421/762	55	6629	1987–90
Boomer Esiason, Mary.	461/850	42	6184	1981–83
Leo Hart, Duke	487/872	23	6116	1968–70
Shane Montgomery, NCS	421/746	31	5298	1986–89
Scott Gardner, Virg.	390/816	33	5218	1972–75
Jay Venuto, WF	412/780	37	5056	1979–80
Neil O'Donnell, Mary.	387/658	26	4989	1987–89
Tommy Suggs, SC	355/672	34	4916	1968–70
Erik Kramer, NCS	344/616	30	4602	1985–86
Dan Henning, Mary.	353/641	24	4560	1985–87
Anthony Dilweg, Duke	342/594	27	4557	1985–88
Dave Buckey, NCS	307/524	25	4286	1972–75
John Dewberry, GT	310/533	27	4193	1983–85
Rodney Williams, Clem.	292/640	16	4082	1985–88
Steve Fuller, Clem.	268/511	22	4078	1975–78
Norm Snead, WF	272/601	27	4040	1958–60
Phil Barnhill, WF	310/656	23	3931	1988–90
Don Majkowski, Virg.	286/579	22	3901	1983–86
Tommy Kendrick, Clem.	303/644	24	3893	1969–71
Tim Esposito, NCS	333/585	18	3847	1983–84
Matt Kupec, NC	305/552	33	3840	1976–79
Mike McGlamry, WF	309/610	17	3684	1974–77

Top Single Game Yards

Shane Montgomery, NCS vs Duke 1989	535
Gary Schofield, WF vs Mary. 1981	504
Dave Brown, Duke vs NC 1989	479
Anthony Dilweg, Duke vs WF 1988	475
Ben Bennett, Duke vs WF 1980	469
Shane Montgomery, NCS vs Duke 1987	468
Steve Slayden, Duke vs NCS 1987	458
Jay Venuto, WF vs SC 1980	447
Dave Brown, Duke vs WF 1989	444
Ben Bennett, Duke vs NCS 1983	442

Top Single Game Completions

Gary Schofield, WF vs Mary. 1981	43
Gary Schofield, WF vs Mary. 1982	40
Ben Bennett, Duke vs WF 1982	38
Shane Montgomery, NCS vs Duke 1987	37
Mike Elkins, WF vs Mary. 1986	35
Ben Bennett, Duke vs Clem. 1983	34
Anthony Dilweg, Duke vs Mary. 1988	34
Steve Slayden, Duke vs NCS 1987	33
Anthony Dilweg, Duke vs NCS 1988	33
Dave Brown, Duke vs NC 1989	33

Receiving Leaders

Annual Leaders

Year	Player, School	Rec	Yards
1953	Clyde, Bennett, SC	23	413
1954	Carl Brazell, SC	29	241
1955	Bill Barnes, WF	31	349
1956	Fred Polzer, Virg.	24	221
1957	Fred Polzer, Virg.	25	232
1958	Sonny Randle, Virg.	47	642
1959	Bob Allen, WF	25	462
1960	Tee Moorman, Duke	46	431
1961	Gary Collins, Mary.	30	428
1962	Tom Brown, Mary.	47	557
1963	Stan Crisson, Duke	48	559
	Bob Lacey, NC	48	553

Year	Player, School	Rec	Yards
1964	Ronnie Jackson, NC	34	512
1965	John Pincavage, Virg.	45	572
1966	Charlie Carr, NC	52	490
1967	Fred Zeigler, SC	35	370
1968	Henley Carter, Duke	65	892
1969	Fred Zeigler, SC	52	658
1970	Wes Chesson, Duke	74	1080
1971	Bill Davis, Virg.	49	617
1972	Dave Sullivan, Virg.	51	662
1973	Harrison Davis, Virg.	44	773
1974	Jimmy Jerome, NC	47	837
1975	Tom Fadden, Virg.	48	620
1976	Tom Hall, Duke	44	594
1977	Steve Young, WF	51	483
1978	Jerry Butler, Clem.	54	864
1979	Wayne Baumgardner, WF	55	1000
1980	Perry Tuttle, Clem.	53	915
1981	Phil Denfield, WF	51	461
1982	Mark Militello, Duke	52	725
1983	Mike Grayson, Duke	66	582
1984	Greg Hill, Mary.	51	820
1985	Mike Ramseur, WF	54	450
1986	James Brim, WF	66	930
1987	Roger Boone, Duke	62	587
1988	Roger Boone, Duke	73	630
1989	Ricky Proehl, WF	65	1053
1990	Frank Wycheck, Mary.	58	509

Career Leaders

Player, School	Years	Rec	TD	Yards
Clarkston Hines, Duke	1986–89	189	38	3318
Ricky Proehl, WF	1986–89	188	25	2949
Herman Moore, Virg.	1988–90	114	27	2504
John Ford, Virg.	1984, 86–88	128	20	2399
Wes Chesson, Duke	1968–70	164	10	2399
Perry Tuttle, Clem.	1978–81	134	14	2329
Wayne Baumgardner, WF	1978–81	135	12	2303
Nasrallah Worthen, NCS	1984–86, 88	131	14	2247
Jerry Butler, Clem.	1975–78	131	11	2115
Doug Green, Duke	1983–87	142	16	2082
James Brim, WF	1983–86	153	12	2040
Mike Quick, NCS	1978–81	116	10	1934

Player, School	Years	Rec	TD	Yards
Azizuddin Abdur-Ra'oof, Mary.	1984–87	108	10	1895
Fred Zeigler, SC	1967–69	146	9	1876
Don Buckey, NCS	1972–75	102	5	1735
Haywood Jeffires, NCS	1983–86	111	14	1733
Cedric Jones, Duke	1978–81	99	21	1732
Barry Johnson, Mary.	1987–90	106	11	1721
Greg Hill, Mary.	1982–84	97	18	1721
Steve Brown, WF	1987–90	122	3	1678
Ferrell Edmunds, Mary.	1984–87	101	10	1641
Earl Winfield, NC	1983–85	107	11	1603
Tim Ryan, WF	1980–83	111	10	1591
Dave Sullivan, Virg.	1970–72	120	12	1578
Bruce McGonnigal, Virg.	1987–90	103	12	1556

Top Single Game Yards

Chris Castor, Duke vs WF 1982	283
Wayne Baumgardner, WF vs SC 1980	271
Clarkston Hines, Duke vs WF 1989	251
Randy Marriott, NC vs GT 1987	247
Ken Shelton, Virg. vs W&M 1974	241
Herman Moore, Virg. vs GT 1990	234
Jim Milling, Mary. vs NC 1984	220
Henley Carter, Duke vs Clem. 1968	209
James Brim, WF vs NCS 1986	194
Greg Lester, GT vs Duke 1987	193

Top Single Game Receptions

Charlie Carr, NC vs Air Force 1966	16
Roger Boone, Duke vs Vanderbilt 1988	15
James Brim, WF vs NCS 1986	15
Robert Lavette, GT vs Notre Dame 1981	14
John Henry Mills, WF vs Duke 1990	14
Frank Wycheck, Mary. vs VPI 1990	14
Henley Carter, Duke vs Clem. 1968	13
Wes Chesson, Duke vs Clem. 1970	13
Mark Militello, Duke vs Clem. 1983	13
Mark Militello, Duke vs GT 1983	13
Roger Boone, Duke vs WF 1988	13

Scoring Leaders

Annual Leaders

Year	Player, School	TD	XP	FG	Pts
1953	Lloyd Caudle, Duke	9			54
	Bernie Faloney, Mary.	9			54
1954	Bob Pascal, Duke	9			54
	Dick Bielski, Mary.	9			54
1955	Ed Vereb, Mary.	16			96
1956	Bill Barnes, WF	7	2		44
1957	Dick Christy, NCS	13	2	1	83
1958	Wray Carlton, Duke	8	8		56
1959	Bill Mathis, Clem.	11	4		70
1960	Bill McGuirt, Clem.	9			54
1961	Ron Scrudato, Clem.	8			48
1962	Billy Gambrell, SC	8	2		50
	Mike Curtis, Duke	8	2		50
	Dan Reeves, SC	8	2		50
1963	Jay Wilkinson, Duke	12			72
1964	Brian Piccolo, WF	17	9		111
1965	Danny Talbott, NC	7	13	5	70
1966	Frank Quayle, Virg.	11			66
1967	Gerald Warren, NCS		19	17	70
1968	Frank Quayle, Virg.	14			84
1969	Ray Yauger, Clem.	11	2		68
1970	Don McCauley, NC	21			126
1971	Larry Russell, WF	15	4		94
1972	Stan Fritts, NCS	17	4		106
1973	Lou Carter, Mary.	14			84
1974	Roland Hooks, NCS	13	4		82
1975	Ted Brown, NCS	13	6		84
1976	Mike Voight, NC	18	2		110
1977	Ted Brown, NCS	14			84
1978	Lester Brown, Clem.	17			102
1979	Scott Smith, NCS	13			78
	James McDougald, WF	13			78
1980	Amos Lawrence, NC	15			90
1981	Kelvin Bryant, NC	18			108
1982	Robert Lavette, GT	19			114
1983	Bob Paulling, Clem.		36	18	90
1984	Rick Badanjek, Mary.	16	6		102
1985	Kenny Flowers, Clem.	13			78
1986	Terrence Flagler, Clem.	13			78
1987	David Treadwell, Clem.		28	18	82

Year	Player, School	TD	XP	FG	Pts
1988	Dan Plocki, Mary.		27	17	78
1989	Clarkston Hines, Duke	17	1		104
1990	Jake McInerney, Virg.		49	15	94

Career Scoring

Player, School	Pts	Years	Player, School	Pts	Years
Ted Brown, NCS	312	1975–78	Don McCauley, NC	210	1968–70
Jess Atkinson, Mary.	308	1981–84	Frank Quayle, Virg.	210	1966–68
Rick Badanjek, Mary.	286	1982–85	Bob Paulling, Clem.	208	1979–83
Obed Ariri, Clem.	276	1977–80	Amos Lawrence, NC	206	1977–80
Robert Lavette, GT	276	1981–84	Jeff Hayes, NC	205	1978–81
Stan Fritts, NCS	256	1972–74	Kenny Stadlin, Virg.	204	1983–85
Mike Voight, NC	254	1973–76	Steve Mike-Mayer, Mary.	203	1972–74
Mike Cofer, NCS	247	1982–86	Mike Ramseur, WF	194	1982–85
Chris Gardocki, Clem.	234	1988–90	Doug Peterson, Duke	193	1986–88
Clarkston Hines, Duke	234	1986–89	Wayne Morrison, Virg.	193	1979–82
Dan Plocki, Mary.	233	1985–88	James McDougald, WF	192	1976–79
Wilson Hoyle, WF	230	1986–89	Steve Atkins, Mary.	192	1975–78
Kelvin Bryant, NC	228	1979–82	Brooks Barwick, NC	188	1981–83
David Treadwell, Clem.	212	1985–87	Lester Brown, Clem.	186	1976–79

Career Field Goals

Player, School	FGs	Years
Jess Atkinson, Mary.	60	1981–84
Obed Ariri, Clem.	60	1977–80
Chris Gardocki, Clem.	56	1988–90
Mike Cofer, NCS	50	1982–86
Dan Plocki, Mary.	47	1985–88
David Treadwell, Clem.	43	1985–87
Wayne Morrison, Virg.	38	1979–82
Brooks Barwick, NC	37	1981–83
Doug Peterson, Duke	37	1986–88
Kenny Stadlin, Virg.	37	1983–85
Steve Mike-Mayer, Mary.	37	1972–74
Wilson Hoyle, WF	37	1986–89

Season Field Goals

Player, School	FGs	Year
Obed Ariri, Clem.	23	1980
Chris Gardocki, Clem.	20	1989
Brooks Barwick, NC	20	1982
Damon Hartman, NCS	19	1989
David Treadwell, Clem.	18	1987
Bob Paulling, Clem.	18	1983
Gerald Warren, NCS	17	1967
Dale Castro, Mary.	17	1979
Dan Plocki, Mary.	17	1988
Donald Igwebuike, Clem.	16	1984
Kenny Stadlin, Virg.	16	1985

Career Extra Points

Player, School	XPs	Years
Jeff Hayes, NC	133	1978–81
Jess Atkinson, Mary.	128	1981–84
Wilson Hoyle, WF	119	1986–89
Bob Paulling, Clem.	106	1979–83
Mike Cofer, NCS	97	1982–86
Obed Ariri, Clem.	96	1977–80
Ellis Alexander, NC	94	1972–74
Kenny Stadlin, Virg.	93	1983–85
Dan Plocki, Mary.	92	1985–88
Steve Mike-Mayer, Mary.	92	1972–74

Season Kick Scoring

Player, School	Pts	Year
Chris Gardocki, Clem.	98	1989
Brooks Barwick, NC	97	1982
Jake McInerney, Virg.	94	1990
Bob Paulling, Clem.	90	1983
Donald Igwebuike, Clem.	89	1984
Jess Atkinson, Mary.	88	1984
Jake McInerney, Virg.	88	1989
Jess Atkinson, Mary.	87	1982
Obed Ariri, Clem.	87	1980
Clint Gwaltney, NC	85	1990

Interception Leaders

Annual Leaders

Year	Player, School	Int	Year	Player, School	Int
1953	Jerry Barger, Duke	6	1973	Mike Devine, NCS	7
1954	Jerry Barger, Duke	6	1974	Dennis Smith, Clem.	6
1955	Dale Boyd, Duke	6	1975	Bob Grupp, Duke	4
1956	Eddie Rushton, Duke	4		Ken Roy, Mary.	4
1957	Reece Whitley, Virg.	5	1976	Bobby Cale, NC	5
1958	Rod Breedlove, Mary.	5	1977	Derrick Glasper, Virg.	5
1959	Charles Reiley, WF	4		James Royster, WF	5
1960	Charles Reiley, WF	4		Steve Ryan, Clem.	5
1961	Tom Brown, Mary.	8	1978	Woodrow Wilson, NCS	5
1962	Tom Brown, Mary.	6		Ronnie Lee, NCS	5
1963	Ernie Arizzi, Mary.	4	1979	Ralph Lary, Mary.	7
	Tom Krebs, Virg.	4	1980	Dennis Tabron, Duke	5
	Bill Edwards, NC	4		Hillery Honeycutt, NCS	5
1964	Sonny Dickinson, SC	5		Bryan Shumock, Virg.	5
	Jimmy Bell, Clem.	5		Steve Streater, NC	5
1965	Bob Sullivan, Mary.	10	1981	Eric Williams, NCS	7
1966	Andy Harper, WF	6	1982	Lendell Jones, Mary.	7
1967	Andy Beath, Duke	6	1983	Clarence Baldwin, Mary.	7
1968	Pat Watson, SC	7	1984	Ray Daly, Virg.	6
1969	Tony Greene, Mary.	5	1985	Keeta Covington, Mary.	6
1970	Bo Davies, SC	8		Larry Griffin, NC	6
1971	Larry Marshall, Mary.	6	1986	Derrick Taylor, NCS	6
1972	Lou Angelo, NC	8		Derrick Donald, NC	6

Year	Player, School	Int	Year	Player, School	Int
1987	Keith McMeans, Virg.	9	1989	Robert O'Neal, Clem.	7
1988	Jesse Campbell, NCS	5	1990	Ken Swilling, GT	5
	Keith McMeans, Virg.	5			

Career Leaders

Player, School	Int	Years	Player, School	Int	Years
Tom Brown, Mary.	17	1960–62	Kevin Cook, Virg.	14	1986–89
Ronnie Burgess, WF	17	1981–84	Ken Schroy, Mary.	13	1972–74
A. J. Greene, WF	17	1985–88	Bob Sullivan, Mary.	13	1963–65
Terry Kinard, Clem.	17	1978–81	James Royster, WF	13	1975–78
Keith McMeans, Virg.	17	1987–90	Jerry Barger, Duke	12	1953–54
Lou Angelo, NC	16	1970–72	Bobby Cale, NC	12	1976–78
Pat Chester, Virg.	16	1978–82	Buddy Curry, NC	12	1977–79
Rich Searl, Duke	16	1969–71	Eddie Gaethers, Clem.	12	1977–80
Eric Williams, NCS	16	1978–82	Lawrence Lowe, GT	12	1977–80
Bob Smith, Mary.	15	1972–74	Bryan Shumock, Virg.	12	1977–80
Lendell Jones, Mary.	14	1981–83	Ted Thurson, GT	12	1979–82

Punting Leaders

Annual Leaders

Year	Player, School	Avg	Year	Player, School	Avg
1953	Dick Lackey, NC	43.4	1969	Jack Anderson, Clem.	40.1
1954	Joe Pagliei, Clem.	36.7	1970	Jack Anderson, Clem.	41.0
1955	Joe Pagliei, Clem.	39.1	1971	Chuck Ramsey, WF	43.5
1956	Wally Vale, NC	41.1	1972	Chuck Ramsey, WF	43.2
1957	Don Coker, NC	39.6	1973	Chuck Ramsey, WF	44.8
1958	Don Coker, NC	43.2	1974	Johnny Evans, NCS	43.5
1959	Wayne Wolff, WF	41.1	1975	Johnny Evans, NCS	44.6
1960	Wayne Wolff, WF	40.5	1976	Johnny Evans, NCS	46.1
1961	Eddie Werntz, Clem.	40.2	1977	Russ Henderson, Virg.	42.5
1962	Eddie Werntz, Clem.	40.7	1978	Russ Henderson, Virg.	42.5
1963	Karl Sweetan, WF	37.3	1979	David Sims, Clem.	44.4
	Bill Edwards, NC	37.3	1980	Steve Streater, NC	43.4
1964	Ron Skosnik, NCS	40.8	1981	Dale Hatcher, Clem.	43.1
1965	Rod Stewart, Duke	42.5	1982	Ron Rice, GT	42.6
1966	Bill Van Heusen, Mary.	39.9		Harry Newsome, WF	42.6
1967	Scott Townsend, SC	39.3	1983	Harry Newsome, WF	45.5
1968	Gary Yount, NCS	39.5	1984	Harry Newsome, WF	44.1

Year	Player, School	Avg	Year	Player, School	Avg
1985	Tommy Barnhardt, NC	41.5	1988	Martin Bailey, WF	43.7
1986	Kelly Hollodick, NCS	42.4	1989	Chris Gardocki, Clem.	42.7
1987	Craig Salmon, NCS	45.0	1990	Chris Gardocki, Clem.	44.3

Career Leaders

Player, School	Avg	Years
Johnny Evans, NCS	44.02	1974–77
Chuck Ramsey, WF	43.95	1971–73
Harry Newsome, WF	43.56	1981–84
Russ Henderson, Virg.	43.30	1975–78
Chris Gardocki, Clem.	43.27	1988–90
Dale Hatcher, Clem.	42.82	1981–84
Scott McAlister, NC	42.08	1988–90
Steve Streater, NC	41.81	1977–80
Tommy Barnhardt, WF	41.75	1983–85
Nick Vidnovic, NC	41.64	1971–73
David Sims, Clem.	41.54	1977–80
Craig Salmon, NCS	41.43	1984–87
Mitch Tyner, Clem.	40.95	1973–74
Jeff Pierce, GT	40.76	1978–81
Bob Grupp, Duke	40.58	1973–75
John Tolish, Duke	40.39	1981–84
Ron Rice, GT	40.27	1980–83
Steve Jones, Duke	40.18	1970–72
Mike Sochko, Mary.	40.17	1975–77
Jeff Hayes, NC	40.14	1978–81
Darryl Wright, Mary.	40.13	1984–87
Preston Poag, NCS	40.11	1988–90
Dale Lydecker, NC	40.07	1972–74
Kenny Miller, NC	40.06	1984–87
Martin Bailey, WF	40.04	1985–88

Punt Return Leaders

Annual Leaders

Year	Player, School	Avg	Year	Player, School	Avg
1953	Eddie West, NCS	10.4	1956	Bill Barnes, WF	19.0
1954	Ron Waller, Mary.	15.3	1957	Dick Hunter, NCS	9.3
1955	Carroll McClain, SC	18.3	1958	Bobby Morgan, Clem.	19.0

Year	Player, School	Avg	Year	Player, School	Avg
1959	George Usry, Clem.	10.8	1975	Troy Slade, Duke	12.3
1960	Jim Davidson, Mary.	10.6	1976	Mel Collins, NC	10.7
1961	Jay Wilkinson, Duke	14.9	1977	George Gawdun, Duke	11.7
1962	Jay Wilkinson, Duke	9.3	1978	Willie Jordan, Clem.	13.9
1963	Hugh Mauldin, Clem.	11.4	1979	Pat Chester, Virg.	9.9
1964	Julian James, NCS	11.3	1980	Pat Chester, Virg.	10.1
1965	Bobby Bryant, SC	14.6	1981	Louie Meadows, NCS	13.1
1966	Bobby Bryant, SC	22.0	1982	Jack Westbrook, GT	12.1
1967	Fred Combs, NCS	19.0	1983	Rick Badanjek, Mary.	11.1
1968	Jack Whitley, NCS	14.1	1984	Keeta Covington, Mary.	10.5
1969	Rusty Culbreth, NC	8.0	1985	Doug Green, Duke	10.3
1970	Don Kelley, Clem.	16.2	1986	Riccardo Ingram, GT	14.6
1971	Larry Marshall, Mary.	10.7	1987	Donnell Woolford, Clem.	15.5
1972	Bob Smith, Mary.	13.4	1988	Eric Blount, NC	9.9
1973	Troy Slade, Duke	11.3	1989	Bren Lowery, Mary.	10.1
1974	Ken Schroy, Mary.	18.7	1990	George Coghill, WF	14.5

Kickoff Return Leaders

Annual Leaders

Year	Player, School	Avg	Year	Player, School	Avg
1953	Ken Keller, NC	23.0	1972	Roland Hooks, NCS	22.8
1954	George Marinkov, NCS	35.3	1973	Tom Lockridge, WF	24.9
1955	Carl Brazell, SC	31.5	1974	Jim Betterson, NC	28.4
1956	Bill Barnes, WF	28.6	1975	John Schultz, Mary.	31.0
1957	Dick Christy, NCS	45.4	1976	Art Gore, Duke	25.6
1958	Sonny Randle, Virg.	24.1	1977	Ralph Stringer, NCS	25.7
1959	Tom Gravins, Virg.	20.4	1978	Sean McCall, Virg.	26.9
1960	Dennis Condie, Mary.	35.2	1979	Cedric Jones, Duke	27.2
1961	Jack Morris, SC	31.3	1980	Dennis Tabron, Duke	22.8
1962	Donnie Frederick, WF	22.8	1981	Robert Lavette, GT	22.9
1963	Darryl Hill, Mary.	24.4	1982	Cleve Pounds, GT	23.4
1964	Bob Davis, Virg.	21.9	1983	Cory Collier, GT	30.0
1965	Ben Galloway, SC	24.4	1984	Mike Atkinson, Duke	22.3
1966	Gary Rowe, NCS	25.5	1985	Keeta Covington, Mary.	23.2
1967	Ken Dutton, Mary.	18.9	1986	Terrence Roulhac, Clem.	33.0
1968	Bobby Hall, NCS	24.9	1987	Randy Marriott, NC	22.5
1969	John Shields, Clem.	21.6	1988	Chris Williams, NCS	26.0
1970	Dick Harris, SC	29.3	1989	Bren Lowery, Mary.	23.9
1971	Larry Marshall, Mary.	26.7	1990	Randy Jones, Duke	28.3

Jacobs Blocking Trophy

This trophy is awarded annually by William and Hugh Jacobs of Clinton, SC, to the player voted the outstanding blocker in the ACC by a poll of the head football coaches. The trophy is given in memory of William P. Jacobs, president of Presbyterian College from 1935 to 1945, by his sons.

1953	Bill Wohrman, SC
1954	Bill Wohrman, SC
1955	Bob Pellegrini, Mary.
1956	Hal McElhaney, Duke
1957	Hal McElhaney, Duke
1958	John Saunders, SC
1959	Doug Cline, Clem.
1960	Dwight Bumgarner, Duke
1961	Art Gregory, Duke and Jim LeCompte, NC
1962	Art Gregory, Duke
1963	Chuck Walker, Duke
1964	Eddie Kesler, NC
1965	John McNabb, Duke
1966	Wayne Mass, Clem.
1967	Harry Olszewski, Clem.
1968	Greg Shelly, Virg.
1969	Ralph Sonntag, Mary.
1970	Dan Ryczek, Virg.
1971	Geof Hamlin, NC
1972	Ron Rusnak, NC
1973	Bill Yoest, NC State
1974	Ken Huff, NC
1975	Billy Bryan, Duke
1976	Billy Bryan, Duke
1977	Joe Bostic, Clem.
1978	Jim Ritcher, NC State
1979	Jim Ritcher, NC State
1980	Ron Wooten, NC
1981	Lee Nanney, Clem.
1982	Dave Pacella, Mary.
1983	James Farr, Clem.
1984	Jim Dombrowski, Virg.
1985	Jim Dombrowski, Virg.
1986	Paul Kiser, WF
1987	John Phillips, Clem.
1988	Jeff Garnica, NC
1989	Chris Port, Duke
1990	Ray Roberts, Virg.

Annual Team Leaders

Total Offense			Rushing Offense			Passing Offense			Scoring Offense		
Year	Team	Avg	Year	Team	Avg	Year	Team	Avg	Year	Team	Avg
1953	Mary.	359.5	1953	Mary.	257.8	1953	Mary.	133.4	1953	Mary.	29.8
1954	Mary.	333.0	1954	Mary.	248.9	1954	Duke	91.7	1954	Mary.	28.0
1955	Clem.	305.7	1955	Clem.	220.0	1955	WF	129.1	1955	Mary.	21.1
1956	Duke	314.3	1956	Duke	254.4	1956	Virg.	91.9	1956	Duke	18.4
1957	Clem.	327.7	1957	Duke	236.6	1957	Clem.	104.5	1957	Clem.	21.6
1958	NC	319.8	1958	Clem.	225.8	1958	Virg.	138.6	1958	NC	19.5
1959	WF	313.9	1959	SC	206.6	1959	WF	149.8	1959	Clem.	26.2
1960	Clem.	306.0	1960	SC	196.9	1960	WF	169.2	1960	Clem.	19.7
1961	Clem.	307.5	1961	Clem.	178.3	1961	Mary.	136.4	1961	Clem.	19.9
1962	Mary.	306.9	1962	Clem.	205.4	1962	Mary.	148.0	1962	Duke	19.9
1963	NC	341.4	1963	Clem.	195.9	1963	NC	160.5	1963	Duke	23.0
1964	WF	316.6	1964	Mary.	186.6	1964	Virg.	164.2	1964	NC	17.8
1965	Duke	346.6	1965	Duke	188.7	1965	Virg.	187.9	1965	Duke	21.6
1966	Virg.	308.3	1966	NCS	168.3	1966	Mary.	162.4	1966	Virg.	21.4
1967	Clem.	312.1	1967	Virg.	209.9	1967	Mary.	114.1	1967	NCS	20.0
1968	Virg.	439.4	1968	Virg.	280.0	1968	Duke	265.3	1968	Virg.	32.8
1969	NC	366.2	1969	NC	261.5	1969	Clem.	175.5	1969	NC	20.0
1970	NC	411.2	1970	NC	285.2	1970	SC	221.8	1970	NC	31.5
1971	NC	365.0	1971	WF	304.0	1971	Mary.	158.9	1971	NC	25.9
1972	NCS	432.5	1972	NC	244.0	1972	NCS	207.8	1972	NCS	32.7
1973	NCS	409.9	1973	NCS	272.3	1973	Virg.	158.3	1973	NCS	33.2
1974	NC	426.5	1974	NC	265.9	1974	Mary.	179.7	1974	NC	30.9
1975	Mary.	375.2	1975	NC	224.2	1975	Clem.	163.5	1975	Mary.	27.2
1976	Mary.	372.0	1976	Mary.	261.3	1976	Virg.	113.9	1976	Mary.	24.8
1977	NCS	380.0	1977	NCS	250.4	1977	Mary.	162.9	1977	Mary.	21.5
1978	Clem.	436.7	1978	Clem.	296.5	1978	WF	164.9	1978	Clem.	31.9
1979	WF	385.1	1979	Clem.	238.4	1979	WF	222.6	1979	NC	24.8
1980	NC	365.3	1980	NC	270.6	1980	WF	239.5	1980	NC	25.5
1981	NC	415.7	1981	NC	274.5	1981	WF	271.5	1981	NC	31.3
1982	Duke	453.6	1982	NC	261.9	1982	Duke	304.5	1982	Mary.	32.1
1983	NC	441.8	1983	NC	276.9	1983	Duke	284.7	1983	Clem.	30.7
1984	Mary.	446.4	1984	GT	235.0	1984	Mary.	236.5	1984	Mary.	32.0
1985	Mary.	326.4	1985	Virg.	246.6	1985	NCS	258.6	1985	Mary.	26.5
1986	NC	436.0	1986	Clem.	273.4	1986	Mary.	248.0	1986	WF	29.5
1987	Duke	419.0	1987	Clem.	244.3	1987	Duke	313.0	1987	Duke	27.4
1988	Duke	464.6	1988	Clem.	277.6	1988	Duke	351.6	1988	Clem.	29.9
1989	Duke	501.7	1989	Clem.	234.9	1989	Duke	323.0	1989	Duke	32.4
1990	Virg.	501.5	1990	Virg.	257.4	1990	Mary.	252.2	1990	Virg.	40.2

Annual Team Leaders

	Total Defense			Rushing Defense			Passing Defense			Scoring Defense	
Year	Team	Avg	Year	Team	Avg	Year	Team	Avg	Year	Team	Avg
1953	Mary.	193.2	1953	Mary.	83.9	1953	NC	78.2	1953	Mary.	3.1
1954	Clem.	176.1	1954	Clem.	96.9	1954	Duke	67.5	1954	Mary.	6.7
1955	Mary.	169.1	1955	Mary.	75.9	1955	Duke	76.5	1955	Mary.	5.7
1956	SC	199.8	1956	SC	152.2	1956	SC	47.6	1956	SC	6.7
1957	Clem.	215.9	1957	Duke	151.8	1957	Clem.	59.7	1957	NCS	6.7
1958	NC	239.7	1958	NC	134.9	1958	Duke	100.9	1958	NC	10.9
1959	Clem.	197.1	1959	Clem.	108.5	1959	WF	62.1	1959	Clem.	9.6
1960	Clem.	212.1	1960	Clem.	112.1	1960	NC	67.6	1960	Duke	10.8
1961	Duke	224.1	1961	Clem.	127.5	1961	NCS	78.4	1961	Duke	10.6
1962	Mary.	229.7	1962	Clem.	121.3	1962	WF	95.9	1962	Duke	10.5
1963	Clem.	184.7	1963	Clem.	93.1	1963	NC	84.4	1963	NCS	9.1
1964	NC	257.3	1964	NC	146.2	1964	NCS	102.5	1964	Mary.	12.6
1965	Clem.	251.5	1965	NCS	125.4	1965	SC	96.8	1965	NCS	11.0
1966	NCS	274.9	1966	WF	134.8	1966	SC	96.8	1966	WF	16.2
1967	NCS	253.3	1967	NCS	132.1	1967	Virg.	91.8	1967	NCS	8.7
1968	NCS	312.5	1968	Virg.	124.2	1968	NCS	146.5	1968	Clem.	17.9
1969	Virg.	235.8	1969	NC	108.5	1969	Virg.	107.3	1969	NC	16.4
1970	NC	260.4	1970	NC	95.3	1970	NCS	127.8	1970	NC	16.3
1971	NC	278.4	1971	NC	134.5	1971	NCS	109.3		NCS	16.3
1972	Mary.	287.8	1972	Mary.	137.5	1972	Duke	131.2	1971	NC	13.2
1973	Mary.	245.1	1973	Mary.	112.1	1973	Duke	99.2	1972	Duke	14.2
1974	Mary.	256.1	1974	Mary.	133.7	1974	NC	108.6	1973	Mary.	11.3
1975	Mary.	249.9	1975	Mary.	154.9	1975	NCS	70.5	1974	Mary.	8.8
1976	Mary.	211.0	1976	Mary.	116.7	1976	Mary.	94.3	1975	Mary.	13.6
1977	NC	238.5	1977	NC	135.2	1977	NC	103.4	1976	Mary.	7.7
1978	Clem.	254.2	1978	Mary.	137.8	1978	Clem.	100.3	1977	NC	7.4
1979	Clem.	237.5	1979	Clem.	117.5	1979	Mary.	88.5	1978	Clem.	10.5
1980	NC	256.5	1980	Mary.	118.8		Virg.	88.5	1979	Clem.	8.4
1981	Clem.	251.3	1981	Mary.	83.9	1980	GT	123.4	1980	NC	11.2
1982	NC	235.5	1982	Mary.	87.2	1981	Duke	123.4	1981	Clem.	8.2
1983	NC	295.8	1983	NC	135.8	1982	NC	135.5	1982	NC	12.6
1984	GT	317.2	1984	GT	147.5	1983	WF	143.6	1983	NC	17.1
1985	Mary.	305.1	1985	Mary.	125.8	1984	WF	165.6	1984	GT	18.3
1986	Clem.	309.5	1986	Clem.	103.5	1985	GT	149.1	1985	GT	10.7
1987	Clem.	240.0	1987	Clem.	80.0	1986	GT	136.9	1986	Clem.	15.1
1988	NCS	264.3	1988	NCS	103.6	1987	WF	158.0	1987	Clem.	15.1
1989	Clem.	267.9	1989	Clem.	94.6	1988	GT	138.9	1988	NCS	12.9
1990	Clem.	216.9	1990	Clem.	71.7	1989	NCS	167.8	1989	Clem.	11.9
						1990	Duke	142.3	1990	Clem.	9.9

ACC Standings

1953

Team	W	L	T	For	Opp	W	L	T	For	Opp
Maryland	3	0	0	70	6	10	1	0	298	38
Duke	4	0	0	105	27	7	2	1	217	81
South Carolina	2	3	0	58	70	7	3	0	198	97
North Carolina	2	3	0	67	99	4	6	0	173	187
Wake Forest	2	3	0	52	75	3	6	1	123	157
Clemson	1	2	0	25	34	3	5	1	139	172
NC State	0	3	0	14	80	1	9	0	80	263
Virginia						1	8	0	75	242

All-Conference First Team	*All-Conference Second Team*
E Clyde Bennett, SC	**E** Dreher Gaskins, Clem.
Howard Pitt, Duke	Bill Walker, Mary.
T Ed Meadows, Duke	**T** Bob Bartholomew, WF
Stan Jones, Mary.	Bob Morgan, Mary.
G Bob Burrows, Duke	**G** Frank Mincevich, SC
Jack Bowersox, Mary.	Bob King, SC
C Leon Cunningham, SC	**C** John Palmer, Duke
B Bernie Faloney, Mary.	**B** Ralph Felton, Mary.
Chet Hanulak, Mary.	Don King, Clem.
James "Red" Smith, Duke	Jerry Barger, Duke
Johnny Gramling, SC	Dick Lackey, NC

Player of the Year: Bernie Faloney, Mary.
Coach of the Year: Jim Tatum, Mary.

1954

Team	W	L	T	For	Opp	W	L	T	For	Opp
Duke	4	0	0	122	47	8	2	1	270	161
Maryland	4	0	1	124	27	7	2	1	280	67
North Carolina	4	2	0	93	126	4	5	1	140	222
South Carolina	3	3	0	86	94	6	4	0	172	153
Clemson	1	2	0	40	49	5	5	0	193	121
Wake Forest	1	4	1	106	107	2	7	1	129	165
Virginia	0	2	0	14	53	3	6	0	113	162
NC State	0	4	0	27	109	2	8	0	104	193

All-Conference First Team

E Will Frye, NC
    Bill Walker, Mary.
T Bob Bartholomew, WF
    Clyde White, Clem.
G Frank Mincevich, SC
    Ralph Torrance, Duke
C Leon Cunningham, SC
B Jerry Barger, Duke
    Dick Bielski, Mary.
    Bob Pascal, Duke
    Ron Waller, Mary.

All-Conference Second Team

E Ed Stowers, WF
    Scott Jackson, Clem.
T Jack Maultsby, NC
    Harry Lovell, SC
G John Polzer, Virg.
    Bob Pellegrini, Mary.
C John Irvine, Mary.
B George Marinkov, NC State
    Mackie Prickett, SC
    Bryant Aldridge, Duke
    Don King, Clem.

Player of the Year: Jerry Barger, Duke
Coach of the Year: Bill Murray, Duke

1955

Team	W	L	T	For	Opp	W	L	T	For	Opp
Maryland	4	0	0	105	26	10	1	0	217	77
Duke	4	0	0	94	14	7	2	1	280	67
Clemson	3	1	0	79	59	7	3	0	206	144
North Carolina	3	3	0	90	102	3	7	0	117	218
Wake Forest	3	3	1	105	100	5	4	1	131	157
South Carolina	1	5	0	75	176	3	6	0	120	209
NC State	0	2	1	36	71	4	5	1	206	193
Virginia	0	4	0	42	80	1	9	0	96	201

All-Conference First Team

E Sonny Sorrell, Duke
    Will Frye, NC
T Mike Sandusky, Mary.
    Bob Bartholomew, WF
G Jack Davis, Mary.
    Jesse Birchfield, Duke
C Bob Pellegrini, Mary.
B Bob Pascal, Duke
    Ed Vereb, Mary.
    Joel Wells, Clem.
    Bill Barnes, WF

All-Conference Second Team

E Bill Walker, Mary.
    Russ Dennis, Mary.
T Doug Knotts, Duke
    Sid Deloatch, Duke
G Al D'Angelo, NC State
    John Polzer, Virg.
C Ronnie Falls, Duke
B Sonny Jurgensen, Duke
    Frank Tamburello, Mary.
    Dick Christy, NC State
    Jim Bakhtiar, Virg.

Player of the Year: Bob Pellegrini, Mary.
Coach of the Year: Jim Tatum, Mary.

1956

Team	W	L	T	For	Opp	W	L	T	For	Opp
Clemson	4	0	1	50	13	7	2	2	167	101
Duke	4	1	0	129	20	5	4	1	184	100
South Carolina	5	2	0	81	34	7	3	0	126	67
Maryland	2	2	1	43	67	2	7	1	68	168
North Carolina	2	3	1	73	80	2	7	1	99	183
NC State	2	4	0	61	106	3	7	0	94	169
Wake Forest	1	5	1	25	75	2	5	3	91	102
Virginia	1	4	0	34	101	3	7	0	92	167

All-Conference First Team	*All-Conference Second Team*
E Buddy Frick, SC	**E** John Collar, NC State
Buddy Bass, Duke	Dalton Rivers, Clem.
T Mike Sandusky, Mary.	**T** Sam DeLuca, SC
Sid Deloatch, Duke	John Szuchan, NC State
G Jack Davis, Mary.	**G** John Grdijan, Clem.
Jim Jones, NC	Roy Hord, Duke
C Jim Keyser, Virg.	**C** Eddie Moore, WF
B Bill Barnes, WF	**B** Sonny Jurgensen, Duke
Joel Wells, Clem.	Hal McElhaney, Duke
Ed Sutton, NC	Mackie Prickett, SC
Jim Bakhtiar, Virg.	Charlie Bussey, Clem.

Player of the Year: Bill Barnes, WF
Coach of the Year: Paul Amen, WF

1957

Team	W	L	T	For	Opp	W	L	T	For	Opp
NC State	5	0	1	130	60	7	1	2	155	67
Duke	5	1	1	148	62	6	3	2	182	135
Clemson	4	3	0	85	65	7	3	0	216	79
North Carolina	4	3	0	109	74	6	4	0	142	129
Maryland	4	3	0	90	101	5	5	0	119	144
Virginia	2	4	0	54	118	3	6	1	117	164
South Carolina	2	5	0	91	113	5	5	0	202	167
Wake Forest	0	7	0	47	161	0	10	0	64	225

All-Conference First Team	*All-Conference Second Team*
E Buddy Payne, NC	**E** Ray Masneri, Clem.
Ed Cooke, Mary.	Bill Thompson, Duke

All-Conference First Team

T	Tom Topping, Duke
	Phil Blazer, NC
G	Roy Hord, Duke
	Rod Breedlove, Mary.
C	Jim Oddo, NC State
B	Dick Christy, NC State
	Wray Carlton, Duke
	Jim Bakhtiar, Virg.
	Harvey White, Clem.

All-Conference Second Team

T	John Kompara, SC
	Darrell Dess, NC State
G	John Grdijan, Clem.
	Bill Rearick, NC State
C	Gene Alderton, Mary.
B	Dick Hunter, NC State
	Hal McElhaney, Duke
	Alex Hawkins, SC
	King Dixon, SC

Player of the Year: Dick Christy, NC State
Coach of the Year: Earle Edwards, NC State

1958

Team	W	L	T	For	Opp	W	L	T	For	Opp
Clemson	5	1	0	87	80	8	3	0	169	138
South Carolina	5	2	0	104	50	7	3	0	168	116
Duke	3	2	0	68	42	5	5	0	128	131
North Carolina	4	3	0	142	61	6	4	0	195	109
Maryland	3	3	0	75	87	4	6	0	132	175
Wake Forest	2	4	0	73	100	3	7	0	124	163
NC State	2	5	0	86	107	2	7	1	120	160
Virginia	1	5	0	64	172	1	9	0	89	301

All-Conference First Team

E	Al Goldstein, NC
	Bob Pepe, NC State
T	Phil Blazer, NC
	Jim Padgett, Clem.
G	Mike McGee, Duke
	Bill Rearick, NC State
C	Ronnie Koes, NC
B	Jack Cummings, NC
	Alex Hawkins, SC
	Wray Carlton, Duke
	John Saunders, SC

All-Conference Second Team

E	Ray Masneri, Clem.
	Pete Manning, WF
T	Ed Pitts, SC
	Fred Cole, Mary.
G	Joe Rodri, NC State
	Rod Breedlove, Mary.
C	Bill Thomas, Clem.
B	Harvey White, Clem.
	Ken Trowbridge, NC State
	Norm Snead, WF
	Wade Smith, NC

Player of the Year: Alex Hawkins, SC
Coach of the Year: Frank Howard, Clem.

1959

Team	W	L	T	For	Opp	W	L	T	For	Opp
Clemson	6	1	0	181	77	9	2	0	285	103
North Carolina	5	2	0	176	71	5	5	0	198	142
Maryland	4	2	0	143	104	5	5	0	184	188
Wake Forest	4	3	0	169	134	6	4	0	218	178
South Carolina	4	3	0	104	129	6	4	0	170	169
Duke	2	3	0	51	98	4	6	0	104	159
NC State	0	6	0	76	122	1	9	0	117	201
Virginia	0	5	0	44	209	0	10	0	80	393

All-Conference First Team	*All-Conference Second Team*
E Pete Manning, WF	**E** Al Goldstein, NC
Gary Barnes, Clem.	Dwight Bumgarner, Duke
T Ed Pitts, SC	**T** Lou Cordileone, Clem.
Harold Olson, Clem.	Jim Gardner, Duke
G Mike McGee, Duke	**G** Tom Gunderman, Mary.
Nick Patella, WF	Frank Marocco, NC State
C Rip Hawkins, NC	**C** Paul Snyder, Clem.
B Norm Snead, WF	**B** Jack Cummings, NC
Bill Mathis, Clem.	Ron Podwika, NC State
Joel Arrington, Duke	Jim Joyce, Mary.
Doug Cline, Clem.	Wade Smith, NC

Player of the Year: Mike McGee, Duke
Coach of the Year: Paul Amen

1960

Team	W	L	T	For	Opp	W	L	T	For	Opp
Duke	5	1	0	129	40	8	3	0	173	114
NC State	4	1	1	77	54	6	3	1	148	113
Maryland	5	2	0	131	94	6	4	0	171	164
Clemson	4	2	0	108	56	6	4	0	197	124
South Carolina	3	3	1	99	92	3	6	1	117	186
North Carolina	2	5	0	79	98	3	7	0	117	161
Wake Forest	2	5	0	100	163	2	8	0	119	215
Virginia	0	6	0	54	180	0	10	0	103	332

All-Conference First Team	*All-Conference Second Team*
E Tee Moorman, Duke	**E** Jim Tapp, NC State
Gary Collins, Mary.	John Schroeder, NC

All-Conference First Team	*All-Conference Second Team*

	All-Conference First Team		*All-Conference Second Team*
T	Dwight Bumgarner, Duke	**T**	Wayne Wolff, WF
	Collice Moore, NC State		Ron Gassert, Virginia
G	Art Browning, Duke	**G**	Alex Gilleskie, NC State
	Jake Bodkin, SC		Dave Lynn, Clem.
C	Rip Hawkins, NC	**C**	Jim Fitzgerald, NC State
B	Roman Gabriel, NC State	**B**	Bob Elliott, NC
	Mark Leggett, Duke		Don Altman, Duke
	Norm Snead, WF		Fred Shepherd, Virg.
	Lowndes Shingler, Clem.		Bill McGuirt, Clem.

Player of the Year: Roman Gabriel, NC State
Coach of the Year: Bill Murray, Duke

1961

Team	W	L	T	For	Opp	W	L	T	For	Opp
Duke	5	1	0	102	35	7	3	0	183	106
North Carolina	4	3	0	99	80	5	5	0	121	141
Maryland	3	3	0	78	97	7	3	0	156	141
Clemson	3	3	0	112	69	5	5	0	199	126
NC State	3	4	0	101	102	4	6	0	129	149
South Carolina	3	4	0	91	121	4	6	0	128	187
Wake Forest	3	4	0	72	92	4	6	0	103	159
Virginia	2	4	0	85	144	4	6	0	123	190

	All-Conference First Team		*All-Conference Second Team*
E	Gary Collins, Mary.	**E**	Bill Hull, WF
	John Morris, NC State		Bill Ruby, WF
T	Art Gregory, Duke	**T**	Ron Gassert, Virg.
	Jim Moss, SC		Roger Shoals, Mary.
G	Jim LeCompte, NC	**G**	Calvin West, Clem.
	Jean Berry, Duke		Bill Kirchiro, Mary.
C	Bob Hacker, Mary.	**C**	Joe Craver, NC
B	Roman Gabriel, NC State	**B**	Jim Parker, Clem.
	Alan White, WF		Mark Leggett, Duke
	Billy Gambrell, SC		Ray Farris, NC
	Bob Elliott, NC		Walt Rappold, Duke

Player of the Year: Roman Gabriel, NC State
Coach of the Year: Bill Elias, Virg.

1962

Team	W	L	T	For	Opp	W	L	T	For	Opp
Duke	6	0	0	134	43	8	2	0	199	105
Clemson	5	1	0	85	60	6	4	0	168	130
Maryland	5	2	0	132	77	6	4	0	170	128
South Carolina	3	4	0	134	91	4	5	1	187	148
NC State	3	4	0	84	80	3	6	1	108	139
North Carolina	3	4	0	92	106	3	7	0	112	206
Virginia	1	4	0	57	127	5	5	0	194	167
Wake Forest	0	7	0	44	178	0	10	0	66	278

All-Conference First Team

E Bob Lacey, NC
    Don Montgomery, NC State
T Art Gregory, Duke
    Don Chuy, Clem.
G Jean Berry, Duke
    Walter Rock, Mary.
C Joe Craver, NC
B Billy Gambrell, SC
    Dick Shiner, Mary.
    Tom Brown, Mary.
    Mike Curtis, Duke

All-Conference Second Team

E Pete Widener, Duke
    John Caskey, SC
T Jim Moss, SC
    Dave Graham, Virg.
G Bill Sullivan, NC State
    Bob Rowley, Virg.
C Paul Bengel, Duke
B Mark Leggett, Duke
    Ken Willard, NC
    Dan Reeves, SC
    Joe Scarpati, NC State

Player of the Year: Billy Gambrell, SC
Coach of the Year: Bill Murray, Duke

1963

Team	W	L	T	For	Opp	W	L	T	For	Opp
North Carolina	6	1	0	107	49	9	2	0	197	103
NC State	6	1	0	149	70	8	3	0	188	107
Duke	5	2	0	177	108	5	4	1	230	198
Clemson	5	2	0	160	75	5	4	1	181	140
Maryland	2	5	0	105	128	3	7	0	148	201
South Carolina	1	5	1	90	114	1	8	1	104	170
Wake Forest	1	5	0	27	189	1	9	0	37	318
Virginia	0	5	1	40	122	2	7	1	76	169

All-Conference First Team

E Bob Lacey, NC
    Stan Crisson, Duke

All-Conference Second Team

E Don Montgomery, NC State
    Lou Fogle, Clem.

All-Conference First Team

T Bert Wilder, NC State
   Chuck Walker, Duke
G Bill Sullivan, NC State
   Billy Weaver, Clem.
C Chris Hanburger, NC
B Jay Wilkinson, Duke
   Ken Willard, NC
   Pat Crain, Clem.
   Jim Rossi, NC State

All-Conference Second Team

T Jack Aaron, Clem.
   Bob Kowalkowski, Virg.
G Turnley Todd, Virg.
   Jerry Cabe, NC
C Ted Bunton, Clem.
B Junior Edge, NC
   Joe Scarpati, NC State
   Dick Shiner, Mary.
   Scotty Glacken, Duke

Player of the Year: Jay Wilkinson, Duke
Coach of the Year: Jim Hickey, NC, and Earle Edwards, NC State

1964

Team	W	L	T	For	Opp	W	L	T	For	Opp
NC State	5	2	0	94	117	5	5	0	119	194
Duke	3	2	1	120	70	4	5	1	148	135
Maryland	4	3	0	125	74	5	5	0	164	126
North Carolina	4	3	0	146	76	5	5	0	172	178
Wake Forest	4	3	0	114	125	5	5	0	172	178
South Carolina	2	3	1	65	90	3	5	2	95	176
Clemson	2	4	0	53	88	3	7	0	105	135
Virginia	1	5	0	74	151	5	5	0	163	214

All-Conference First Team

E Rich Cameron, WF
   Ray Barlow, NC State
T Glenn Sasser, NC State
   Dan Lonon, Duke
G Jerry Fishman, Mary.
   Bennett Williams, NC State
C Chris Hanburger, NC
B Brian Piccolo, WF
   Ken Willard, NC
   Bob Davis, Virg.
   Mike Curtis, Duke

All-Conference Second Team

E Chuck Drulis, Duke
   J. R. Wilburn, SC
T Bob Kowalkowski, Virg.
   Olaf Drozdov, Mary.
G Richy Zarro, NC
   Jim McCarthy, Duke
C Ted Bunton, Clem.
B Bo Hickey, Mary.
   Dan Reeves, SC
   John Mackovic, WF
   Hal Davis, Clem.

Player of the Year: Brian Piccolo, WF
Coach of the Year: Bill Tate, WF

1965

Team	W	L	T	For	Opp	W	L	T	For	Opp
Duke	4	2	0	117	60	6	4	0	216	157
South Carolina*	4	2	0	114	84	5	5	0	151	167
NC State	4	3	0	97	62	6	4	0	134	110
Clemson	4	3	0	99	76	5	5	0	117	137
North Carolina	3	3	0	73	97	4	6	0	146	195
Maryland	3	3	0	87	95	4	6	0	132	164
Virginia	2	4	0	82	115	4	6	0	170	189
Wake Forest	1	5	0	57	137	3	7	0	88	204

Forfeited all ACC wins

All-Conference Offensive Team		*All-Conference Defensive Team*	
E	J. R. Wilburn, SC	E	Butch Sursavage, Clem.
	Chuck Drulis, Duke		Pete Sokalsky, NC State
T	John Boyette, Clem.	T	Dennis Byrd, NC State
	Bill Jones, Duke		Chuck Stavins, Duke
G	John McNabb, Duke	MG	Joe Fratangelo, NC
	John Stec, NC State	LB	Bob Matheson, Duke
C	Ed Stringer, NC		Bill Hecht, Clem.
B	Hugh Mauldin, Clem.	B	Tony Golmont, NC State
	Danny Talbott, NC		Ben Galloway, SC
	Jay Calabrese, Duke		Joe Carazo, WF
	Shelby Mansfield, NC State		Bob Sullivan, Mary.

Player of the Year: Danny Talbott, NC
Coach of the Year: Earle Edwards, NC State

1966

Team	W	L	T	For	Opp	W	L	T	For	Opp
Clemson	6	1	0	162	108	6	4	0	174	177
NC State	5	2	0	165	116	5	5	0	191	168
Virginia	3	3	0	150	150	4	6	0	214	235
Maryland	3	3	0	117	107	4	6	0	180	204
Duke	2	3	0	100	96	5	5	0	164	237
Wake Forest	2	4	0	63	102	3	7	0	90	162
South Carolina	1	3	0	49	80	1	9	0	95	216
North Carolina	1	4	0	52	99	2	8	0	90	196

All-Conference Offensive Team

E Ed Carrington, Virg.
   Dave Dunaway, Duke
T Wayne Mass, Clem.
   Bill Gentry, NC State
G Harry Olszewski, Clem.
   John Stec, NC State
C Bob Oplinger, WF
B Bob Davis, Virg.
   Gary Rowe, NC State
   Don DeArment, NC State
   Jim Addison, Clem.

All-Conference Defensive Team

E Butch Sursavage, Clem.
   Dick Absher, Mary.
T Dennis Byrd, NC State
   Robert Grant, WF
MG Bob Foyle, Duke
LB Bob Matheson, Duke
   Dave Everett, NC State
B Art McMahon, NC State
   Andy Harper, WF
   Bobby Bryant, SC
   Wayne Page, Clem.

Player of the Year: Bob Davis, Virg.
Coach of the Year: Frank Howard, Clem.

1967

Team	W	L	T	For	Opp	W	L	T	For	Opp
Clemson	6	0	0	118	38	6	4	0	166	128
NC State	5	1	0	132	52	9	2	0	214	94
South Carolina	4	2	0	125	108	5	5	0	159	166
Virginia	3	3	0	103	103	5	5	0	172	169
Wake Forest	3	4	0	128	140	4	6	0	175	256
Duke	2	4	0	84	101	4	6	0	143	153
North Carolina	2	5	0	78	115	2	8	0	104	182
Maryland	0	6	0	40	151	0	9	0	46	231

All-Conference Offensive Team

E Harry Martell, NC State
   Rick Decker, WF
T Wayne Mass, Clem.
   Greg Shelly, Virg.
G Harry Olszewski, Clem.
   Norm Cates, NC State
C Mike Murphy, Duke
B Freddie Summers, WF
   Buddy Gore, Clem.
   Frank Quayle, Virg.
   Warren Muir, SC
PK Gerald Warren, NC State

All-Conference Defensive Team

E Mark Capuano, NC State
   Ronnie Ducworth, Clem.
T Dennis Byrd, NC State
   Don Somma, SC
MG Bob Foyle, Duke
LB Tim Bice, SC
   Jimmy Catoe, Clem.
B Andy Beath, Duke
   Fred Combs, NC State
   Frank Liberatore, Clem.
   Jack Davenport, NC

Player of the Year: Buddy Gore, Clem.
Coach of the Year: Earle Edwards, NC State

1968

Team	W	L	T	For	Opp	W	L	T	For	Opp
NC State	6	1	0	170	74	6	4	0	205	185
Clemson	4	1	1	126	82	4	5	1	184	179
Virginia	3	2	0	147	117	7	3	0	329	222
South Carolina	4	3	0	160	150	4	6	0	204	226
Duke	3	4	0	133	169	4	6	0	214	287
Wake Forest	2	3	1	136	127	2	7	1	212	228
Maryland	2	5	0	130	186	2	8	0	171	299
North Carolina	1	6	0	133	230	3	7	0	178	272

All-Conference Offensive Team	*All-Conference Defensive Team*
E Henley Carter, Duke	**E** Mark Capuano, NC State
Fred Zeigler, SC	Ronnie Ducworth, Clem.
T Greg Shelly, Virg.	**T** John Cagle, Clem.
Joe Lhotsky, Clem.	Ron Carpenter, NC State
G Don Jordan, NC State	**MG** Bob Paczkowski, Virg.
Chuck Hammer, Virg.	**LB** Jimmy Catoe, Clem.
C Carey Metts, NC State	Dick Biddle, Duke
B Frank Quayle, Virg.	**B** Wally Orrel, SC
Leo Hart, Duke	Gary Yount, NC State
Buddy Gore, Clem.	Jack Whitley, NC State
Bobby Hall, NC State	Digit Laughridge, WF

Player of the Year: Frank Quayle, Virg.
Coach of the Year: George Blackburn, Virg.

1969

Team	W	L	T	For	Opp	W	L	T	For	Opp
South Carolina	6	0	0	130	61	7	4	0	189	195
NC State	3	2	1	127	78	3	6	1	183	201
Clemson	3	3	0	144	121	4	6	0	178	250
Duke	3	3	1	130	142	3	6	1	161	224
Maryland	3	3	0	63	116	3	7	0	100	249
North Carolina	3	3	0	89	59	5	5	0	200	164
Wake Forest	2	5	0	102	163	3	7	0	125	279
Virginia	1	5	0	59	104	3	7	0	115	270

All-Conference Offensive Team	*All-Conference Defensive Team*
E Fred Zeigler, SC	**E** Judge Mattocks, NC
Charlie Waters, Clem.	Ivan Southerland, Clem.

All-Conference Offensive Team

T Dave DeCamilla, SC
    Ralph Sonntag, Mary.
G Ed Chalupka, NC
    Don Jordan, NC State
C Joe Dobner, WF
B Leo Hart, Duke
    Don McCauley, NC
    Ray Yauger, Clem.
    Warren Muir, SC
PK Billy DuPre, SC

Player of the Year: Don McCauley, NC
Coach of the Year: Paul Dietzel, SC

All-Conference Defensive Team

T Ron Carpenter, NC State
    Jimmy Poston, SC
LB Bill Richardson, NC
    John Mazalewski, WF
    Mike Hilka, NC State
B Pat Watson, SC
    Jack Whitley, NC State
    Rich Searl, Duke
    Gary Yount, NC State

1970

Team	W	L	T	For	Opp	W	L	T	For	Opp
Wake Forest	5	1	0	128	110	6	5	0	191	241
Duke	5	2	0	163	160	6	5	0	229	252
North Carolina	5	2	0	237	125	8	4	0	372	227
South Carolina	3	2	1	176	130	4	6	1	285	253
NC State	2	3	1	53	80	3	7	1	90	179
Clemson	2	4	0	120	165	3	8	0	164	313
Maryland	2	4	0	81	125	2	9	0	112	241
Virginia	0	6	0	76	139	5	6	0	240	187

All-Conference Offensive Team

E Wes Chesson, Duke
    Jim Mitchell, SC
T Paul Hoolahan, NC
    Dave DeCamilla, SC
G Bill Bobbora, WF
    Dave Thompson, Clem.
C Dan Ryczek, Virg.
B Don McCauley, NC
    Leo Hart, Duke
    Larry Hopkins, WF
    Larry Russell, WF
PK Tracy Lounsbury, WF

Player of the Year: Don McCauley, NC
Coach of the Year: Cal Stoll, WF

All-Conference Defensive Team

E Guy Roberts, Mary.
    Bruce Mills, Duke
T Win Headley, WF
    Flip Ray, NC
LB Dick Biddle, Duke
    George Smith, NC State
    Ed Stetz, WF
B Dick Harris, SC
    Jack Whitley, NC State
    Rich Searl, Duke
    Don Kelley, Clem.

1971

Team	W	L	T	For	Opp	W	L	T	For	Opp
North Carolina	6	0	0	165	57	9	3	0	288	152
Clemson	4	2	0	101	95	5	6	0	155	202
Duke	2	3	0	76	77	6	5	0	170	149
Virginia	2	3	0	78	129	3	8	0	134	272
Wake Forest	2	3	0	67	59	6	5	0	218	178
NC State	2	4	0	89	154	3	8	0	147	274
Maryland	1	4	0	104	109	2	9	0	224	283

All-Conference Offensive Team

E John McMakin, Clem.
Dan Bungori, Mary.
T Ed Newman, Duke
Jerry Sain, NC
G Bill Bobbora, WF
Ron Rusnak, NC
C Bob Thornton, NC
B Larry Hopkins, WF
Larry Russell, WF
Paul Miller, NC
Lewis Jolley, NC
PK Ken Craven, NC

All-Conference Defensive Team

E Bill Brafford, NC
Wayne Baker, Clem.
T Bud Grissom, NC
Andy Selfridge, Virg.
LB John Bunting, NC
Ed Stetz, WF
Larry Hefner, Clem.
B Ernie Jackson, Duke
Rich Searl, Duke
Bill Hanenberg, Duke
Steve Bowden, WF

Player of the Year: Ernie Jackson, Duke
Coach of the Year: Bill Dooley, NC

1972

Team	W	L	T	For	Opp	W	L	T	For	Opp
North Carolina	6	0	0	149	72	11	1	0	324	210
NC State	4	1	1	193	102	8	3	1	409	240
Maryland	3	2	1	142	104	5	5	1	243	217
Duke	3	3	0	71	67	5	6	0	132	156
Clemson	2	4	0	101	127	4	7	0	143	245
Virginia	1	5	0	89	168	4	7	0	199	276
Wake Forest	1	5	0	34	139	2	9	0	88	339

All-Conference Offensive Team

E Dave Sullivan, Virg.
Pat Kenney, NC State
T Rick Druschel, NC State

All-Conference Defensive Team

E Gene Brown, NC
Mel Parker, Duke
T Ed Newman, Duke

<table>
<tr><td colspan="2">*All-Conference Offensive Team*</td><td colspan="2">*All-Conference Defensive Team*</td></tr>
</table>

	All-Conference Offensive Team		*All-Conference Defensive Team*
	Jerry Sain, NC		Eric Hyman, NC
G	Ron Rusnak, NC		Frank Wirth, Clem.
	Bill Yoest, NC State	LB	Mike Mansfield, NC
C	Dale Grimes, Duke		Paul Vellano, Mary.
QB	Bruce Shaw, NC State		Jimmy DeRatt, NC
RB	Steve Jones, Duke		Nick Arcaro, WF
	Stan Fritts, NC State	B	Bill Hanenberg, Duke
	Willie Burden, NC State		Lou Angelo, NC
K	Chuck Ramsey, WF		Mike Stultz, NC State
			Bob Smith, Mary.

Player of the Year: Steve Jones, Duke
Coach of the Year: Lou Holtz, NC State

1973

Team	W	L	T	For	Opp	W	L	T	For	Opp
NC State	6	0	0	197	93	9	3	0	396	251
Maryland	5	1	0	173	50	8	4	0	335	141
Clemson	4	2	0	147	129	5	6	0	231	263
Virginia	3	3	0	122	161	4	7	0	199	300
Duke	1	4	1	58	99	2	8	1	132	204
North Carolina	1	5	0	150	159	4	7	0	242	266
Wake Forest	0	5	1	38	194	1	9	1	73	326

	All-Conference Offensive Team		*All-Conference Defensive Team*
E	Harrison Davis, Virg.	DL	Paul Vellano, Mary.
	Charlie Waddell, NC		Randy White, Mary.
T	Rick Druschel, NC State		John Ricca, Duke
	Bob Pratt, NC		Ernie Clark, Duke
G	Bill Yoest, NC State	LB	Dick Ambrose, Virg.
	Ken Peeples, Clem.		Keith Stoneback, Duke
C	Paul Ryczek, Virg.		Jimmy DeRatt, NC
QB	Ken Pengitore, Clem.	DB	Bob Smith, Mary.
RB	Willie Burden, NC State		Mike Stultz, NC State
	Sammy Johnson, NC		Peanut Martin, Clem.
	Lou Carter, Mary.		Bobby Pilz, NC State
K	Chuck Ramsey, WF		

Player of the Year: Willie Burden, NC State
Coach of the Year: Jerry Claiborne, Mary.

1974

Team	W	L	T	For	Opp	W	L	T	For	Opp
Maryland	6	0	0	198	35	8	4	0	312	150
NC State	4	2	0	145	120	9	2	1	317	241
Clemson	4	2	0	130	135	7	4	0	246	250
North Carolina	4	2	0	146	115	7	5	0	364	279
Duke	2	4	0	110	136	6	5	0	201	208
Virginia	1	5	0	61	111	4	7	0	207	239
Wake Forest	0	6	0	31	169	1	10	0	74	348

All-Conference Offensive Team

WR	Jimmy Jerome, NC
TE	Bennie Cunningham, Clem.
T	Stan Rogers, Mary.
	Ken Peeples, Clem.
G	Ken Huff, NC
	Bob Blanchard, NC State
C	Justus Everett, NC State
QB	Chris Kupec, NC
RB	Stan Fritts, NC State
	Lou Carter, Mary.
	Jim Betterson, NC
PK	Steve Mike-Mayer, Mary.

All-Conference Defensive Team

DL	Randy White, Mary.
	Willie Anderson, Clem.
	Dennis Turner, Duke
	Ronnie Robinson, NC
LB	Dick Ambrose, Virg.
	Keith Stoneback, Duke
	Harry Walters, Mary.
DB	Bob Smith, Mary.
	Jeff Christopher, Duke
	Mike Devine, NC State
	Jim Ness, Clem.
KR	Troy Slade, Duke

Player of the Year: Randy White, Mary.
Coach of the Year: Jim Parker, Clem.

1975

Team	W	L	T	For	Opp	W	L	T	For	Opp
Maryland	5	0	0	182	73	9	2	1	312	150
Duke	3	0	2	131	84	4	5	2	197	212
NC State	2	2	1	131	115	7	4	1	260	210
Wake Forest	3	3	0	145	137	3	8	0	221	264
Clemson	2	3	0	102	141	2	9	0	177	381
North Carolina	1	4	1	119	159	3	7	1	207	272
Virginia	0	5	0	98	226	1	10	0	175	428

All-Conference Offensive Team

SE	Don Buckey, NC State
TE	Bennie Cunningham, Clem.
	Pat Hovance, NC State

All-Conference Defensive Team

DL	Tom Higgins, NC State
	Paul Divito, Mary.
	Dave Dusek, Duke

All-Conference Offensive Team

T	Gary Pellom, Duke
	Marion Koprowski, Mary.
G	Tom Serfass, NC State
	Tom Glassic, Virg.
C	Billy Bryan, Duke
QB	Dave Buckey, NC State
RB	Mike Voight, NC
	Ted Brown, NC State
	Clark Gaines, WF
K	Mike Sochko, Mary.

All-Conference Defensive Team

	Joe Campbell, Mary.
LB	Dave Meier, Duke
	Leroy Hughes, Mary.
	Kevin Benson, Mary.
DB	Bill Armstrong, WF
	Jim Brechbiel, Mary.
	Ralph Stringer, NC State
	Bob Grupp, Duke
KR	Troy Slade, Duke

Player of the Year: Mike Voight, NC
Coach of the Year: Jerry Claiborne, Mary.

1976

Team	W	L	T	For	Opp	W	L	T	For	Opp
Maryland	5	0	0	111	24	11	1	0	294	115
North Carolina	4	1	0	144	102	9	3	0	243	220
Wake Forest	3	3	0	124	118	5	6	0	177	206
Duke	2	3	1	125	145	5	5	1	234	245
NC State	2	3	0	97	98	3	7	1	205	258
Virginia	1	4	0	40	111	2	9	0	106	266
Clemson	0	4	1	76	123	3	6	2	172	237

All-Conference Offensive Team

SE	Tom Hall, Duke
TE	Steve Young, WF
T	Tom Schick, Mary.
	Mike Fagan, NC State
G	Ed Fulton, Mary.
	Craig Funk, NC
C	Billy Bryan, Duke
QB	Mark Manges, Mary.
RB	Ted Brown, NC State
	Mike Voight, NC
	James McDougald, WF
PK	Vince Fusco, Duke

All-Conference Defensive Team

DL	Joe Campbell, Mary.
	Dee Hardison, NC
	Bill Perdue, NC
	Larry Seder, Mary.
LB	Brad Carr, Mary.
	Carl McGee, Duke
	Don Cervi, WF
DB	Bill Armstrong, WF
	Ken Roy, Mary.
	Ronny Johnson, NC
	Bob Grupp, Duke
KR	Del Powell, NC

Player of the Year: Mike Voight, NC
Coach of the Year: Jerry Claiborne, Mary.

1977

Team	W	L	T	For	Opp	W	L	T	For	Opp
North Carolina	5	0	1	131	54	8	3	1	251	102
Clemson	4	1	1	108	48	8	3	1	228	163
NC State	4	2	0	133	100	8	4	0	259	181
Maryland	4	2	0	142	74	8	4	0	254	179
Duke	2	4	0	128	122	5	6	0	231	221
Virginia	1	5	0	33	149	1	9	1	56	280
Wake Forest	0	6	0	48	176	1	10	0	113	270

All-Conference Offensive Team

SE	Jerry Butler, Clem.
TE	Steve Young, WF
T	Lacy Brumley, Clem.
	John Patterson, Duke
G	Joe Bostic, Clem.
	Mike Salzano, NC
C	Larry Tearry, WF
QB	Steve Fuller, Clem.
RB	Ted Brown, NC State
	Amos Lawrence, NC
	James McDougald, WF
P	Russ Henderson, Virg.

All-Conference Defensive Team

DL	Dee Hardison, NC
	Rod Broadway, NC
	Ken Sheets, NC
	Jonathan Brooks, Clem.
	Ted Klaube, Mary.
LB	Randy Scott, Clem.
	Buddy Curry, NC
DB	Alan Caldwell, NC
	Steve Ryan, Clem.
	Richard Carter, NC State
	Ralph Stringer, NC State

Player of the Year: Steve Fuller, Clem.
Coach of the Year: Charley Pell, Clem.

1978

Team	W	L	T	For	Opp	W	L	T	For	Opp
Clemson	6	0	0	183	71	11	1	0	368	131
Maryland	5	1	0	159	62	9	3	0	261	167
NC State	4	2	0	133	112	9	3	0	280	208
North Carolina	3	3	0	124	132	5	6	0	199	216
Duke	2	4	0	56	108	4	7	0	108	247
Wake Forest	1	5	0	59	161	1	10	0	104	274
Virginia	0	6	0	75	143	2	9	0	139	236

All-Conference Offensive Team

SE	Jerry Butler, Clem.
TE	Bob Loomis, NC
T	Steve Kenney, Clem.

All-Conference Defensive Team

DL	Jonathan Brooks, Clem.
	Bruce Palmer, Mary.
	Charlie Johnson, Mary.

All-Conference Offensive Team

	Chris Dieterich, NC State
G	Joe Bostic, Clem.
	Mike Salzano, NC
C	Jim Ritcher, NC State
QB	Steve Fuller, Clem.
RB	Ted Brown, NC State
	Steve Atkins, Mary.
	Lester Brown, Clem.
PK	Nathan Ritter, NC State

Player of the Year: Steve Fuller, Clem.
Coach of the Year: Charley Pell, Clem.

All-Conference Defensive Team

	Simon Gupton, NC State
	Jim Stuckey, Clem.
LB	Bubba Brown, Clem.
	Randy Scott, Clem.
DB	Woodrow Wilson, NC State
	Lloyd Burruss, Mary.
	Steve Ryan, Clem.
	Ricky Barden, NC
P	Russ Henderson, Virg.

1979

Team	W	L	T	For	Opp	W	L	T	For	Opp
NC State	5	1	0	120	96	7	4	0	258	213
Clemson	4	2	0	108	62	8	4	0	205	116
Maryland	4	2	0	97	53	7	4	0	198	135
Wake Forest	4	2	0	99	112	8	4	0	240	283
North Carolina	3	3	0	128	104	8	3	1	290	167
Virginia	2	4	0	98	108	6	5	0	258	134
Duke	0	6	0	59	167	2	8	1	152	264
Georgia Tech						4	6	1	152	190

All-Conference Offensive Team

SE	Wayne Baumgardner, WF
TE	Mike Chatham, NC
T	Steve Junkmann, NC
	Larry Stewart, Mary.
G	Jeff Bostic, Clem.
	Chris Dieterich, NC State
C	Jim Ritcher, NC State
QB	Jay Venuto, WF
RB	James McDougald, WF
	Charlie Wysocki, Mary.
	Tommy Vigorito, Virg.
PK	Dale Castro, Mary.

Player of the Year: Jay Venuto, WF
Coach of the Year: John Mackovic, WF

All-Conference Defensive Team

DL	Steve Potter, Virg.
	Jim Stuckey, Clem.
	Steve Durham, Clem.
	Simon Gupton, NC State
	Jim Parker, WF
LB	Buddy Curry, NC
	Bubba Brown, Clem.
DB	Woodrow Wilson, NC State
	Ricky Barden, NC
	Rex Varn, Clem.
	Tony Blount, Virg.
P	David Sims, Clem.

1980

Team	W	L	T	For	Opp	W	L	T	For	Opp
North Carolina	6	0	0	166	63	11	1	0	297	130
Maryland	5	1	0	120	48	8	4	0	211	165
NC State	3	3	0	104	133	6	5	0	222	212
Clemson	2	4	0	125	173	6	5	0	217	222
Virginia	2	4	0	84	149	4	7	0	144	259
Wake Forest	2	4	0	127	128	5	6	0	251	213
Duke	1	5	0	131	163	2	9	0	214	296
Georgia Tech						1	9	1	113	260

	All-Conference Offensive Team		*All-Conference Defensive Team*
SE	Perry Tuttle, Clem.	**DL**	Bubba Green, NC State
TE	John Brinkman, Duke		Lawrence Taylor, NC
T	Chris Koehne, NC State		Donnell Thompson, NC
	Lee Nanney, Clem.		Stuart Anderson, Virg.
G	Ron Wooten, NC		Marlin Van Horn, Mary.
	Bill Ard, WF	**LB**	Darrell Nicholson, NC
C	Rick Donnalley, NC		Carlos Bradley, WF
QB	Jay Venuto, WF	**DB**	Steve Streater, NC
RB	Charlie Wysocki, Mary.		Dennis Tabron, Duke
	Amos Lawrence, NC		Lloyd Burruss, Mary.
	Kelvin Bryant, NC		Bryan Shumock, Virg.
PK	Obed Ariri, Clem.	**P**	Steve Streater, NC

Player of the Year: Lawrence Taylor, NC
Coach of the Year: Dick Crum, NC

1981

Team	W	L	T	For	Opp	W	L	T	For	Opp
Clemson	6	0	0	195	56	12	0	0	338	105
North Carolina	5	1	0	142	64	10	2	0	375	140
Maryland	4	2	0	168	108	4	6	1	232	194
Duke	3	3	0	118	134	6	5	0	210	230
NC State	2	4	0	91	136	4	7	0	182	223
Wake Forest	1	5	0	124	255	4	7	0	217	365
Virginia	0	6	0	90	175	1	10	0	127	261
Georgia Tech						1	10	0	124	308

	All-Conference Offensive Team		*All-Conference Defensive Team*
WR	Cedric Jones, Duke	**DL**	Jeff Bryant, Clem.
	Perry Tuttle, Clem.		Bill Fuller, NC

TE	Phil Denfield, WF
T	Lee Nanney, Clem.
	Chris Koehne, NC State
G	Dave Drechsler, NC
	Ron Spruill, NC
C	Tony Berryhill, Clem.
QB	Homer Jordan, Clem.
RB	Joe McIntosh, NC State
	Kelvin Bryant, NC
PK	Todd Auten, NC State

	Stuart Anderson, Virg.
	Dan Benish, Clem.
	Charles Bowser, Duke
LB	Jeff Davis, Clem.
	Lee Shaffer, NC
DB	Terry Kinard, Clem.
	Dennis Tabron, Duke
	Donnie LeGrande, NC State
	Greg Poole, NC
P	Jeff Hayes, NC

Player of the Year: Jeff Davis, Clem.
Coach of the Year: Danny Ford, Clem.

1982

Team	W	L	T	For	Opp	W	L	T	For	Opp
Clemson	6	0	0	196	95	9	1	1	289	147
Maryland	5	1	0	222	121	8	4	0	373	220
North Carolina	3	3	0	146	100	8	4	0	348	149
Duke	3	3	0	172	179	6	5	0	307	290
NC State	3	3	0	111	131	6	5	0	206	255
Virginia	1	5	0	92	214	2	9	0	208	320
Wake Forest	0	6	0	91	186	3	8	0	200	286
Georgia Tech						6	5	0	239	286

WR	Chris Castor, Duke
	Tim Ryan, WF
TE	Phil Denfield, WF
T	Dave Pacella, Mary.
	Robert Oxendine, Duke
G	Dave Drechsler, NC
	Ron Spruill, NC
C	Phil Ebinger, Duke
QB	Ben Bennett, Duke
RB	Cliff Austin, Clem.
	Robert Lavette, GT
PK	Jess Atkinson, Mary.

DL	Bill Fuller, NC
	William Perry, Clem.
	Mark Duda, Mary.
	Mike Wilcher, NC
	Andy Headen, Clem.
LB	Johnny Rembert, Clem.
	Chris Ward, NC
DB	Terry Kinard, Clem.
	Eric Williams, NC State
	Pat Chester, Virg.
	Willie Harris, NC
P	Harry Newsome, WF

Player of the Year: Chris Castor, Duke
Coach of the Year: Bobby Ross, Mary.

1983

Team	W	L	T	For	Opp	W	L	T	For	Opp
Maryland	6	0	0	154	71	8	4	0	316	253
North Carolina	4	2	0	184	117	8	4	0	337	216
Georgia Tech	3	2	0	147	140	3	8	0	222	313
Duke	3	3	0	150	183	3	8	0	246	350
Virginia	3	3	0	145	150	6	5	0	252	280
NC State	1	5	0	108	159	3	8	0	236	246
Wake Forest	1	5	0	150	218	4	7	0	257	281
Clemson						9	1	1	338	200

All-Conference Offensive Team

WR Mark Militello, Duke
Mark Smith, NC
TE K. D. Dunn, Clem.
T Brian Blados, NC
Jim Dombrowski, Virg.
G Ron Solt, Mary.
James Farr, Clem.
C Phil Ebinger, Duke
QB Ben Bennett, Duke
RB Ethan Horton, NC
Mike Grayson, Duke
Joe McIntosh, NC State

All-Conference Defensive Team

DL Bill Fuller, NC
William Perry, Clem.
Jim Robinson, Clem.
Pete Koch, Mary.
Ed Pickett, Clem.
LB Vaughan Johnson, NC State
Eric Wilson, Mary.
DB Clarence Baldwin, Mary.
Lester Lyles, Virg.
Willie Harris NC
Rod McSwain, Clem.
PK Bob Paulling, Clem.

Player of the Year: Ben Bennett, Duke
Coach of the Year: George Welsh, Virg.

1984

Team	W	L	T	For	Opp	W	L	T	For	Opp
Maryland	6	0	0	204	102	9	3	0	380	280
Virginia	3	1	2	189	108	8	2	2	337	216
North Carolina	3	2	1	119	125	5	5	1	234	274
Wake Forest	3	3	0	91	124	6	5	0	205	232
Georgia Tech	2	2	1	114	81	6	4	1	296	201
Duke	1	5	0	67	162	2	9	0	128	301
NC State	1	5	0	97	179	3	8	0	263	311
Clemson						7	4	0	346	215

All-Conference Offensive Team

WR Greg Hill, Mary.
Terrance Roulhac, Clem.

All-Conference Defensive Team

DL William Perry, Clem.
Ron Mattes, Virg.

All-Conference Offensive Team

TE	Ken Whisenhunt, GT
T	Jim Dombrowski, Virg.
	Joe Milnichik, NC State
G	Bob Olderman, Virg.
	Steve Reese, Clem.
C	Kevin Glover, Mary.
QB	John Dewberry, GT
RB	Ethan Horton, NC
	Robert Lavette, GT
PK	Donald Igwebuike, Clem.

All-Conference Defensive Team

	Gary Baldinger, WF
	Dave Bond, Virg.
	Bruce Mesner, Mary.
LB	Eric Wilson, Mary.
	Micah Moon, NC
DB	Lester Lyles, Virg.
	Ronnie Burgess, WF
	Al Covington, Mary.
	Ron Watson, Clem.
P	Dale Hatcher, Clem.

Player of the Year: William Perry, Clem.
Coach of the Year: George Welsh, Virg.

1985

Team	W	L	T	For	Opp	W	L	T	For	Opp
Maryland	6	0	0	192	92	9	3	0	326	192
Georgia Tech	5	1	0	136	55	9	2	1	252	132
Clemson	4	3	0	167	122	6	6	0	244	222
Virginia	4	3	0	172	150	6	5	0	262	217
North Carolina	3	4	0	129	154	5	6	0	224	223
Duke	2	5	0	94	174	4	7	0	193	252
NC State	2	5	0	121	189	3	8	0	186	305
Wake Forest	1	6	0	99	174	4	7	0	212	249

All-Conference Offensive Team

WR	Earl Winfield, NC
	James Brim, WF
TE	Jim Riggs, Clem.
T	Jim Dombrowski, Virg.
	John Maarleveld, Mary.
G	Steve Reese, Clem.
	Len Lynch, Mary.
C	Harold Garren, Virg.
QB	Erik Kramer, NC State
RB	Barry Word, Virg.
	Kenny Flowers, Clem.
PK	Kenny Stadlin, Virg.

All-Conference Defensive Team

DL	Pat Swilling, GT
	Bruce Mesner, Mary.
	Gary Baldinger, WF
	Steve Berlin, Clem.
	Reuben Davis, NC
LB	Ted Roof, GT
	Chuck Faucette, Mary.
DB	Cleve Pounds, GT
	Al Covington, Mary.
	Larry Griffin, NC
	Keeta Covington, Mary.
P	Tommy Barnhardt, NC

Player of the Year: Barry Word, Virg.
Coach of the Year: Bill Curry, GT

1986

Team	W	L	T	For	Opp	W	L	T	For	Opp
Clemson	5	1	1	179	97	8	2	2	296	187
North Carolina	5	2	0	206	195	7	5	0	305	279
NC State	5	2	0	198	185	8	3	1	328	274
Georgia Tech	3	3	0	165	113	5	5	1	282	211
Maryland	2	3	1	153	133	5	5	1	262	211
Duke	2	5	0	136	216	4	7	0	200	284
Virginia	2	5	0	111	192	3	8	0	198	315
Wake Forest	2	5	0	203	220	5	6	0	325	295

All-Conference Offensive Team

WR	James Brim, WF
	Nasrallah Worthen, NC State
TE	Jim Riggs, Clem.
T	Harris Barton, NC
	Tim Morrison, WF
G	John Phillips, Clem.
	Paul Kiser, WF
C	John Davis, GT
QB	Erik Kramer, NC State
RB	Terrence Flagler, Clem.
	Derrick Fenner, NC
PK	Mike Cofer, NC State

All-Conference Defensive Team

DL	Terence Mack, Clem.
	Michael Dean Perry, Clem.
	Bruce Mesner, Mary.
	Tim Goad, NC
	Kyle Ambrose, GT
LB	Mike Junkin, Duke
	Chuck Faucette, Mary.
DB	Delton Hall, Clem.
	Keeta Covington, Mary.
	Riccardo Ingram, GT
	Walter Bailey, NC
P	Kelly Hollodick, NC State

Player of the Year: Erik Kramer, NC State
Coach of the Year: Dick Sheridan, NC State

1987

Team	W	L	T	For	Opp	W	L	T	For	Opp
Clemson	6	1	0	205	116	10	2	0	333	176
Virginia	5	2	0	194	159	8	4	0	292	276
Wake Forest	4	3	0	144	130	7	4	0	201	185
NC State	4	3	0	184	159	4	7	0	212	302
Maryland	3	3	0	102	155	4	7	0	194	301
North Carolina	3	4	0	125	131	5	6	0	214	207
Duke	2	5	0	194	183	5	6	0	301	243
Georgia Tech	0	6	0	69	184	2	9	0	199	275

All-Conference Offensive Team

E	John Ford, Virg.
	Clarkston Hines, Duke

All-Conference Defensive Team

DL	Michael Dean Perry, Clem.
	Carlton Bailey, NC

All-Conference Offensive Team

	Ferrell Edmunds, Mary.
T	Jeff Nunamacher, Clem.
	Chris Minear, Virg.
G	John Phillips, Clem.
	Pat Crowley, NC
C	Chuck Massaro, NC State
QB	Scott Secules, Virg.
RB	Terry Allen, Clem.
	Mark Young, WF
PK	David Treadwell, Clem.

All-Conference Defensive Team

	Tim Goad, NC
	Sean Scott, Virg.
	Tony Stephens, Clem.
LB	Kevin Walker, Mary.
	Jimmie Simmons, WF
DB	Norris Davis, NC
	Donnell Woolford, Clem.
	A. J. Greene, WF
	Kevin Cook, Virg.
P	Craig Salmon, NC State

Player of the Year: Michael Dean Perry, Clem.
Coach of the Year: Bill Dooley, WF

1988

Team	W	L	T	For	Opp	W	L	T	For	Opp
Clemson	6	1	0	216	107	10	2	0	342	157
Virginia	5	2	0	162	139	7	4	0	251	244
NC State	4	2	1	169	110	8	3	1	312	175
Wake Forest	4	3	0	173	174	6	4	1	282	238
Maryland	4	3	0	190	196	5	6	0	260	304
Duke	3	3	1	204	245	7	3	1	324	324
North Carolina	1	6	0	152	247	1	10	0	217	391
Georgia Tech	0	7	0	105	153	3	8	0	200	194

All-Conference Offensive Team

E	Clarkston Hines, Duke
	Nasrallah Worthen, NC State
	Dave Colonna, Duke
T	Jeff Nunamacher, Clem.
	Chris Port, Duke
G	Roy Brown, Virg.
	Pat Crowley, NC
C	Jeff Garnica, NC
QB	Anthony Dilweg, Duke
RB	Terry Allen, Clem.
	Ken Martin, NC
PK	Dan Plocki, Mary.

All-Conference Defensive Team

DL	Ray Agnew, NC State
	Mark Drag, Clem.
	Warren Powers, Mary.
	Willis Crockett, GT
	Scott Auer, NC State
LB	Jeff Lageman, Virg.
	Fred Stone, NC State
DB	Donnell Woolford, Clem.
	A. J. Greene, WF
	Jesse Campbell, NC State
	Cedric Stallworth, GT
P	Martin Bailey, WF

Player of the Year: Anthony Dilweg, Duke
Coach of the Year: Steve Spurrier, Duke

1989

Team	W	L	T	For	Opp	W	L	T	For	Opp
Virginia	6	1	0	251	147	10	3	0	371	272
Duke	6	1	0	253	171	8	4	0	377	335
Clemson	5	2	0	205	101	10	2	0	368	138
Georgia Tech	4	3	0	175	151	7	4	0	265	213
NC State	4	3	0	160	142	7	5	0	290	230
Maryland	2	5	0	148	170	3	7	1	215	238
Wake Forest	1	6	0	128	256	2	8	1	194	319
North Carolina	0	7	0	56	238	1	10	0	138	297

All-Conference Offensive Team

WR	Clarkston Hines, Duke
	Ricky Proehl, WF
TE	Bruce McGonnigal, Virg.
T	Chris Port, Duke
	Stacy Long, Clem.
G	Pat Crowley, NC
	Roy Brown, Virg.
C	Carey Metts, Duke
QB	Shawn Moore, Virg.
RB	Jerry Mays, GT
	Randy Cuthbert, Duke
PK	Chris Gardocki, Clem.

All-Conference Defensive Team

DL	Ray Agnew, NC State
	Vance Hammond, Clem.
	Ray Savage, Virg.
	Bobby Houston, NC State
	Cecil Gray, NC
LB	Doug Brewster, Clem.
	Eric Thomas, GT
DB	Jesse Campbell, NC State
	Ken Swilling, GT
	James Lott, Clem.
	Robert O'Neal, Clem.
P	Chris Gardocki, Clem.

Player of the Year: Clarkston Hines, Duke
Coach of the Year: Steve Spurrier, Duke

1990

Team	W	L	T	For	Opp	W	L	T	For	Opp
Georgia Tech	6	0	1	217	124	11	0	1	379	186
Clemson	5	2	0	138	91	10	2	0	333	109
Virginia	5	2	0	251	107	8	4	0	464	227
Maryland	4	3	0	142	158	6	5	1	237	284
North Carolina	3	3	1	124	125	6	4	1	227	186
NC State	3	4	0	90	113	7	5	0	298	189
Duke	1	6	0	137	216	4	7	0	240	295
Wake Forest	0	7	0	99	264	3	8	0	247	351

All-Conference Offensive Team

WR	Herman Moore, Virg.
	Barry Johnson, Mary.

All-Conference Defensive Team

DL	Vance Hammond, Clem.
	Chris Slade, Virg.

All-Conference Offensive Team

TE	John Henry Mills, WF
T	Stacy Long, Clem.
	Ray Roberts, Virg.
G	Joe Siffri, GT
	Eric Harmon, Clem.
C	Trevor Ryals, Virg.
QB	Shawn Moore, Virg.
RB	Terry Kirby, Virg.
	Ronald Williams, Clem.
PK	Chris Gardocki, Clem.

All-Conference Defensive Team

	Rob Bodine, Clem.
	Marco Coleman, GT
	Levon Kirkland, Clem.
LB	Calvin Tiggle, GT
	Dwight Hollier, NC
DB	Ken Swilling, GT
	Dexter Davis, Clem.
	Jesse Campbell, NC State
	Willie Clay, GT
P	Chris Gardocki, Clem.

Player of the Year: Shawn Moore, Virg.
Coach of the Year: Bobby Ross, GT

1991

Team	W	L	T	For	Opp	W	L	T	For	Opp
Clemson	6	0	1	180	90	9	2	1	317	181
NC State	5	2	0	163	150	9	3	0	304	222
Georgia Tech	5	2	0	165	91	8	5	0	283	214
Virginia	4	2	1	185	90	8	3	1	327	167
North Carolina	3	4	0	131	118	7	4	0	282	199
Maryland	2	5	0	87	163	2	9	0	138	302
Wake Forest	1	6	0	86	194	3	8	0	195	300
Duke	1	6	0	106	207	4	6	1	231	280
Florida State						11	2	0	449	188

All-Conference Offensive Team

WR	Terry Smith, Clem.
	Charles Davenport, NC State
TE	John Henry Mills, WF
T	Ray Roberts, Virg.
	Mike Mooney, GT
G	Jeb Flesch, Clem.
	Brian Bollinger, NC
C	Mike Brown, Clem.
QB	Matt Blundin, Virg.
RB	Terry Kirby, Virg.
	Natrone Means, NC
PK	Nelson Welch, Clem.

All-Conference Defensive Team

DL	Coleman Rudolph, GT
	Rob Bodine, Clem.
	Chester McGlockton, Clem.
	Marco Coleman, GT
	Levon Kirkland, Clem.
LB	Ed McDaniel, Clem.
	Tommy Thigpen, NC
DB	Willie Clay, GT
	Sebastian Savage, NC State
	Robert O'Neal, Clem.
	George Coghill, WF
P	Ed Garno, Virg.

Player of the Year: Matt Blundin, Virg.
Coach of the Year: George Welsh, Virg.

Clemson

Location: Clemson, SC
Colors: Purple and Orange
Stadium: Memorial (1942), 79,854 capacity, natural turf.

Enrollment: 14,794
Nickname: Tigers

Head Coaches

Walter Riggs 1896, 1899
William Williams, 1897
John Penton 1898
John Heisman 1900–03
Shack Shealy 1904
Eddie Cochems 1905
Bob Williams 1906, 1909, 1913–15
Frank Shaughnessy 1907
John Stone 1908
Frank Dobson 1910–12
Wayne Hart 1916

Ed Donahue 1917–20
Doc Stewart 1921–22
Bud Saunders 1923–26
Josh Cody 1927–30
Jess Neely 1931–39
Frank Howard 1940–69
Hootie Ingram 1970–72
Jim "Red" Parker 1973–76
Charley Pell 1977–78
Danny Ford 1979–89
Ken Hatfield 1990–91

All–American Players

Banks McFadden 1939 tailback
Joe Blalock 1940–41 end
Ralph Jenkins 1945 center
Bobby Gage 1948 tailback
Jackie Calvert 1950 tailback
Tom Barton 1952 def. guard
Lou Cordileone 1959 tackle
Wayne Mass 1966 tackle
Harry Olszewski 1967 guard
Dave Thompson 1970 center
Bennie Cunningham 1974–75 end
Joe Bostic 1977–78 guard
Jerry Butler 1978 end
Jim Stuckey 1979 def. tackle
Obed Ariri 1980 place-kicker
Jeff Bryant 1981 def. tackle

Jeff Davis 1981 linebacker
Terry Kinard 1981–82 def. back
Lee Nanney 1981 tackle
Perry Tuttle 1981 end
Jim Robinson 1983 def. tackle
William Perry 1983–84 nose guard
Dale Hatcher 1984 punter
Steve Reese 1985 guard
Terrence Flagler 1986 halfback
John Phillips 1986–87 guard
David Treadwell 1987 place-kicker
Michael Dean Perry 1987 def. tackle
Donnell Woolford 1987–88 def. back
Stacy Long 1989–90 tackle
Chris Gardocki 1990 place-kicker
Jeb Flesch 1991 guard

Scores

1896 (2-1-0)

14	Furman	6
6	South Carolina	12
16	Wofford	0

1897 (2-2-0)

0	Georgia	24
10	Charlotte YMCA	0
0	North Carolina	28
18	South Carolina	6

1898 (3-1-0)

8	Georgia	20
55	Bingham	0
24	South Carolina	0
23	Georgia Tech	0

1899 (4-2-0)

0	Georgia	11
10	Davidson	0
0	Auburn	34
34	South Carolina	0
24	NC State	0
41	Georgia Tech	5

1900 (6-0-0)

64	Davidson	0
21	Wofford	0
51	South Carolina	0
39	Georgia	5
12	Virginia Tech	5
35	Alabama	0

1901 (3-1-1)

122	Guilford	0
6	Tennessee	6
29	Georgia	5
11	Virginia Tech	17
22	North Carolina	0

1902 (6-1-0)

11	NC State	5
44	Georgia Tech	5
28	Furman	0
6	South Carolina	12
36	Georgia	0
16	Auburn	0
11	Tennessee	0

1903 (4-1-1)

29	Georgia	0
73	Georgia Tech	0
24	NC State	0
6	North Carolina	11
24	Davidson	0
11	Cumberland	11

1904 (3-3-1)

18	Alabama	0
0	Auburn	5
10	Georgia	0
5	Sewanee	11
11	Georgia Tech	11
6	Tennessee	0
0	NC State	18

1905 (3-2-1)

5	Tennessee	5
35	Georgia	0
25	Alabama	0
26	Auburn	0
0	Vanderbilt	41
10	Georgia Tech	17

1906 (4-0-3)

0	Virginia Tech	0
6	Georgia	0
0	NC State	0
0	Davidson	0
6	Auburn	4
16	Tennessee	0
10	Georgia Tech	0

1907 (4-4-0)

5	Gordon	0
35	Maryville	0
0	Tennessee	4
15	North Carolina	6
0	Auburn	12
0	Georgia	8
6	Davidson	10
6	Georgia Tech	5

1908 (1-6-0)

15	Gordon	0
0	Virginia Tech	6
0	Vanderbilt	41
0	Davidson	13
0	Georgia	8
5	Tennessee	6
6	Georgia Tech	30

1909 (6-3-0)

26	Gordon	0
0	Virginia Tech	6
17	Davidson	5
0	Alabama	3
19	Port Royal	0
6	South Carolina	0
5	Georgia	0
17	The Citadel	0
3	Georgia Tech	29

1910 (4-3-1)

26	Gordon	0
0	Mercer	3
24	Howard	0
32	The Citadel	0
0	Auburn	17
24	South Carolina	0
0	Georgia	0
0	Georgia Tech	34

***Opposite:* Memorial Stadium, Clemson, SC**

1911 (3-5-0)

0	Auburn	29
15	Howard	0
5	Florida	6
27	South Carolina	0
18	The Citadel	0
0	Georgia	22
6	Mercer	20
0	Georgia Tech	31

1912 (4-4-0)

59	Howard	0
26	Riverside	0
6	Auburn	27
52	The Citadel	14
7	South Carolina	22
6	Georgia	27
21	Mercer	13
0	Georgia Tech	20

1913 (4-4-0)

6	Davidson	3
0	Alabama	20
0	Auburn	20
32	South Carolina	0
15	Georgia	18
7	The Citadel	3
52	Mercer	0
0	Georgia Tech	34

1914 (5-3-1)

0	Davidson	0
0	Tennessee	27
0	Auburn	28
57	Furman	0
29	South Carolina	6
14	The Citadel	0
35	Georgia	13
27	VMI	23
6	Georgia Tech	26

1915 (2-4-2)

94	Furman	0
6	Davidson	6
3	Tennessee	0
0	Auburn	14
0	South Carolina	0
7	North Carolina	9
3	VMI	6
0	Georgia	13

1916 (3-6-0)

7	Furman	6
0	Georgia	26
0	Tennessee	14
0	Auburn	28
27	South Carolina	0
7	VMI	37
0	The Citadel	3
40	Presbyterian	0
0	Davidson	33

1917 (6-2-0)

13	Presbyterian	0
38	Furman	0
0	Auburn	7
21	South Carolina	13
27	Wofford	16
20	The Citadel	0
55	Florida	7
9	Davidson	21

1918 (5-2-0)

65	Camp Sevier	0
0	Georgia Tech	28
39	South Carolina	0
13	Camp Hancock	66
7	The Citadel	0
68	Furman	7
7	Davidson	0

1919 (6-2-2)

52	Erskine	0
7	Davidson	0
0	Georgia Tech	28
0	Auburn	7
14	Tennessee	0
19	South Carolina	6
19	Presbyterian	7
33	The Citadel	0
7	Furman	7
0	Georgia	0

1920 (4-6-1)

26	Erskine	0
7	Presbyterian	7
26	Newberry	6
13	Wofford	7
0	Auburn	21
0	Tennessee	26
0	South Carolina	3
0	Georgia Tech	7
26	The Citadel	0
0	Furman	14
0	Georgia	55

1921 (1-6-2)

0	Centre	14
34	Presbyterian	0
0	Auburn	56
0	Furman	0
0	South Carolina	21
7	Georgia Tech	48
7	The Citadel	7
0	Erskine	13
0	Georgia	28

1922 (5-4-0)

0	Centre	21
57	Newberry	0
13	Presbyterian	0
3	South Carolina	0
7	Georgia Tech	21
18	The Citadel	0
52	Erskine	0
6	Furman	20
14	Florida	47

1923 (5-2-1)

0	Auburn	0
32	Newberry	0
7	Centre	28
7	South Carolina	6
6	Virginia Tech	25
12	Davidson	0
20	Presbyterian	0
7	Furman	6

1924 (2-6-0)

60	Elon	0
0	Auburn	13
14	Presbyterian	0
0	South Carolina	3
6	Virginia Tech	50
0	Davidson	7
0	The Citadel	20
0	Furman	3

1925 (1-7-0)

9	Presbyterian	14
6	Auburn	13
6	Kentucky	19
0	South Carolina	33
0	Wofford	13
0	Florida	42
6	The Citadel	0
0	Furman	26

1926 (2-7-0)

7	Erskine	0
0	Presbyterian	14
0	Auburn	47
7	NC State	3
0	South Carolina	24
0	Wofford	3
0	Florida	33
6	The Citadel	15
0	Furman	30

1927 (5-3-1)

0	Presbyterian	0
3	Auburn	0
6	NC State	18
25	Erskine	6
20	South Carolina	0
6	Wofford	0
13	The Citadel	0
0	Georgia	32
0	Furman	28

1928 (8-3-0)

30	Newberry	0
6	Davidson	0
6	Auburn	0
7	NC State	0
52	Erskine	0
32	South Carolina	0
7	Mississippi	26
12	VMI	0
6	Florida	27
27	Furman	12
7	The Citadel	12

1929 (8-3-0)

68	Newberry	0
32	Davidson	14
26	Auburn	7
26	NC State	0
30	Wofford	0
21	South Carolina	14
6	Kentucky	44
0	VMI	12
7	Florida	13
13	The Citadel	0
7	Furman	6

1930 (8-2-0)

28	Presbyterian	7
32	Wofford	0
13	The Citadel	7
27	NC State	0
75	Newberry	0
20	South Carolina	7
0	Tennessee	27
32	VMI	0
0	Florida	27
12	Furman	7

1931 (1-6-2)

0	Presbyterian	0
0	Tennessee	44
6	NC State	0
0	The Citadel	6
0	South Carolina	21
0	Oglethorpe	12
6	VMI	7
7	Alabama	74
0	Furman	0

1932 (3-5-1)

13	Presbyterian	0
14	Georgia Tech	32
0	NC State	13
19	Erskine	0
0	South Carolina	14
7	Davidson	7
18	The Citadel	6
18	Georgia	32
0	Furman	7

1933 (3-6-2)

6	Presbyterian	6
2	Georgia Tech	39
9	NC State	0
0	George Wash.	0
0	South Carolina	7
0	Mississippi	13
13	Wake Forest	0
13	Wofford	14
0	Mercer	13

1934 (5-4-0)

6	Presbyterian	0
7	Georgia Tech	12
6	Duke	20
0	Kentucky	7
19	South Carolina	0
12	NC State	6
0	Alabama	40
32	Mercer	0
7	Furman	0

1933 (cont.)

7	The Citadel	0
0	Furman	6

1935 (6-3-0)

26	Presbyterian	6
28	Virginia Tech	7
13	Wake Forest	7
12	Duke	38
44	South Carolina	0
13	Mercer	0
0	Alabama	33
6	The Citadel	0
6	Furman	8

1936 (5-5-0)

19	Presbyterian	0
20	Virginia Tech	0
0	Alabama	32
0	Duke	25
0	Wake Forest	6
19	South Carolina	0
14	Georgia Tech	13
20	The Citadel	0
6	Kentucky	7
0	Furman	12

1937 (4-4-1)

46	Presbyterian	0
0	Tulane	7
6	Army	21
0	Georgia	14
34	South Carolina	6
32	Wake Forest	0
0	Georgia Tech	7
10	Florida	9
0	Furman	0

1938 (7-1-1)

26	Presbyterian	0
13	Tulane	10
7	Tennessee	20
7	VMI	7
34	South Carolina	12
7	Wake Forest	0
27	George Wash.	0
14	Kentucky	0
10	Furman	7

1939 (9-1-0)

18	Presbyterian	0
6	Tulane	7
25	NC State	6
27	South Carolina	0
15	Navy	7
13	George Wash.	6
20	Wake Forest	7
21	Southwestern	6
14	Furman	3
6	Boston College (Cotton Bowl)	3

1940 (6-2-1)

38	Presbyterian	0
26	Wofford	0
26	NC State	7
39	Wake Forest	0
21	South Carolina	13
0	Tulane	13
7	Auburn	21
12	Southwestern	12
13	Furman	7

1941 (7-2-0)

41	Presbyterian	12
36	VMI	7
27	NC State	6
26	Boston College	13
14	South Carolina	18
19	George Wash.	0
29	Wake Forest	0
34	Furman	6
7	Auburn	28

1942 (3-6-1)

32	Presbyterian	13
0	VMI	0
6	NC State	7
7	Boston College	14
18	South Carolina	6
6	Wake Forest	19
0	George Wash.	7
6	Jax. NAS	24
12	Furman	7
13	Auburn	41

1943 (2-6-0)

12	Presbyterian	13
19	NC State	7
7	VMI	12
6	South Carolina	33
12	Wake Forest	41
26	Davidson	6
6	Ga. Pre-Flight	32
6	Georgia Tech	41

1944 (4-5-0)

34	Presbyterian	0
0	Georgia Tech	51
13	NC State	7
20	South Carolina	13

1945 (6-3-1)

76	Presbyterian	0
0	Georgia	20
13	NC State	0
7	Pensacola NAS	6

1946 (4-5-0)

39	Presbyterian	0
12	Georgia	35
7	NC State	14
7	Wake Forest	19

1944 (cont.)		
7	Tennessee	26
7	Wake Forest	13
57	VMI	12
20	Tulane	36
7	Georgia	21

1945 (cont.)		
0	South Carolina	0
6	Miami (FL)	7
35	Virginia Tech	0
47	Tulane	20
21	Georgia Tech	7
6	Wake Forest	13

1946 (cont.)		
14	South Carolina	26
14	Virginia Tech	7
13	Tulane	54
20	Furman	6
21	Auburn	13

1947 (4-5-0)		
42	Presbyterian	0
22	Boston College	32
14	Wake Forest	16
0	NC State	18
19	South Carolina	21
6	Georgia	21
35	Furman	7
34	Duquesne	13
34	Auburn	18

1948 (11-0-0)		
53	Presbyterian	0
6	NC State	0
21	Miss. State	7
13	South Carolina	7
26	Boston College	19
41	Furman	0
21	Wake Forest	14
42	Duquesne	0
7	Auburn	6
20	The Citadel	0
24	Missouri	23
	(Gator Bowl)	

1949 (4-4-2)		
69	Presbyterian	0
7	Rice	33
7	NC State	6
7	Miss. State	7
13	South Carolina	27
21	Wake Forest	35
27	Boston College	40
33	Duquesne	20
28	Furman	21
20	Auburn	20

1950 (9-0-1)		
55	Presbyterian	0
34	Missouri	0
27	NC State	0
14	South Carolina	14
13	Wake Forest	12
53	Duquesne	20
35	Boston College	14
57	Furman	2
41	Auburn	0
15	Miami (FL)	14
	(Orange Bowl)	

1951 (7-3-0)		
53	Presbyterian	6
20	Rice	14
6	NC State	0
7	Pacific	21
0	South Carolina	20
21	Wake Forest	6
21	Boston College	2
34	Furman	14
34	Auburn	0
0	Miami (FL)	14
	(Gator Bowl)	

1952 (2-6-1)		
53	Presbyterian	13
7	Villanova	14
0	Maryland	28
13	Florida	54
0	South Carolina	6
13	Boston College	0
12	Fordham	12
14	Kentucky	27
0	Auburn	3

1953 (3-5-1)		
33	Presbyterian	7
14	Boston College	14
0	Maryland	20
7	Miami (FL)	39
7	South Carolina	14
18	Wake Forest	0
7	Georgia Tech	20
34	The Citadel	13
19	Auburn	45

1954 (5-5-0)		
33	Presbyterian	0
7	Georgia	14
7	Virginia Tech	18
14	Florida	7
8	South Carolina	13
32	Wake Forest	20
27	Furman	6
0	Maryland	16
6	Auburn	27
59	The Citadel	0

1955 (7-3-0)		
33	Presbyterian	0
20	Virginia	7
26	Georgia	7
7	Rice	21
28	South Carolina	14
19	Wake Forest	13
21	Virginia Tech	16
12	Maryland	25
0	Auburn	21
40	Furman	20

1956 (7-2-2)

27	Presbyterian	7
20	Florida	20
13	NC State	7
17	Wake Forest	0
7	South Carolina	0
21	Virginia Tech	6
6	Maryland	6
0	Miami (FL)	21
7	Virginia	0
28	Furman	7
21	Colorado	27
	(Orange Bowl)	

1957 (7-3-0)

66	Presbyterian	0
0	North Carolina	26
7	NC State	13
20	Virginia	6
13	South Carolina	0
20	Rice	7
26	Maryland	7
6	Duke	7
13	Wake Forest	6
45	Furman	6

1958 (8-3-0)

20	Virginia	15
26	North Carolina	21
8	Maryland	0
12	Vanderbilt	7
6	South Carolina	26
14	Wake Forest	12
0	Georgia Tech	13
13	NC State	6
34	Boston College	12
36	Furman	19
0	LSU	7
	(Sugar Bowl)	

1959 (9-2-0)

20	North Carolina	18
47	Virginia	0
6	Georgia Tech	16
23	NC State	0
27	South Carolina	0
19	Rice	0
6	Duke	0
25	Maryland	28
33	Wake Forest	31
56	Furman	3
23	TCU	7
	(Bluebonnet Bowl)	

1960 (6-4-0)

28	Wake Forest	7
13	Virginia Tech	7
21	Virginia	7
17	Maryland	19
6	Duke	21
20	Vanderbilt	22
24	North Carolina	0
12	South Carolina	2
14	Boston College	25
42	Furman	14

1961 (5-5-0)

17	Florida	21
21	Maryland	24
27	North Carolina	0
13	Wake Forest	17
17	Duke	7
14	Auburn	24
21	Tulane	6
14	South Carolina	21
35	Furman	6
20	NC State	0

1962 (6-4-0)

9	Georgia Tech	26
7	NC State	0
24	Wake Forest	7
16	Georgia	24
0	Duke	16
14	Auburn	17
17	North Carolina	6
44	Furman	3
17	Maryland	14
20	South Carolina	17

1963 (5-4-1)

14	Oklahoma	31
0	Georgia Tech	27
3	NC State	7
7	Georgia	7
30	Duke	35
35	Virginia	0
36	Wake Forest	0
11	North Carolina	7
21	Maryland	6
24	South Carolina	20

1964 (3-7-0)

28	Furman	0
0	NC State	9
7	Georgia Tech	14
7	Georgia	19
21	Wake Forest	2
10	TCU	14
29	Virginia	7
0	North Carolina	29
0	Maryland	34
3	South Carolina	7

1965 (5-5-0)

21	NC State	7
20	Virginia	14
6	Georgia Tech	28
9	Georgia	23

1966 (6-4-0)

40	Virginia	35
12	Georgia Tech	13
0	Alabama	26
9	Duke	6

1967 (6-4-0)

23	Wake Forest	6
17	Georgia	24
0	Georgia Tech	10
21	Auburn	43

1965 (cont.)

3	Duke	2
3	TCU	0
26	Wake Forest	13
13	North Carolina	17
0	Maryland	6
16	South Carolina	17

1968 (4-5-1)

20	Wake Forest	20
13	Georgia	31
21	Georgia Tech	24
10	Auburn	21
39	Duke	22
14	Alabama	21
24	NC State	19
16	Maryland	0
24	North Carolina	14
3	South Carolina	7

1971 (5-6-0)

10	Kentucky	13
0	Georgia	28
14	Georgia Tech	24
3	Duke	0
32	Virginia	15
13	Auburn	35
10	Wake Forest	9
13	North Carolina	26
20	Maryland	14
23	NC State	31
17	South Carolina	7

1974 (7-4-0)

0	Texas A&M	24
10	NC State	31
21	Georgia Tech	17
28	Georgia	24
0	Maryland	41
17	Duke	13
28	Tennessee	29
21	Wake Forest	9
54	North Carolina	32
28	Virginia	9
39	South Carolina	21

1966 (cont.)

0	Southern Cal	30
23	Wake Forest	21
27	North Carolina	3
14	Maryland	10
14	NC State	23
35	South Carolina	10

1969 (4-6-0)

21	Virginia	14
0	Georgia	30
21	Georgia Tech	10
0	Auburn	51
28	Wake Forest	14
13	Alabama	38
40	Maryland	0
27	Duke	34
15	North Carolina	32
13	South Carolina	27

1972 (4-7-0)

13	The Citadel	0
10	Rice	29
3	Oklahoma	52
9	Georgia Tech	31
0	Duke	7
37	Virginia	21
31	Wake Forest	0
10	North Carolina	26
6	Maryland	31
17	NC State	42
7	South Carolina	6

1975 (2-9-0)

13	Tulane	17
0	Alabama	56
28	Georgia Tech	33
7	Georgia	35
16	Wake Forest	14
21	Duke	25
7	NC State	45
7	Florida State	43
38	North Carolina	35
20	Maryland	22
20	South Carolina	56

1967 (cont.)

13	Duke	7
10	Alabama	13
17	North Carolina	0
28	Maryland	7
14	NC State	6
23	South Carolina	12

1970 (3-8-0)

24	The Citadel	0
27	Virginia	17
0	Georgia	38
7	Georgia Tech	28
0	Auburn	44
20	Wake Forest	36
10	Duke	21
24	Maryland	11
13	Florida State	38
7	North Carolina	42
32	South Carolina	38

1973 (5-6-0)

14	The Citadel	12
14	Georgia	31
21	Georgia Tech	29
15	Texas A&M	30
32	Virginia	27
24	Duke	8
6	NC State	29
35	Wake Forest	8
37	North Carolina	29
13	Maryland	28
20	South Carolina	32

1976 (3-6-2)

10	The Citadel	7
0	Georgia	41
24	Georgia Tech	24
19	Tennessee	21
14	Wake Forest	20
18	Duke	18
21	NC State	38
15	Florida State	12
23	North Carolina	27
0	Maryland	20
28	South Carolina	9

1977 (8-3-1)

14	Maryland	21
7	Georgia	6
31	Georgia Tech	14
31	Virginia Tech	13
31	Virginia	0
17	Duke	11
7	NC State	3
26	Wake Forest	0
13	North Carolina	13
17	Notre Dame	21
31	South Carolina	27
3	Pitt	34
	(Gator Bowl)	

1978 (11-1-0)

58	The Citadel	3
0	Georgia	12
31	Villanova	0
38	Virginia Tech	7
30	Virginia	14
28	Duke	8
33	NC State	10
51	Wake Forest	6
13	North Carolina	9
28	Maryland	24
41	South Carolina	23
17	Ohio State	15
	(Gator Bowl)	

1979 (8-4-0)

21	Furman	0
0	Maryland	19
12	Georgia	7
17	Virginia	7
21	Virginia Tech	0
28	Duke	10
13	NC State	16
31	Wake Forest	0
19	North Carolina	10
16	Notre Dame	10
9	South Carolina	13
18	Baylor	24
	(Peach Bowl)	

1980 (6-5-0)

19	Rice	3
16	Georgia	20
17	W. Carolina	10
13	Virginia Tech	10
27	Virginia	24
17	Duke	34
20	NC State	24
35	Wake Forest	33
19	North Carolina	24
7	Maryland	34
27	South Carolina	6

1981 (12-0-0)

45	Wofford	10
13	Tulane	5
13	Georgia	3
21	Kentucky	3
27	Virginia	0
38	Duke	10
17	NC State	7
82	Wake Forest	24
10	North Carolina	8
21	Maryland	7
29	South Carolina	13
22	Nebraska	15
	(Orange Bowl)	

1982 (9-1-1)

7	Georgia	13
17	Boston College	17
21	W. Carolina	10
24	Kentucky	6
48	Virginia	0
49	Duke	14
38	NC State	29
16	North Carolina	13
24	Maryland	22
24	South Carolina	6
21	Wake Forest	17

1983 (9-1-1)

44	W. Carolina	10
16	Boston College	31
16	Georgia	16
41	Georgia Tech	14
42	Virginia	21
38	Duke	31
27	NC State	17
24	Wake Forest	17
16	North Carolina	3
52	Maryland	27
22	South Carolina	13

1984 (7-4-0)

40	App. State	7
55	Virginia	0
23	Georgia	26
21	Georgia Tech	28
20	North Carolina	12
54	Duke	21
35	NC State	34
37	Wake Forest	14
17	Virginia Tech	10
23	Maryland	41
21	South Carolina	22

1985 (6-6-0)

20	Virginia Tech	17
13	Georgia	20
3	Georgia Tech	14
7	Kentucky	26
27	Virginia	24
21	Duke	9
39	NC State	10
26	Wake Forest	10
20	North Carolina	21
31	Maryland	34
24	South Carolina	17
13	Minnesota	20
	(Independence Bowl)	

1986 (8-2-2)

14	Virginia Tech	20
31	Georgia	28
27	Georgia Tech	3
24	The Citadel	0
31	Virginia	17
35	Duke	3
3	NC State	27
28	Wake Forest	20
38	North Carolina	10
17	Maryland	17
21	South Carolina	21
27	Stanford	21
	(Gator Bowl)	

1987 (10-2-0)

43	W. Carolina	0
22	Virginia Tech	10
21	Georgia	20
33	Georgia Tech	12
38	Virginia	21
17	Duke	10
28	NC State	30
31	Wake Forest	17
13	North Carolina	10
45	Maryland	16
7	South Carolina	20
35	Penn State	10
	(Citrus Bowl)	

1988 (10-2-0)

40	Virginia Tech	7
23	Furman	3
21	Florida State	24
30	Georgia Tech	13
10	Virginia	7
49	Duke	17
3	NC State	10
38	Wake Forest	21
37	North Carolina	14
49	Maryland	25
29	South Carolina	10
13	Oklahoma	6
	(Citrus Bowl)	

1989 (10-2-0)

30	Furman	0
34	Florida State	23
27	Virginia Tech	7
31	Maryland	7
17	Duke	21
34	Virginia	20
14	Georgia Tech	30
30	NC State	10
44	Wake Forest	10
35	North Carolina	3
45	South Carolina	0
27	West Virginia	7
	(Gator Bowl)	

1990 (10-2-0)

59	Long Beach St.	0
7	Virginia	20
18	Maryland	17
48	App. State	0
26	Duke	7
34	Georgia	3
19	Georgia Tech	21
24	NC State	17
24	Wake Forest	6
20	North Carolina	3
24	South Carolina	15
30	Illinois	0
	(Hall of Fame Bowl)	

1991 (9-2-1)

34	App. State	0
37	Temple	7
9	Georgia Tech	7
12	Georgia	27
20	Virginia	20
29	NC State	19
28	Wake Forest	10
21	North Carolina	6
40	Maryland	7
41	South Carolina	24
33	Duke	21
13	California	37
	(Citrus Bowl)	

Duke

Location: Durham, NC   Enrollment: 6,000
Colors: Royal Blue and White   Nickname: Blue Devils
Stadium: Wallace Wade (1929), 33,941 capacity, natural turf.

Head Coaches

John Crowell 1888–89
No head coach 1890–94
Floyd Egan 1920
James Baldwin 1921

Herman Steiner 1922
Stewart Alexander 1923
Howard Jones 1924
Pat Herron 1925

Wallace Wade Stadium, Durham, NC

Jimmy DeHart 1926–30
Wallace Wade 1931–41, 1946–50
Eddie Cameron 1942–45
Bill Murray 1951–65
Tom Harp 1966–70

Mike McGee 1971–78
Red Wilson 1979–82
Steve Sloan 1983–86
Steve Spurrier 1987–89
Barry Wilson 1990–91

All–American Players

Fred Crawford 1932–33 tackle
Earle Wentz 1934 end
Ace Parker 1935–36 tailback
Elmore Hackney 1937 tailback
Joe Brunansky 1937 tackle
Dan Hill 1938 center
Eric Tipton 1938 halfback
George McAfee 1939 halfback
Tony Ruffa 1940 tackle
Steve Lach 1941 halfback
Bob Gantt 1942 end
Pat Preston 1943 tackle
Tom Davis 1944 fullback
Ernie Knotts 1945 guard
Bill Milner 1943, 1946 guard
Al DeRogatis 1948 tackle
Blaine Earon 1950 end

Ed Meadows 1952–53 tackle
Bob Burrows 1953 guard
Roy Hord 1957 end
Mike McGee 1959 guard
Tee Moorman 1960 end
Jean Berry 1962 guard
Art Gregory 1962 tackle
Jay Wilkinson 1963 halfback
Bob Matheson 1966 linebacker
Ernie Jackson 1971 def. back
Billy Bryan 1976 center
Cedric Jones 1981 end
Chris Castor 1982 end
Robert Oxendine 1982 tackle
Mike Junkin 1986 linebacker
Clarkston Hines 1988–89 end
Chris Port 1989 tackle

Scores

1888 (1-0-0)

16	North Carolina	0

1889 (2-2-0)

25	North Carolina	17
0	Wake Forest	32
0	North Carolina	1
8	Wake Forest	4

1890 (0-1-0)

4	Virginia	10

1891 (3-0-0)

96	Furman	0
6	North Carolina	4
20	Virginia	0

1892 (1-3-0)

0	North Carolina	24
0	VMI	32
4	Virginia	46
34	Auburn	6

1893 (3-1-0)

12	Wake Forest	6
6	North Carolina	4
70	Tennessee	0
0	Virginia	30

1894 (0-1-0)

0	North Carolina	28

1920 (4-0-1)

20	Guilford	7
7	Emory & Henry	0

1921 (6-1-2)

14	Lynchburg	13
0	William & Mary	12

Football banned by
faculty 1895–1919

1920 (cont.)

13	Lynchburg	7
13	Elon	6
0	Wofford	0

1921 (cont.)

6	Randolph Macon	0
7	Emory & Henry	0
0	Elon	0
28	Guilford	0
17	Wake Forest	0
7	NYU	7
68	Wofford	0

1922 (7-2-1)

43	Guilford	0
27	Hampden-Sydney	0
0	North Carolina	20
7	William & Mary	13
12	Davidson	0
7	Oglethorpe	6
3	Wake Forest	0
25	Randolph Macon	12
6	Presbyterian	6
26	Wofford	0

1923 (5-4-0)

68	Guilford	0
54	Randolph Macon	0
6	North Carolina	14
0	William & Mary	21
0	Virginia	35
39	Elon	0
6	Wake Forest	16
20	Newberry	14
18	Davidson	6

1924 (4-5-0)

0	NC State	14
33	Guilford	6
0	North Carolina	6
14	Richmond	0
3	William & Mary	21
54	Elon	0
0	Wake Forest	32
12	Wofford	0
13	Davidson	20

1925 (4-5-0)

33	Guilford	0
0	NC State	13
0	North Carolina	41
0	William & Mary	41
10	Richmond	0
6	Elon	0
3	Wake Forest	21
6	Wofford	0
0	Davidson	26

1926 (3-6-0)

32	Guilford	0
7	Richmond	9
32	Elon	0
0	North Carolina	6
0	Wake Forest	21
0	Columbia	24
19	NC State	26
34	Wofford	0
0	Davidson	20

1927 (4-5-0)

7	Furman	13
25	Boston College	9
7	Wash. & Lee	12
72	Richmond	0
6	Navy	32
32	Wake Forest	6
18	NC State	20
0	North Carolina	18
48	Davidson	7

1928 (5-5-0)

0	Furman	6
25	South Dakota	6
0	Boston College	19
0	Navy	6
0	Georgetown	35
38	Mercer	18
38	Wake Forest	0
14	NC State	12
33	Davidson	0
7	North Carolina	14

1929 (4-6-0)

19	Mercer	6
7	Pitt	52
13	Navy	45
12	Villanova	58
12	Boston College	20
32	LSU	6
19	NC State	12
20	Wake Forest	0
12	Davidson	13
7	North Carolina	48

1930 (8-1-2)

0	South Carolina	22
32	Virginia	0
12	Davidson	0
18	Navy	0
14	Wofford	0
12	Villanova	6
14	Kentucky	7
18	NC State	0
13	Wake Forest	13
14	Wash. & Lee	0
0	North Carolina	0

1931 (5-3-2)

0	South Carolina	7
13	VMI	0
18	Villanova	0
0	Davidson	0
28	Wake Forest	0
2	Tennessee	25
7	Kentucky	0
0	NC State	14
0	North Carolina	0
6	Wash. & Lee	0

1932 (7-3-0)

13	Davidson	0
44	VMI	0
7	Auburn	18
34	Maryland	0
9	Wake Forest	0
13	Tennessee	16
13	Kentucky	0
0	NC State	6
7	North Carolina	0
13	Wash. & Lee	0

1933 (9-1-0)

37	VMI	6
22	Wake Forest	0
10	Tennessee	2
19	Davidson	7
14	Kentucky	7
13	Auburn	7
38	Maryland	7
21	North Carolina	0
7	NC State	0
0	Georgia Tech	6

1934 (7-2-0)

46	VMI	0
20	Clemson	6
20	Georgia Tech	0
20	Davidson	0
6	Tennessee	14
13	Auburn	6
28	Wake Forest	7
0	North Carolina	7
32	NC State	0

1935 (8-2-0)

26	Wake Forest	7
47	South Carolina	0
26	Wash. & Lee	0
38	Clemson	12
0	Georgia Tech	6
0	Auburn	7
19	Tennessee	6
26	Davidson	7
25	North Carolina	0
7	NC State	0

1936 (9-1-0)

13	Davidson	0
6	Colgate	0
21	South Carolina	0
25	Clemson	0
19	Georgia Tech	6
13	Tennessee	15
51	Wash. & Lee	0
20	Wake Forest	0
27	North Carolina	7
13	NC State	0

1937 (7-2-1)

25	Virginia Tech	0
34	Davidson	6
0	Tennessee	0
20	Georgia Tech	19
13	Colgate	0
43	Wash. & Lee	0
67	Wake Forest	0
6	North Carolina	14
20	NC State	7
0	Pitt	10

1938 (9-1-0)

18	Virginia Tech	0
27	Davidson	0
7	Colgate	0
6	Georgia Tech	0
7	Wake Forest	0
14	North Carolina	0
21	Syracuse	0
7	NC State	0
7	Pitt	0
3	Southern Cal	7
	(Rose Bowl)	

1939 (8-1-0)

26	Davidson	6
37	Colgate	0
13	Pitt	14
33	Syracuse	6
6	Wake Forest	0
7	Georgia Tech	6
20	VMI	7
13	North Carolina	3
28	NC State	0

1940 (7-2-0)

23	VMI	0
0	Tennessee	13
13	Colgate	0
23	Wake Forest	0
41	Georgia Tech	7
46	Davidson	13
3	North Carolina	6
42	NC State	6

1941 (9-1-0)

43	Wake Forest	14
19	Tennessee	0
50	Maryland	0
27	Colgate	14
27	Pitt	7
14	Georgia Tech	0
56	Davidson	0
20	North Carolina	0

1942 (5-4-1)

21	Davidson	0
7	Wake Forest	20
12	Ga. Pre-Flight	26
34	Colgate	0
28	Pitt	0
7	Georgia Tech	26
42	Maryland	0
13	North Carolina	13

1940 (cont.)

12	Pitt	7

1941 (cont.)

55	NC State	6
16	Oregon State	20
	(Rose Bowl)	

1942 (cont.)

47	NC State	0
0	Jax. NAS	13

1943 (8-1-0)

40	Camp Lejeune	0
61	Richmond	0
42	NC Pre-Flight	0
13	Navy	14
14	North Carolina	7
14	Georgia Tech	7
75	NC State	0
49	Virginia	0
27	North Carolina	6

1944 (6-4-0)

61	Richmond	7
7	Penn	18
6	NC Pre-Flight	13
0	Navy	7
7	Army	27
19	Georgia Tech	13
34	Wake Forest	0
34	South Carolina	7
33	North Carolina	0
29	Alabama	26
	(Sugar Bowl)	

1945 (6-2-0)

60	South Carolina	0
76	Bogue Field	0
0	Navy	21
26	Wake Forest	19
13	Army	48
14	Georgia Tech	6
26	NC State	13
14	North Carolina	7

1946 (4-5-0)

6	NC State	13
7	Tennessee	12
21	Navy	6
41	Richmond	0
0	Army	19
0	Georgia Tech	14
13	Wake Forest	0
39	South Carolina	0
7	North Carolina	22

1947 (4-3-2)

7	NC State	0
19	Tennessee	7
14	Navy	14
19	Maryland	7
13	Wake Forest	6
0	Georgia Tech	7
7	Missouri	28
0	South Carolina	0
0	North Carolina	21

1948 (4-3-2)

0	NC State	0
7	Tennessee	7
28	Navy	7
13	Maryland	12
7	Virginia Tech	0
7	Georgia Tech	19
20	Wake Forest	27
62	George Wash.	0
0	North Carolina	20

1949 (6-3-0)

67	Richmond	0
21	Tennessee	7
14	Navy	28
14	NC State	13
55	Virginia Tech	7
27	Georgia Tech	14
7	Wake Forest	27
35	George Wash.	0
20	North Carolina	21

1950 (7-3-0)

14	South Carolina	0
28	Pitt	14
7	Tennessee	28
7	NC State	0
41	Richmond	0
14	Maryland	26
30	Georgia Tech	21
7	Wake Forest	13
47	Virginia Tech	6
7	North Carolina	0

1951 (5-4-1)

34	South Carolina	6
19	Pitt	14
0	Tennessee	26
27	NC State	21
55	Virginia Tech	6
7	Virginia	30
14	Georgia Tech	14
13	Wake Forest	19
13	William & Mary	14
19	North Carolina	7

1952 (8-2-0)

34	Wash. & Lee	0
14	SMU	7
7	Tennessee	0
33	South Carolina	7

1953 (7-2-1)

20	South Carolina	7
19	Wake Forest	0
21	Tennessee	7
20	Purdue	14

1954 (8-2-1)

52	Penn	0
7	Tennessee	6
13	Purdue	13
14	Army	28

1952 (cont.)

57	NC State	0
21	Virginia	7
7	Georgia Tech	28
6	Navy	16
14	Wake Forest	7
34	North Carolina	0

1953 (cont.)

13	Army	14
31	NC State	0
48	Virginia	6
0	Navy	0
10	Georgia Tech	13
35	North Carolina	20

1954 (cont.)

21	NC State	7
21	Georgia Tech	20
7	Navy	40
28	Wake Forest	21
26	South Carolina	7
47	North Carolina	12
34	Nebraska	7
	(Orange Bowl)	

1955 (7-2-1)

33	NC State	7
21	Tennessee	0
47	William & Mary	7
20	Ohio State	14
7	Pitt	26
0	Georgia Tech	27
7	Navy	7
41	South Carolina	7
14	Wake Forest	0
6	North Carolina	0

1956 (5-4-1)

0	South Carolina	7
40	Virginia	7
20	Tennessee	33
14	SMU	6
14	Pitt	27
42	NC State	0
0	Georgia Tech	7
7	Navy	7
26	Wake Forest	0
21	North Carolina	6

1957 (6-3-2)

26	South Carolina	14
40	Virginia	0
14	Maryland	0
7	Rice	6
34	Wake Forest	7
14	NC State	14
0	Georgia Tech	13
6	Navy	6
7	Clemson	6
13	North Carolina	21
21	Oklahoma	48
	(Orange Bowl)	

1958 (5-5-0)

0	South Carolina	8
12	Virginia	15
15	Illinois	13
12	Baylor	7
7	Notre Dame	9
20	NC State	13
8	Georgia Tech	10
18	LSU	50
29	Wake Forest	0
7	North Carolina	6

1959 (4-6-0)

7	South Carolina	12
13	Ohio State	14
24	Rice	7
0	Pitt	12
6	Army	21
17	NC State	15
10	Georgia Tech	7
0	Clemson	6
27	Wake Forest	15
0	North Carolina	50

1960 (8-3-0)

31	South Carolina	0
20	Maryland	7
6	Michigan	31
17	NC State	13
21	Clemson	6
6	Georgia Tech	0
19	Navy	10
34	Wake Forest	7
6	North Carolina	7
6	UCLA	27
7	Arkansas	6
	(Cotton Bowl)	

1961 (7-3-0)

7	South Carolina	6
42	Virginia	0
23	Wake Forest	3
0	Georgia Tech	21
7	Clemson	17
17	NC State	6
14	Michigan	28

1962 (8-2-0)

7	Southern Cal	14
21	South Carolina	8
28	Florida	21
21	California	7
16	Clemson	0
21	NC State	14
9	Georgia Tech	20

1963 (5-4-1)

22	South Carolina	14
30	Virginia	8
30	Maryland	12
22	California	22
35	Clemson	30
7	NC State	21
6	Georgia Tech	30

1961 (cont.)

30	Navy	9
6	North Carolina	3
37	Notre Dame	13

1964 (4-5-1)

9	South Carolina	9
30	Virginia	0
24	Maryland	17
35	NC State	3
6	Army	0
8	Georgia Tech	21
7	Wake Forest	20
14	Navy	27
15	North Carolina	21
9	Tulane	17

1967 (4-6-0)

31	Wake Forest	13
7	Michigan	10
17	South Carolina	21
10	Army	7
13	Virginia	6
7	Clemson	13
7	NC State	28
7	Georgia Tech	19
35	Navy	16
9	North Carolina	20

1970 (6-5-0)

19	Florida	21
13	Maryland	12
17	Virginia	7
10	Ohio State	34
21	West Virginia	13
22	NC State	6
21	Clemson	10
16	Georgia Tech	24
14	Wake Forest	28
42	South Carolina	38
34	North Carolina	59

1973 (2-8-1)

17	Tennessee	21
23	Washington	21
3	Virginia	7

1962 (cont.)

10	Maryland	7
50	Wake Forest	0
16	North Carolina	14

1965 (6-4-0)

21	Virginia	7
20	South Carolina	15
41	Rice	21
21	Pitt	13
2	Clemson	3
14	Illinois	28
23	Georgia Tech	35
0	NC State	21
40	Wake Forest	7
34	North Carolina	7

1968 (4-6-0)

14	South Carolina	7
10	Michigan	31
30	Maryland	28
20	Virginia	50
22	Clemson	39
25	Army	57
46	Georgia Tech	30
15	NC State	17
18	Wake Forest	3
14	North Carolina	25

1971 (6-5-0)

12	Florida	6
28	South Carolina	12
28	Virginia	0
9	Stanford	3
0	Clemson	3
41	NC State	13
14	Navy	15
0	Georgia Tech	21
31	West Virginia	15
7	Wake Forest	23
0	North Carolina	38

1974 (6-5-0)

21	NC State	35
20	South Carolina	14
27	Virginia	7

1963 (cont.)

39	Wake Forest	7
25	Navy	38
14	North Carolina	16

1966 (5-5-0)

34	West Virginia	15
14	Pitt	7
27	Virginia	8
19	Maryland	21
6	Clemson	9
7	NC State	33
7	Georgia Tech	48
9	Navy	7
0	Notre Dame	64
41	North Carolina	25

1969 (3-6-1)

20	South Carolina	27
0	Virginia	10
12	Pitt	14
27	Wake Forest	20
7	Maryland	20
25	NC State	25
7	Georgia Tech	20
34	Clemson	27
12	Virginia Tech	48
17	North Carolina	13

1972 (5-6-0)

12	Alabama	35
6	Washington	14
6	Stanford	10
37	Virginia	13
0	NC State	17
7	Clemson	0
20	Maryland	14
17	Navy	16
20	Georgia Tech	14
7	Wake Forest	9
0	North Carolina	14

1975 (4-5-2)

7	Southern Cal	35
16	South Carolina	24
26	Virginia	11

1973 (cont.)

7	Purdue	27
17	Tulane	24
8	Clemson	24
10	Maryland	30
10	Georgia Tech	12
7	Wake Forest	7
3	NC State	21
27	North Carolina	10

1976 (5-5-1)

21	Tennessee	18
6	South Carolina	24
21	Virginia	6
31	Pitt	44
20	Miami (FL)	7
18	Clemson	18
3	Maryland	30
31	Georgia Tech	7
17	Wake Forest	38
28	NC State	14
38	North Carolina	39

1979 (2-8-1)

28	E. Carolina	14
0	South Carolina	35
12	Virginia	30
17	Army	17
34	Richmond	7
10	Clemson	28
0	Maryland	27
14	Georgia Tech	24
14	Wake Forest	17
7	NC State	28
16	North Carolina	37

1982 (6-5-0)

25	Tennessee	24
30	South Carolina	17
51	Virginia	17
21	Navy	27
21	Virginia Tech	22
14	Clemson	49
22	Maryland	49
38	Georgia Tech	21
46	Wake Forest	26

1974 (cont.)

16	Purdue	14
33	Army	14
13	Clemson	17
13	Florida	30
9	Georgia Tech	0
23	Wake Forest	7
13	Maryland	56
13	North Carolina	14

1977 (5-6-0)

16	E. Carolina	17
9	Michigan	21
31	Virginia	7
28	Navy	16
25	South Carolina	21
11	Clemson	17
13	Maryland	31
25	Georgia Tech	24
38	Wake Forest	14
32	NC State	37
3	North Carolina	16

1980 (2-9-0)

10	E. Carolina	35
28	Auburn	35
17	Virginia	20
21	Indiana	31
7	South Carolina	20
34	Clemson	17
14	Maryland	17
17	Georgia Tech	12
24	Wake Forest	27
21	NC State	38
21	North Carolina	44

1983 (3-8-0)

30	Virginia	38
10	Indiana	15
24	South Carolina	31
17	Miami (FL)	56
14	Virginia Tech	27
31	Clemson	38
3	Maryland	38
32	Georgia Tech	26
31	Wake Forest	21

1975 (cont.)

0	Pitt	14
21	Army	10
25	Clemson	21
16	Florida	24
6	Georgia Tech	21
42	Wake Forest	14
21	NC State	21
17	North Carolina	17

1978 (4-7-0)

28	Georgia Tech	10
16	South Carolina	12
0	Michigan	52
20	Virginia	13
8	Navy	31
8	Clemson	28
0	Maryland	27
0	Tennessee	34
3	Wake Forest	0
10	NC State	24
15	North Carolina	16

1981 (6-5-0)

13	Ohio State	34
3	South Carolina	17
29	Virginia	24
24	E. Carolina	14
14	Virginia Tech	7
10	Clemson	38
21	Maryland	24
38	Georgia Tech	24
31	Wake Forest	10
17	NC State	7
10	North Carolina	31

1984 (2-9-0)

31	Indiana	24
0	South Carolina	21
9	Army	13
10	Virginia	38
0	Virginia Tech	27
21	Clemson	54
7	Maryland	43
3	Georgia Tech	31
16	Wake Forest	20

1982 (cont.)

16	NC State	21
23	North Carolina	17

1985 (4-7-0)

40	Northwestern	17
18	West Virginia	20
34	Ohio	13
14	Virginia	37
7	South Carolina	28
9	Clemson	21
10	Maryland	40
0	Georgia Tech	9
7	Wake Forest	27
31	NC State	19
23	North Carolina	21

1988 (7-3-1)

31	Northwestern	21
31	Tennessee	26
41	The Citadel	17
38	Virginia	34
17	Vanderbilt	15
17	Clemson	49
24	Maryland	34
31	Georgia Tech	21
16	Wake Forest	35
43	NC State	43
35	North Carolina	29

1983 (cont.)

27	NC State	26
27	North Carolina	34

1986 (4-7-0)

17	Northwestern	6
7	Georgia	31
22	Ohio	7
20	Virginia	13
18	Vanderbilt	24
3	Clemson	35
19	Maryland	27
6	Georgia Tech	34
38	Wake Forest	36
15	NC State	29
35	North Carolina	42

1989 (8-4-0)

21	South Carolina	27
41	Northwestern	31
6	Tennessee	28
28	Virginia	49
21	Clemson	17
35	Army	29
46	Maryland	25
30	Georgia Tech	19
52	Wake Forest	35
35	NC State	26
41	North Carolina	0
21	Texas Tech	49
	(All–American	
	Bowl)	

1984 (cont.)

16	NC State	13
15	North Carolina	17

1987 (5-6-0)

41	Colgate	6
31	Northwestern	16
35	Vanderbilt	31
17	Virginia	42
0	Rutgers	7
10	Clemson	17
22	Maryland	23
48	Georgia Tech	14
27	Wake Forest	30
45	NC State	47
25	North Carolina	10

1990 (4-7-0)

10	South Carolina	21
27	Northwestern	24
0	Virginia	59
7	Clemson	26
17	Army	16
49	W. Carolina	18
20	Maryland	23
31	Georgia Tech	48
57	Wake Forest	20
0	NC State	16
22	North Carolina	24

1991 (4-6-1)

24	South Carolina	24
42	Rutgers	22
42	Colgate	14
3	Virginia	34
17	Vanderbilt	13
17	Maryland	13
6	Georgia Tech	17
14	Wake Forest	31
31	NC State	32
14	North Carolina	47
21	Clemson	33

Georgia Tech

Location: Atlanta, GA
Colors: Old Gold and White
Stadium: Bobby Dodd/Grant Field (1914), 46,000 cap., artificial turf.

Enrollment: 11,900
Nickname: Yellow Jackets

Head Coaches

Ernest West 1892
Leonard Wood and Frank Spain
  1893–94
No team 1895
Volunteer coaches 1896–97, 1900,
  1903
Rufus Nally 1898–99
Cyrus Strickler 1901
John McKee 1902

John Heisman 1904–19
Bill Alexander 1920–44
Bobby Dodd 1945–66
Bud Carson 1967–71
Bill Fulcher 1972–73
Pepper Rodgers 1974–79
Bill Curry 1980–86
Bobby Ross 1987–91

All–American Players

Everett Strupper 1917 halfback
Walker Carpenter 1917 tackle
Ashel "Bum" Day 1918 center
Joe Guyon 1918 halfback
Bill Fincher 1918, 1920 end
Warner Mizell 1928 halfback
Pete Pund 1928 center
Frank Speer 1928 tackle
Bob Ison 1939 end
Harvey Hardy 1942 guard
John Steber 1943 guard
Phil Tinsley 1944 end
Paul Duke 1946 center
Bob Davis 1947 tackle
George Brodnax 1948 end
Bill Healy 1948 def. guard
Ray Beck 1951 guard
Lamar Wheat 1951 def. tackle
Pete Brown 1952 center
Hal Miller 1952 tackle
Buck Martin 1952 end

Bobby Moorhead 1952 def. back
Leon Hardeman 1952 halfback
George Morris 1952 linebacker
Larry Morris 1953 center
Don Stephenson 1956–57 center
Maxie Baughan 1959 center
Rufus Guthrie 1962 guard
Billy Lothridge 1963 quarterback
Billy Martin 1963 end
Gerry Bussell 1964 def. back
Jim Breland 1966 center
Lenny Snow 1966 tailback
Rock Perdoni 1970 def. tackle
Smylie Gebhart 1971 def. end
Randy Rhino 1972–74 def. back
Lucius Sanford 1977 linebacker
Don Bessillieu 1978 def. back
John Davis 1985 tackle
Pat Swilling 1985 def. end
Ken Swilling 1990 def. back

Scores

1892 (0-3-0)

0	Mercer	12
10	Vanderbilt	20
0	Auburn	26

1893 (2-1-1)

28	Georgia	6
0	Auburn	0
0	St. Alban's	6
10	Mercer	6

1894 (0-3-0)

0	Savannah A. A.	8
0	Auburn	94
0	Ft. McPherson	34

1896 (1-1-1)

6	Mercer	4
0	Auburn	45
4	Mercer	4

1897 (0-1-0)

0	Georgia	28

1898 (0-3-0)

6	Auburn	29
0	Clemson	23
0	Georgia	15

1899 (0-5-0)

0	Auburn	63
0	Sewanee	30
0	Nashville	15
5	Clemson	41
0	Georgia	20

1900 (0-4-0)

0	Georgia	12
0	Nashville	23
0	Sewanee	34
6	Davidson	38

1901 (4-0-1)

29	Gordon	0
17	Furman	0
33	Wofford	0
5	Furman	5
13	South Carolina	0

1902 (0-6-2)

6	Auburn	18
5	Clemson	44
0	Georgia	0
0	Furman	0
0	St. Alban's	17
6	Davidson	7
6	Tennessee	10
0	Alabama	26

1903 (2-5-0)

0	Clemson	73
0	Georgia	38
37	Howard	0
17	Florida State	0
5	Auburn	10
0	Tennessee	11
0	South Carolina	16

1904 (8-1-1)

11	Ft. McPherson	5
35	Florida State	0
51	Mooney	0
77	Florida	0
2	Tennessee	0
0	Auburn	12
11	Clemson	11
23	Georgia	6
59	Tenn. Medical	0
18	Cumberland	0

1905 (6-0-1)

54	Dahlonega	0
17	Clemson	10
12	Alabama	5
15	Cumberland	0
45	Tennessee	0
18	Sewanee	18
46	Georgia	0

1906 (5-3-1)

18	Grant	0
0	Sewanee	16
4	Davidson	0
11	Auburn	0
17	Georgia	0
6	Vanderbilt	37
0	Clemson	10
6	Maryville	6
11	Dahlonega	0

1907 (4-4-0)

51	Gordon	0
72	Dahlonega	0
6	Tennessee	4
6	Auburn	12
10	Georgia	6
0	Sewanee	18
0	Vanderbilt	54
5	Clemson	6

Opposite: **Bobby Dodd Stadium/Grant Field, Atlanta, GA**

1908 (6-3-0)

32	Gordon	0
30	Mooney	0
23	Miss. A&M	0
11	Alabama	6
5	Tennessee	6
0	Auburn	44
0	Sewanee	6
16	Mercer	6
30	Clemson	6

1909 (7-2-0)

18	Gordon	6
35	Mooney	0
59	South Carolina	0
0	Sewanee	15
29	Tennessee	0
0	Auburn	9
12	Georgia	6
35	Mercer	0
29	Clemson	3

1910 (5-3-0)

57	Gordon	0
18	Chattanooga	0
48	Mercer	0
36	Alabama	0
0	Auburn	16
0	Vanderbilt	23
6	Georgia	11
34	Clemson	0

1911 (6-2-1)

22	11th Cavalry	5
28	Howard	0
24	Tennessee	0
17	Mercer	0
0	Alabama	0
6	Auburn	11
23	Sewanee	0
0	Georgia	5
32	Clemson	0

1912 (5-3-1)

0	11th Cavalry	0
20	The Citadel	16
20	Alabama	3
14	Florida	7
16	Mercer	6
7	Auburn	27
0	Sewanee	7
0	Georgia	20
23	Clemson	0

1913 (7-2-0)

19	Ft. McPherson	0
47	The Citadel	0
71	Chattanooga	6
33	Mercer	0
13	Florida	3
33	Sewanee	0
0	Auburn	20
0	Georgia	14
34	Clemson	0

1914 (6-2-0)

20	South Carolina	0
105	Mercer	0
0	Alabama	13
28	VMI	7
20	Sewanee	0
0	Auburn	14
7	Georgia	0
26	Clemson	6

1915 (7-0-1)

52	Mercer	0
27	Davidson	7
67	Transylvania	0
36	LSU	7
23	North Carolina	3
21	Alabama	7
0	Georgia	0
7	Auburn	0

1916 (8-0-1)

61	Mercer	0
222	Cumberland	0
9	Davidson	0
10	North Carolina	6
7	Wash. & Lee	7
45	Tulane	0
13	Alabama	0
21	Georgia	0
33	Auburn	7

1917 (9-0-0)

33	Wake Forest	0
25	Furman	0
41	Penn	0
32	Davidson	10
63	Wash. & Lee	0
83	Vanderbilt	0
48	Tulane	0
98	Carlisle	0
68	Auburn	7

1918 (6-1-0)

28	Clemson	0
118	Furman	0
28	Camp Gordon	0
119	11th Cavalry	0
128	NC State	0
0	Pitt	32
41	Auburn	0

1919 (7-3-0)

48	5th Division	0
74	Furman	0
14	Wake Forest	0
28	Clemson	0
20	Vanderbilt	0
6	Pitt	16
33	Davidson	0
0	Wash. & Lee	3
27	Georgetown	0
7	Auburn	14

1920 (8-1-0)

44	Wake Forest	0
55	Oglethorpe	0
66	Davidson	0
44	Vanderbilt	0
3	Pitt	10
24	Centre	0
7	Clemson	0
35	Georgetown	6
34	Auburn	0

1921 (8-1-0)

42	Wake Forest	0
41	Oglethorpe	0
70	Davidson	0
69	Furman	0
48	Rutgers	14
7	Penn State	28
48	Clemson	7
21	Georgetown	7
14	Auburn	0

1922 (7-2-0)

31	Oglethorpe	6
19	Davidson	0
33	Alabama	7
0	Navy	13
3	Notre Dame	13
19	Georgetown	7
21	Clemson	7
14	Auburn	6
17	NC State	0

1923 (3-2-4)

28	Oglethorpe	13
10	VMI	7
7	Florida	7
20	Georgetown	10
7	Notre Dame	35
0	Alabama	0
0	Penn State	7
3	Kentucky	3
0	Auburn	0

1924 (5-3-1)

19	Oglethorpe	0
3	VMI	0
7	Florida	7
15	Penn State	13
0	Alabama	14
3	Notre Dame	34
28	LSU	7
0	Vanderbilt	3
7	Auburn	0

1925 (6-2-1)

13	Oglethorpe	7
33	VMI	0
16	Penn State	7
23	Florida	7
0	Alabama	7
0	Notre Dame	13
7	Vanderbilt	0
3	Georgia	0
7	Auburn	7

1926 (4-5-0)

6	Oglethorpe	7
13	VMI	0
9	Tulane	6
0	Alabama	21
19	Wash. & Lee	7
0	Notre Dame	12
7	Vanderbilt	13
13	Georgia	14
20	Auburn	7

1927 (8-1-1)

7	VMI	0
13	Tulane	6
13	Alabama	0
13	North Carolina	0
7	Notre Dame	26
0	Vanderbilt	0
23	LSU	0
19	Oglethorpe	7
18	Auburn	0
12	Georgia	0

1928 (10-0-0)

13	VMI	0
12	Tulane	0
13	Notre Dame	0
20	North Carolina	7
32	Oglethorpe	7
19	Vanderbilt	7
33	Alabama	13
51	Auburn	0
20	Georgia	6
8	California	7
	(Rose Bowl)	

1929 (3-6-0)

27	Miss. A&M	13
7	North Carolina	18
19	Florida	6
14	Tulane	20
6	Notre Dame	26
7	Vanderbilt	23
0	Alabama	14
19	Auburn	6
6	Georgia	12

1930 (2-6-1)

45	South Carolina	0
0	Carnegie Tech	31
14	Auburn	12
0	Tulane	28
6	North Carolina	6
0	Vanderbilt	6
7	Penn	34
7	Florida	55
0	Georgia	13

1931 (2-7-1)

25	South Carolina	13
0	Carnegie Tech	13
0	Auburn	13
0	Tulane	33
7	Vanderbilt	49
19	North Carolina	19
12	Penn	13
23	Florida	0
6	Georgia	35
6	California	9

1932 (4-5-1)

32	Clemson	14
6	Kentucky	12
0	Auburn	6
43	North Carolina	14
0	Vanderbilt	12
14	Tulane	20
6	Alabama	0
6	Florida	0
0	Georgia	0
7	California	27

1933 (5-5-0)

39	Clemson	2
6	Kentucky	7
16	Auburn	6
0	Tulane	7
10	North Carolina	6
6	Vanderbilt	9
19	Florida	7
9	Alabama	12
6	Georgia	7
6	Duke	0

1934 (1-9-0)

12	Clemson	7
12	Vanderbilt	27
0	Duke	20
2	Michigan	9
12	Tulane	20
0	North Carolina	26
6	Auburn	18
0	Alabama	40
12	Florida	13
0	Georgia	7

1935 (5-5-0)

33	Presbyterian	0
32	Sewanee	0
6	Kentucky	25
6	Duke	0
13	Vanderbilt	14
0	North Carolina	19
7	Auburn	33
7	Alabama	38
39	Florida	6
19	Georgia	7

1936 (5-5-1)

55	Presbyterian	0
58	Sewanee	0
34	Kentucky	0
6	Duke	19
0	Vanderbilt	0
13	Clemson	14
12	Auburn	13
16	Alabama	20
38	Florida	14
6	Georgia	16
13	California	7

1937 (6-3-1)

59	Presbyterian	0
28	Mercer	0
32	Kentucky	0
19	Duke	20
0	Auburn	21
14	Vanderbilt	0
7	Clemson	0
0	Alabama	7
12	Florida	0
6	Georgia	6

1938 (3-4-3)

19	Mercer	0
6	Notre Dame	14
0	Duke	6
7	Auburn	6
7	Vanderbilt	13
19	Kentucky	18
14	Alabama	14
0	Florida	0
0	Georgia	0
0	California	13

1939 (8-2-0)

14	Notre Dame	17
35	Howard	0
14	Vanderbilt	6
6	Alabama	0
6	Duke	7
13	Kentucky	6
7	Auburn	6
21	Florida	7
13	Georgia	0
21	Missouri	7
	(Orange Bowl)	

1940 (3-7-0)

27	Howard	0
20	Notre Dame	26
19	Vanderbilt	0
7	Auburn	16
7	Duke	41
7	Kentucky	26
13	Alabama	14
7	Florida	16
19	Georgia	21
13	California	0

1941 (3-6-0)

20	Chattanooga	0
0	Notre Dame	20
7	Vanderbilt	14
28	Auburn	14
0	Duke	14
20	Kentucky	13
0	Alabama	20

1942 (9-2-0)

15	Auburn	0
13	Notre Dame	6
30	Chattanooga	6
33	Davidson	0
21	Navy	0
26	Duke	7
47	Kentucky	7

1943 (8-3-0)

20	North Carolina	7
13	Notre Dame	55
35	Ga. Pre-Flight	7
27	Ft. Benning	0
14	Navy	28
7	Duke	14
42	LSU	7

1941 (cont.)

7	Florida	14
0	Georgia	21

1942 (cont.)

7	Alabama	0
20	Florida	7
0	Georgia	34
7	Texas	14
	(Cotton Bowl)	

1943 (cont.)

33	Tulane	0
41	Clemson	6
48	Georgia	0
20	Tulsa	18
	(Sugar Bowl)	

1944 (8-3-0)

51	Clemson	0
28	North Carolina	0
27	Auburn	0
17	Navy	15
13	Ga. Pre-Flight	7
13	Duke	19
34	Tulane	7
14	LSU	6
0	Notre Dame	21
44	Georgia	0
12	Tulsa	26
	(Orange Bowl)	

1945 (4-6-0)

20	North Carolina	14
7	Notre Dame	40
43	Howard	0
6	Navy	20
20	Auburn	7
6	Duke	14
41	Tulane	7
7	LSU	9
7	Clemson	21
0	Georgia	33

1946 (9-2-0)

9	Tennessee	13
32	VMI	6
24	Mississippi	7
26	LSU	7
27	Auburn	6
14	Duke	0
28	Navy	20
35	Tulane	7
41	Furman	7
7	Georgia	35
41	St. Mary's	19
	(Oil Bowl)	

1947 (10-1-0)

27	Tennessee	0
20	Tulane	0
20	VMI	0
27	Auburn	7
38	The Citadel	0
7	Duke	0
16	Navy	14
7	Alabama	14
51	Furman	0
7	Georgia	0
20	Kansas	14
	(Orange Bowl)	

1948 (7-3-0)

13	Vanderbilt	0
13	Tulane	7
27	Wash. & Lee	0
27	Auburn	0
42	Florida	7
19	Duke	7
6	Tennessee	13
12	Alabama	14
54	The Citadel	0
13	Georgia	21

1949 (7-3-0)

12	Vanderbilt	7
0	Tulane	18
36	Wash. & Lee	0
35	Auburn	21
43	Florida	14
14	Duke	27
30	Tennessee	13
7	Alabama	20
13	South Carolina	3
7	Georgia	6

1950 (5-6-0)

13	SMU	33
0	South Carolina	7
16	Florida	13
13	LSU	0
20	Auburn	0
14	Kentucky	28
21	Duke	30
13	VMI	14
19	Alabama	54
46	Davidson	14

1951 (11-0-1)

21	SMU	7
27	Florida	0
13	Kentucky	7
25	LSU	7
27	Auburn	7
8	Vanderbilt	7
14	Duke	14
34	VMI	7
27	Alabama	7
34	Davidson	7

1952 (12-0-0)

54	The Citadel	6
17	Florida	14
20	SMU	7
14	Tulane	0
33	Auburn	0
30	Vanderbilt	0
28	Duke	7
45	Army	7
7	Alabama	3
30	Florida State	0

1950 (cont.)

7	Georgia	0

1951 (cont.)

48	Georgia	6
17	Baylor	14
	(Orange Bowl)	

1952 (cont.)

23	Georgia	9
24	Mississippi	7
	(Sugar Bowl)	

1953 (9-2-1)

53	Davidson	0
0	Florida	0
6	SMU	4
27	Tulane	13
36	Auburn	6
14	Notre Dame	27
43	Vanderbilt	0
20	Clemson	7
6	Alabama	13
13	Duke	10
28	Georgia	12
42	West Virginia	19
	(Sugar Bowl)	

1954 (8-3-0)

28	Tulane	0
12	Florida	13
10	SMU	7
30	LSU	20
14	Auburn	7
6	Kentucky	13
20	Duke	21
28	Tennessee	7
20	Alabama	0
7	Georgia	3
14	Arkansas	6
	(Cotton Bowl)	

1955 (9-1-1)

14	Miami (FL)	6
14	Florida	7
20	SMU	7
7	LSU	0
12	Auburn	14
34	Florida State	0
27	Duke	0
7	Tennessee	7
26	Alabama	2
21	Georgia	3
7	Pitt	0
	(Sugar Bowl)	

1956 (10-1-0)

14	Kentucky	6
9	SMU	7
39	LSU	7
28	Auburn	7
40	Tulane	0
7	Duke	0
0	Tennessee	6
27	Alabama	0
28	Florida	0
35	Georgia	0
21	Pitt	14
	(Gator Bowl)	

1957 (4-4-2)

13	Kentucky	0
0	SMU	0
13	LSU	20
0	Auburn	3
20	Tulane	13
13	Duke	0
6	Tennessee	21
10	Alabama	7
0	Florida	0
0	Georgia	7

1958 (5-4-1)

0	Kentucky	13
17	Florida State	3
14	Tulane	0
21	Tennessee	7
7	Auburn	7
0	SMU	20
10	Duke	8
13	Clemson	0
8	Alabama	17
3	Georgia	16

1959 (6-5-0)

14	Kentucky	12
16	SMU	12
16	Clemson	6
14	Tennessee	7
6	Auburn	7
21	Tulane	13
7	Duke	10
14	Notre Dame	10
7	Alabama	9
14	Georgia	21
7	Arkansas	14
	(Gator Bowl)	

1960 (5-5-0)

23	Kentucky	13
16	Rice	13
17	Florida	18
6	LSU	2
7	Auburn	9
14	Tulane	6
0	Duke	6
14	Tennessee	7
15	Alabama	16
6	Georgia	7

1961 (7-4-0)

27	Southern Cal	7
24	Rice	0
0	LSU	10
21	Duke	0
7	Auburn	6
35	Tulane	0
20	Florida	0
6	Tennessee	10
0	Alabama	10
22	Georgia	7
15	Penn State	30
	(Gator Bowl)	

1962 (7-3-1)

26	Clemson	9
17	Florida	0
7	LSU	10
17	Tennessee	0
14	Auburn	17
42	Tulane	12
20	Duke	9
14	Florida State	14
7	Alabama	6
37	Georgia	6
10	Missouri	14
	(Bluebonnet Bowl)	

1963 (7-3-0)

9	Florida	0
27	Clemson	0
6	LSU	7
23	Tennessee	7
21	Auburn	29
17	Tulane	3
30	Duke	6
15	Florida State	7
11	Alabama	27
14	Georgia	3

1964 (7-3-0)

14	Vanderbilt	2
20	Miami (FL)	0
14	Clemson	7
17	Navy	0
7	Auburn	3
7	Tulane	6
21	Duke	8
14	Tennessee	22
7	Alabama	24
0	Georgia	7

1965 (7-3-1)

10	Vanderbilt	10
10	Texas A&M	14
38	Clemson	6
13	Tulane	10
23	Auburn	14
37	Navy	16
35	Duke	23
7	Tennessee	21
42	Virginia	19
7	Georgia	17
31	Texas Tech	21
	(Gator Bowl)	

1966 (9-2-0)

38	Texas A&M	3
42	Vanderbilt	0
13	Clemson	12
6	Tennessee	3
17	Auburn	3
35	Tulane	17
48	Duke	7
14	Virginia	13
21	Penn State	0
14	Georgia	23
12	Florida	27
	(Orange Bowl)	

1967 (4-6-0)

17	Vanderbilt	10
24	TCU	7
10	Clemson	0
13	Tennessee	24
10	Auburn	28
12	Tulane	23
19	Duke	7
7	Miami (FL)	49
3	Notre Dame	36
14	Georgia	21

1968 (4-6-0)

17	TCU	7
7	Miami (FL)	10
24	Clemson	21
7	Tennessee	24
21	Auburn	20
23	Tulane	19
30	Duke	46
15	Navy	35
6	Notre Dame	34
8	Georgia	47

1969 (4-6-0)

24	SMU	21
17	Baylor	10
10	Clemson	21
8	Tennessee	26
14	Auburn	17
18	Southern Cal	29
20	Duke	7
7	Tulane	14
20	Notre Dame	38
6	Georgia	0

1970 (9-3-0)

23	South Carolina	20
23	Florida State	13
31	Miami (FL)	21
28	Clemson	7
6	Tennessee	17
7	Auburn	31
20	Tulane	6
24	Duke	16
30	Navy	8
7	Notre Dame	10
17	Georgia	7
17	Texas Tech	9
	(Sun Bowl)	

1971 (6-6-0)

7	South Carolina	24
10	Michigan State	0

1972 (7-4-1)

3	Tennessee	34
34	South Carolina	6

1973 (5-6-0)

28	South Carolina	41
6	Southern Cal	23

1971 (cont.)

13	Army	16
24	Clemson	14
6	Tennessee	10
14	Auburn	31
24	Tulane	16
21	Duke	0
34	Navy	21
12	Florida State	6
24	Georgia	28
18	Mississippi	41
	(Peach Bowl)	

1972 (cont.)

21	Michigan State	16
36	Rice	36
31	Clemson	9
14	Auburn	24
21	Tulane	7
14	Duke	20
42	Boston College	10
30	Navy	7
7	Georgia	27
31	Iowa State	30
	(Liberty Bowl)	

1973 (cont.)

29	Clemson	21
14	Army	10
14	Tennessee	20
10	Auburn	24
14	Tulane	23
12	Duke	10
36	VMI	7
26	Navy	22
3	Georgia	10

1974 (6-5-0)

7	Notre Dame	31
35	South Carolina	20
17	Pitt	27
17	Clemson	21
28	Virginia	24
29	North Carolina	28
22	Auburn	31
27	Tulane	7
0	Duke	9
22	Navy	0
34	Georgia	14

1975 (7-4-0)

17	South Carolina	23
38	Miami (FL)	23
33	Clemson	28
30	Florida State	0
38	VMI	10
27	Auburn	31
23	Tulane	0
21	Duke	6
3	Notre Dame	24
14	Navy	13
26	Georgia	42

1976 (4-6-1)

17	South Carolina	27
14	Pitt	42
24	Clemson	24
35	Virginia	14
7	Tennessee	42
28	Auburn	10
28	Tulane	16
7	Duke	31
23	Notre Dame	14
28	Navy	34
10	Georgia	13

1977 (6-5-0)

0	South Carolina	17
10	Miami (FL)	6
14	Clemson	31
30	Air Force	3
24	Tennessee	8
38	Auburn	21
38	Tulane	14
24	Duke	25
14	Notre Dame	69
16	Navy	20
16	Georgia	7

1978 (7-5-0)

10	Duke	28
22	California	34
27	Tulane	17
28	The Citadel	0
6	South Carolina	3
24	Miami (FL)	19
24	Auburn	10
17	Florida	13
42	Air Force	21
21	Notre Dame	38
28	Georgia	29
21	Purdue	41
	(Peach Bowl)	

1979 (4-6-1)

6	Alabama	30
7	Florida	7
33	William & Mary	7
13	Notre Dame	21
0	Tennessee	31
14	Auburn	38
7	Tulane	12
24	Duke	14
21	Air Force	0
24	Navy	14
3	Georgia	16

1980 (1-9-1)

3	Alabama	26
12	Florida	45
17	Memphis State	8
0	North Carolina	33

1981 (1-10-0)

24	Alabama	21
6	Florida	27
15	Memphis State	28
7	North Carolina	28

1982 (6-5-0)

7	Alabama	45
36	The Citadel	7
24	Memphis State	20
0	North Carolina	41

1980 (cont.)

10	Tennessee	23
14	Auburn	17
14	Tulane	31
12	Duke	17
3	Notre Dame	3
8	Navy	19
20	Georgia	38

1983 (3-8-0)

7	Alabama	20
14	Furman	17
14	Clemson	41
21	North Carolina	38
20	NC State	10
13	Auburn	31
3	Tennessee	37
26	Duke	32
31	Virginia	27
49	Wake Forest	33
24	Georgia	27

1986 (5-5-1)

17	Furman	17
28	Virginia	14
3	Clemson	27
20	North Carolina	21
59	NC State	21
10	Auburn	31
14	Tennessee	13
34	Duke	6
52	VMI	6
21	Wake Forest	24
24	Georgia	31

1989 (7-4-0)

28	NC State	38
10	Virginia	17
10	South Carolina	21
28	Maryland	24
30	Clemson	14
17	North Carolina	14
19	Duke	30

1981 (cont.)

7	Tennessee	10
7	Auburn	31
10	Tulane	27
24	Duke	38
3	Notre Dame	35
14	Navy	20
7	Georgia	44

1984 (6-4-1)

16	Alabama	6
48	The Citadel	3
28	Clemson	21
22	NC State	27
20	Virginia	20
34	Auburn	48
21	Tennessee	24
31	Duke	3
17	North Carolina	24
24	Wake Forest	7
35	Georgia	18

1987 (2-9-0)

51	The Citadel	12
23	North Carolina	30
12	Clemson	33
0	NC State	17
38	Indiana State	0
10	Auburn	20
15	Tennessee	29
14	Duke	48
14	Virginia	23
6	Wake Forest	33
16	Georgia	30

1990 (11-0-1)

21	NC State	13
44	UT–Chattanooga	9
27	South Carolina	6
31	Maryland	3
21	Clemson	19
13	North Carolina	13
48	Duke	31

1982 (cont.)

19	Tulane	13
0	Auburn	24
31	Tennessee	21
21	Duke	38
38	Virginia	32
45	Wake Forest	7
18	Georgia	38

1985 (9-2-1)

28	NC State	18
13	Virginia	24
14	Clemson	3
31	North Carolina	0
24	W. Carolina	17
14	Auburn	17
6	Tennessee	6
9	Duke	0
35	UT–Chattanooga	7
41	Wake Forest	10
20	Georgia	16
17	Michigan State (All–American Bowl)	14

1988 (3-8-0)

24	UT–Chattanooga	10
16	Virginia	17
13	Clemson	30
6	NC State	14
8	Maryland	13
34	South Carolina	0
17	North Carolina	20
21	Duke	31
34	VMI	7
24	Wake Forest	28
3	Georgia	24

1991 (8-5-0)

22	Penn State	34
30	Boston College	14
24	Virginia	21
7	Clemson	9
21	NC State	28
34	Maryland	10
14	South Carolina	23

Maryland

Location: College Park, MD   Enrollment: 29,800
Colors: Red, White, Black, Gold   Nickname: Terps
Stadium: Byrd (1950), 45,000 capacity, natural turf.

Head Coaches

Will Skinner 1892*
Sam Harding 1893*
George Harris 1894*
No team 1895
Grenville Lewis 1896*
John Lillibridge 1897*
Frank Kenley 1898*
Sam Cooke 1899*
Frank Peters 1900*
Emmons Dunbar 1901*
John Markey 1902–04
Fred Nielsen 1905–06
Calvin Church and Charles Melick 1907
Bill Lang 1908
Barney Cooper and Pat Larkin 1909
Roy Alston 1910

Charles Donnelly 1911
Curley Byrd 1912–34
Jack Faber 1935–36
Frank Dobson 1937–39
Jack Faber, Al Heagy, and Al Woods 1940
Al Woods 1941
Clark Shaughnessy 1942, 1946
Clarence "Doc" Spears 1943–44
Paul "Bear" Bryant 1945
Jim Tatum 1947–55
Tommy Mont 1956–58
Tom Nugent 1959–65
Lou Saban 1966
Bob Ward 1967–68
Roy Lester 1969–71
Jerry Claiborne 1972–81
Bobby Ross 1982–86
Joe Krivak 1987–91

team captain

All–American Players

Bill Supplee 1923 end
Snitz Snyder 1928 fullback

Ray Krouse 1948 tackle
Bob Ward 1950–51 guard

Ed Modzelewski 1951 fullback
Dick Modzelewski 1951–52 def. tackle
Tom Cosgrove 1952 center
Jack Scarbath 1952 quarterback
Stan Jones 1953 tackle
Bernie Faloney 1953 quarterback
Chet Hanulak 1953 halfback
Bill Walker 1954–55 end
Bob Pellegrini 1955 center
Mike Sandusky 1955 tackle
Ed Vereb 1955 halfback
Gary Collins 1961 end

Paul Vellano 1973 def. guard
Randy White 1973–74 def. tackle
Lou Carter 1974 halfback
Steve Mike-Mayer 1974 place-kicker
Joe Campbell 1976 def. tackle
Dale Castro 1979 kicker
Boomer Esiason 1983 quarterback
Ron Solt 1983 guard
Eric Wilson 1984 linebacker
Kevin Glover 1984 center
John Maarleveld 1985 tackle

Scores

1892 (0-3-0)

0	St. John's	50
0	Johns Hopkins	62
0	Episcopal Hi	16

1893 (6-0-0)

36	Eastern Hi	0
10	Central Hi	0
18	Balt. City	0
6	St. John's	0
18	W. Maryland	10
16	Orient Ath Club	6

1894 (3-3-0)

52	W. Maryland	0
12	Washington Col	0
6	St. John's	22
6	Georgetown	4
0	Columbia Ath Club	26
0	Mt. St. Mary's	24

1896 (6-2-2)

0	Eastern Hi	6
0	Gallaudet	0
32	Business Hi	0
10	Central Hi	6
18	Alexandria Hi	0
20	Bethel Mil Acad	10
0	Episcopal Hi	6
16	W. Maryland	6
14	Central Hi	0
0	MD–Balt.	0

1897 (2-4-0)

24	Central Hi	6
4	Eastern Hi	0
6	Johns Hopkins	30
4	St. John's	6
6	Gallaudet	16
0	Balt. Medical	10

1898 (2-5-0)

5	Columbian*	17
0	W. Maryland	32
36	Eastern Hi	0
0	Gallaudet	34
0	Johns Hopkins	16
0	Episcopal Hi	37
27	Rock Hill	0

*now George Wash.

1899 (1-4-0)

0	W. Maryland	21
26	Eastern Hi	0
0	Johns Hopkins	40
0	Delaware	34
0	St. John's	62

1900 (3-4-1)

0	Western Hi	0
0	Gibraltar Ath Club	17
0	Georgetown Prep	5
6	Episcopal Hi	34

1901 (1-7-0)

6	Delaware	24
10	Gallaudet Reserves	11
0	Johns Hopkins	6
6	Rock Hill	11
0	Central Hi	11

1900 (cont.)

5	Gonzaga Hi	11
15	Georgetown Prep	0
21	Gonzaga Hi	0
21	Charlotte Hall Mil Acad	0

1901 (cont.)

27	Wash DC Marines	0
0	Walbrook Ath Club	36
0	W. Maryland	30

1902 (3-5-2)

0	Georgetown	27
5	Mt. St. Joseph's	0
11	Columbian	10
6	Olympia Ath Cl	0
0	Washington Col	0
0	Mt. St. Mary's	5
6	W. Maryland	26
0	MD – Balt.	5
0	Johns Hopkins	17
0	Delaware	0

1903 (7-4-0)

0	Georgetown	28
5	Clifton Ath Cl	0
21	Gunton Temple Bapt Church	0
0	St. John's	18
28	Washington Col	0
27	Technical Hi	0
0	Mt. St. Mary's	2
6	W. Maryland	0
11	MD – Balt.	0
0	Delaware	16
6	Columbian	0

1904 (2-4-2)

0	Georgetown	22
0	Randolph Macon	0
0	Ft. Monroe	0
11	Mt. St. Mary's	6
0	W. Maryland	5
23	Gallaudet	5
0	MD – Balt.	6
0	Delaware	18

1905 (6-4-0)

20	Balt Poly Inst	0
16	Gallaudet	0
0	W. Maryland	10
0	Navy	17
17	William & Mary	0
28	Mt. St. Joseph's	0
27	St. John's	5
0	Washington Col	17
23	MD – Balt.	5
0	Delaware	12

1906 (5-3-0)

5	Technical Hi	0
22	Balt. City	0
0	Navy	12
0	Georgetown	28
0	Mt. Wash.	29
20	St. John's	4
16	Rock Hill	0
35	Washington Col	0

1907 (3-6-0)

13	Technical Hi	0
0	Georgetown	10
5	Richmond	11
0	Navy	12
6	Mt. St. Mary's	12
10	George Wash.	0
10	Washington Col	5
0	St. John's	16
0	Gallaudet	5

1908 (3-8-0)

5	Central Hi	0
5	Technical Hi	6
0	Richmond	22
0	Johns Hopkins	10
0	Navy	57
5	Gallaudet	0
0	Fredericksburg	10
12	Balt Poly Inst	6
0	St. John's	31

1909 (2-5-0)

0	Richmond	12
0	Johns Hopkins	9
0	Technical Hi	11
5	Rock Hill	0
0	George Wash.	26
0	NC State	31
14	Gallaudet	12

1910 (4-3-1)

12	Central Hi	0
20	Richmond	0
11	Johns Hopkins	11
21	Catholic	0
11	George Wash.	0
0	VMI	8
0	St. John's	6
3	W. Maryland	17

Opposite: **Byrd Stadium & Cole Field House, College Park, MD**

1908 (cont.)

0	Washington Col	11
0	George Wash.	57

1911 (4-4-2)

6	Technical Hi	0
0	Richmond	0
5	Fredericksburg	0
0	Central Hi	14
3	Johns Hopkins	6
6	Catholic	6
0	St. John's	27
5	Washington Col	17
6	W. Maryland	0
6	Gallaudet	2

1912 (6-1-1)

31	Technical Hi	6
46	Richmond	0
58	MD – Balt.	0
13	Johns Hopkins	0
0	St. John's	27
13	Gallaudet	6
17	W. Maryland	7
13	Penn Military*	13

*now Widener

1913 (6-3-0)

27	Balt. City	10
45	Richmond	0
26	Johns Hopkins	0
46	W. Maryland	0
0	Navy	76
13	St. John's	0
26	Washington Col	0
0	Gallaudet	13
7	Penn Military	27

1914 (5-3-0)

0	Balt Poly Inst	6
6	Catholic	0
13	W. Maryland	20
14	Johns Hopkins	0
10	St. John's	0
3	Washington Col	0
0	Gallaudet	23
26	Penn Military	0

1915 (6-3-0)

31	Balt Poly Inst	0
0	Haverford	7
0	Catholic	16
10	Gallaudet	3
14	Penn Military	13
27	St. John's	14
28	Washington Col	13
51	W. Maryland	0
0	Johns Hopkins	3

1916 (6-2-0)

6	Dickinson	0
7	Navy	14
15	VMI	9
6	Haverford	7
31	St. John's	6
10	NYU	7
13	Catholic	9
54	Johns Hopkins	0

1917 (4-3-1)

20	Delaware	0
0	Navy	62
14	VMI	14
29	Wake Forest	13
6	NC State	10
13	St. John's	3
0	Penn State	57
7	Johns Hopkins	0

1918 (4-1-1)

6	American	13
7	VMI	6
19	W. Maryland	0
6	NYU	2
19	St. John's	14
0	Johns Hopkins	0

1919 (5-4-0)

6	Swarthmore	10
13	Virginia	0
0	West Virginia	27
0	Virginia Tech	6
0	Yale	31
27	St. John's	0
13	Catholic	0
20	W. Maryland	0
14	Johns Hopkins	0

1920 (7-2-0)

54	Randolph Macon	0
0	Rutgers	6
0	Princeton	35
14	Catholic	0
27	Washington Col	0
7	Virginia Tech	0
13	North Carolina	0

1921 (3-5-1)

3	Rutgers	0
0	Syracuse	42
3	St. John's	7
10	Virginia Tech	7
7	North Carolina	16
0	Yale	28
16	Catholic	0

1922 (4-5-1)

7	Third Army	0
0	Richmond	0
0	Penn	12
0	Princeton	26
3	North Carolina	27
0	Virginia Tech	21
3	Yale	45

1920 (cont.)

10	Syracuse	7
24	Johns Hopkins	7

1923 (7-2-1)

53	Randolph Macon	0
3	Penn	0
23	Richmond	0
7	Virginia Tech	16
14	North Carolina	0
26	St. John's	0
14	Yale	16
26	NC State	12
40	Catholic	6
6	Johns Hopkins	6

1926 (5-4-1)

63	Washington Col	0
0	South Carolina	12
0	Chicago	21
8	Virginia Tech	24
14	North Carolina	6
38	Gallaudet	7
15	Yale	0
6	Virginia	6
0	Wash. & Lee	3
17	Johns Hopkins	14

1929 (4-4-2)

34	Washington Col	7
0	North Carolina	43
6	South Carolina	26
13	Gallaudet	6
6	VMI	7
13	Virginia	13
13	Yale	13
24	Virginia Tech	0
39	Johns Hopkins	6
0	W. Maryland	12

1932 (5-6-0)

63	Washington Col	0
6	Virginia	7

1921 (cont.)

0	Carnegie Tech	21
6	NC State	6

1924 (3-3-3)

23	Washington Col	0
7	Wash. & Lee	19
38	Richmond	0
0	Virginia Tech	12
6	North Carolina	0
0	Catholic	0
0	Yale	47
0	NC State	0
0	Johns Hopkins	0

1927 (4-7-0)

80	Washington Col	0
26	South Carolina	0
6	North Carolina	7
13	Virginia Tech	7
10	VMI	6
6	Wash. & Lee	13
6	Yale	30
0	Virginia	21
20	Vanderbilt	39
13	Johns Hopkins	14
6	Florida	7

1930 (7-5-0)

60	Washington Col	6
13	Yale	40
21	North Carolina	28
21	St. John's	13
20	VMI	0
14	Virginia	6
41	Wash. & Lee	7
13	Virginia Tech	7
0	Navy	6
21	Johns Hopkins	0
7	Vanderbilt	22
0	W. Maryland	7

1933 (3-7-0)

20	St. John's	0
0	Virginia Tech	14

1922 (cont.)

54	Catholic	0
7	NC State	6

1925 (2-5-1)

13	Washington Col	0
16	Rutgers	0
0	Virginia Tech	3
0	Virginia	6
0	North Carolina	16
14	Yale	43
3	Wash. & Lee	7
7	Johns Hopkins	7

1928 (6-3-1)

31	Washington Col	0
19	North Carolina	26
7	South Carolina	21
13	W. Maryland	6
0	VMI	0
6	Virginia Tech	9
6	Yale	0
18	Virginia	2
6	Wash. & Lee	0
26	Johns Hopkins	6

1931 (8-1-1)

13	Washington Col	0
7	Virginia	6
6	Navy	0
6	Kentucky	6
41	VMI	20
20	Virginia Tech	0
12	Vanderbilt	39
13	Wash. & Lee	7
35	Johns Hopkins	14
41	W. Maryland	6

1934 (7-3-0)

13	St. John's	0
0	Wash. & Lee	7

1932 (cont.)

0	Virginia Tech	23
0	Duke	34
24	St. John's	7
12	VMI	7
0	Vanderbilt	13
7	Navy	28
6	Wash. & Lee	0
23	Johns Hopkins	0
7	W. Maryland	39

1933 (cont.)

0	Tulane	20
13	VMI	19
7	W. Maryland	13
0	Virginia	6
7	Duke	38
27	Johns Hopkins	7
33	Wash. & Lee	13
0	Florida	19

1934 (cont.)

13	Navy	16
14	Virginia Tech	9
21	Florida	0
20	Virginia	0
23	VMI	0
14	Indiana	17
6	Georgetown	0
19	Johns Hopkins	0

1935 (7-2-2)

39	St. John's	6
7	Virginia Tech	0
0	North Carolina	33
6	VMI	0
20	Florida	6
14	Virginia	7
7	Indiana	13
0	Wash. & Lee	0
12	Georgetown	6
0	Syracuse	0
22	W. Maryland	7

1936 (6-5-0)

20	St. John's	0
6	Virginia Tech	0
0	North Carolina	14
21	Virginia	0
12	Richmond	0
20	Syracuse	0
6	Florida	7
7	VMI	13
6	Georgetown	7
19	Wash. & Lee	6
0	W. Maryland	12

1937 (8-2-0)

28	St. John's	0
21	Penn	28
6	W. Maryland	6
3	Virginia	0
13	Syracuse	0
13	Florida	7
9	VMI	7
14	Penn State	21
12	Georgetown	2
8	Wash. & Lee	0

1938 (2-7-0)

6	Richmond	19
0	Penn State	33
0	Syracuse	53
14	W. Maryland	8
19	Virginia	27
14	VMI	47
7	Florida	21
7	Georgetown	14
19	Wash. & Lee	13

1939 (2-7-0)

26	Hampden-Sydney	0
12	W. Maryland	0
7	Virginia	12
12	Rutgers	25
0	Florida	14
0	Georgetown	20
0	Penn State	12
0	VMI	13
7	Syracuse	10

1940 (2-6-1)

6	Hampden-Sydney	7
0	Penn	51
6	Virginia	19
0	Florida	19
6	W. Maryland	0
0	Georgetown	41
0	VMI	20
14	Rutgers	7
7	Wash. & Lee	7

1941 (3-5-1)

18	Hampden-Sydney	0
6	W. Maryland	6
0	Duke	50
13	Florida	12
6	Penn	55
0	Georgetown	26
0	Rutgers	20
0	VMI	27
6	Wash. & Lee	0

1942 (7-2-0)

34	Connecticut	0
14	Lakehurst NAS	0
27	Rutgers	13
0	VMI	29
51	W. Maryland	0
13	Florida	0
0	Duke	42
27	Virginia	12
32	Wash. & Lee	28

1943 (4-5-0)

7	Curtis Bay CG	13
13	Wake Forest	7
19	Richmond AAB	7
2	West Virginia	6
0	Penn State	45
43	Greenville AAB	18
0	Virginia	39
0	Bainbridge NTS	46
39	VMI	14

1944 (1-7-1)

0	Hampden-Sydney	12
0	Wake Forest	39
6	West Virginia	6
0	Michigan State	8
6	Florida	14
7	Virginia	18
0	Michigan State	33
19	Penn State	34
8	VMI	6

1945 (6-2-1)

60	Guilford	6
21	Richmond	0
22	Merch Mar Acad	6
13	Virginia Tech	21
13	West Virginia	13
14	William & Mary	33
38	VMI	0
19	Virginia	13
19	South Carolina	13

1946 (3-6-0)

54	Bainbridge NTS	0
7	Richmond	37
0	North Carolina	33
6	Virginia Tech	0
7	William & Mary	41
17	South Carolina	21
24	Wash. & Lee	7
14	Michigan State	26
7	NC State	28

1947 (7-2-2)

19	South Carolina	13
43	Delaware	19
18	Richmond	6
7	Duke	19
21	Virginia Tech	19
27	West Virginia	0
32	Duquesne	0
0	North Carolina	19
20	Vanderbilt	6
0	NC State	0
20	Georgia (Gator Bowl)	20

1948 (6-4-0)

19	Richmond	0
21	Delaware	0
28	Virginia Tech	0
12	Duke	13
47	George Wash.	0
27	Miami (FL)	13
19	South Carolina	7
20	North Carolina	49
0	Vanderbilt	34
14	West Virginia	16

1949 (9-1-0)

34	Virginia Tech	7
33	Georgetown	7
7	Michigan State	14
14	NC State	6
44	South Carolina	7
40	George Wash.	14
14	Boston Univ.	13
47	West Virginia	7
13	Miami (FL)	0
20	Missouri (Gator Bowl)	7

1950 (7-2-1)

7	Georgia	27
35	Navy	21
34	Michigan State	7
25	Georgetown	14
13	NC State	16
26	Duke	14
23	George Wash.	7
7	North Carolina	7
41	West Virginia	0
63	Virginia Tech	7

1951 (10-0-0)

54	Wash. & Lee	14
33	George Wash.	6
43	Georgia	7
14	North Carolina	7
27	LSU	0
35	Missouri	0
40	Navy	21
53	NC State	0
54	West Virginia	7
28	Tennessee (Sugar Bowl)	13

1952 (7-2-0)

13	Missouri	10
13	Auburn	7
28	Clemson	0
37	Georgia	0
38	Navy	7
34	LSU	6
34	Boston Univ.	7
14	Mississippi	21
7	Alabama	27

1953 (10-1-0)

20	Missouri	6
52	Wash. & Lee	0
20	Clemson	0
40	Georgia	13
26	North Carolina	0
30	Miami (FL)	0

1954 (7-2-1)

24	Kentucky	0
7	UCLA	12
13	Wake Forest	13
33	North Carolina	0
7	Miami (FL)	9
20	South Carolina	0

1955 (10-1-0)

13	Missouri	12
7	UCLA	0
20	Baylor	6
28	Wake Forest	7
25	North Carolina	7
34	Syracuse	13

1953 (cont.)

24	South Carolina	6
27	George Wash.	6
38	Mississippi	0
21	Alabama	0
0	Oklahoma	7
	(Orange Bowl)	

1956 (2-7-1)

12	Syracuse	26
6	Wake Forest	0
0	Baylor	14
6	Miami (FL)	13
6	North Carolina	34
7	Tennessee	34
0	Kentucky	14
6	Clemson	6
0	South Carolina	13
25	NC State	14

1959 (5-5-0)

27	West Virginia	7
0	Texas	26
0	Syracuse	29
7	Wake Forest	10
14	North Carolina	7
6	South Carolina	22
14	Navy	22
28	Clemson	25
55	Virginia	12
33	NC State	28

1962 (6-4-0)

7	SMU	0
13	Wake Forest	2
14	NC State	6
31	North Carolina	13
24	Miami (FL)	28
13	South Carolina	11
7	Penn State	23
7	Duke	10
14	Clemson	17
40	Virginia	18

1965 (4-6-0)

24	Ohio	7
7	Syracuse	24

1954 (cont.)

42	NC State	14
16	Clemson	0
48	George Wash.	6
74	Missouri	13

1957 (5-5-0)

13	Texas A&M	21
13	NC State	48
0	Duke	14
27	Wake Forest	0
21	North Carolina	7
0	Tennessee	16
10	South Carolina	6
7	Clemson	26
16	Miami (FL)	6
12	Virginia	0

1960 (6-4-0)

31	West Virginia	8
0	Texas	34
7	Duke	20
10	NC State	13
19	Clemson	17
14	Wake Forest	13
15	South Carolina	0
9	Penn State	28
22	North Carolina	19
44	Virginia	12

1963 (3-7-0)

14	NC State	36
13	South Carolina	21
12	Duke	30
7	North Carolina	14
21	Air Force	14
32	Wake Forest	0
15	Penn State	17
7	Navy	42
6	Clemson	21
21	Virginia	6

1966 (4-6-0)

7	Penn State	15
34	Wake Forest	7

1955 (cont.)

27	South Carolina	0
13	LSU	0
25	Clemson	12
19	George Wash.	0
6	Oklahoma	20
	(Orange Bowl)	

1958 (4-6-0)

0	Wake Forest	34
21	NC State	6
0	Clemson	8
10	Texas A&M	14
0	North Carolina	27
7	Auburn	20
10	South Carolina	6
14	Navy	40
26	Miami (FL)	14
44	Virginia	6

1961 (7-3-0)

14	SMU	6
24	Clemson	21
22	Syracuse	21
8	North Carolina	14
21	Air Force	0
10	South Carolina	20
21	Penn State	17
10	NC State	7
10	Wake Forest	7
16	Virginia	28

1964 (5-5-0)

3	Oklahoma	13
24	South Carolina	6
13	NC State	14
17	Duke	24
10	North Carolina	9
17	Wake Forest	21
9	Penn State	17
27	Navy	22
34	Clemson	0
10	Virginia	0

1967 (0-9-0)

0	Oklahoma	35
3	Syracuse	7

1965 (cont.)

10	Wake Forest	7
10	North Carolina	12
7	NC State	29
27	South Carolina	14
7	Navy	19
6	Clemson	0
27	Virginia	33
7	Penn State	19

1968 (2-8-0)

14	Florida State	24
14	Syracuse	32
28	Duke	30
33	North Carolina	24
21	South Carolina	19
11	NC State	31
14	Wake Forest	38
0	Clemson	16
13	Penn State	57
23	Virginia	28

1971 (2-9-0)

13	Villanova	28
35	NC State	7
14	North Carolina	35
14	Wake Forest	18
13	Syracuse	21
6	South Carolina	35
23	Florida	27
38	VMI	0
27	Penn State	63
14	Clemson	20
27	Virginia	29

1974 (8-4-0)

16	Alabama	21
10	Florida	17
24	North Carolina	12
31	Syracuse	0
41	Clemson	0
47	Wake Forest	0
20	NC State	10

1966 (cont.)

7	Syracuse	28
21	Duke	19
28	West Virginia	9
14	South Carolina	2
21	NC State	24
10	Clemson	14
17	Virginia	41
21	Florida State	45

1969 (3-7-0)

7	West Virginia	31
7	NC State	24
19	Wake Forest	14
9	Syracuse	20
20	Duke	7
0	South Carolina	17
0	Clemson	40
21	Miami (Ohio)	34
0	Penn State	48
17	Virginia	14

1972 (5-5-1)

24	NC State	24
26	North Carolina	31
28	VMI	16
12	Syracuse	16
23	Wake Forest	0
37	Villanova	7
14	Duke	20
24	Virginia	23
16	Penn State	46
31	Clemson	6
8	Miami (FL)	28

1975 (9-2-1)

41	Villanova	0
8	Tennessee	26
34	North Carolina	7
10	Kentucky	10
24	Syracuse	7
37	NC State	22
27	Wake Forest	0

1967 (cont.)

9	NC State	31
0	North Carolina	14
0	South Carolina	31
3	Penn State	38
7	Clemson	28
17	Wake Forest	35
7	Virginia	12

1970 (2-9-0)

3	Villanova	21
12	Duke	13
20	North Carolina	53
11	Miami (FL)	18
7	Syracuse	23
21	South Carolina	15
0	NC State	6
11	Clemson	24
0	Penn State	34
17	Virginia	14
10	West Virginia	20

1973 (8-4-0)

13	West Virginia	20
23	North Carolina	3
31	Villanova	3
38	Syracuse	0
22	NC State	24
37	Wake Forest	0
30	Duke	10
22	Penn State	42
33	Virginia	0
28	Clemson	13
42	Tulane	9
16	Georgia	17
	(Peach Bowl)	

1976 (11-1-0)

31	Richmond	7
24	West Virginia	3
42	Syracuse	28
20	Villanova	9
16	NC State	6
17	Wake Forest	15
30	Duke	3

1974 (cont.)

17	Penn State	24
41	Villanova	0
56	Duke	13
10	Virginia	0
3	Tennessee	7
	(Liberty Bowl)	

1977 (8-4-0)

21	Clemson	14
16	West Virginia	24
9	Penn State	27
20	NC State	24
24	Syracuse	10
35	Wake Forest	7
31	Duke	13
7	North Carolina	16
19	Villanova	13
27	Richmond	24
28	Virginia	0
17	Minnesota	7
	(Hall of Fame Bowl)	

1980 (8-4-0)

7	Villanova	3
31	Vanderbilt	6
14	West Virginia	11
3	North Carolina	17
9	Pitt	38
10	Penn State	24
11	Wake Forest	10
17	Duke	14
24	NC State	0
34	Clemson	7
31	Virginia	0
20	Florida	35
	(Tangerine Bowl)	

1983 (8-4-0)

21	Vanderbilt	14
21	West Virginia	31
13	Pitt	7
23	Virginia	3
34	Syracuse	13
36	Wake Forest	33

1975 (cont.)

13	Penn State	15
21	Cincinnati	19
22	Clemson	20
62	Virginia	24
13	Florida	0
	(Gator Bowl)	

1978 (9-3-0)

31	Tulane	7
24	Louisville	17
21	North Carolina	20
20	Kentucky	3
31	NC State	7
24	Syracuse	9
39	Wake Forest	0
27	Duke	0
3	Penn State	27
17	Virginia	7
24	Clemson	28
0	Texas	42
	(Sun Bowl)	

1981 (4-6-1)

17	Vanderbilt	23
13	West Virginia	17
34	NC State	9
17	Syracuse	17
10	Florida	15
45	Wake Forest	33
24	Duke	21
10	North Carolina	17
7	Tulane	14
7	Clemson	21
48	Virginia	7

1984 (9-3-0)

7	Syracuse	23
14	Vanderbilt	23
20	West Virginia	17
38	Wake Forest	17
24	Penn State	25
44	NC State	21

1976 (cont.)

24	Kentucky	14
21	Cincinnati	0
20	Clemson	0
28	Virginia	0
21	Houston	30
	(Cotton Bowl)	

1979 (7-4-0)

24	Villanova	20
19	Clemson	0
35	Miss. State	14
7	Kentucky	14
7	Penn State	27
0	NC State	7
17	Wake Forest	25
27	Duke	0
17	North Carolina	14
28	Louisville	7
17	Virginia	7

1982 (8-4-0)

31	Penn State	39
18	West Virginia	19
23	NC State	6
26	Syracuse	3
38	Indiana State	0
52	Wake Forest	31
49	Duke	22
31	North Carolina	24
18	Miami (FL)	17
22	Clemson	24
45	Virginia	14
20	Washington	21
	(Aloha Bowl)	

1985 (9-3-0)

18	Penn State	20
31	Boston College	13
28	West Virginia	0
0	Michigan	20
31	NC State	17
26	Wake Forest	3

1983 (cont.)

38	Duke	3
28	North Carolina	26
23	Auburn	25
27	Clemson	52
29	NC State	6
23	Tennessee	30
	(Citrus Bowl)	

1984 (cont.)

43	Duke	7
34	North Carolina	23
42	Miami (FL)	40
41	Clemson	23
45	Virginia	34
28	Tennessee	27
	(Sun Bowl)	

1985 (cont.)

40	Duke	10
28	North Carolina	10
22	Miami (FL)	29
34	Clemson	31
33	Virginia	21
35	Syracuse	18
	(Cherry Bowl)	

1986 (5-5-1)

10	Pitt	7
35	Vanderbilt	21
24	West Virginia	3
16	NC State	28
25	Boston College	30
21	Wake Forest	27
27	Duke	19
30	North Carolina	32
15	Penn State	17
17	Clemson	17
42	Virginia	10

1987 (4-7-0)

11	Syracuse	25
21	Virginia	19
25	West Virginia	20
14	NC State	42
16	Miami (FL)	46
14	Wake Forest	0
23	Duke	22
14	North Carolina	27
16	Penn State	21
16	Clemson	45
24	Vanderbilt	34

1988 (5-6-0)

27	Louisville	16
24	West Virginia	55
30	NC State	26
9	Syracuse	20
13	Georgia Tech	8
24	Wake Forest	27
34	Duke	24
41	North Carolina	38
10	Penn State	17
25	Clemson	49
23	Virginia	24

1989 (3-7-1)

6	NC State	10
10	West Virginia	14
23	W. Michigan	0
7	Clemson	31
21	Michigan	41
24	Georgia Tech	28
27	Wake Forest	7
25	Duke	46
38	North Carolina	0
13	Penn State	13
21	Virginia	48

1990 (6-5-1)

20	Virginia Tech	13
14	West Virginia	10
17	Clemson	18
13	NC State	12
17	Michigan	45
3	Georgia Tech	31
41	Wake Forest	13
23	Duke	20
10	North Carolina	34
10	Penn State	24
35	Virginia	30
34	Louisiana Tech	34
	(Independence Bowl)	

1991 (2-9-0)

17	Virginia	6
17	Syracuse	31
7	West Virginia	37
20	Pitt	24
10	Georgia Tech	34
23	Wake Forest	22
13	Duke	17
0	North Carolina	24
7	Penn State	47
7	Clemson	40
17	NC State	20

North Carolina

Location: Chapel Hill, NC
Colors: Blue and White
Stadium: Kenan (1927), 52,000 capacity, natural turf.

Enrollment: 21,757
Nickname: Tar Heels

Head Coaches

No coach 1888, 1892–93
Hector Cowan 1889 (spring)
No team 1890, 1917–18
Billy Graves 1891
Vernon Irvine 1894
Tom Trenchard 1895, 1913–15
Gordon Johnston 1896
Will Reynolds 1897–1900
Charles Jenkins 1901
Herman Olcutt 1902–03
Robert Brown 1904
William Warner 1905
Willis Keinholz 1906
Otis Lamson 1907
Ed Green 1908
Art Brides 1909–10

Branch Bocock 1911
William Martin 1912
Thomas Campbell 1916, 1919
Myron Fuller 1920
Bill and Bob Fetzer 1921–25
Chuck Collins 1926–33
Carl Snavely 1934–35, 1945–52
Ray Wolf 1936–41
Jim Tatum 1942, 1956–58
Tom Young 1943
Gene McEver 1944
George Barclay 1953–55
Jim Hickey 1959–66
Bill Dooley 1967–77
Dick Crum 1978–87
Mack Brown 1988–91

All–American Players

George Barclay 1934 guard
Don Jackson 1935 tailback
Andy Bershak 1937 end
Steve Maronic 1938 tackle
Paul Severin 1939–40 end
Ray Poole 1943 end
Charlie Justice 1946–49 tailback
Art Weiner 1948–49 end
Len Szafaryn 1948 tackle
Ken Powell 1949 end
Irv Holdash 1950 center
Al Goldstein 1958 end
Bob Lacey 1963 end
Don McCauley 1970 tailback

Ron Rusnak 1972 guard
Ken Huff 1974 guard
Charlie Waddell 1974 end
Mike Voight 1976 tailback
Dee Hardison 1977 def. tackle
Lawrence Taylor 1980 linebacker
Ron Wooten 1980 guard
Rick Donnalley 1980 center
Dave Drechsler 1981–82 guard
Greg Poole 1981 def. back
Bill Fuller 1982–83 def. tackle
Brian Blados 1983 tackle
Ethan Horton 1984 tailback
Harris Barton 1986 tackle

Scores

1888 (0-2-0)

4	Wake Forest	6
0	Trinity	16

1889 (2-2-0)

33	Wake Forest	0
17	Trinity	25
8	Wake Forest	18
1	Trinity	0

1891 (0-2-0)

0	Wake Forest	1
4	Trinity	6

Opposite: **Kenan Stadium, Chapel Hill, NC**

1892 (5-1-0)

40	Richmond	0
18	Virginia	30
24	Trinity	0
64	Auburn	0
24	Vanderbilt	0
26	Virginia	0

1893 (3-4-0)

44	Wash. & Lee	0
4	VMI	10
4	Trinity	6
60	Tennessee	0
40	Wake Forest	0
0	Lehigh	34
0	Virginia	16

1894 (6-3-0)

44	NC A&M	0
16	NC A&M	0
28	Trinity	0
36	Sewanee	4
6	Lehigh	24
0	Rutgers	5
20	Georgetown	4
28	Richmond	0
0	Virginia	34

1895 (7-1-1)

36	NC A&M	0
34	Richmond	0
6	Georgia	0
12	Vanderbilt	0
0	Sewanee	0
10	Georgia	6
16	Wash. & Lee	0
32	Virginia Tech	5
0	Virginia	6

1896 (3-4-1)

26	Guilford	4
34	Guilford	0
0	Virginia Tech	0
16	Georgia	24
0	Charlotte Ath. Club	8
0	Hampton Ath Cl	18
30	Greensboro Ath. Assoc.	0
0	Virginia	46

1897 (7-3-0)

40	NC A&M	0
16	Guilford	0
24	Greensboro Ath. Assoc.	0
28	Clemson	0
0	Virginia Tech	4
12	Sewanee	6
0	Vanderbilt	31
16	Tennessee	0
14	Bingham	0
0	Virginia	12

1898 (9-0-0)

18	Guilford	0
34	NC A&M	0
11	Greensboro Ath. Assoc.	0
11	Oak Ridge	0
28	Virginia Tech	6
11	Davidson	0
53	Georgia	0
29	Auburn	0
6	Virginia	2

1899 (7-3-1)

34	NC A&M	0
16	Oak Ridge	0
45	Guilford	0
10	Davidson	0
46	Horner	0
11	NC A&M	11
6	MD–Balt.	0
0	Navy	12
0	Princeton	30
5	Georgia	0
0	Sewanee	5

1900 (4-1-3)

38	Morganton Inst	0
0	Virginia Tech	0
22	Tennessee	5
48	Vanderbilt	0
0	Sewanee	0
55	Georgia	0
0	Virginia	17
0	Georgetown	0

1901 (7-2-0)

28	Oak Ridge	0
39	NC A&M	0
42	Guilford	0
6	Davidson	0
27	Georgia	0
10	Auburn	0
30	NC A&M	0

1902 (5-1-3)

16	Guilford	0
35	Oak Ridge	0
10	Furman	0
27	Davidson	0
0	Virginia Tech	0
17	VMI	10
0	NC A&M	0

1903 (6-3-0)

15	Guilford	0
45	Oak Ridge	0
17	South Carolina	0
28	VMI	6
0	Georgetown	33
5	Kentucky	6
0	Virginia Tech	21

1901 (cont.)

6	Virginia	23
10	Clemson	22

1904 (5-2-2)

29	Guilford	0
0	Davidson	0
50	Bingham	0
27	South Carolina	0
41	Norfolk Ath. Assoc.	0
6	Virginia Tech	0
0	Georgetown	16
6	NC A&M	6
11	Virginia	12

1907 (4-4-1)

0	Penn	37
0	Wash. & Lee	0
38	Oak Ridge	0
14	William & Mary	0
4	Virginia	9
6	Clemson	15
12	Georgetown	5
13	Richmond	11
6	Virginia Tech	20

1910 (3-6-0)

6	VMI	0
0	Kentucky	11
0	Davidson	6
37	Wake Forest	0
0	Georgetown	12
0	Virginia Tech	20
0	Wash. & Lee	5
27	South Carolina	6
0	Virginia	7

1913 (5-4-0)

7	Wake Forest	0
15	Virg. Medical	0
7	Davidson	0
13	South Carolina	3
7	Virginia Tech	14
6	Georgia	19
0	Wash. & Lee	14

1902 (cont.)

5	Georgetown	12
12	Virginia	12

1905 (4-3-1)

6	Davidson	0
0	Penn	17
0	Navy	38
6	Virginia Tech	35
36	Georgetown	0
0	NC A&M	0
17	VMI	0
17	Virginia	0

1908 (3-3-3)

17	Wake Forest	0
0	Tennessee	12
0	Wash. & Lee	0
0	Davidson	0
6	Georgetown	6
17	Richmond	12
0	Virginia Tech	10
22	South Carolina	0
0	Virginia	31

1911 (6-1-1)

12	Wake Forest	3
12	Bingham	0
5	Davidson	0
12	USS Franklin	0
0	Virginia Tech	0
21	South Carolina	0
4	Wash. & Lee	0
0	Virginia	28

1914 (10-1-0)

41	Richmond	0
65	Virg. Medical	0
53	Wake Forest	0
48	South Carolina	0
41	Georgia	6
40	Riverside	0
10	Vanderbilt	9

1903 (cont.)

11	Clemson	6
16	Virginia	0

1906 (1-4-2)

0	Davidson	0
0	Penn	11
12	Richmond	0
6	Lafayette	28
0	Virginia Tech	0
0	Georgetown	4
0	Navy	40

1909 (5-2-0)

18	Wake Forest	0
3	Tennessee	0
0	VMI	3
5	Georgetown	0
22	Richmond	0
0	Virginia Tech	15
6	Wash. & Lee	0

1912 (3-4-1)

13	Davidson	0
9	Wake Forest	2
47	Bingham	0
0	Virginia Tech	26
10	Georgetown	37
6	South Carolina	6
0	Wash. & Lee	31
0	Virginia	66

1915 (4-3-1)

14	The Citadel	7
35	Wake Forest	0
0	Georgetown	38
3	VMI	3
3	Georgia Tech	23
9	Clemson	7
41	Davidson	6

1913 (cont.)		
29	Wake Forest	0
7	Virginia	26

1914 (cont.)		
16	Davidson	3
30	VMI	7
12	Wake Forest	7
3	Virginia	20

1915 (cont.)		
0	Virginia	14

1916 (5-4-0)		
20	Wake Forest	0
0	Princeton	29
0	Harvard	21
6	Georgia Tech	10
38	VMI	13
7	Virginia Tech	14
10	Davidson	6
46	Furman	0
7	Virginia	0

1919 (4-3-1)		
0	Rutgers	19
7	Yale	34
6	Wake Forest	0
13	NC State	12
0	Tennessee	0
7	VMI	29
10	Davidson	0
6	Virginia	0

1920 (2-6-0)		
6	Wake Forest	0
0	Yale	21
7	South Carolina	0
3	NC State	13
0	Maryland	13
0	VMI	23
0	Davidson	7
0	Virginia	14

1921 (5-2-2)		
21	Wake Forest	0
0	Yale	34
7	South Carolina	7
0	NC State	7
16	Maryland	7
20	VMI	7
0	Davidson	0
7	Virginia	3
14	Florida	10

1922 (9-1-0)		
62	Wake Forest	3
0	Yale	18
20	Trinity	0
10	South Carolina	7
14	NC State	9
27	Maryland	3
19	Tulane	12
9	VMI	7
29	Davidson	6
10	Virginia	7

1923 (5-3-1)		
22	Wake Forest	0
0	Yale	53
14	Trinity	6
14	NC State	0
0	Maryland	14
13	South Carolina	0
0	VMI	9
14	Davidson	3
0	Virginia	0

1924 (4-5-0)		
6	Wake Forest	7
0	Yale	27
6	Trinity	0
10	NC State	0
0	Maryland	6
7	South Carolina	10
3	VMI	0
6	Davidson	0
0	Virginia	7

1925 (7-1-1)		
0	Wake Forest	6
7	South Carolina	0
41	Duke	0
17	NC State	0
3	Mercer	0
16	Maryland	0
23	VMI	11
13	Davidson	0
3	Virginia	3

1926 (4-5-0)		
0	Wake Forest	13
0	Tennessee	34
7	South Carolina	0
6	Duke	0
6	Maryland	14
12	NC State	0
28	VMI	0
0	Davidson	10
0	Virginia	3

1927 (4-6-0)		
8	Wake Forest	9
0	Tennessee	26
7	Maryland	6
6	South Carolina	14
0	Georgia Tech	13

1928 (5-3-2)		
65	Wake Forest	0
26	Maryland	19
0	Harvard	20
14	Virginia Tech	16
7	Georgia Tech	20

1929 (9-1-0)		
48	Wake Forest	0
43	Maryland	0
18	Georgia Tech	7
12	Georgia	19
38	Virginia Tech	13

1927 (cont.)

6	NC State	19
0	VMI	7
27	Davidson	0
18	Duke	0
14	Virginia	13

1930 (5-3-2)

13	Wake Forest	7
39	Virginia Tech	21
28	Maryland	21
0	Georgia	26
7	Tennessee	9
6	Georgia Tech	6
13	NC State	6
6	Davidson	7
41	Virginia	0
0	Duke	0

1933 (4-5-0)

6	Davidson	0
13	Vanderbilt	20
0	Georgia	30
0	Florida	9
6	Georgia Tech	10
6	NC State	0
26	Wake Forest	0
0	Duke	21
14	Virginia	0

1936 (8-2-0)

14	Wake Forest	7
14	Tennessee	6
14	Maryland	0
14	NYU	13
7	Tulane	21
21	NC State	6
26	Davidson	6
7	Duke	27
14	South Carolina	0
59	Virginia	14

1939 (8-1-1)

50	The Citadel	0
36	Wake Forest	6
13	Virginia Tech	6

1928 (cont.)

6	NC State	6
0	South Carolina	0
30	Davidson	7
24	Virginia	20
14	Duke	7

1931 (4-3-3)

37	Wake Forest	0
0	Vanderbilt	13
0	Florida	0
7	Georgia	32
0	Tennessee	7
18	NC State	15
19	Georgia Tech	19
20	Davidson	0
0	Duke	0
13	Virginia	6

1934 (7-1-1)

21	Wake Forest	0
7	Tennessee	19
14	Georgia	0
6	Kentucky	0
7	NC State	7
26	Georgia Tech	0
12	Davidson	2
7	Duke	0
25	Virginia	6

1937 (7-1-1)

13	South Carolina	13
20	NC State	0
19	NYU	6
28	Wake Forest	0
13	Tulane	0
0	Fordham	14
26	Davidson	0
14	Duke	6
40	Virginia	0

1940 (6-4-0)

56	Appalachian	6
0	Wake Forest	12
27	Davidson	7

1929 (cont.)

32	NC State	0
40	South Carolina	0
26	Davidson	7
41	Virginia	7
48	Duke	7

1932 (3-5-2)

0	Wake Forest	0
7	Vanderbilt	39
7	Tennessee	20
6	Georgia	6
14	Georgia Tech	43
13	NC State	0
18	Florida	13
12	Davidson	0
0	Duke	7
7	Virginia	14

1935 (8-1-0)

14	Wake Forest	0
38	Tennessee	13
33	Maryland	0
14	Davidson	0
19	Georgia Tech	0
35	NC State	6
56	VMI	0
0	Duke	25
61	Virginia	0

1938 (6-2-1)

14	Wake Forest	6
21	NC State	0
14	Tulane	17
7	NYU	0
34	Davidson	0
0	Duke	14
7	Virginia Tech	0
0	Fordham	0
20	Virginia	0

1941 (3-7-0)

42	Lenoir Rhyne	6
7	South Carolina	13
20	Davidson	0

1939 (cont.)

14	NYU	7
14	Tulane	14
30	Penn	6
17	NC State	0
32	Davidson	0
3	Duke	13
19	Virginia	0

1940 (cont.)

21	TCU	14
13	NC State	7
13	Tulane	14
0	Fordham	14
13	Richmond	14
6	Duke	3
10	Virginia	7

1941 (cont.)

14	Fordham	27
6	Tulane	52
0	Wake Forest	13
7	NC State	13
27	Richmond	0
0	Duke	20
7	Virginia	28

1942 (5-2-2)

6	Wake Forest	0
18	South Carolina	6
0	Fordham	0
13	Duquesne	6
14	Tulane	29
14	NC State	21
43	Davidson	14
13	Duke	13
28	Virginia	13

1943 (6-3-0)

7	Georgia Tech	20
19	Penn State	0
23	Jax. NATTC	0
7	Duke	14
27	NC State	13
21	South Carolina	6
9	Penn	6
6	Duke	27
54	Virginia	7

1944 (1-7-1)

0	Wake Forest	7
0	Army	46
0	Georgia Tech	28
20	Cherry Pt MCAS	14
0	South Carolina	6
0	William & Mary	0
6	Yale	13
0	Duke	33
7	Virginia	26

1945 (5-5-0)

6	Camp Lee	0
14	Georgia Tech	20
14	Virginia Tech	0
0	Penn	49
20	Cherry Pt MCAS	14
6	Tennessee	20
6	William & Mary	0
13	Wake Forest	14
7	Duke	14
27	Virginia	18

1946 (8-2-1)

14	Virginia Tech	14
21	Miami (FL)	0
33	Maryland	0
21	Navy	14
40	Florida	19
14	Tennessee	20
21	William & Mary	7
26	Wake Forest	14
22	Duke	7
49	Virginia	14
10	Georgia (Sugar Bowl)	20

1947 (8-2-0)

14	Georgia	7
0	Texas	34
7	Wake Forest	19
13	William & Mary	7
35	Florida	7
20	Tennessee	6
41	NC State	6
19	Maryland	0
21	Duke	0
40	Virginia	7

1948 (9-1-1)

34	Texas	7
21	Georgia	14
28	Wake Forest	6
14	NC State	0
34	LSU	7
14	Tennessee	7
7	William & Mary	7
49	Maryland	20
20	Duke	0
34	Virginia	12

1949 (7-4-0)

26	NC State	6
21	Georgia	14
28	South Carolina	13
28	Wake Forest	14
7	LSU	13
6	Tennessee	35
20	William & Mary	14
6	Notre Dame	42
21	Duke	20
14	Virginia	7

1950 (3-5-2)

13	NC State	7
7	Notre Dame	14
0	Georgia	0
7	Wake Forest	13
40	William & Mary	7
0	Tennessee	16
7	Maryland	7
14	South Carolina	7
0	Duke	7
13	Virginia	44

1948 (cont.)		1949 (cont.)	
6 Oklahoma	14	13 Rice	27
(Sugar Bowl)		(Cotton Bowl)	

1951 (2 8 0)		1952 (2-6-0)		1953 (4-6-0)	
21 NC State	0	7 Texas	28	29 NC State	7
16 Georgia	28	7 Wake Forest	9	39 Wash. & Lee	0
20 Texas	45	14 Notre Dame	34	18 Wake Forest	13
21 South Carolina	6	14 Tennessee	41	0 Maryland	26
7 Maryland	14	7 Virginia	34	14 Georgia	27
7 Wake Forest	39	27 South Carolina	19	6 Tennessee	20
0 Tennessee	27	0 Duke	34	0 South Carolina	18
14 Virginia	34	34 Miami (FL)	7	14 Notre Dame	34
7 Notre Dame	12			33 Virginia	7
7 Duke	19			20 Duke	35

1954 (4-5-1)		1955 (3-7-0)		1956 (2-7-1)	
20 NC State	6	6 Oklahoma	13	6 NC State	26
7 Tulane	7	25 NC State	18	0 Oklahoma	36
7 Georgia	21	7 Georgia	28	0 South Carolina	14
0 Maryland	33	7 Maryland	25	12 Georgia	26
14 Wake Forest	7	0 Wake Forest	25	34 Maryland	6
20 Tennessee	26	7 Tennessee	48	6 Wake Forest	6
21 South Carolina	19	32 South Carolina	14	0 Tennessee	20
13 Notre Dame	42	7 Notre Dame	27	21 Virginia	7
26 Virginia	14	26 Virginia	14	14 Notre Dame	21
12 Duke	47	0 Duke	6	6 Duke	21

1957 (6-4-0)		1958 (6-4-0)		1959 (5-5-0)	
0 NC State	7	14 NC State	21	18 Clemson	20
26 Clemson	0	21 Clemson	26	8 Notre Dame	28
13 Navy	7	8 Southern Cal	7	20 NC State	12
20 Miami (FL)	13	6 South Carolina	0	19 South Carolina	6
7 Maryland	21	27 Maryland	0	7 Maryland	14
14 Wake Forest	7	26 Wake Forest	7	21 Wake Forest	19
0 Tennessee	35	21 Tennessee	7	7 Tennessee	29
28 South Carolina	6	42 Virginia	0	7 Miami (FL)	14
21 Duke	13	24 Notre Dame	34	41 Virginia	0
13 Virginia	20	6 Duke	7	50 Duke	0

1960 (3-7-0)		1961 (5-5-0)		1962 (3-7-0)	
0 NC State	3	27 NC State	22	6 NC State	7
12 Miami (FL)	29	0 Clemson	27	7 Ohio State	41
12 Notre Dame	7	14 Maryland	8	6 Michigan State	38
12 Wake Forest	13	17 South Carolina	0	13 Maryland	31
6 South Carolina	22	0 Miami (FL)	10	19 South Carolina	14

1960 (cont.)			1961 (cont.)			1962 (cont.)		
14	Tennessee	27	22	Tennessee	21	23	Wake Forest	14
0	Clemson	24	0	LSU	30	6	Clemson	17
19	Maryland	22	3	Duke	6	11	Virginia	7
7	Duke	6	14	Wake Forest	17	7	Notre Dame	21
35	Virginia	8	24	Virginia	0	14	Duke	16

1963 (9-2-0)			1964 (5-5-0)			1965 (4-6-0)		
11	Virginia	7	13	NC State	14	24	Michigan	31
0	Michigan State	31	21	Michigan State	15	14	Ohio State	3
21	Wake Forest	0	23	Wake Forest	0	17	Virginia	21
14	Maryland	7	3	LSU	20	10	NC State	7
31	NC State	10	9	Maryland	10	12	Maryland	10
7	South Carolina	0	24	South Carolina	6	10	Wake Forest	12
28	Georgia	7	8	Georgia	24	35	Georgia	47
7	Clemson	11	29	Clemson	0	17	Clemson	13
27	Miami (FL)	16	27	Virginia	31	0	Notre Dame	17
16	Duke	14	21	Duke	15	7	Duke	34
35	Air Force	0						
	(Gator Bowl)							

1966 (2-8-0)			1967 (2-8-0)			1968 (3-7-0)		
0	Kentucky	10	7	NC State	13	6	NC State	38
10	NC State	7	10	South Carolina	16	27	South Carolina	32
21	Michigan	7	11	Tulane	36	8	Vanderbilt	7
0	Notre Dame	32	7	Vanderbilt	21	24	Maryland	33
0	Wake Forest	3	8	Air Force	10	22	Florida	7
3	Georgia	28	14	Maryland	0	31	Wake Forest	48
3	Clemson	27	10	Wake Forest	20	15	Air Force	28
14	Air Force	20	0	Clemson	17	6	Virginia	41
25	Duke	41	17	Virginia	40	14	Clemson	24
14	Virginia	21	20	Duke	9	25	Duke	14

1969 (5-5-0)			1970 (8-4-0)			1971 (9-3-0)		
3	NC State	10	20	Kentucky	10	28	Richmond	0
6	South Carolina	14	19	NC State	0	27	Illinois	0
38	Vanderbilt	22	53	Maryland	20	35	Maryland	14
10	Air Force	20	10	Vanderbilt	7	27	NC State	7
2	Florida	52	21	South Carolina	35	29	Tulane	37
23	Wake Forest	3	17	Tulane	24	0	Notre Dame	16
12	Virginia	0	13	Wake Forest	14	7	Wake Forest	3
61	VMI	11	30	Virginia	15	36	William & Mary	35
32	Clemson	15	62	VMI	13	26	Clemson	13
13	Duke	17	42	Clemson	7	32	Virginia	20
			59	Duke	34	38	Duke	0

1970 (cont.)

26	Arizona State	48
	(Peach Bowl)	

1971 (cont.)

3	Georgia	7
	(Gator Bowl)	

1972 (11-1-0)

28	Richmond	18
31	Maryland	26
34	NC State	33
14	Ohio State	29
31	Kentucky	20
21	Wake Forest	0
26	Clemson	10
23	Virginia	3
14	Duke	0
42	E. Carolina	19
28	Florida	24
32	Texas Tech	28
	(Sun Bowl)	

1973 (4-7-0)

34	William & Mary	27
3	Maryland	23
14	Missouri	27
26	NC State	28
16	Kentucky	10
0	Tulane	16
28	E. Carolina	27
40	Virginia	44
29	Clemson	37
42	Wake Forest	0
10	Duke	27

1974 (7-5-0)

42	Ohio	7
31	Wake Forest	0
12	Maryland	24
45	Pitt	29
28	Georgia Tech	29
33	NC State	14
23	South Carolina	31
24	Virginia	10
32	Clemson	54
56	Army	42
14	Duke	13
24	Miss. State	26
	(Sun Bowl)	

1975 (3-7-1)

33	William & Mary	7
7	Maryland	34
7	Ohio State	32
31	Virginia	28
14	Notre Dame	21
20	NC State	21
17	E. Carolina	38
9	Wake Forest	21
35	Clemson	38
17	Tulane	15
17	Duke	17

1976 (9-3-0)

14	Miami (Ohio)	10
24	Florida	21
12	Northwestern	0
34	Army	32
3	Missouri	24
13	NC State	21
12	E. Carolina	10
34	Wake Forest	14
27	Clemson	23
31	Virginia	6
39	Duke	38
0	Kentucky	21
	(Peach Bowl)	

1977 (8-3-1)

7	Kentucky	10
31	Richmond	0
41	Northwestern	7
7	Texas Tech	10
24	Wake Forest	3
27	NC State	14
17	South Carolina	0
16	Maryland	7
13	Clemson	13
35	Virginia	14
16	Duke	3
17	Nebraska	21
	(Liberty Bowl)	

1978 (5-6-0)

14	E. Carolina	10
20	Maryland	21
16	Pitt	20
3	Miami (Ohio)	7
34	Wake Forest	29
7	NC State	34
24	South Carolina	22
18	Richmond	27
9	Clemson	13
38	Virginia	20
16	Duke	15

1979 (8-3-1)

28	South Carolina	0
17	Pitt	7
41	Army	3
35	Cincinnati	14
19	Wake Forest	24
35	NC State	21
24	E. Carolina	24
14	Maryland	17
10	Clemson	19
13	Virginia	7
37	Duke	16

1980 (11-1-0)

35	Furman	13
9	Texas Tech	3
17	Maryland	3
33	Georgia Tech	0
27	Wake Forest	9
28	NC State	8
31	E. Carolina	3
7	Oklahoma	41
24	Clemson	19
26	Virginia	3
44	Duke	21

1979 (cont.)

17	Michigan	15
	(Gator Bowl)	

1980 (cont.)

16	Texas	7
	(Bluebonnet Bowl)	

1981 (10-2-0)

56	E. Carolina	0
49	Miami (Ohio)	7
56	Boston College	14
28	Georgia Tech	7
48	Wake Forest	10
21	NC State	10
13	South Carolina	31
17	Maryland	10
8	Clemson	10
17	Virginia	14
31	Duke	10
31	Arkansas	27
	(Gator Bowl)	

1982 (8-4-0)

6	Pitt	7
34	Vanderbilt	10
62	Army	8
41	Georgia Tech	0
24	Wake Forest	7
41	NC State	9
24	Maryland	31
13	Clemson	16
27	Virginia	14
17	Duke	23
33	Bowling Green	14
26	Texas	10
	(Sun Bowl)	

1983 (8-4-0)

24	South Carolina	8
24	Memphis State	10
48	Miami (Ohio)	17
51	William & Mary	20
38	Georgia Tech	21
30	Wake Forest	10
42	NC State	14
26	Maryland	28
3	Clemson	16
14	Virginia	17
34	Duke	27
3	Florida State	28
	(Peach Bowl)	

1984 (5-5-1)

30	Navy	33
20	Boston College	52
23	Kansas	17
12	Clemson	20
3	Wake Forest	14
28	NC State	21
30	Memphis State	27
23	Maryland	34
24	Georgia Tech	17
24	Virginia	24
17	Duke	15

1985 (5-6-0)

21	Navy	19
13	LSU	23
51	VMI	7
0	Georgia Tech	31
34	Wake Forest	14
21	NC State	14
10	Florida State	20
10	Maryland	28
21	Clemson	20
22	Virginia	24
21	Duke	23

1986 (7-5-0)

45	The Citadel	14
20	Kansas	0
10	Florida State	10
21	Georgia Tech	20
40	Wake Forest	30
34	NC State	35
3	LSU	30
32	Maryland	30
10	Clemson	38
27	Virginia	7
42	Duke	35
21	Arizona	30
	(Aloha Bowl)	

1987 (5-6-0)

34	Illinois	14
0	Oklahoma	28
30	Georgia Tech	23
45	Navy	14
10	Auburn	20
14	Wake Forest	22
17	NC State	14
27	Maryland	14
10	Clemson	13

1988 (1-10-0)

10	South Carolina	31
0	Oklahoma	28
34	Louisville	38
21	Auburn	47
24	Wake Forest	42
3	NC State	48
20	Georgia Tech	17
38	Maryland	41
14	Clemson	37

1989 (1-10-0)

49	VMI	7
6	Kentucky	13
6	NC State	40
7	Navy	12
16	Wake Forest	17
17	Virginia	50
14	Georgia Tech	17
0	Maryland	38
3	Clemson	35

1987 (cont.)		1988 (cont.)		1989 (cont.)	
17 Virginia	20	24 Virginia	27	20 South Carolina	27
10 Duke	25	29 Duke	35	0 Duke	41

1990 (6-4-1)		1991 (7-4-0)	
34 Miami (Ohio)	0	51 Cincinnati	16
5 South Carolina	27	20 Army	12
48 Connecticut	21	7 NC State	24
16 Kentucky	13	59 William & Mary	36
9 NC State	12	24 Wake Forest	10
31 Wake Forest	24	9 Virginia	14
13 Georgia Tech	13	14 Georgia Tech	35
34 Maryland	10	24 Maryland	0
6 Clemson	24	6 Clemson	21
10 Virginia	24	21 South Carolina	17
24 Duke	22	47 Duke	14

North Carolina State

Location: Raleigh, NC

Enrollment: 24,265

Colors: Red and White

Nickname: Wolfpack

Stadium: Carter-Finley (1966), 47,000 capacity, natural turf.

Head Coaches

Bart Gatling 1892–95

Perrin Busbee 1896–97

Bill Riddick 1898–99

John McKee 1900–01

Art Devlin 1902–03

Willis Keinholz 1904

George Whitney 1905

Willie Heston 1906

Mickey Whitehurst 1907–08

Eddie Greene 1909–13

Jack Hegarty 1914–15

Britt Patterson 1916

Harry Hartsell 1917, 1921–23

Tal Stafford 1918

Bill Fetzer 1919–20

Buck Shaw 1924

Gus Tebell 1925–29

John Van Liew 1930

John "Clipper" Smith 1931–33

Hunk Anderson 1934–36

Doc Newton 1937–43

Beattie Feathers 1944–51

Horace Hendrickson 1952–53

Earle Edwards 1954–70

Al Michaels 1971

Lou Holtz 1972–75

Bo Rein 1976–79

Monte Kiffin 1980–82

Tom Reed 1983–85

Dick Sheridan 1986–91

All–American Players

John Ripple 1918 tackle	Ron Carpenter 1968 tackle
Steve Sabol 1935 center	Carey Metts 1968 center
Ty Coon 1939 tackle	Bill Yoest 1973 guard
Elmer Costa 1950 tackle	Stan Fritts 1974 fullback
Dick Christy 1957 halfback	Don Buckey 1975 end
Roman Gabriel 1960–61 quarterback	Ted Brown 1978 halfback
Don Montgomery 1963 end	Jim Ritcher 1978–79 center
Dennis Byrd 1966–67 tackle	Vaughan Johnson 1983 linebacker
Fred Combs 1967 def. back	Nasrallah Worthen 1986, 1988 end
Gerald Warren 1967–68 kicker	Jesse Campbell 1990 def. back

Scores

1892 (1-0-0)

14	Raleigh Acad.	6

1893 (1-0-0)

13	Raleigh Acad.	0

1894 (0-2-0)

0	North Carolina	44
0	North Carolina	16

1895 (1-2-1)

0	North Carolina	36
4	Wake Forest	4
6	VMI	42
40	Richmond	0

1896 (1-0-0)

6	Guilford	0

1897 (1-1-0)

0	North Carolina	40
19	Davidson	0

1898 (0-1-0)

0	North Carolina	34

1899 (1-2-2)

0	North Carolina	34
18	Bingham	0
11	North Carolina	11
0	Davidson	0
0	Clemson	24

1900 (0-4-0)

2	Virginia Tech	18
5	South Carolina	17
0	Davidson	17
0	South Carolina	12

1901 (1-2-0)

0	North Carolina	39
0	North Carolina	30
27	Davidson	6

1902 (3-4-2)

5	Clemson	11
0	Furman	0
2	Furman	5
6	Virginia Tech	11
10	St. Alban's	0
28	Guilford	5
0	North Carolina	0
0	Davidson	5
30	Richmond	5

1903 (4-4-0)

50	Guilford	0
0	VMI	6
0	Virginia Tech	21
33	Danville Military Inst	0
0	Clemson	24
0	Kentucky	18
6	South Carolina	5
53	Richmond	0

Opposite: **Carter-Finley Stadium at North Carolina State in Raleigh.**

1904 (3-1-2)

69	Guilford	0
6	VMI	0
0	Virginia	5
0	South Carolina	0
6	North Carolina	6
18	Clemson	0

1905 (4-1-1)

5	VMI	0
0	Virginia	10
29	South Carolina	0
0	North Carolina	0
21	Wash. & Lee	0
10	Davidson	0

1906 (3-1-4)

39	Randolph Macon	0
0	Virginia	0
0	Richmond	0
17	VMI	0
4	Wash. & Lee	4
40	William & Mary	0
0	Clemson	0
0	Virginia Tech	6

1907 (6-0-1)

20	Randolph Macon	0
7	Richmond	4
22	Roanoke	0
11	Richmond	0
6	Davidson	0
5	NC All Stars	5
10	Virginia	4

1908 (6-1-0)

25	Wake Forest	0
24	William & Mary	0
5	Georgetown	0
0	Virginia	6
21	Davidson	0
76	Wake Forest	0
6	Virginia Tech	5

1909 (6-1-0)

39	Maryville	0
12	Maryland Ath Cl	0
15	Kentucky	6
31	Maryland	0
3	Wash. & Lee	0
5	USS Franklin	0
5	Virginia Tech	18

1910 (4-0-2)

0	Georgetown	0
33	Eastern	0
28	Wake Forest	3
5	Virginia Tech	3
53	Richmond	0
6	Villanova	6

1911 (5-3-0)

23	USS Franklin	0
6	Bucknell	0
15	Wash. & Lee	3
13	Wake Forest	5
5	VMI	6
16	Tennessee	0
6	Navy	17
6	Virginia Tech	3

1912 (4-3-0)

21	USS Franklin	0
7	Virg. Medical	0
0	Georgetown	48
7	Davidson	0
12	Wake Forest	0
0	Navy	40
6	Wash. & Lee	16

1913 (6-1-0)

26	Davidson	6
6	Wash. & Lee	0
37	Wake Forest	0
13	Virg. Medical	7
12	Georgetown	0
7	VMI	14
54	USS Franklin	0

1914 (2-3-1)

12	Navy	14
0	Virginia Tech	3
0	Wash. & Lee	7
7	Georgetown	7
51	Wake Forest	0
26	West Virginia	13

1915 (3-3-1)

7	Wake Forest	0
14	Navy	12
0	Georgetown	28
13	Wash. & Lee	48
10	South Carolina	19
0	Roanoke	0
27	Gallaudet	0

1916 (2-5-0)

13	Roanoke	3
0	Davidson	16
6	Wake Forest	0
0	Virginia Tech	40
0	Navy	50
5	Georgetown	61
0	Wash. & Lee	21

1917 (6-2-1)

19	Guilford	0
7	Davidson	3
28	Roanoke	0
17	Wake Forest	6
7	Wash. & Lee	27
10	Maryland	6
17	VMI	0

1918 (1-3-0)

54	Guilford	0
0	Georgia Tech	128
0	Virginia Tech	25
0	Wake Forest	21

1917 (cont.)

7	Virginia Tech	7
0	West Virginia	21

1919 (7-2-0)

80	Guilford	0
0	Navy	49
100	Hampton Roads	0
78	Roanoke	0
12	North Carolina	13
21	VMI	0
36	Davidson	6
3	Virginia Tech	0
21	Wake Forest	7

1920 (7-3-0)

23	Davidson	0
14	Navy	7
0	Penn State	41
13	North Carolina	3
0	VMI	14
81	William & Mary	0
14	Virginia Tech	6
0	Georgetown	27
90	Wofford	7
49	Wake Forest	7

1921 (3-3-3)

21	Randolph Macon	0
0	Navy	40
0	Penn State	35
7	North Carolina	0
7	VMI	7
3	Davidson	3
3	Virginia Tech	7
14	Wake Forest	0
6	Maryland	6

1922 (4-6-0)

20	Randolph Macon	2
6	Wash. & Lee	14
13	Roanoke	0
9	North Carolina	14
0	VMI	14
15	Davidson	0
0	Virginia Tech	24
0	Georgia Tech	17
32	Wake Forest	0
6	Maryland	7

1923 (3-7-0)

6	Roanoke	0
0	Penn State	16
7	South Carolina	0
0	North Carolina	14
7	VMI	22
12	Davidson	6
0	Virginia Tech	16
12	Maryland	26
0	Wake Forest	14
12	Wash. & Lee	20

1924 (2-6-2)

14	Duke	0
6	Penn State	51
0	South Carolina	10
0	North Carolina	10
7	VMI	17
10	Davidson	10
6	Virginia Tech	3
0	Maryland	0
0	Wake Forest	12
0	Wash. & Lee	34

1925 (3-5-1)

20	Richmond	0
13	Duke	0
6	South Carolina	7
0	North Carolina	17
0	Davidson	9
6	VMI	27
0	Virginia Tech	0
6	Wake Forest	0
0	Wash. & Lee	14

1926 (4-6-0)

10	Elon	0
0	Furman	31
0	Davidson	3
0	VMI	7
0	North Carolina	12
6	Lenoir Rhyne	0
26	Duke	19
14	South Carolina	20
7	Wake Forest	3
3	Clemson	7

1927 (9-1-0)

39	Elon	0
0	Furman	20
18	Clemson	6
30	Wake Forest	7
12	Florida	6
19	North Carolina	6
25	Davidson	6
20	Duke	18
34	South Carolina	0
19	Michigan State	0

1928 (4-5-1)

57	Elon	0
6	Wash. & Lee	38
0	Clemson	7
37	Wake Forest	0
7	Florida	14

1929 (1-8-0)

6	Wash. & Lee	27
0	Clemson	26
8	Wake Forest	6
6	Michigan State	40
0	North Carolina	32

1930 (2-8-0)

37	High Point	0
0	Davidson	12
0	Florida	27
0	Clemson	27
0	Wake Forest	7

1928 (cont.)		
6	North Carolina	6
14	Davidson	7
12	Duke	14
0	Michigan State	7
18	South Carolina	7

1929 (cont.)		
0	Davidson	13
12	Duke	19
6	Villanova	24
6	South Carolina	20

1930 (cont.)		
14	Miss. State	0
0	Presbyterian	2
6	North Carolina	13
0	Duke	18
0	South Carolina	19

1931 (3-6-0)		
18	Davidson	7
0	Florida	34
0	Clemson	6
0	Wake Forest	6
7	Catholic	12
15	North Carolina	18
6	Miss. State	0
14	Duke	0
0	South Carolina	21

1932 (6-1-2)		
31	Appalachian	0
9	Richmond	0
13	Clemson	0
0	Wake Forest	0
17	Florida	6
0	North Carolina	13
7	Davidson	3
6	Duke	0
7	South Carolina	7

1933 (1-5-3)		
7	Catawba	0
10	Georgia	20
0	Clemson	9
0	Florida	0
0	Wake Forest	0
6	Davidson	6
0	North Carolina	6
0	South Carolina	14
0	Duke	7

1934 (2-6-1)		
7	Davidson	0
12	Wake Forest	13
6	South Carolina	0
0	Florida	14
7	North Carolina	7
6	Clemson	12
6	Virginia Tech	7
0	Georgia	27
0	Duke	32

1935 (6-4-0)		
14	Davidson	7
14	South Carolina	0
21	Wake Forest	6
0	Georgia	13
20	Manhattan	0
6	North Carolina	35
6	Virginia Tech	0
6	Richmond	0
0	Duke	7
0	Catholic	8

1936 (3-7-0)		
12	Elon	0
2	Davidson	6
0	Wake Forest	9
6	Manhattan	13
27	Furman	0
13	Virginia Tech	0
6	North Carolina	21
3	Boston College	7
6	Catholic	7
0	Duke	13

1937 (5-3-1)		
6	Davidson	2
0	North Carolina	20
7	Furman	7
13	Virginia Tech	7
20	Wake Forest	0
12	Boston College	7
26	The Citadel	14
0	Manhattan	15
7	Duke	20

1938 (3-7-1)		
19	Davidson	7
0	North Carolina	21
0	Alabama	14
19	Wake Forest	7
7	Furman	7
0	Virginia Tech	7
0	Manhattan	3
0	Detroit	7
0	Duke	7
0	Carnegie Tech	14
14	The Citadel	6

1939 (2-8-0)		
18	Davidson	14
0	Tennessee	13
6	Clemson	25
0	Wake Forest	32
6	Detroit	21
0	North Carolina	17
0	Duquesne	7
12	Furman	7
0	Duke	28
7	Miami (FL)	27

1940 (3-6-0)		
16	William & Mary	0
34	Davidson	0

1941 (4-5-2)		
14	Richmond	7
6	Davidson	6

1942 (4-4-2)		
0	Davidson	0
13	Richmond	0

1940 (cont.)

7	Clemson	26
7	North Carolina	13
10	Miss. State	26
6	Furman	20
14	Wake Forest	20
20	The Citadel	14
6	Duke	42

1941 (cont.)

6	Clemson	27
0	Furman	0
0	Wake Forest	7
44	Newberry	0
13	North Carolina	7
13	Virginia Tech	14
7	Georgetown	20
6	Duke	55
13	William & Mary	0

1942 (cont.)

7	Clemson	6
7	NC Pre-Flight	19
0	Wake Forest	0
0	Holy Cross	28
21	North Carolina	14
2	Miami (FL)	0
20	Georgetown	28
0	Duke	47

1943 (3-6-0)

18	Newport News	0
7	Clemson	19
0	Camp Davis	27
6	Wake Forest	54
7	Greenville AAB	6
13	North Carolina	27
0	Duke	75
10	Davidson	0
7	NC Pre-Flight	19

1944 (7-2-0)

27	Milligan	7
13	Virginia	0
7	Clemson	13
12	Catawba	7
7	Wake Forest	21
19	William & Mary	2
21	VMI	6
28	Miami (FL)	7
39	Richmond	0

1945 (3-6-0)

47	Milligan	12
6	Virginia	26
0	Clemson	13
14	VMI	21
18	Wake Forest	19
20	William & Mary	6
6	Virginia Tech	0
13	Duke	26
7	Miami (FL)	21

1946 (8-3-0)

13	Duke	6
14	Clemson	7
25	Davidson	0
14	Wake Forest	6
6	Virginia Tech	14
49	VMI	7
0	Vanderbilt	7
27	Virginia	7
37	Florida	6
28	Maryland	7
13	Oklahoma	34
	(Gator Bowl)	

1947 (5-3-1)

0	Duke	7
14	Davidson	0
18	Clemson	0
6	Florida	7
21	Chattanooga	0
6	North Carolina	41
20	Wake Forest	0
7	Virginia	2
0	Maryland	0

1948 (3-6-1)

0	Duke	0
0	Clemson	6
40	Davidson	0
0	North Carolina	14
7	Chattanooga	0
13	Wake Forest	34
20	Duquesne	6
14	Virginia	21
6	William & Mary	26
7	Villanova	21

1949 (3-7-0)

6	North Carolina	26
6	Clemson	7
14	Davidson	20
13	Duke	14
6	Maryland	14
14	Virginia Tech	13
20	Richmond	6
27	Wake Forest	14

1950 (5-4-1)

7	North Carolina	13
7	Catawba	6
0	Clemson	27
0	Duke	7
16	Maryland	13
34	Virginia Tech	6
7	Richmond	0
15	Davidson	7

1951 (3-7-0)

34	Catawba	0
0	North Carolina	21
6	Wake Forest	21
21	Duke	27
28	William & Mary	35
19	Virginia Tech	14
2	Louisville	26
0	Clemson	6

1949 (cont.)
21	Villanova	45
7	William & Mary	33

1952 (3-7-0)
0	George Wash.	39
0	Georgia	49
28	Davidson	6
0	Duke	57
13	Florida State	7
6	Wake Forest	21
25	Wash. & Lee	14
6	Pitt	48
6	William & Mary	41
7	Texas Tech	54

1955 (4-5-1)
0	Florida State	7
7	Duke	33
18	North Carolina	25
13	Wake Forest	13
34	Villanova	13
33	Furman	7
40	Boston Univ.	13
26	Virginia Tech	34
28	William & Mary	21
7	West Virginia	27

1958 (2-7-1)
21	North Carolina	14
6	Maryland	21
26	Virginia	14
7	Wake Forest	13
6	William & Mary	13
13	Duke	20
14	Virginia Tech	14
14	Southern Miss.	26
6	Clemson	13
7	South Carolina	12

1961 (4-6-0)
14	Wyoming	15
22	North Carolina	27
21	Virginia	14
7	Alabama	26
7	Wake Forest	0

1950 (cont.)
6	Wake Forest	6
0	William & Mary	34

1953 (1-9-0)
7	North Carolina	29
7	George Wash.	20
27	Davidson	7
7	Wake Forest	20
0	Duke	31
6	William & Mary	7
6	Pitt	40
0	West Virginia	61
13	Florida State	23
7	Army	27

1956 (3-7-0)
26	North Carolina	6
6	Virginia Tech	35
7	Clemson	13
0	Florida State	14
20	Dayton	0
0	Duke	42
0	Wake Forest	13
14	South Carolina	7
7	Penn State	14
14	Maryland	25

1959 (1-9-0)
15	Virginia Tech	13
12	North Carolina	20
0	Clemson	23
14	Wake Forest	17
15	Duke	17
0	Wyoming	26
14	Southern Miss.	19
12	UCLA	21
7	South Carolina	12
28	Maryland	33

1962 (3-6-1)
7	North Carolina	6
0	Clemson	7
6	Maryland	14
14	Nebraska	19
0	Southern Miss.	30

1951 (cont.)
31	Davidson	0
0	Maryland	53

1954 (2-8-0)
21	Virginia Tech	30
6	North Carolina	20
0	Wake Forest	26
26	William & Mary	0
7	Florida State	13
7	Duke	21
6	Furman	7
14	Maryland	42
14	Richmond	6
3	West Virginia	28

1957 (7-1-2)
7	North Carolina	0
48	Maryland	13
13	Clemson	7
7	Florida State	0
0	Miami (FL)	0
14	Duke	14
19	Wake Forest	0
6	William & Mary	7
12	Virginia Tech	0
29	South Carolina	26

1960 (6-3-1)
29	Virginia Tech	14
3	North Carolina	0
26	Virginia	7
13	Maryland	10
13	Duke	17
20	Southern Miss.	13
0	UCLA	7
14	Wake Forest	12
22	Arizona State	25
8	South Carolina	8

1963 (8-3-0)
36	Maryland	14
14	Southern Miss.	0
7	Clemson	3
18	South Carolina	6
10	North Carolina	31

1961 (cont.)

6	Duke	17
7	Southern Miss.	6
7	Maryland	10
38	South Carolina	14
0	Clemson	20

1962 (cont.)

14	Duke	21
10	Georgia	10
6	South Carolina	17
24	Virginia	12
27	Wake Forest	3

1963 (cont.)

21	Duke	7
15	Virginia	9
13	Virginia Tech	7
0	Florida State	14
42	Wake Forest	0
12	Miss. State	16
	(Liberty Bowl)	

1964 (5-5-0)

14	North Carolina	13
9	Clemson	0
14	Maryland	13
0	Alabama	21
3	Duke	35
24	Virginia	15
17	South Carolina	14
19	Virginia Tech	28
6	Florida State	28
13	Wake Forest	27

1965 (6-4-0)

7	Clemson	21
13	Wake Forest	11
7	South Carolina	13
7	North Carolina	10
6	Florida	28
29	Maryland	7
13	Virginia	0
21	Duke	0
3	Florida State	0
28	Iowa	20

1966 (5-5-0)

10	Michigan State	28
7	North Carolina	10
15	Wake Forest	12
21	South Carolina	31
10	Florida	17
33	Duke	7
42	Virginia	21
24	Maryland	21
6	Southern Miss.	7
23	Clemson	14

1967 (9-2-0)

13	North Carolina	7
24	Buffalo	6
20	Florida State	10
16	Houston	6
31	Maryland	9
24	Wake Forest	7
28	Duke	7
30	Virginia	8
8	Penn State	13
6	Clemson	14
14	Georgia	7
	(Liberty Bowl)	

1968 (6-4-0)

10	Wake Forest	6
38	North Carolina	6
14	Oklahoma	28
14	SMU	35
36	South Carolina	12
19	Virginia	0
31	Maryland	11
19	Clemson	24
17	Duke	15
7	Florida State	48

1969 (3-6-1)

21	Wake Forest	22
10	North Carolina	3
24	Maryland	7
13	Miami (FL)	23
16	South Carolina	21
31	Virginia	0
25	Duke	25
13	Houston	34
22	Florida State	33
8	Penn State	33

1970 (3-7-1)

6	Richmond	21
0	North Carolina	19
7	South Carolina	7
6	Florida	14
23	E. Carolina	6
6	Duke	22
6	Maryland	0
2	Kentucky	27
21	Virginia	16
13	Wake Forest	16

1971 (3-8-0)

21	Kent State	23
7	Maryland	35
6	South Carolina	24
7	North Carolina	27
21	Wake Forest	14
13	Duke	41
15	E. Carolina	31
10	Virginia	14
13	Miami (FL)	7
3	Penn State	35

1972 (8-3-1)

24	Maryland	24
43	Syracuse	20
33	North Carolina	34
22	Georgia	28
17	Duke	0
42	Wake Forest	13
38	E. Carolina	16
42	South Carolina	24
35	Virginia	14
22	Penn State	37

1970 (cont.)		1971 (cont.)		1972 (cont.)	
0 Tulane	31	31 Clemson	23	42 Clemson	17
				49 West Virginia	13
				(Peach Bowl)	

1973 (9-3-0)		1974 (9-2-1)		1975 (7-4-1)	
57 E. Carolina	8	33 Wake Forest	15	26 E. Carolina	3
43 Virginia	23	35 Duke	21	22 Wake Forest	30
14 Nebraska	31	31 Clemson	10	8 Florida	7
12 Georgia	31	28 Syracuse	22	15 Michigan State	37
28 North Carolina	26	24 E. Carolina	20	27 Indiana	0
24 Maryland	22	22 Virginia	21	22 Maryland	37
29 Clemson	6	14 North Carolina	33	21 North Carolina	20
56 South Carolina	35	10 Maryland	20	45 Clemson	7
29 Penn State	35	42 South Carolina	27	28 South Carolina	21
21 Duke	3	12 Penn State	7	15 Penn State	14
52 Wake Forest	13	35 Arizona State	14	21 Duke	21
31 Kansas	18	31 Houston	31	10 West Virginia	13
(Liberty Bowl)		(Astro-Blue-		(Peach Bowl	
		bonnet Bowl)			

1976 (3-7-1)		1977 (8-4-0)		1978 (9-3-0)	
12 Furman	18	23 E. Carolina	28	29 E. Carolina	13
18 Wake Forest	20	14 Virginia	0	27 Syracuse	19
14 E. Carolina	23	38 Syracuse	0	29 West Virginia	15
31 Michigan State	31	41 Wake Forest	14	34 Wake Forest	10
24 Indiana	21	24 Maryland	20	7 Maryland	31
6 Maryland	16	17 Auburn	15	34 North Carolina	7
21 North Carolina	13	14 North Carolina	27	10 Clemson	33
38 Clemson	21	3 Clemson	7	22 South Carolina	13
7 South Carolina	27	7 South Carolina	3	10 Penn State	19
20 Penn State	41	17 Penn State	21	24 Duke	10
14 Duke	28	37 Duke	32	24 Virginia	21
		24 Iowa State	14	30 Pitt	17
		(Peach Bowl)		(Tangerine Bowl)	

1979 (7-4-0)		1980 (6-5-0)		1981 (4-7-0)	
34 E. Carolina	20	42 William & Mary	0	27 Richmond	21
31 Virginia	27	27 Virginia	13	28 Wake Forest	23
38 West Virginia	14	7 Wake Forest	27	31 E. Carolina	10
17 Wake Forest	14	10 South Carolina	30	9 Maryland	34
31 Auburn	44	17 App. State	14	30 Virginia	24
7 Maryland	0	8 North Carolina	28	10 North Carolina	21
21 North Carolina	35	24 Clemson	20	7 Clemson	17
16 Clemson	13	0 Maryland	24	12 South Carolina	20
28 South Carolina	30	13 Penn State	21	15 Penn State	22

1979 (cont.)

| 7 | Penn State | 9 |
| 28 | Duke | 7 |

1982 (6-5-0)

26	Furman	0
33	E. Carolina	26
30	Wake Forest	0
6	Maryland	23
16	Virginia	13
9	North Carolina	41
29	Clemson	38
33	South Carolina	3
0	Penn State	54
21	Duke	16
3	Miami (FL)	41

1985 (3-8-0)

14	E. Carolina	33
18	Georgia Tech	28
20	Wake Forest	17
20	Furman	42
17	Maryland	31
10	Pitt	24
14	North Carolina	21
10	Clemson	39
21	South Carolina	17
23	Virginia	22
19	Duke	31

1988 (8-3-1)

45	W. Carolina	6
14	Wake Forest	6
26	Maryland	30
14	Georgia Tech	6
49	E. Tenn. State	0
48	North Carolina	3
10	Clemson	3
7	South Carolina	23
14	Virginia	19
43	Duke	43
14	Pitt	3
28	Iowa	23
	(Peach Bowl)	

1980 (cont.)

| 38 | Duke | 21 |
| 36 | E. Carolina | 14 |

1983 (3-8-0)

16	E. Carolina	22
45	The Citadel	0
14	Virginia	26
38	Wake Forest	15
10	Georgia Tech	20
14	North Carolina	42
17	Clemson	27
17	South Carolina	31
33	App. State	7
26	Duke	27
6	Maryland	29

1986 (8-3-1)

38	E. Carolina	10
14	Pitt	14
42	Wake Forest	38
28	Maryland	16
21	Georgia Tech	59
35	North Carolina	34
27	Clemson	3
23	South Carolina	22
16	Virginia	20
29	Duke	15
31	W. Carolina	18
24	Virginia Tech	25
	(Peach Bowl)	

1989 (7-5-0)

10	Maryland	6
38	Georgia Tech	28
27	Wake Forest	17
40	North Carolina	6
42	Kent State	22
35	Middle Tenn St	14
10	Clemson	30
20	South Carolina	10
9	Virginia	20
26	Duke	35
23	Virginia Tech	25
10	Arizona	17
	(Copper Bowl)	

1981 (cont.)

| 7 | Duke | 17 |
| 6 | Miami (FL) | 14 |

1984 (3-8-0)

43	Ohio	6
30	Furman	34
15	Wake Forest	24
31	E. Carolina	22
27	Georgia Tech	22
21	Maryland	44
21	North Carolina	28
34	Clemson	35
28	South Carolina	35
0	Virginia	45
13	Duke	16

1987 (4-7-0)

14	E. Carolina	32
0	Pitt	34
3	Wake Forest	21
42	Maryland	14
17	Georgia Tech	0
14	North Carolina	17
30	Clemson	28
0	South Carolina	48
14	E. Tenn. State	29
47	Duke	45
31	Virginia	34

1990 (7-5-0)

67	W. Carolina	0
13	Georgia Tech	21
20	Wake Forest	15
12	Maryland	13
12	North Carolina	9
56	App. State	0
0	Virginia	31
17	Clemson	24
38	South Carolina	29
16	Virginia Tech	20
16	Duke	0
31	Southern Miss.	27
	(All–American Bowl)	

1991 (9-3-0)

7	Virginia Tech	0
47	Kent State	0
30	Wake Forest	3
24	North Carolina	7
28	Georgia Tech	21
15	Marshall	14
19	Clemson	29
38	South Carolina	21
10	Virginia	42
32	Duke	31
20	Maryland	17
34	E. Carolina	37
	(Peach Bowl)	

Virginia

Location: Charlottesville, VA Enrollment: 17,200
Colors: Orange and Blue Nickname: Cavaliers
Stadium: Scott (1931), 42,000 capacity, artificial turf.

Head Coaches

Frank Meacham 1888*
Sid Neely 1889*
Bill Taggett 1890*
Oliver Catchings 1891*
R. H. Thomas 1892*
John Poe 1893–94
Harry Mackey 1895
Martin Bergen 1896–97
Joe Massie 1898
Archie Hoxton 1899–1900
Wes Abbott 1901
John DeSaulles 1902
Gresham Poe 1903
Foster Sanford 1904
Bill Cole 1905–06
Ed Johnson 1907
Merritt T. Cooke 1908
Johnny Neff 1909

team captain

Charles Crawford 1910
Kemper Yancey 1911
Speed Elliott 1912
Rice Warren 1913, 1920–21
Joe Wood 1914
Harry Varner 1915
Peyton Evans 1916
No team 1917–18
Harris Coleman 1919
Thomas Campbell 1922
Earle Neale 1923–28
Earl Abell 1929–30
Fred Dawson 1931–33
Gus Tebell 1934–36
Frank Murray 1937–45
Art Guepe 1946–52
Ned McDonald 1953–55
Ben Martin 1956–57
Dick Vorhis 1958–60
Bill Elias 1961–64

George Blackburn 1965–70   Dick Bestwick 1976–81
Don Lawrence 1971–73   George Welsh 1982–91
Sonny Randle 1974–75

All–American Players

Gene Mayer 1915 halfback   Russ Henderson 1978 punter
Bill Dudley 1941 halfback   Lester Lyles 1984 def. back
Henry Walker 1944 end   Jim Dombrowski 1985 tackle
John Papit 1949 halfback   Roy Brown 1989 guard
Joe Palumbo 1951 guard   Herman Moore 1990 end
Tom Scott 1952 end   Shawn Moore 1990 quarterback
Jim Bakhtiar 1957 halfback

Scores

1888 (2-1-0)
20	Pantops Acad.	0
16	Episcopal Hi	0
0	Johns Hopkins	26

1889 (4-2-0)
44	Pantops Acad.	0
32	Georgetown	0
58	Johns Hopkins	0
12	Lehigh	24
46	Wake Forest	4
12	Navy	22

1890 (5-2-0)
12	Dickinson	0
0	Penn	72
0	Princeton	115
20	Lafayette	6
136	Randolph Macon	0
46	Wash. & Lee	0
10	Trinity	4

1891 (2-1-2)
34	St. John's	0
16	Schuylkill Navy	16
6	Lafayette	6
12	Princeton JV	0
0	Trinity	20

1892 (3-2-1)
0	Penn	32
30	North Carolina	18
30	Sewanee	0
4	Georgetown	4
46	Trinity	0
0	North Carolina	26

1893 (8-3-0)
34	Richmond	4
0	Penn State	6
20	Washington YMCA	0
0	Navy	28
28	Johns Hopkins	12
24	Georgetown	28
30	Trinity	0
58	Georgetown	0
12	Navy	0
22	VMI	0
16	North Carolina	0

1894 (8-2-0)
48	Richmond	0
36	Balt. City	0
0	Princeton	12
28	Richmond	0

1895 (9-2-0)
30	Miller	0
38	Virginia Tech	0
0	Princeton	36
20	Maryland Ath Cl	0

1896 (7-2-2)
10	Hampton Ath Cl	10
26	Miller	2
0	Penn	20
48	St. John's	0

1894 (cont.)

76	Johns Hopkins	0
6	Penn	14
20	Rutgers	4
102	Ft. Monroe	0
64	W Phil Ath Cl	0
34	North Carolina	0

1897 (6-2-1)

38	Frank & Marsh	0
14	St. Alban's	0
0	Penn	42
17	Georgia	4
20	Gallaudet	4
0	Navy	4
10	George Wash.	0
12	North Carolina	0
0	Vanderbilt	0

1900 (7-2-1)

51	Richmond	0
2	Carlisle	17
20	Johns Hopkins	0
0	VMI	0
28	Wash. & Lee	0
34	Gallaudet	0
17	Virginia Tech	5
0	Georgetown	10
17	North Carolina	0
17	Sewanee	5

1903 (7-2-1)

16	St. Alban's	0
37	Randolph Macon	0
16	Wash. & Lee	0
5	Navy	6
6	Kentucky	0
21	Virginia Tech	0
22	Davidson	0
48	St. John's	6
6	Carlisle	6
6	North Carolina	16

1895 (cont.)

0	Penn	54
16	Gallaudet	6
14	Roanoke	0
14	St. Alban's	4
62	Richmond	0
6	Vanderbilt	4
6	North Carolina	0

1898 (6-5-0)

16	St. Alban's	0
0	Penn	40
16	Gallaudet	0
47	George Wash.	0
0	Princeton	12
6	Mary. Medical	0
12	Georgetown	0
18	Vanderbilt	0
0	West Virginia	6
0	Navy	6
2	North Carolina	6

1901 (8-2-0)

28	Wash. & Lee	0
68	Roanoke	0
39	St. Alban's	0
24	Gallaudet	0
5	Penn	20
16	Virginia Tech	0
28	VMI	0
16	Georgetown	17
23	North Carolina	6
23	Sewanee	5

1904 (6-3-0)

16	Randolph Macon	0
17	Wash. & Lee	0
0	Penn	24
17	VMI	0
5	NC State	0
5	Virginia Tech	0
6	Carlisle	14
0	Navy	5
12	North Carolina	11

1896 (cont.)

0	Princeton	48
44	Virginia Tech	0
6	St. Alban's	0
46	VMI	0
6	Hampton Ath Cl	6
6	Gallaudet	0
48	North Carolina	0

1899 (4-3-2)

10	St. Alban's	0
33	Episcopal Hi	6
6	Penn	33
0	Mary. Medical	0
5	Gallaudet	11
0	Michigan	38
28	Virginia Tech	0
0	Georgetown	0
10	Lehigh	0

1902 (8-1-1)

16	Wash. & Lee	0
15	St. Alban's	0
27	Nashville	0
12	Kentucky	0
22	St. John's	0
35	Davidson	0
6	Lehigh	34
6	Virginia Tech	0
6	Carlisle	5
12	North Carolina	12

1905 (5-4-0)

59	Randolph Macon	0
30	St. John's	5
10	NC State	0
0	Carlisle	12
15	Bucknell	11
0	Virginia Tech	11
55	George Wash.	0
0	Navy	22
0	North Carolina	17

1906 (7-2-2)

11	St. John's	0
22	Richmond	0
0	NC State	0
38	Randolph Macon	0
38	Hampden-Sydney	5
4	VMI	0
12	Richmond	6
5	Bucknell	12
12	Georgetown	0
0	George Wash.	0
17	Carlisle	18

1907 (6-3-1)

5	Davidson	5
38	Richmond	0
22	St. John's	4
40	Gallaudet	0
18	VMI	17
9	North Carolina	4
0	Sewanee	12
5	Wash. & Lee	6
28	Georgetown	6
4	NC State	10

1908 (7-0-1)

11	William & Mary	0
18	St. John's	9
22	Randolph Macon	0
12	Davidson	0
0	Sewanee	0
6	NC State	0
6	Georgetown	0
31	North Carolina	0

1909 (7-1-0)

30	William & Mary	0
37	Hampden-Sydney	0
11	Davidson	0
12	St. John's	0
7	Lehigh	11
5	Navy	0
32	VMI	0
21	Georgetown	0

1910 (6-2-0)

10	William & Mary	0
17	Randolph Macon	0
21	Roanoke	0
29	St. John's	0
28	VMI	0
5	Carlisle	22
0	Georgetown	15
7	North Carolina	0

1911 (8-2-0)

23	Hampden-Sydney	0
81	William & Mary	0
31	Randolph Macon	0
8	Swarthmore	9
6	St. John's	0
22	VMI	6
29	Wake Forest	6
34	Johns Hopkins	0
0	Georgetown	9
28	North Carolina	0

1912 (6-3-0)

60	William & Mary	0
45	Randolph Macon	0
10	Hampden-Sydney	0
19	South Carolina	0
0	VMI	19
7	Norfolk Blues	0
0	Vanderbilt	13
13	Georgetown	16
66	North Carolina	0

1913 (7-1-0)

40	Randolph Macon	0
54	South Carolina	0
53	Hampden-Sydney	0
38	VMI	7
13	Georgia	6
34	Vanderbilt	0
7	Georgetown	8
26	North Carolina	7

1914 (8-1-0)

39	Randolph Macon	0
0	Yale	21
62	Richmond	0
49	South Carolina	0
28	Georgia	0
20	Vanderbilt	7
88	St. John's	0
47	Swarthmore	0
20	North Carolina	3

1915 (8-1-0)

20	Randolph Macon	0
10	Yale	0
74	Richmond	0
0	Harvard	9
9	Georgia	7
44	VMI	0

1916 (4-5-0)

14	Davidson	0
3	Yale	61
21	Richmond	0
7	Georgia	13
6	Vanderbilt	27
0	Harvard	51

1919 (2-5-2)

12	Randolph Macon	2
0	Richmond	0
0	Maryland	13
7	VMI	0
0	Harvard	47
7	Centre	49

1915 (cont.)

35	Vanderbilt	10
13	South Carolina	0
14	North Carolina	0

1920 (5-2-2)

27	William & Mary	0
65	Randolph Macon	0
6	VMI	22
14	Johns Hopkins	0
7	Rutgers	0
0	Harvard	24
0	Georgia	0
7	Vanderbilt	7
14	North Carolina	0

1923 (3-5-1)

10	Furman	13
9	Richmond	0
32	St. John's	7
0	VMI	35
33	Trinity	0
0	Wash. & Lee	7
0	Georgia	13
3	Virginia Tech	6
0	North Carolina	0

1926 (6-2-2)

0	Hampden-Sydney	0
7	Georgia	27
38	Lynchburg	0
14	VMI	7
0	Virginia Tech	6
6	South Carolina	0
30	Wash. & Lee	7
6	Maryland	6
57	Randolph Macon	0
3	North Carolina	0

1929 (4-3-2)

27	Randolph Macon	6
6	South Carolina	0
12	Swarthmore	7
7	VMI	20

1916 (cont.)

35	South Carolina	6
20	VMI	7
0	North Carolina	7

1921 (5-4-0)

28	Davidson	0
28	George Wash.	0
14	Richmond	0
14	VMI	7
14	Johns Hopkins	7
0	Princeton	34
0	Georgia	21
0	West Virginia	7
3	North Carolina	7

1924 (5-4-0)

13	Hampden-Sydney	9
0	Harvard	14
26	Randolph Macon	6
13	VMI	0
0	Penn	27
7	Wash. & Lee	20
0	Georgia	7
6	Virginia Tech	0
7	North Carolina	0

1927 (5-4-0)

38	Hampden-Sydney	6
0	Georgia	32
12	South Carolina	13
13	VMI	8
7	Virginia Tech	0
0	Tennessee	42
13	Wash. & Lee	7
21	Maryland	0
13	North Carolina	14

1930 (4-6-0)

37	Roanoke	0
48	Randolph Macon	0
0	Duke	32
6	Penn	40

1919 (cont.)

7	Georgia	7
6	Vanderbilt	10
0	North Carolina	6

1922 (4-4-1)

34	George Wash.	0
0	Princeton	5
14	Richmond	6
0	VMI	14
19	Johns Hopkins	0
22	Wash. & Lee	6
6	Georgia	6
0	West Virginia	13
7	North Carolina	10

1925 (7-1-1)

40	Hampden-Sydney	0
7	Georgia	6
19	Richmond	0
18	VMI	10
6	Maryland	0
0	Wash. & Lee	12
10	Virginia Tech	0
41	Randolph Macon	0
3	North Carolina	3

1928 (2-6-1)

66	Randolph Macon	0
13	South Carolina	24
0	Princeton	0
0	VMI	9
0	Vanderbilt	34
20	Wash. & Lee	13
0	Virginia Tech	20
2	Maryland	18
20	North Carolina	24

1931 (1-7-2)

18	Roanoke	0
7	Randolph Macon	7
6	Maryland	7
0	Sewanee	3

1929 (cont.)

32	St. John's	7
13	Maryland	13
12	Virginia Tech	32
13	Wash. & Lee	13
7	North Carolina	41

1932 (5-4-0)

32	Hampden-Sydney	0
7	Maryland	6
12	Roanoke	0
6	Columbia	22
4	VMI	6
20	St. John's	6
0	Wash. & Lee	7
0	Virginia Tech	13
14	North Carolina	7

1935 (1-5-4)

0	William & Mary	0
7	Hampden-Sydney	12
0	Davidson	0
7	Navy	26
18	St. John's	0
0	VMI	0
7	Maryland	14
0	Wash. & Lee	20
0	Virginia Tech	0
0	North Carolina	61

1938 (4-4-1)

12	VMI	12
13	Wash. & Lee	0
0	Navy	33
14	Virginia Tech	6
27	Maryland	19
34	William & Mary	0
0	Columbia	39
13	Harvard	40
0	North Carolina	20

1930 (cont.)

13	VMI	0
0	Kentucky	47
6	Maryland	14
13	Virginia Tech	31
21	Wash. & Lee	7
0	North Carolina	41

1933 (2-6-2)

7	Hampden-Sydney	7
39	Randolph Macon	0
0	Ohio State	75
6	Columbia	15
7	Navy	13
12	VMI	13
6	Maryland	0
0	Wash. & Lee	6
6	Virginia Tech	6
0	North Carolina	14

1936 (2-7-0)

26	Hampden-Sydney	10
7	William & Mary	0
14	Navy	35
0	Maryland	21
0	Wash. & Lee	13
6	VMI	12
0	Harvard	65
6	Virginia Tech	7
14	North Carolina	59

1939 (5-4-0)

26	Hampden-Sydney	0
12	Navy	14
12	Maryland	7
13	VMI	16
26	William & Mary	6
47	Chicago	0
7	Wash. & Lee	0
0	Virginia Tech	13
0	North Carolina	19

1931 (cont.)

3	VMI	18
0	Wash. & Lee	18
0	Harvard	19
0	Columbia	27
0	Virginia Tech	0
6	North Carolina	13

1934 (3-6-0)

8	Hampden-Sydney	0
6	Navy	21
27	St. John's	6
0	Dartmouth	27
17	VMI	13
0	Maryland	20
0	Wash. & Lee	20
6	Virginia Tech	19
6	North Carolina	25

1937 (2-7-0)

13	Hampden-Sydney	7
0	Princeton	26
13	Navy	40
0	Maryland	3
7	VMI	26
6	William & Mary	0
6	Wash. & Lee	13
7	Virginia Tech	14
0	North Carolina	40

1940 (4-5-0)

32	Lehigh	0
19	Yale	14
19	Maryland	6
0	VMI	7
6	William & Mary	13
0	Virginia Tech	6
20	Wash. & Lee	6
14	Tennessee	41
7	North Carolina	10

1941 (8-1-0)

41	Hampden-Sydney	0
25	Lafayette	0
19	Yale	21
44	Richmond	0
27	VMI	7
34	Virginia Tech	0
27	Wash. & Lee	7
34	Lehigh	0
28	North Carolina	7

1942 (2-6-1)

12	Hampden-Sydney	0
0	Navy	35
18	VMI	38
7	Richmond	7
13	Lafayette	19
14	Virginia Tech	20
34	Wash. & Lee	7
12	Maryland	27
13	North Carolina	28

1943 (3-4-1)

7	Richmond AAB	7
6	West Virginia	0
7	Richmond	16
6	Apprentice Sch	7
34	VMI	0
39	Maryland	0
0	Duke	49
7	North Carolina	54

1944 (6-1-2)

37	Hampden-Sydney	0
0	NC State	13
24	West Virginia	6
13	NC Pre-Flight	13
34	VMI	0
18	Maryland	7
39	Richmond	0
6	Yale	6
26	North Carolina	7

1945 (7-2-0)

39	Coast Guard	0
26	NC State	6
40	VMI	7
31	Virginia Tech	13
13	West Virginia	7
45	Richmond	0
40	Oceana NAS	0
13	Maryland	19
18	North Carolina	27

1946 (4-4-1)

71	Hampden-Sydney	0
21	Virginia Tech	21
19	VMI	8
0	Penn	40
7	Richmond	19
20	Princeton	6
7	NC State	27
21	West Virginia	0
14	North Carolina	49

1947 (7-3-0)

33	George Wash.	13
41	Virginia Tech	7
47	Harvard	0
32	Wash. & Lee	7
35	VMI	6
34	Richmond	0
7	Penn	19
6	West Virginia	0
2	NC State	7
7	North Carolina	40

1948 (5-3-1)

14	Miami (Ohio)	14
28	Virginia Tech	0
12	George Wash.	20
41	Wash. & Lee	6
26	VMI	14
14	Princeton	55
21	NC State	14
7	West Virginia	0
12	North Carolina	34

1949 (7-2-0)

27	George Wash.	13
21	Miami (Ohio)	18
26	Virginia Tech	0
27	Wash. & Lee	7
32	VMI	13
19	West Virginia	14
26	Penn	14
14	Tulane	28
7	North Carolina	14

1950 (8-2-0)

19	George Wash.	0
7	Penn	21
45	Virginia Tech	6
26	Wash. & Lee	21
26	VMI	13
28	West Virginia	21
34	The Citadel	14
13	William & Mary	0

1951 (8-1-0)

20	George Wash.	0
33	Virginia Tech	0
14	Wash. & Lee	42
34	VMI	14
30	Duke	7
39	The Citadel	0
34	North Carolina	14
28	South Carolina	27

1952 (8-2-0)

27	Vanderbilt	0
42	Virginia Tech	0
50	George Wash.	0
33	VMI	14
7	Duke	21
14	South Carolina	21
34	North Carolina	7
49	Richmond	0

1950 (cont.)

18	Tulane	42
44	North Carolina	14

1953 (1-8-0)

6	Virginia Tech	20
0	South Carolina	19
24	George Wash.	20
6	VMI	21
13	Vanderbilt	28
6	Duke	48
0	Pitt	26
13	Wash. & Lee	27
7	North Carolina	33

1956 (4-6-0)

18	VMI	0
7	Duke	40
7	Wake Forest	6
13	South Carolina	27
24	Lehigh	12
7	Virginia Tech	14
2	Vanderbilt	6
7	North Carolina	21
7	Navy	34
0	Clemson	7

1959 (0-10-0)

0	William & Mary	37
0	Clemson	47
10	Florida	55
12	VMI	19
14	Virginia Tech	40
0	Vanderbilt	33
12	Wake Forest	34
20	South Carolina	32
0	North Carolina	41
12	Maryland	55

1962 (5-5-0)

19	William & Mary	7
15	Virginia Tech	20
28	VMI	6
14	Wake Forest	12
34	Davidson	7

1951 (cont.)

46	William & Mary	0

1954 (3-6-0)

27	Lehigh	21
14	George Wash.	13
7	Penn State	34
21	VMI	0
0	Virginia Tech	6
20	Army	21
0	South Carolina	27
14	North Carolina	26
10	West Virginia	14

1957 (3-6-1)

6	West Virginia	6
0	Duke	40
28	Wake Forest	20
6	Clemson	20
38	Virginia Tech	7
12	Army	20
7	VMI	20
0	South Carolina	13
0	Maryland	12
20	North Carolina	13

1960 (0-10-0)

21	William & Mary	41
7	NC State	26
7	Clemson	21
16	VMI	30
6	Virginia Tech	40
20	Wake Forest	28
6	Navy	41
12	Maryland	44
8	North Carolina	35
0	South Carolina	26

1963 (2-7-1)

7	North Carolina	11
8	Duke	30
0	Virginia Tech	10
6	VMI	0
10	South Carolina	10

1952 (cont.)

21	Wash. & Lee	14
20	William & Mary	13

1955 (1-9-0)

7	Clemson	20
0	George Wash.	13
7	Penn State	26
20	VMI	13
13	Virginia Tech	17
7	Vanderbilt	34
7	Pitt	18
7	Wake Forest	13
14	North Carolina	26
14	South Carolina	21

1958 (1-9-0)

15	Clemson	20
15	Duke	12
14	NC State	26
13	Virginia Tech	22
6	Army	35
6	Vanderbilt	39
0	VMI	33
0	North Carolina	42
14	South Carolina	28
6	Maryland	44

1961 (4-6-0)

21	William & Mary	6
0	Duke	42
14	NC State	21
14	VMI	7
0	Virginia Tech	20
15	Wake Forest	21
28	South Carolina	20
3	Navy	13
28	Maryland	16
0	North Carolina	24

1964 (5-5-0)

21	Wake Forest	31
0	Duke	30
20	Virginia Tech	17
20	VMI	19
35	Army	14

1962 (cont.)			**1963 (cont.)**			**1964 (cont.)**		
6	South Carolina	40	0	Clemson	35	15	NC State	24
7	North Carolina	11	9	NC State	15	7	Clemson	29
12	NC State	24	9	William & Mary	7	14	William & Mary	13
18	Maryland	40	21	Boston College	30	31	North Carolina	27
41	Rutgers	0	6	Maryland	21	0	Maryland	10

1965 (5-5-0)			**1966 (4-6-0)**			**1967 (5-5-0)**		
7	Duke	21	24	Wake Forest	10	7	Army	26
14	Clemson	20	35	Clemson	40	35	Buffalo	12
21	North Carolina	17	8	Duke	27	14	Wake Forest	12
14	VMI	10	6	Tulane	20	6	Duke	13
41	West Virginia	0	38	VMI	27	23	South Carolina	24
14	Virginia Tech	22	7	Virginia Tech	24	13	VMI	18
0	NC State	13	21	NC State	42	8	NC State	30
7	South Carolina	17	13	Georgia Tech	14	40	North Carolina	17
19	Georgia Tech	42	41	Maryland	17	14	Tulane	10
33	Maryland	27	21	North Carolina	14	12	Maryland	7

1968 (7-3-0)			**1969 (3-7-0)**			**1970 (5-6-0)**		
6	Purdue	44	14	Clemson	21	7	Virginia Tech	0
47	VMI	0	10	Duke	0	17	Clemson	27
41	Davidson	14	28	William & Mary	15	7	Duke	17
50	Duke	20	28	VMI	10	7	Wake Forest	27
0	NC State	19	0	NC State	31	49	VMI	10
24	Navy	0	0	Navy	10	21	Army	20
28	South Carolina	49	0	North Carolina	12	33	William & Mary	6
41	North Carolina	6	21	Wake Forest	23	15	North Carolina	30
63	Tulane	47	0	Tulane	31	16	NC State	21
28	Maryland	23	14	Maryland	17	54	Colgate	12
						14	Maryland	17

1971 (3-8-0)			**1972 (4-7-0)**			**1973 (4-7-0)**		
6	Navy	10	24	South Carolina	16	16	VMI	0
0	Michigan	56	24	Virginia Tech	20	23	NC State	43
0	Duke	28	10	West Virginia	48	7	Missouri	31
27	Vanderbilt	23	13	Duke	37	7	Duke	3
14	South Carolina	34	7	Vanderbilt	10	22	Vanderbilt	39
15	Clemson	32	45	VMI	14	27	Clemson	32
9	Army	14	21	Clemson	37	15	Virginia Tech	27
14	NC State	10	23	Maryland	24	21	Wake Forest	10
0	Virginia Tech	6	14	NC State	35	44	North Carolina	40
20	North Carolina	32	3	North Carolina	23	0	Maryland	33
29	Maryland	27	15	Wake Forest	12	17	West Virginia	42

1974 (4-7-0)

28	Navy	35
38	William & Mary	28
7	Duke	27
24	Georgia Tech	28
21	NC State	22
28	Virginia Tech	27
14	Wake Forest	0
10	North Carolina	24
28	VMI	10
9	Clemson	28
0	Maryland	10

1975 (1-10-0)

14	Navy	42
22	VMI	21
11	Duke	26
28	North Carolina	31
14	South Carolina	41
17	Virginia Tech	24
21	Wake Forest	66
14	Vanderbilt	17
10	E. Carolina	61
0	Syracuse	37
24	Maryland	62

1976 (2-9-0)

17	Washington	38
0	William & Mary	14
6	Duke	21
14	Georgia Tech	35
7	South Carolina	35
10	Virginia Tech	14
18	Wake Forest	17
7	VMI	13
21	Lehigh	20
6	North Carolina	31
0	Maryland	28

1977 (1-9-1)

0	NC State	14
0	Texas	68
7	Duke	31
0	West Virginia	13
0	Clemson	31
14	Virginia Tech	14
12	Wake Forest	10
3	Syracuse	6
6	VMI	30
14	North Carolina	35
0	Maryland	28

1978 (2-9-0)

0	Wake Forest	14
0	Navy	32
21	Army	17
9	VMI	17
13	Duke	20
14	Clemson	30
17	Virginia Tech	7
17	West Virginia	20
7	Maryland	17
20	North Carolina	38
21	NC State	24

1979 (6-5-0)

31	Richmond	0
27	NC State	31
19	VMI	0
30	Duke	12
7	Clemson	17
69	James Madison	9
10	Navy	17
31	Georgia	0
20	Virginia Tech	18
7	North Carolina	13
7	Maryland	17

1980 (4-7-0)

6	Navy	3
13	NC State	27
20	Duke	17
21	West Virginia	45
24	Clemson	27
0	Virginia Tech	30
24	Wake Forest	21
16	Tennessee	13
17	Rutgers	19
3	North Carolina	26
0	Maryland	31

1981 (1-10-0)

18	West Virginia	32
0	Rutgers	3
24	Duke	29
24	NC State	30
0	Clemson	27
3	South Carolina	21
21	Wake Forest	24
13	VMI	10
14	North Carolina	17
7	Maryland	48
3	Virginia Tech	20

1982 (2-9-0)

16	Navy	30
17	James Madison	21
17	Duke	51
13	NC State	16
0	Clemson	48
34	Wake Forest	27
37	VMI	6
32	Georgia Tech	38
14	North Carolina	27
14	Maryland	45
14	Virginia Tech	21

1983 (6-5-0)

38	Duke	30
27	Navy	16
21	James Madison	14
26	NC State	14
3	Maryland	23
21	Clemson	42

1984 (8-2-2)

0	Clemson	55
35	VMI	7
21	Navy	9
26	Virginia Tech	23
38	Duke	10
20	Georgia Tech	20

1985 (6-5-0)

40	VMI	15
24	Georgia Tech	13
13	Navy	17
37	Duke	14
24	Clemson	27
10	Virginia Tech	28

1983 (cont.)
38	VMI	10
34	Wake Forest	38
27	Georgia Tech	31
17	North Carolina	14
0	Virginia Tech	48

1984 (cont.)
28	Wake Forest	9
27	West Virginia	7
45	NC State	0
24	North Carolina	24
34	Maryland	45
27	Purdue	24
	(Peach Bowl)	

1985 (cont.)
20	Wake Forest	18
27	West Virginia	7
22	NC State	23
24	North Carolina	22
21	Maryland	33

1986 (3-8-0)
30	South Carolina	20
10	Navy	20
14	Georgia Tech	28
13	Duke	20
30	Wake Forest	28
17	Clemson	31
10	Virginia Tech	42
37	William & Mary	41
20	NC State	16
7	North Carolina	27
10	Maryland	42

1987 (8-4-0)
22	Georgia	30
19	Maryland	21
14	Virginia Tech	13
42	Duke	17
30	VMI	0
21	Clemson	38
10	South Carolina	58
35	Wake Forest	21
23	Georgia Tech	14
20	North Carolina	17
34	NC State	31
22	Brigham Young	16
	(All–American	
	Bowl)	

1988 (7-4-0)
31	William & Mary	23
14	Penn State	42
17	Georgia Tech	16
34	Duke	38
7	Clemson	10
28	Louisville	30
34	Wake Forest	14
16	Virginia Tech	10
19	NC State	14
27	North Carolina	24
24	Maryland	23

1989 (10-3-0)
13	Notre Dame	36
14	Penn State	6
17	Georgia Tech	10
49	Duke	28
24	William & Mary	12
20	Clemson	34
50	North Carolina	17
47	Wake Forest	28
16	Louisville	15
20	NC State	9
32	Virginia Tech	25
48	Maryland	21
21	Illinois	31
	(Citrus Bowl)	

1990 (8-4-0)
59	Kansas	10
20	Clemson	7
56	Navy	14
59	Duke	0
63	William & Mary	35
31	NC State	0
49	Wake Forest	14
38	Georgia Tech	41
24	North Carolina	10
30	Maryland	35
13	Virginia Tech	38
22	Tennessee	23
	(Sugar Bowl)	

1991 (8-3-1)
6	Maryland	17
17	Navy	10
21	Georgia Tech	24
34	Duke	3
31	Kansas	19
20	Clemson	20
14	North Carolina	9
48	Wake Forest	7
42	VMI	0
42	NC State	10
38	Virginia Tech	0
14	Oklahoma	48
	(Gator Bowl)	

Wake Forest

Location: Winston-Salem, NC   Enrollment: 3,400
Colors: Old Gold and Black   Nickname: Deacons
Stadium: Groves (1968), 31,500 capacity, natural turf.

Head Coaches

Carey Dowd 1888*
Bill Riddick 1889
No team 1890, 1894, 1896–1907
Walter Sikes 1891–93
John Gore 1895*
A. P. Hall 1908
A. T. Myers 1909
Reddy Rowe 1910
Frank Thompson 1911–13
Wilbur Smith 1914–15
Gil Billings 1916
Ed MacDonnell 1917
Harry Rabenhorst 1918–19*
James White 1920–21
George Levene 1922

Hank Garrity 1923–25
James Baldwin 1926–27
Stan Cofall 1928
Pat Miller 1929–32
James H. Weaver 1933–36
Doug "Peahead" Walker 1937–50
Tom Rogers 1951–55
Paul Amen 1956–59
Billy Hildebrand 1960–63
Bill Tate 1964–68
Cal Stoll 1969–71
Tom Harper 1972
Chuck Mills 1973–77
John Mackovic 1978–80
Al Groh 1981–86
Bill Dooley 1987–91

team captain

All–American Players

Bill George 1949 tackle
Jim Staton 1950 tackle
Bob Bartholomew 1955 tackle
Bill Barnes 1956 halfback
Norm Snead 1960 quarterback
Brian Piccolo 1964 fullback

Win Headley 1970 tackle
Chuck Ramsey 1973 punter
Bill Armstrong 1976 def. back
Bill Ard 1980 guard
Paul Kiser 1986 guard

Scores

1888 (1-0-0)

6	North Carolina	4

1889 (3-3-0)

0	North Carolina	33
32	Trinity	0
18	North Carolina	8
4	Trinity	8
4	Virginia	46
32	Richmond	14

1891 (1-0-0)

1	North Carolina	0

1892 (4-0-1)

40	Asheville Ath	0
12	VMI	12
16	Wash. & Lee	0
16	Richmond	0
10	Tennessee	6

1893 (1-2-0)

6	Trinity	12
64	Tennessee	0
0	North Carolina	40

1895 (0-0-1)

4	NC A&M	4

1908 (1-4-0)

0	Davidson	31
0	NC A&M	25
0	North Carolina	17
0	NC A&M	76
21	Warrenton Prep	0

1909 (2-4-0)

0	North Carolina	18
3	Maryville	0
0	Wash. & Lee	17
8	South Carolina	0
0	Richmond	5
0	NC Medical	5

1910 (1-7-0)

0	Davidson	32
3	NC A&M	28
0	North Carolina	37
28	Horner	0
0	Norfolk Blues	31
0	South Carolina	6
5	The Citadel	9
0	USS Franklin	11

1911 (3-5-0)

52	Warrenton Prep	0
3	North Carolina	12
62	Roanoke	0
5	Wash. & Lee	18
6	Virginia	29
0	Davidson	9
26	USS Franklin	0
6	NC A&M	13

1912 (2-6-0)

33	NC Medical	0
3	South Carolina	10
2	North Carolina	9
0	Wash. & Lee	20
0	NC A&M	12
49	Horner	0
14	Virg. Medical	23
7	Davidson	13

1913 (0-8-0)

0	Davidson	6
0	North Carolina	7
13	Richmond	14
10	South Carolina	27
0	Wash. & Lee	33
0	NC A&M	37
7	Gallaudet	47
0	North Carolina	29

1914 (3-6-0)

0	NC A&M	51
13	USS Franklin	0
0	North Carolina	53
0	Wash. & Lee	72
19	Roanoke	0
0	South Carolina	26
7	North Carolina	12
6	Davidson	7
41	Wofford	0

1915 (3-4-0)

7	Davidson	21
80	Florence YMCA	0
28	Gallaudet	6
0	NC A&M	7
40	Richmond Blues	0
6	VMI	21
0	North Carolina	35

1916 (2-3-0)

33	Guilford	0
0	NC A&M	6
0	North Carolina	20
33	South Carolina	0
0	Virginia Tech	52

1917 (1-6-1)

0	Georgia Tech	33
6	Furman	7
20	Guilford	0
6	NC State	17
13	Maryland	29
0	Virginia Tech	50
7	Davidson	72
7	Hampden-Sydney	7

1918 (1-2-0)

0	Virginia Tech	27
7	Wash. & Lee	20
21	NC State	0

1919 (2-6-0)

0	Georgia Tech	14
0	Davidson	21
7	Furman	37
65	Guilford	0
7	NC State	21
39	Sewanee Cl (VA)	3
0	Virginia Tech	40
0	North Carolina	6

1920 (2-7-0)

0	Georgia Tech	44
0	Wash. & Lee	27
7	Davidson	27

1921 (2-8-0)

10	Davidson	7
0	Trinity	17
0	Georgia Tech	42

1922 (3-5-2)

34	Atlantic Christian	0
6	Davidson	6

Opposite: **Groves Stadium, Winston-Salem, NC**

1920 (cont.)

0	Furman	17
40	Guilford	0
29	Elon	0
7	Richmond	20
7	NC State	49
0	North Carolina	6

1921 (cont.)

28	Guilford	0
0	NC State	14
0	Richmond	41
0	VMI	20
14	William & Mary	21
0	North Carolina	21
14	Hampden-Sydney	39

1922 (cont.)

0	Trinity	3
3	Elon	0
3	North Carolina	62
0	Guilford	0
7	Lynchburg	20
0	NC State	32
0	William & Mary	18
9	Hampden-Sydney	3

1923 (6-3-0)

0	North Carolina	22
41	Guilford	0
25	Lynchburg	0
6	Davidson	0
7	Florida	16
16	Trinity	6
9	Elon	6
14	NC State	0
7	South Carolina	14

1924 (7-2-0)

32	Duke	0
41	Elon	0
67	Guilford	0
37	Lynchburg	7
12	NC State	0
0	South Carolina	7
7	North Carolina	6
10	Wash. & Lee	8
0	Florida	34

1925 (6-2-1)

6	North Carolina	0
7	Davidson	7
3	Florida	24
21	Duke	3
49	Lenoir Rhyne	0
25	Guilford	0
0	NC State	6
9	Furman	6
65	Elon	0

1926 (5-4-1)

13	North Carolina	0
27	Wofford	0
0	Furman	10
0	Presbyterian	13
3	Davidson	3
21	Duke	0
53	Elon	0
6	William & Mary	13
60	Guilford	0
3	NC State	7

1927 (2-6-2)

9	North Carolina	8
0	Elon	0
7	Presbyterian	14
7	NC State	30
13	Davidson	13
6	Duke	32
0	Furman	53
10	Quantico Mar.	39
13	High Point	0
0	Mercer	34

1928 (2-6-2)

0	North Carolina	65
7	Presbyterian	12
0	William & Mary	0
0	NC State	37
25	Davidson	6
0	Furman	18
0	Duke	38
7	Wofford	7
12	Mercer	14
13	Miami (FL)	6

1929 (6-5-1)

20	Catawba	0
0	North Carolina	48
19	Richmond	0
25	Elon	6
6	NC State	8
0	Furman	12
6	Davidson	0
18	Wofford	0
0	Navy	61
0	Presbyterian	0

1930 (5-3-1)

7	North Carolina	13
20	Guilford	0
44	Baltimore	0
7	NC State	0
21	Mercer	0
0	Temple	36
0	Presbyterian	13
13	Duke	13
13	Davidson	2

1931 (4-4-0)

0	North Carolina	37
6	Furman	36
6	NC State	0
0	Duke	28
13	Erskine	0
12	Presbyterian	0
0	Oglethorpe	37
7	Davidson	0

1929 (cont.)

0	Duke	20
13	Mercer	0

1932 (3-3-2)

0	North Carolina	0
6	South Carolina	0
0	NC State	0
0	Duke	9
7	Delaware	0
6	Catholic	14
20	Carson-Newman	6
0	Davidson	7

1933 (0-5-1)

0	Duke	22
0	NC State	0
0	Catholic	12
0	Clemson	13
0	North Carolina	26
13	Davidson	20

1934 (3-7-0)

62	Guilford	0
0	North Carolina	21
13	NC State	12
2	Furman	3
14	Presbyterian	6
2	George Wash.	6
0	Emory & Henry	13
7	Duke	28
6	Richmond	39
12	Davidson	13

1935 (2-7-0)

7	Duke	26
0	North Carolina	14
6	NC State	21
7	Clemson	13
18	Presbyterian	0
0	Furman	9
7	George Wash.	6
0	Miami (FL)	3
7	Davidson	14

1936 (5-4-0)

7	North Carolina	14
9	NC State	0
32	Wofford	0
6	Clemson	0
12	George Wash.	13
19	Presbyterian	0
0	Duke	20
19	Erskine	6
6	Davidson	19

1937 (3-6-0)

0	Tennessee	32
6	George Wash.	34
19	Erskine	0
0	North Carolina	28
0	Clemson	32
0	NC State	20
0	Duke	67
24	Wofford	0
19	Davidson	7

1938 (4-5-1)

57	Randolph Macon	6
6	North Carolina	14
31	The Citadel	0
20	South Carolina	19
7	NC State	19
0	Duke	7
0	Clemson	7
6	VMI	6
13	W. Maryland	0
21	Davidson	0

1939 (7-3-0)

34	Elon	0
19	South Carolina	7
6	North Carolina	36
33	Miami (FL)	0
32	NC State	0
66	W. Maryland	0
0	Duke	6
14	Marshall	13
7	Clemson	20
46	Davidson	7

1940 (7-3-0)

79	William Jewell	0
12	North Carolina	0
19	Furman	0
0	Clemson	39
31	Marshall	19
0	Duke	23
18	George Wash.	0
20	NC State	14
7	Texas Tech	12
7	South Carolina	6

1941 (5-5-1)

66	Camp Davis	0
14	Duke	43
52	Furman	13
6	South Carolina	6
7	NC State	0
13	North Carolina	0

1942 (6-2-1)

0	North Carolina	6
20	Duke	7
14	Furman	6
0	NC State	0
0	Boston College	27
19	Clemson	6

1943 (4-5-0)

20	Camp Davis	24
7	Maryland	13
0	Georgia	7
54	NC State	6
21	VMI	0
41	Clemson	12

1941 (cont.)

6	Marshall	16
6	Boston College	26
0	Clemson	29
42	George Wash.	0
6	Texas Tech	35

1944 (8-1-0)

7	North Carolina	0
14	Georgia	7
39	Maryland	0
38	VMI	7
21	NC State	7
27	Miami (FL)	0
13	Clemson	7
0	Duke	34
19	South Carolina	13

1947 (6-4-0)

6	Georgetown	0
16	Clemson	14
19	North Carolina	7
39	George Wash.	7
6	Duke	13
0	William & Mary	21
14	Boston College	13
0	NC State	20
33	Duquesne	0
0	South Carolina	6

1950 (6-1-2)

7	Boston College	7
43	Richmond	0
47	William & Mary	0
13	North Carolina	7
13	George Wash.	7
12	Clemson	13
13	Duke	7
6	NC State	6
14	South Carolina	7

1953 (3-6-1)

14	William & Mary	16
0	Duke	19

1942 (cont.)

28	VMI	0
20	George Wash.	0
33	South Carolina	14

1945 (5-3-1)

6	Tennessee	7
0	Army	54
19	Duke	26
19	NC State	18
53	Presbyterian	9
14	North Carolina	13
13	South Carolina	13
13	Clemson	6
26	South Carolina (Gator Bowl)	14

1948 (6-4-0)

27	George Wash.	13
9	Boston College	26
21	William & Mary	12
6	North Carolina	28
41	Duquesne	15
34	NC State	13
27	Duke	20
14	Clemson	21
38	South Carolina	0
7	Baylor (Dixie Bowl)	20

1951 (6-4-0)

20	Boston College	6
21	NC State	6
56	Richmond	6
6	William & Mary	7
27	George Wash.	13
39	North Carolina	7
6	Clemson	21
19	Duke	13
0	Baylor	42
6	South Carolina	21

1954 (2-7-1)

14	George Wash.	0
0	Virginia Tech	32

1943 (cont.)

20	NC Pre-Flight	12
0	Greensboro AAB	14
2	South Carolina	13

1946 (6-3-0)

12	Boston College	6
19	Georgetown	6
19	Clemson	7
6	NC State	14
19	Tennessee	6
32	Chattanooga	14
0	Duke	13
14	North Carolina	26
35	South Carolina	0

1949 (4-6-0)

22	Duquesne	7
7	SMU	13
7	Boston College	13
6	Georgetown	12
14	North Carolina	28
55	William & Mary	28
35	Clemson	21
27	Duke	7
14	NC State	27
20	South Carolina	27

1952 (5-4-1)

14	Baylor	17
28	William & Mary	21
7	Boston College	7
0	Villanova	20
9	North Carolina	7
21	NC State	6
9	TCU	27
7	Duke	14
28	Furman	0
39	South Carolina	14

1955 (5-4-1)

13	Virginia Tech	0
34	South Carolina	19

1953 (cont.)

18	Villanova	12
13	North Carolina	18
20	NC State	7
13	Richmond	13
0	Clemson	18
7	Boston College	20
10	Furman	21
19	South Carolina	13

1956 (2-5-3)

39	William & Mary	0
0	Maryland	6
6	Virginia	7
0	Clemson	17
14	Florida State	14
6	North Carolina	6
13	NC State	0
13	Virginia Tech	13
0	Duke	26
0	South Carolina	13

1959 (6-4-0)

22	Florida State	20
27	Virginia Tech	18
0	Tulane	6
10	Maryland	7
17	NC State	14
19	North Carolina	21
34	Virginia	12
15	Duke	27
31	Clemson	33
43	South Carolina	20

1962 (0-10-0)

14	Army	40
2	Maryland	13
7	Clemson	24
6	South Carolina	27
12	Virginia	14
14	North Carolina	23
0	Tennessee	23
8	Virginia Tech	37
0	Duke	50
3	NC State	27

1954 (cont.)

26	NC State	0
13	Maryland	13
7	North Carolina	14
20	Clemson	32
0	Richmond	13
21	Duke	28
9	William & Mary	13
19	South Carolina	20

1957 (0-10-0)

0	Florida	7
20	Virginia	28
0	Maryland	27
7	Duke	34
7	North Carolina	14
0	NC State	19
3	Virginia Tech	10
14	West Virginia	27
6	Clemson	13
7	South Carolina	26

1960 (2-8-0)

7	Clemson	28
6	Florida State	14
13	Virginia Tech	22
13	North Carolina	12
13	Maryland	14
28	Virginia	20
12	NC State	14
7	Duke	34
0	LSU	16
20	South Carolina	41

1963 (1-9-0)

10	E. Carolina	20
0	Virginia Tech	27
0	North Carolina	21
0	Florida State	35
0	Army	47
0	Maryland	32
0	Clemson	36
7	Duke	39
20	South Carolina	19
0	NC State	42

1955 (cont.)

0	West Virginia	46
7	Maryland	28
13	NC State	13
25	North Carolina	0
13	Clemson	19
13	William & Mary	19
13	Virginia	7
0	Duke	14

1958 (3-7-0)

34	Maryland	0
13	Virginia Tech	6
24	Florida State	27
13	NC State	7
7	Villanova	9
7	North Carolina	26
12	Clemson	14
0	Duke	29
7	Auburn	21
7	South Carolina	24

1961 (4-6-0)

0	Baylor	31
7	South Carolina	10
3	Duke	23
17	Clemson	13
0	NC State	7
21	Virginia	15
7	Auburn	21
24	Virginia Tech	15
7	Maryland	10
17	North Carolina	14

1964 (5-5-0)

31	Virginia	21
38	Virginia Tech	21
0	North Carolina	23
6	Vanderbilt	9
2	Clemson	21
21	Maryland	17
14	Memphis State	23
20	Duke	7
13	South Carolina	23
27	NC State	13

1965 (3-7-0)

3	Virginia Tech	12
11	NC State	13
7	Vanderbilt	0
7	Maryland	10
7	South Carolina	38
12	North Carolina	10
13	Clemson	26
0	Florida State	35
7	Duke	40
21	Memphis State	20

1966 (3-7-0)

10	Virginia	24
7	Maryland	34
12	NC State	15
6	Auburn	14
10	South Carolina	6
3	North Carolina	0
21	Clemson	23
0	Virginia Tech	11
21	Memphis State	7
0	Florida State	28

1967 (4-6-0)

13	Duke	31
6	Clemson	23
6	Houston	50
12	Virginia	14
10	Memphis State	42
7	NC State	24
20	North Carolina	10
35	South Carolina	21
31	Tulsa	24
35	Maryland	17

1968 (2-7-1)

6	NC State	10
20	Clemson	20
19	Minnesota	24
6	Virginia Tech	7
27	Purdue	28
48	North Carolina	31
38	Maryland	14
21	South Carolina	24
3	Duke	18
24	Florida State	42

1969 (3-7-0)

22	NC State	21
0	Auburn	57
16	Virginia Tech	10
14	Maryland	19
20	Duke	27
14	Clemson	28
3	North Carolina	23
23	Virginia	21
6	South Carolina	24
7	Miami (FL)	49

1970 (6-5-0)

12	Nebraska	36
7	South Carolina	43
14	Florida State	19
27	Virginia	7
28	Virginia Tech	9
36	Clemson	20
14	North Carolina	13
7	Tennessee	41
28	Duke	14
16	NC State	13
2	Houston	26

1971 (6-5-0)

27	Davidson	7
20	Virginia Tech	9
10	Miami (FL)	29
18	Maryland	14
14	NC State	21
51	Tulsa	21
3	North Carolina	7
9	Clemson	10
36	William & Mary	29
23	Duke	7
7	South Carolina	24

1972 (2-9-0)

26	Davidson	20
10	SMU	56
6	Tennessee	45
0	Maryland	23
13	NC State	42
0	North Carolina	21
0	Clemson	31
3	South Carolina	35
9	Duke	7
12	Virginia	15
9	Virginia Tech	44

1973 (1-9-1)

9	Florida State	7
14	William & Mary	15
0	Richmond	41
0	Texas	41
12	South Carolina	28
0	Maryland	37
10	Virginia	21
8	Clemson	35
7	Duke	7
0	North Carolina	42
13	NC State	52

1974 (1-10-0)

15	NC State	33
6	William & Mary	17
0	North Carolina	31
0	Oklahoma	63
0	Penn State	55
0	Maryland	47
0	Virginia	14

1975 (3-8-0)

7	SMU	14
30	NC State	22
17	App. State	19
16	Kansas State	17
14	Clemson	16
0	Maryland	27
66	Virginia	21

1976 (5-6-0)

6	Virginia Tech	23
20	NC State	18
24	Vanderbilt	27
13	Kansas State	0
0	Michigan	31
20	Clemson	14
15	Maryland	17

1974 (cont.)

9	Clemson	21
7	Duke	23
21	South Carolina	34
16	Furman	10

1977 (1-10-0)

24	Furman	13
0	Vanderbilt	3
14	NC State	41
17	Purdue	26
3	North Carolina	24
7	Maryland	35
10	Virginia	12
0	Clemson	26
14	Duke	38
14	South Carolina	24
10	Virginia Tech	28

1980 (5-6-0)

7	Virginia Tech	16
24	The Citadel	7
27	NC State	7
27	William & Mary	7
9	North Carolina	27
10	Maryland	11
21	Virginia	24
33	Clemson	35
27	Duke	24
38	South Carolina	39
28	App. State	16

1983 (4-7-0)

25	App. State	27
13	Virginia Tech	6
21	W. Carolina	0
31	Richmond	6
15	NC State	38
10	North Carolina	30
33	Maryland	36
38	Virginia	34
17	Clemson	24
21	Duke	31
33	Georgia Tech	49

1975 (cont.)

21	North Carolina	9
14	Duke	42
26	South Carolina	37
10	Virginia Tech	40

1978 (1-10-0)

14	Virginia	0
6	Virginia Tech	28
11	LSU	13
10	NC State	34
7	Purdue	14
29	North Carolina	34
0	Maryland	39
7	Auburn	21
6	Clemson	51
0	Duke	3
14	South Carolina	37

1981 (4-7-0)

6	South Carolina	23
23	NC State	28
24	Auburn	21
14	Virginia Tech	30
15	App. State	14
10	North Carolina	48
33	Maryland	45
24	Virginia	21
24	Clemson	82
10	Duke	31
34	Richmond	22

1984 (6-5-0)

20	Virginia Tech	21
17	App. State	13
24	NC State	15
17	Maryland	38
29	Richmond	16
14	North Carolina	3
9	Virginia	28
34	William & Mary	21
14	Clemson	37
20	Duke	16
7	Georgia Tech	24

1976 (cont.)

17	Virginia	18
14	North Carolina	34
38	Duke	17
10	South Carolina	7

1979 (8-4-0)

30	App. State	23
22	Georgia	21
23	E. Carolina	20
14	NC State	17
19	Virginia Tech	14
24	North Carolina	19
25	Maryland	17
42	Auburn	38
0	Clemson	31
17	Duke	14
14	South Carolina	35
10	LSU	34
	(Tangerine Bowl)	

1982 (3-8-0)

31	W. Carolina	10
10	Auburn	28
0	NC State	30
31	App. State	22
13	Virginia Tech	10
7	North Carolina	24
31	Maryland	52
27	Virginia	34
26	Duke	46
7	Georgia Tech	45
17	Clemson	21

1985 (4-7-0)

30	William & Mary	23
30	Boston Univ.	0
17	NC State	20
24	App. State	21
29	Tennessee	31
14	North Carolina	34
6	Maryland	23
18	Virginia	20
10	Clemson	26
27	Duke	7
10	Georgia Tech	41

1986 (5-6-0)

21	App. State	13
31	Boston Univ.	0
38	NC State	42
49	Army	14
28	Virginia	30
30	North Carolina	40
27	Maryland	21
20	Clemson	28
36	Duke	38
21	South Carolina	48
24	Georgia Tech	21

1987 (7-4-0)

24	Richmond	0
21	NC State	3
16	App. State	12
17	Army	13
22	North Carolina	14
0	Maryland	14
21	Virginia	35
17	Clemson	31
30	Duke	27
0	South Carolina	30
33	Georgia Tech	6

1988 (6-4-1)

31	Villanova	11
35	Illinois State	0
6	NC State	14
9	Michigan	19
42	North Carolina	24
27	Maryland	24
14	Virginia	34
21	Clemson	38
35	Duke	16
28	Georgia Tech	24
34	App. State	34

1989 (2-8-1)

10	App. State	15
17	NC State	27
10	Army	14
17	Rice	17
17	North Carolina	16
7	Maryland	27
28	Virginia	47
10	Clemson	44
35	Duke	52
29	Tulsa	17
14	Georgia Tech	43

1990 (3-8-0)

17	Rice	33
23	App. State	12
15	NC State	20
52	Army	14
24	North Carolina	31
13	Maryland	41
14	Virginia	49
6	Clemson	24
20	Duke	57
7	Georgia Tech	42
56	Vanderbilt	28

1991 (3-8-0)

40	W. Carolina	24
3	NC State	30
14	Northwestern	41
3	App. State	17
10	North Carolina	24
22	Maryland	23
7	Virginia	48
10	Clemson	28
31	Duke	14
3	Georgia Tech	27
52	Navy	24

Bibliography

Attner, Paul. *The Terrapins*. Huntsville, AL: Strode, 1975.

Bolton, Clyde. *The Crimson Tide*. Huntsville, AL: Strode, 1972.

Corrie, Bruce A. *The Atlantic Coast Conference*. Durham, NC: Carolina Academic Press, 1978.

Danzig, Allison. *The History of American Football*. Englewood Cliffs, NJ: Prentice-Hall, 1956.

DiMarco, Anthony C. *The Big Bowl Football Guide*. New York, NY: G. P. Putnam's Sons, 1976.

Hunter, Jim. *The Gamecocks*. Huntsville, AL: Strode, 1975.

McCallum, John D. *Big Eight Football*. New York, NY: Charles Scribner's Sons, 1979.

McEwen, Tom. *The Gators*. Huntsville, AL: Strode, 1974.

Mann, Ted. *A Story of Glory*. Greenville, SC: Doorway, 1985.

Mumau, Thad. *Go Wolfpack*. Huntsville, AL: Strode, 1981.

Perrin, Tom. *Football: A College History*. Jefferson, NC: McFarland, 1987.

Rappoport, Ken. *Tar Heel*. Huntsville, AL: Strode, 1976.

Sahadi, Lou. *The Clemson Tigers*. New York, NY: William Morrow, 1983.

Thomy, Al. *The Ramblin' Wreck*. Huntsville, AL: Strode, 1973.

Index

Italics denotes a photo.